Spain 1936
YEAR ZERO

Sussex Studies in Spanish History

General Editor: Nigel Townson, Universidad Complutense, Madrid
Consultant Editor: José Álvarez-Junco, Universidad Complutense, Madrid
Advisory Editors: Pamela Radcliff, University of California, San Diego
Tim Rees, University of Exeter

José Álvarez-Junco, *The Emergence of Mass Politics in Spain: Populist Demagoguery and Republican Culture, 1890–1910.*

Tom Buchanan, *The Impact on the Spanish Civil War on Britain: War, Loss and Memory.*

Miguel Ángel Ruiz Carnicer (ed.), *From Franco to Freedom: The Roots of the Transition to Democracy in Spain, 1962–1982.*

Andrew Dowling, *Catalonia since the Spanish Civil War: Reconstructing the Nation.**

Ferran Gallego and Francisco Morente (eds), *The Last Survivor: Cultural and Social Projects Underlying Spanish Fascism, 1931–1975.*

Hugo García, *The Truth about Spain!: Mobilizing British Public Opinion, 1936–1939.*

Irene González González, *Spanish Education in Morocco, 1912–1956: Cultural Interactions in a Colonial Context .*

Aitana Guia, *The Muslim Struggle for Civil Rights in Spain: Promoting Democracy through Migrant Engagement, 1985–2010.*

Patricia Hertel, *The Crescent Remembered: Islam and Nationalism on the Iberian Peninsula.*

Silvina Schammah Gesser, *Madrid's Forgotten Avant-Garde: Between Essentialism and Modernity.*

David Messenger, *L'Espagne Républicaine: French Policy and Spanish Republicanism in Liberated France.*

Javier Moreno-Luzón, *Modernizing the Nation: Spain during the Reign of Alfonso XIII, 1902–1931.*

Inbal Ofer, *Señoritas in Blue: The Making of a Female Political Elite in Franco's Spain.*

Stanley G. Payne, *Alcalá Zamora and the Failure of the Spanish Republic, 1931–1936.*

Raanan Rein and Joan Maria Thomàs (eds), *Spain 1936: Year Zero.*

Mario Ojeda Revah, *Mexico and the Spanish Civil War: Domestic Politics and the Republican Cause.*

Elizabeth Roberts, *"Freedom, Faction, Fame and Blood": British Soldiers of Conscience in Greece, Spain and Finland.*

Julius Ruiz, *'Paracuellos': The Elimination of the 'Fifth Column' in Republican Madrid during the Spanish Civil War.*

Guy Setton, *Spanish–Israeli Relations, 1956–1992: Ghosts of the Past and Contemporary Challenges in the Middle East.*

Manuel Álvarez Tardío, *José María Gil-Robles: Leader of the Catholic Right during the Spanish Second Republic.*

Manuel Álvarez Tardío and Fernando del Rey Reguillo (eds.), *The Spanish Second Republic Revisited.*

Nigel Townson, *The Crisis of Democracy in Spain: Centrist Politics under the Second Republic, 1931–1936.*

Nigel Townson (ed.), *Is Spain Different?: A Comparative Look at the 19th and 20th Centuries.*

* Published in association with the Cañada Blanch Centre for Contemporary Spanish Studies and the Catalan Observatory, London School of Economics.

A full list of titles in the series is available on the Press website.

Spain 1936
YEAR ZERO

Edited by
RAANAN REIN and JOAN MARIA THOMÀS

sussex
ACADEMIC
PRESS
Brighton • Chicago • Toronto

2 4 6 8 10 9 7 5 3 1

First published *in Great Britain by*
SUSSEX ACADEMIC PRESS
PO Box 139
Eastbourne BN24 9BP

Distributed in North America by
SUSSEX ACADEMIC PRESS
Independent Publishers Group
814 N. Franklin Street
Chicago, IL 60610

British Library Cataloguing in Publication Data
A CIP catalogue record for this book is available from the British Library.

Library of Congress Cataloging-in-Publication Data
Names: Rein, Raanan, 1960– editor. | Thomàs, Joan Maria, editor.
Title: Spain 1936 : year zero / edited by Raanan Rein and Joan Maria Thomàs.
Description: Brighton : Sussex Academic Press, 2018. | Series: Sussex studies in Spanish history | Includes bibliographical references and index.
Identifiers: LCCN 2017059921 | ISBN 9781845198923 (hbk : alk. paper)
Subjects: LCSH: Spain—History—Civil War, 1936–1939. | Spain—History—Civil War, 1936–1939—Causes. | Spain—History—Civil War, 1936–1939—Public opinion, Foreign. | Spain—History—Civil War, 1936–1939—Participation, Foreign. | Spain—Foreign relations—1931–1939.
Classification: LCC DP257 .S625 2018 | DDC 946.081—dc23
LC record available at https://lccn.loc.gov/2017059921

MIX
Paper | Supporting responsible forestry
FSC® C013604

Typeset & designed by Sussex Academic Press, Brighton & Eastbourne.
Printed and bound by CPI Group (UK) Ltd, Croydon, CR0 4YY

Contents

The Cover Illustrations ix
Preface by Series Editor Nigel Townson x

Introduction 1
Raanan Rein and Joan Maria Thomàs

1 1936: The Eruption of Revolutionary Anti-Fascism in Spain 13
Michael Seidman

2 The Pioneers of International Defense of the Republic: The Athletes of Barcelona's Popular Olympiad 34
Raanan Rein

3 The Political Evolution of the Nationalist Zone in 1936: The Construction of the Francoist State 56
Joan Maria Thomàs

4 Spanish Fascists and Nazi Germany, 1931–1940: From Fascination to Intervention 75
Xosé M. Núñez Seixas

5 Women and the Spanish Civil War: The Radical Months 93
Inbal Ofer

6 Taking sides: Salazar's Estado Novo, the Nationalist uprising and the Spanish Civil War 114
Pedro Aires Oliveira

7 Italy 1936: From Consensus to First Doubts about the Regime 133
Luciano Casali

8 From Marginalization to Mobilization: The Soviet Union and the Spanish Republic 152
Daniel Kowalsky

9 An Engagé in 1936 Spain: Commitment and Its Downside in Rafael Alberti's Philo-Sovietism 174
Silvina Schammah Gesser and Alexandra Cheveleva Dergacheva

10 Solidarity and Non-intervention: France and the Spanish Civil War 198
David A. Messenger

11 Chimerical Thoughts? Winston Churchill and Spain 216
Emilio Sáenz-Francés San Baldomero

12 The Impact of the Spanish Civil War on Imperial Japan, 1936–1940 232
Haruo Tohmatsu

13 Argentina's Diplomatic and Naval Asylum Policy in the Spanish Civil War 251
Leonardo Senkman

14 Spanish Destiny: Renzo Giua and Giustizia e Libertà – *In Memoriam* 269
Manuela Consonni

The Editors and Contributors 291
Index 295

The Cover Illustrations

A visit by Francisco Largo Caballero and Wenceslao Carrillo Alonso-Forjador to the front. This photo was taken in Collado Villalba, north of Madrid. Courtesy of José Ramón García Gandía.

Children from Madrid saluting in Fascist style after the capture of the capital by the nationalist army in 1939. Courtesy of Archivo Regional de la Comunidad de Madrid/ Fondo Martín Santos Yubero).

A poster of the 80th Anniversary of the Barcelona Popular Olympics. Courtesy of CRAI Biblioteca Pavelló de la República (Universitat de Barcelona).

Series Editor's Preface

A colleague once told me that when he was at school in the 1990s his father objected to one of the boys in his group of friends, telling his son to dissociate himself from this particular youth. "What's the problem? He's a nice guy", the son pleaded, to which the father retorted: "His grandfather was a Nationalist". The fact that feelings still run deep eighty years after the Civil War of 1936–39 and that it continues to shape social relations, cultural attitudes and political choices is hardly surprising. In contrast, say, to the Civil War of the United States of America (1861-65), the victors in the Spanish conflict did not seek the reconciliation of the two warring sides in an endeavour to restore national unity. On the contrary, the Franco dictatorship, in an attempt to justify its own insurgent origins and in consonance with the patrimonial politics that had hitherto dominated Spain, sought retaliation, retribution and revenge. Not only were the vanquished to be punished, but also the diverse political, social and cultural values which they had upheld were to be extirpated from Spanish society. This translated into a widespread repression, with up to 30,000 'Reds' being executed after hostilities were over and hundreds of thousands of republicans spending years in jail. Yet this is only part of the story. Many Spaniards lost their jobs, land, houses and other property because they had either chosen to support the Republic or because they had simply found themselves in the republican zone during the conflict. Many people were excluded from their chosen profession and found it extremely difficult to find alternative employment, often taking up positions that were patently inferior to their training or qualifications. The beneficiaries of the plots of land, houses, cars and jobs that were wrenched from the hands of the 'Reds' were of course those that had actively supported the Nationalists or had found themselves in the Nationalist zone during the war. Small wonder, then, that in the 1990s the Civil War continued to provoke feelings of hatred or hostility between Spaniards.

A further consequence of this deep-seated division within Spanish society is that it has powerfully shaped the research and writing on the Civil War. Much of the work on the war remains strongly politicised. Many of the thousands of books on the subject are vitiated by the rerunning of battles that first took place in the 1930s, left-wing historians often defending the historical cause of the left, with right-wing historians frequently doing exactly the same for the historical right. If, however, we are to understand the Civil War in all its complexity, and the most salutary lessons possible are to be extracted from it, then a conscious and strenous effort must be made to set aside the ongoing political battles. The chief virtue of *Spain 1936:Year Zero* is that it endeavours to revisit the early months of the Civil War in a dispassionate spirit that eschews the politically-charged approach of many other studies. Further, over the course of its fourteen chapters, *Spain 1936:Year Zero* covers a multitude of topics, ranging from the ideologies and politics of the two sides to the war's international reverberations, the experience of women in both zones, and the changing perceptions of prominent individuals, including the Communist poet Rafael Alberti and the Conservative politician Winston Churchill. In doing so, the book reevaluates long-held assumptions about the conflict, such as the unity of the Nationalist camp or the different trajectories of women in the two camps. Particular attention is paid to the international dimension of the war, the book tackling not just well-known players such as Germany, Italy, France and the USSR, but also those that have received short shrift, such as Argentina, Japan and Portugal. In short, *Spain 1936:Year Zero* offers new research, new topics and new ideas on the early months of the Civil War, revealing in the process that, despite the profusion of books on the subject, Spain's paramount tragedy of the 20th century continues to merit further research and reflection.

NIGEL TOWNSON
Universidad Complutense, Madrid

Introduction

Raanan Rein and Joan Maria Thomàs

The ghosts of the Spanish Civil War (1936–39) continue to haunt Spain, forming an integral part of public discussions, historiographical debates, and political struggles. It is no wonder, then, that more than 80 years after General Francisco Franco's troops launched a military uprising against the elected Republican government of Santiago Casares Quiroga in July 1936, there is still no museum in Spain offering a comprehensive picture of the 1930s and representing all sides to the civil war. Unlike in Germany, the legacy in Spain of the recent traumatic past is a source of contention and controversy, and the battles for memory of the Spanish Civil War are still being passionately waged.

In May 2017, the Spanish parliament voted in favor of removing the remains of the dictator Franco from the state-founded Valley of the Fallen mausoleum, 40 miles outside of the capital Madrid.[1] The non-binding decision was approved by a large majority of 198 to 1, but no less important was the abstention of 140 deputies, most of them members of the ruling conservative Partido Popular of Mariano Rajoy, who argued that such a move would only open old wounds. Parliamentarians who insisted that it was precisely the mausoleum in its present form that was keeping old wounds open, also called to remove the remaining symbols of dictatorship from around Spain and to establish an investigatory committee to look into the fate of more than one hundred thousand people still considered missing since the end of this fratricidal war.

The Valley of the Fallen was built between the years 1940 and 1959 by order of the dictator as a tribute to fallen "heroes" of the crusade he had led against the Spanish Republic in the period 1936–39. Thousands of Republican prisoners were forced to dig the mausoleum out of rock, transforming the memorial site and mass grave into a monument to Republican suffering as well.[2] Alongside Franco, José Antonio Primo de Rivera, the founder of the Spanish Falange, is also entombed there.[3] Some 40,000 individuals are buried in the huge underground basilica, which is larger than St Peter's in Rome. For many years, on November 20, right-wing militants would mark there the anniversaries of both Primo de Rivera's and Franco's deaths.[4] The monument also became a pilgrimage site for those who looked back with nostalgia to the Franco years. The Socialist Party explained that the new parliamentary decision was aimed at transforming the site so that it ceased "to be a place of Francoist and National-Catholic memory and is remade as a space for the culture of reconciliation and collective democratic memory, where the victims of the civil war and the dictatorship are recognized and treated in dignity."[5]

A few days before the Spanish parliament's vote, the city council of Madrid decided to change the names of 52 streets, squares, and public spaces that glorified Francoist heroes, Nationalist victories in the bloody civil war, and National-Catholic values on which the dictatorship was founded.[6] Aiming to put an end to the urban topography of terror, the council renamed places honoring Franco and other generals, Millán Astray, founder of the Spanish Legion, and Juan Yagüe, a leading Falange member, among others. Similarly, Calle de los Caídos de la División Azul, the street name memoralizing the soldiers of the Blue Division who fought alongside Hitler's Wehrmacht against the Soviet Union in World War II, was also erased.[7] The Arco de la Victoria Avenue became the Avenida de la Memoria.

New names included the Memorial del 11 de marzo de 2004, commemorating those killed in the March 2004 jihadist terrorist attack on Madrid's Atocha train station. Intellectuals and artists such as Max Aub, Diego Torres Villarroel, Simone Veil, the French politician of Jewish origin who died in 2017, and photo-journalist Robert Capa, were also marked in this way. Fifty-seven council members voted in favor of these name changes, 36 against, and the Partido Popular representatives abstained again in the intensifying debate on the material legacy of the Franco dictatorship. It seems that there are still two Spains when it comes to re-examining the civil war and its legacy.

As we were preparing this volume, the Basque town of Guernica commemorated the eightieth anniversary of the Nazi bombing that devastated it – an atrocity that inspired Pablo Picasso's renowned painting, which is still considered the most famous depiction of the horrors of war. The Condor Legion, a unit of the German Luftwaffe, was sent by Adolf Hitler to help the Nationalists destroy the Republic and, at the same time, practice blitzkrieg tactics. For four hours on April 26, 1937, they raided this small market town, dropping 31 tons of bombs and killing a large number of people (most sources estimate the numbers in hundreds).[8]

Eighty years later, the city council of Madrid decided to dismantle a mausoleum in La Almudena cemetery, where seven pilots of the German

Condor Legion are buried.[9] The monument's façade, stating "German aviators who died for God and for Spain. Present!" was removed at the request of the German embassy in Madrid. It was replaced by seven small plaques, identifying the pilots buried there.

To a large extent, all these initiatives are a result of the 2007 Law of Historical Memory, adopted by the then Socialist government of José Luis Rodríguez Zapatero. This law – a public divorce from the so called pact of oblivion (*pacto de olvido*)[10] – condemned the 40-year-long dictatorship, offering greater recognition to victims of political, religious, and ideological violence on both sides of the civil war. It also supported efforts to locate the remains of missing people and to seek the moral restitution and recovery of their personal and family memory. The Law of Historical Memory, however, did not repeal the 1977 Amnesty law, which forbids the pressing of charges against the perpetrators of crimes against humanity committed during the Franco regime. In any event, after coming to power in 2011, the conservative government put a halt to most of these initiatives.

The historiography of the Spanish Civil War is ever growing. A new generation of Spanish scholars who had little or no experience of the dictatorship, the grandchildren of those who killed or were killed in the conflict, are now contributing to a plethora of regional and local studies on the atrocities and repression during and after the war, thus preventing silence and forgetting.[11] Searches in former battlefields conducted by Emilio Silva's Association for the Recovery of Historical Memory have led to the retrieval of the remains of thousands of victims of Francoist killings.[12]

Still, there is much work to be done. Spain has yet to declassify many state files from the period 1931–68. For several years now, the authorities have rejected petitions to declassify thousands of official records covering the times of Spain's Second Republic, the civil war, and a large part of the Franco dictatorship. This material was classified under the 1968 Official Secrets Act, while the dictatorship was still in full swing, leaving them beyond the reach of historians. There is no legal time limit for their declassification.

Although former minister Fernando Morán had agreed to give historians access to these files back in the 1980s, recent governments have not considered this "a priority." They claim that they lack the technical means and the necessary employees to carry out "such a difficult task."[13] In 2012, Pedro Morenés, then minister of defense, explained that "we will not declassify documents whose content we are ignorant about because the government is not going to take risks of state security issues."[14] Spain is one of the few democracies that does not have an established time limit after which classified information must be released to the public. Access to these documents might shed new light on various aspects of a wide range of experiences in a crucial period of Spain's history.

In the introduction to a debate on "Public Memory, Political Violence and the Spanish Civil War," published recently in the *Journal of Contemporary History*, historian Richard Evans adopted a comparative perspective, stating:

> The overwhelming majority of serious historians are agreed on the horrors of the Nazi extermination of Europe's Jews, the cruelties and massacres of Stalin's reign of terror, and other mass murders that disfigured the face of twentieth-century Europe, but in the case of the Spanish Civil War, they seem to be as far from agreement as ever . . . only in Spain have the deep divisions in public memory found an echo in the work of the historical profession.[15]

And indeed, in the past few years there has been a continuous output of revisionist texts in Spain that question the democratic nature of the Second Republic and put the blame for the outbreak of the civil war on the revolutionary and unstable nature of the Republic. Several books recycled traditional Francoist arguments as to the Republic and the civil war, claiming that Spain had to be "saved from the threat of communism." These non-academic histories became at times best-sellers. A notable example of such literature is Pío Moa's *Los orígenes de la Guerra Civil* (1999). The popularity of such arguments points to the deep roots of certain, Francoist interpretations of history in Spanish society.

A different kind of controversy was provoked recently by Roberto Villa García and Manuel Álvarez Tardío's book.[16] The authors claim that the elections won by the Popular Front in February 1936 were tainted by fraud and violence. This claim was interpreted by some critics as a "neo-Francoist" argument against the legitimacy of the Republic. The bitter disputes around the book were similar to those inflamed a couple of years previously by Stanley Payne and Jesús Palacios' *Franco: Una biografía personal y política*.[17] The latter was described as a "manipulation" by a group of historians, led by Ángel Viñas, in a special issue of the journal *Hispania Nova*.

Based on a conference marking the eightieth anniversary of the outbreak of the Spanish Civil War, the present volume looks at the initial moments of the fratricidal conflict and the immediate impact they had on both Spaniards and the contemporary European powers. The contributors re-examine the crystallization of political alliances formed in both the Nationalist Zone (Joan Maria Thomàs) and the Republican Zone

(Michael Seidman); the support mobilized by the two warring camps; and the different attitudes and policies adopted by neighboring (Portugal and France) and more distant countries (such as the Soviet Union, Great Britain, Germany, Italy, Japan and Argentina).

Spain 1936 aims at going beyond and against some of the commonly held assumptions regarding the supposed unity of the Nationalist camp vis-à-vis the fragmentation of the Republican one, the initial support of the military by Nazi Germany (Xosé M. Núñez Seixas), and Soviet support of the beleaguered Republic (Daniel Kowalsky). Situating the Iberian conflict in the larger international context, senior and junior scholars from various countries joined together to challenge various accepted ideas about the beginning of the Spanish Civil War, which exerted a terrible human cost. To the loss of hundreds of thousands killed in the war and the waves of repression and terror that followed must be added hundreds of thousands of exiles, invalids, political prisoners, and those labeled Reds who were barred from employment in various sectors.

This volume brings to the discussion on the Spanish Civil War less known perspectives by including Argentina (Leonardo Senkman), Japan (Haruo Tohmatsu), and Jewish Palestine (Raanan Rein), as well as less heard voices of women (Inbal Ofer), intellectuals (Silvina Schammah Gesser and Alexandra Cheveleva), and athletes (Raanan Rein).

Chronologically speaking, following the opening chapter of Michael Seidman which sets the stage, Raanan Rein's contribution is devoted to one of the last anti-Fascist gestures of the Republic. On July 19, 1936, a few hours before the scheduled opening ceremony of the Peoples' Olympiad, the military uprising against the elected government of the Second Republic broke out. Most of the athletes who had come to Barcelona departed quickly. However, some of them remained in Spain and became the first international volunteers to help in the defense of the Republic.

The Barcelona games had been planned as a response to the Olympics, which were about to open in Berlin and had been hijacked to serve the Nazi propaganda. Since the Peoples' Olympiad did not take place, historiography has devoted only scant attention to this attempt at an anti-Fascist, counter-Olympics. In addition, the chapter looks at Catalan nationalism and international solidarity, and focuses on the delegation of athletes from Jewish Palestine, mostly members of the Hapoel Sports Federation. This was the first expression of the Jewish Yishuv's solidarity with the Spanish Republic and the anti-Fascist struggle.

Joan Maria Thomàs explores the beginnings of the construction of the Francoist state in the so-called Nationalist Zone during the first months of the conflict. His chapter analyzes the ways in which the military achieved hegemony in the growing territories of the rebels, marginalizing the civilian forces that had supported the uprising. Taking advantage of the accidental death of General José Sanjurjo, who was supposed to head the rebels' junta, and of the execution of Falange founder José Antonio Primo de Rivera by the Republicans, General Franco was quick to engineer a plan, installing himself as both the military leader of the Nationalists – Generalísimo – and head of state. Still, he had to go a long way in order to impose unity on a political camp that was no less fragmented and divided than the Republican one.

Michael Seidman's chapter shifts attention to struggles that took place in the Republican zone between Communists, Socialists, anarchists, and their allied trade unionists. The eruption of an unprecedented revolutionary zeal was expressed in part in the effort to elaborate a revolutionary culture which was not exempt from violence. The outbreak of the Spanish Civil War also led to the rise of a trans-Atlantic revolutionary anti-Fascism, explored in more detail in subsequent chapters.

The relationship between gender and spatial practices is the focus of Inbal Ofer's chapter. By looking at women from the two warring camps, Ofer emphasizes that this fratricidal war was experienced and portrayed by both Republican and Nationalist women as a moment of rapture, a time when spatial, generational, and even gender divisions were momentarily suspended. Her essay highlights the fact that women's war-time mobilization did not differ significantly whichever side they were on.

The debate regarding the nature and characterization of the Franco regime has accompanied it from its initial stages. Was it a Fascist dictatorship? Was it a totalitarian regime, or an authoritarian one, as suggested in the 1960s by Juan Linz?[18] In his chapter, Xosé Manoel Núñez Seixas argues that although Fascism has been defined as a transnational phenomenon, the ideological tenets of National Socialism were barely assimilated by radical Falangism or Catholic tradionalism. Albeit Nationalist Spain was profoundly and increasingly pro-German prior to the outbreak of the war, and became even more so as a result of the critical military support offered by Nazi Germany to the rebels, still, Spanish Nationalists oscillated between the shaping of an autonomous ideological core and the critical reception of foreign influences. Italian Fascism and German National Socialism had an impact, but while several of their ideological notions were appropriated, they were reinterpreted in the Nationalist Zone.

The support provided by Fascist Italy and Nazi Germany to the Nationalist crusade was decisive in assuring the military victory of Franco's forces. The assistance offered by neighboring Portugal, however, was of a special importance. In his chapter, Pedto Aires Oliveira highlights the strained relations between the two Iberian countries during the years of the Second Spanish Republic. The authoritarian, corporatist government established in Lisbon in 1926 was far from enthusiastic about the democratization and radicalization processes that had been taking place in Spain since April 1931. Portugal's strongman, António de Oliveira Salazar, perceived the victory of the Popular Front in Spain in February 1936 as an existential threat to his own regime, and therefore opted to back outright the Nationalist camp in the civil war.

Luciano Casali's chapter ties Italian involvement in Spain with the waning of internal consensus around Mussolini's regime. The year 1936 was no less crucial for Italy as well. It represented the zenith of the regime, with the establishment of an African empire contributing to its consolidation. The involvement in the Spanish Civil War, however, fostered significant anti-Fascist dissent in the country.

Renzo Giua was one such opponent of the regime. Manuela Consonni uses his trajectory as a lens to study the anti-Fascist resistance, both in Italy and in Spain, where Giua fought alongside the Republicans against the Nationalists, supported by Italian troops. This battle, claims Consonni, later laid the foundations for the partisan struggle in Italy against the Mussolini government between 1943 and 1945

Although Spain formally recognized the Soviet Union in 1933, during the years of the Second Republic bilateral relations between the two countries were very limited, including in the political, commercial, and cultural fields. The Spanish Communist Party was small and of little influence. The July 1936 uprising quickly transformed Soviet-Spanish relations. As analyzed by Daniel Kowalsky in his chapter, diplomacy was renewed, friendship societies flourished, and within a few weeks Moscow initiated a solidarity campaign, which included military, as well as humanitarian assistance to the beleaguered Republic. In early November, Soviet tanks, airplanes, and advisors were already present in Spain, and the International Brigades, organized by the Comintern, were able to change the course of events in the Battle of Madrid. By the end of 1936, Soviet commitment to the Loyalist cause was clear to all.

Soviet support had a crucial impact on Spanish intellectuals, many of them, such as the poet Rafael Alberti, had identified with revolutionary messages emanating from Moscow before the outbreak of the war. Silvina Schammah Gesser and Alexandra Cheveleva Dergacheva explore in their chapter the political and moral conflicts exposed during the poet's visit to the Soviet capital during the early stages of the civil war. Torn between a growing awareness of Stalinist terror and gratitude for Soviet assistance to the Republicans, Alberti was troubled by this dilemma for the rest of his life.

The similarities between the Popular Front governments of Spain and France in 1936 gave rise to expectations for swift and decisive French support for the legally established Spanish Republic. Public opinion in France, however, was divided and the Blum government lacked firm backing. Its dependency on British foreign policy, in the shadow of a rising German power, also limited its room for maneuver. David Messenger maps the various currents within French society and the way they reacted to the Spanish crisis. In a polarized society, as reflected in the political party system and the contemporary press, France was divided among those, mainly on the left, who expressed solidarity with the Republican government, those who supported the Nationalist rebels, and many who feared the eruption of a civil war at home and therefore opted for non-intervention.

Focusing on conservative attitudes toward Spain, and especially Winston Churchill's approach, Emilio Sáenz-Francés explores how anti-Communist feelings, sympathies with the possibility of a return to monarchy, and contemporary suspicions of Fascism shaped British responses to events in Spain. Churchill's realistic views on the Iberian Peninsula, which led him to support appeasement and non-intervention, are traced from the outbreak of the civil war to World War II.

Argentina formally adhered to the non-intervention policy as well, but in fact its diplomats showed marked sympathy for the Nationalists. Leonardo Senkman analyzes the practices of diplomatic and maritime asylum offered by Argentina during the initial phases of the Spanish Civil War. Based on the Latin American legal tradition of the right of asylum, Argentine diplomats gave shelter to and then evacuated mostly supporters of the insurgents. Two Argentine warships bore away important figures on the Franco side between July 1936 and late 1937; most of them returned to Spain once the Nationalists won the war.

The Spanish Civil War coincided with a turning point in Japan's political history. A failed coup in February 1936 led to an increase in military influence and to greater involvement of army officers in decision-making processes. Haruo Tohmatsu's chapter explores the impact of the Spanish Civil War on Japanese politics, diplomacy, and strategy on the eve of World War II. The crystallization of the Franco regime during the first months of the conflict became a model for several Japanese, who yearned for an authoritarian regime supported by a monarchy. Gathering information on weapons used in the Iberian battlefields helped the Japanese army in its preparations to deal with the Red Army in the Soviet–Mongolian–Manchuko border disputes of 1938–39. Based in Salamanca in late 1936, Captain Susumu Nishiura, an artillery officer of the Imperial Japanese Army, observed the Spanish Civil War and sent reports to

Tokyo which contributed to the shaping of the Japanese army's views on the Axis powers and the Soviet Union.

In 1948, audiences all over Europe were stunned by Roberto Rosselini's new movie, *Germany Year Zero* (*Germania anno zero*). This was the last film in Rossellini's unofficial war trilogy, following *Rome, Open City*, and *Paisà*. Unlike the other films, which transpire in German-occupied Rome or during the Allied invasion of Italy, *Germany Year Zero* takes place in postwar Germany. In the movie, Rossellini tried to convey the reality there, the year after its near total destruction in World War II. The film contains dramatic images of bombed-out Berlin and of the human struggle for survival following the defeat of the Third Reich.

We, the co-editors of this volume, had Rossellini's movie in mind when we discussed the main theme of the conference on which our book is based. We decided to focus on 1936, the year "when it all began." We also discussed Ian Buruma's 2014 book *Year Zero: A History of 1945*, which examines the attempts to "return to normality" after a devastating world war, as well as Felix Luna's Argentine classic, *El 45: Crónica de un año decisivo.*[19] In all three works we discerned an effort to look at a brief, intense, and crucial historical moment, during which, to a large extent, many of the social and political events in subsequent decades were determined – a year full of unique, probably unrepeatable, events.

There is no way to understand present-day Spain without looking back to the beginnings of the civil war, which transformed social and political cleavages into a Manichean struggle between two antagonistic camps, each one believing it represented the utmost good and was fighting the utmost evil.

The transition to democracy tended at first to let bygones be bygones. Following the death of the Caudillo, Spain's leading politicians negotiated an informal agreement to put aside the most difficult episodes of Spanish history: the atrocities, massacres, and mass murders of the civil war and early Francoism – coined by Paul Preston "the Spanish Holocaust."[20] Far from seeking "justice," "truth," or "reconciliation," Spain chose to forget and move on, adopting a comprehensive amnesty law to avoid prosecuting the human rights abuses of the old regime. This policy of dis-remembering was evident already in 1986, under the Socialist government of Felipe González, during the events to commemorate the fiftieth anniversary of the start of the civil war.

There were obviously many reasons for this. Unlike similar regimes that arose in Europe in the interwar period, the Franco regime was never defeated by its opponents but instead abolished itself by enacting a political reform law in 1976. Moreover, there was a "natural" fear of provoking a renewed confrontation. "In Spain there is only one way to reach democracy, which is to forget the past," the Communist leader Santiago Carrillo said in 1975.

The topic has continued to touch a sensitive nerve in Spanish society until this very day. In late 2016, for example, in his annual Christmas Eve speech, King Felipe VI urged Spaniards to remain united as the nation faced an uncertain political future. The monarch spoke of coexistence between young and old, in the workplace, and between men and women. These are not times for internal bickering but for building on the diversity of thought that makes Spain great, he said in the televised address. The speech provoked a complaint by the Association for the Recovery of Historical Memory (Asociación para la recuperación de la Memoria Histórica). In a letter to the ombudsman (*defensor del pueblo*), they claimed that the king's call not to intensify old resentments or to reopen unhealed wounds violated the rights of the victims of Francoism.

The editors of this volume would like to express their gratitude to Tel Aviv University for hosting the conference in which several of the papers included here were first presented. The S. Daniel Abraham Center for International and Regional Studies, as well as the Elías Sourasky Chair of Latin American and Spanish History, and the Kahn Institute for History of the Mediterranean Basin, supported this project both financially and administratively. The Israel Institute of Washington, DC, sponsored the research for the chapter on Jewish athletes who traveled from Palestine to Spain to participate in the People's Olympiad that never took place. Haruo Tohmatsu is grateful for the Japan International Relations Association's support.

We are indebted to Pablo Bornstein for his help in organizing the conference and taking care of the correspondence with authors, reviewers, and editors. We are also grateful to Talma Kinarti, Omri Elmaleh, and Maayan Nahari for their help. Many thanks to Beryl Belsky for style editing the texts, and to Tony Grahame and the staff at Sussex Academic Press for their excellent editorial work. It has been a pleasure working with them.

Tel Aviv, December 2017

Notes

1 "Spain Parliament Calls for Franco's Remains to Be Moved," *The New York Times*, May 11, 2017; "'It's Shameful for Franco's Victims': Spanish MPs Vote to Exhume Dictator," *The Guardian*, May 11, 2017.

2 On the construction of the country's largest monument, surmounted by a 150-meter-high cross, see Andrea Hepworth, "Site of Memory and Dismemory: The Valley of the Fallen in Spain," *Journal of Genocide Research* 16,

no. 4 (2014): 463–65; Katherine Hite, "The Valley of the Fallen: Tales from the Crypt," *Forum for Modern Language Studies* 44, no. 2 (2008): 110–26; Daniel Sueiro, *El Valle de los Caídos. Los secretos de la cripta franquista* (Madrid: La Esfera de los Libros, 2006).

3 For a recent biography of Primo de Rivera, see Joan Maria Thomàs, *José Antonio: Realidad y mito* (Barcelona: Debate Penguin Random House, 2017).

4 José Luis Rodríguez Jiménez, *La extrema derecho española en el siglo xx* (Madrid: Alianza, 1997).

5 "Spanish MPs Vote to Exhume Dictator," *The Guardian.*

6 "Madrid aprueba el cambio de nombre de 52 calles de referencias franquistas," *El País*, April 28, 2017; "Madrid cambiará el nombre de 52 calles franquistas la próxima semana," *El Español*, April 28, 2017.

7 For recent studies of the División Azul, see Xose Manoel Núñez Seixas, *Camarada invierno: Experiencia y memoria de la División Azul (1941–1945)* (Barcelona: Crítica, 2016); Xavier Moreno Juliá, *The Blue Division: Spanish Blood in Russia, 1941–1945* (Brighton: Sussex Academic Press, 2015).

8 See among others, Paul Preston, *The Destruction of Guernica* (London: HarperCollins, 2012); Robert Stradling, *Your Children Will Be Next: Bombing and Propaganda in the Spanish Civil War, 1936–1939* (Cardiff: University of Wales Press, 2008).

9 "Guernica Massacre: Madrid Removes Façade that Glorified Nazi Role," *The Guardian*, 26 April, 2017.

10 Paloma Aguilar Fernández, *Memory and Amnesia: The Role of the Spanish Civil War in the Transition to Democracy* (Oxford: Berghahn Books, 2002); Santos Julia, coord., *Víctimas de la Guerra Civil* (Madrid: Temas de Hoy, 1999).

11 On the third and fourth generations of Spaniards and their contemporary role in dealing with their country's violent past, see Paloma Aguilar and Clara Ramírez-Barat, "Generational Dynamics in Spain: Memory Transmission of a Turbulent Past," *Memory Studies* (2016): 1–17; Andrea Hepworth, "From Survivor to Fourth-Generation Memory: Literal and Discursive Sites of Memory in Post-Dictatorship Germany and Spain, *Journal of Contemporary History* (2017): 1–24.

12 See, for example, Layla Renshaw, *Exhuming Loss: Memory, Materiality and Mass Graves of the Spanish Civil War* (Walnut Creek, CA: Left Coast Press, 2011); Alejandro Baer and Natan Sznaider, *Memory and Forgetting in the Post-Holocaust Era* (Oxford: Routledge, 2017).

13 "Spain Refuses to Declassify State Files from 1931 to 1968," *El País* (in English), June 24, 2015; "Congress Set to Approve Reform of Spain's Franco-Era Secrecy Laws," *El País* (in English), November 29, 2016; "PP y PSOE dejan en el limbo la nueva ley de Secretos Oficiales," *El País*, May 1, 2017.

14 "Spain Refuses to Declassify State Files," *El País.*

15 "Symposium Introduction," *Journal of Contemporary History* 52, no. 1 (2017): 118–20.

16 Roberto Villa García y Álvarez Tardío, *1936. Fraude y violencia en las elecciones del Frente Popular* (Barcelona: S.L.U. Espasa, 2017).
17 Stanley G. Payne and Jesús Palacios, *Franco: Una biografía personal y política* (Barcelona: S.L.U. Espasa, 2014). An English edition was published simultaneously by University of Wisconsin Press, 2014: *Franco: A Personal and Political Biography*.
18 Thomas Jeffrey Miley, "Franquism as Authoritarianism: Juan Linz and his Critics," *Politics, Religion & Ideology* 12, no. 1 (2011): 27–50.
19 Ian Buruma, *Year Zero: A History of 1945* (New York: Penguin Group, 2013); Félix Luna, *El 45: Crónica de un año decisivo* (Buenos Aires: Editorial Jorge Alvarez, 1969).
20 Paul Preston, *The Spanish Holocaust* (London: HarperPress, 2013).

1

1936: The Eruption of Revolutionary Anti-Fascism in Spain

MICHAEL SEIDMAN

The emphasis on a single year often reflects a Western revolutionary consciousness, which began with the French Revolution. The year 1789 became the date conventionally accepted as the beginning of the first modern revolution on the European continent. In fact, in 1939 the great historian of the revolution, Georges Lefebvre, authored a book, *Quatre-Vingt-Neuf*, which was published with the assistance of the Comité national de célébration du 150e anniversaire de la Révolution française. The name of the book's sponsor is significant because the committee wished not merely to commemorate the year but to celebrate it. Lefebvre's volume has been translated into many languages, usually with the title *1789: The Year of the Revolution*, or *1789: French Revolution.* Hence, the French spread this idea of the single revolutionary year – a great break with the past, or the "old regime" – to the rest of the world. In fact, the concept of dramatic rupture or revolution is probably France's most important conceptual export during the last several hundred years. It may be, in part, because of the French that we speak of what the Germans call the "magical date" (*magische Datum*).[1]

Historians have wrestled with the meaning and significance of a single, supposedly seminal, year. Alexis de Tocqueville analyzed 1789 as the result of the state building of the *ancien régime*, and Arthur Marwick regarded another magical date, 1968, as the zenith of the cultural revolution of the "long sixties."[2] Likewise, it makes sense to see 1936 as part of a larger period of revolutionary upheaval, even if 1936 has not achieved the prominence of 1789 or 1968. The year 1936 is rather equivalent to 1917, a date which is largely identified with the Russian Revolution. Similarly, 1936 was subsumed by the outbreak of the Spanish Civil War.[3]

Of course, like all magical dates, 1917 and 1936 belong to a larger era, and both years experienced the culmination of past tensions in the form of revolution and counterrevolution. War – a global conflict in the Russian case and a civil one in the Spanish case – once again provoked revolution. The specter of another "proletarian revolution," all of which had been defeated in Hungary, Finland, Germany, and China after World War I, inspired and frightened many. The year 1936 meant that the Russian Revolution was no longer isolated as it had been after 1919. In fact, many in the European establishment feared the spread of revolution to neighboring France, where a Popular Front government also ruled. In hindsight, they were wrong since a much more conservative, if not counterrevolutionary, anti-Fascism marked the French Popular Front and would develop rapidly after the Spanish Civil War ended in 1939.

In January 1936, an electoral coalition of Socialists, Republicans, POUM (Partido Obrero de Unificación Marxista), UGT (Unión General de Trabajadores), Catalan nationalists, and PCE (Partido Comunista de España) composed the Spanish Popular Front. Its victory in February 1936 encouraged violent revolutionary and counterrevolutionary movements.[4] The Popular Front parliament amnestied the hundreds, if not thousands, of revolutionaries imprisoned following the 1934 Asturias revolt, and the government decreed that they be readmitted immediately to their former jobs. At the same time, its supporters demanded that those who had suppressed the Asturias rebellion be put on trial.[5] During the Popular Front period, 153 religious establishments suffered severe destruction, usually by arson.[6] Anti-clerical militants damaged and pillaged hundreds more, and frequently intimidated clergymen.[7] Between the Popular Front electoral victory and the outbreak of the civil war, peasants illegally took over seven times more land than they had occupied since the establishment of the Second Republic in 1931.[8] In urban areas, "proletarian shoppers" assaulted stores, entering and leaving without paying for the commodities taken.[9] In Andalusia, many pilfered from shops and neglected to pay rent.[10] The fall in rent receipts led urban landlords in Seville and throughout Spain to neglect to meet their fiscal obligations. Strikes were continuous and nearly countless.[11] Some industrialists abandoned their enterprises because of a fear of the coming "Red Revolution."[12] A cross-class coalition of Catholics and large and small property owners feared the onset or expansion of the revolution.

Leaders of the PCE believed that the Popular Front had begun the transition to a proletarian revolution. "In the Communist texts of the Popular Front, anti-Fascism was a synonym for revolution, in the same way that Fascism meant counterrevolution."[13] Furthermore, the breakdown of public order was apparent to many, including Comintern leaders, who feared that it might provoke a military coup to overturn the Popular Front government.[14] In April 1936, a well-placed leftist journalist observed the inability of the parliamentary regime to contain its foes:

> Everyone – from the most intelligent to the dumbest – knows that each day the country becomes more divided into two irreconcilable and antagonistic parts: revolution and counterrevolution . . . which are warring bodies that are not compatible within a parliamentary democracy.[15]

The Popular Front government was perceived – often correctly – as repressing the radical Right more than the revolutionary Left.[16] The most telling example was the assassination on July 13 of the extreme right leader José Calvo Sotelo. For the first time in the history of parliamentary regimes, a detachment of state police murdered a leader of the parliamentary opposition.[17] The assassins were close to the "moderate" Socialist leader, Indalecio Prieto, who protected them from any investigation. Another leading Socialist, Margarita Nelken, hid the killers, one of whom later became a powerful Republican security chief during the civil war. The magnicide helped to convince a wavering General Francisco Franco to join the conspiracy against the Republic. Political and social violence in Spain reflected the underdeveloped and polarized nature of Spanish society and the inability of its weak state to control either supporters or opponents. The absence of what important sectors of the Right considered to be a neutral and efficient state encouraged them to rebel.

The Popular Front prime minister, Santiago Casares Quiroga (May 13–July 19), was forced to confront the military rebellion of July 17–18. He consciously avoided replaying the role of Alexander Kerensky, often considered responsible for failing to block the Bolsheviks, and resigned on the evening of July 18 rather than allow revolutionary groups to arm. His successor, Diego Martínez Barrio, desperately attempted to convince the rebel officers of his government's desire to restore order, but General Emilio Mola rejected negotiations with the Republican authorities and made the bloody conflict inevitable. Martínez Barrio resigned on the same day that he took office. Given the officers' commitment to continue the *pronunciamiento*, President Manuel Azaña and the new prime minister, José Giral (July 19–September 4), felt compelled to arm the revolutionaries, who already possessed large amounts of weapons. In major urban centers, professional Republican forces of order often joined these amateur militiamen. Sensing the feelings of their fellow urban residents, soldiers and police in the principal cities were often wary of supporting the military revolt. For example, 15 companies or 3,000 security and assault guards stationed in Barcelona declared themselves unconditionally loyal to the Generalitat, the Catalan regional government.[18] The Republic's overwhelming victory in Barcelona resonated throughout the nation.[19] The major cities and the wealthiest regions remained in Republican hands.

The partial failure of military revolt unleashed the Spanish Civil War (1936–39). The conflict in Spain brought anti-Fascism to worldwide attention in dramatic fashion, and the relatively new mass media of radio and photojournalism broadcast the anti-Fascist struggle throughout the globe. On a greater scale than any previous conflicts, including the Ethiopian War of 1935–36, the Republic offered anti-Fascists across the globe an opportunity to work and fight against their enemies. From its onset, the Spanish Civil War eclipsed all other international events until the Munich crisis of September 1938. Forty thousand persons – many of them Communists – from all over the globe volunteered to fight for the Spanish Republic in the International Brigades, and tens of thousands more worked in their native lands in a host of pro-Republican and anti-Fascist organizations.

In Republican Spain itself, the most intense and spontaneous revolution that any European country would ever experience occurred in the Republican zone during the Spanish Civil War, especially in 1936. Throughout Republican Spain, rekindled iconoclastic fervor abused the people and property of the Church. Church burnings destroyed the symbols and rituals of the old order as revolutionary firing squads "executed" holy statues. Priests suffered their greatest massacre since the French Revolution. Nearly 7,000 members of the Catholic clergy were killed. Local revolutionaries might spare the lives of the rich and right-wingers, but they were usually implacable with priests. Clerics possessed the unfortunate qualities of being hated and easily identified. Furthermore, "fascist" clergymen gained a highly embellished reputation for firing on revolutionaries from church towers. As in other major European civil wars – English, French, and Russian – religion both created and revealed the gap between revolutionaries and counterrevolutionaries. The revolutionaries' massacres and numerous acts of iconoclasm demonstrated their desire to replace the old religion with their new secular faith. Nationalist sympathizers reported brutal ceremonies that recalled the rough justice of the French Revolution. The Spanish conflict became the greatest European war of religion in the twentieth century. The inability of the Second Spanish Republic to integrate a large body of Catholics did it great harm both domestically and internationally. As a result, Catholicism became the most cohesive cultural force in the Nationalist zone and the most important source of *franquista* support in Britain, France, and the United States.

Both revolutionaries and counterrevolutionaries coined the term *paseos*, a word derived from American gangster movies. During these "walks," organized gangs would eliminate their ideological enemies by forcing them into a vehicle – usually requisitioned from the comfortable classes – and driving them to their final destination.[20] Alternatively, an ambulatory squad knocked at the door, politely requested the victim to accompany it, and, when out of sight, shot him. In addition to the Catholic clergy, the targets were potentially rebellious military officers, Rightists, and bourgeois citizens. A mixture of social, political, and religious hatreds spurred killers of all persuasions to begin the bloody birthing of a new society cleansed of its enemies. As in the postwar civil wars in Finland and Hungary, when revolutionaries also confronted counterrevolutionaries, the Right proved more murderous than the Left. During the Spanish conflict, the Nationalists would assassinate 130,000 Leftists; the Republicans 50,000 Rightists. Although later in the war some officials did make efforts to stop *paseos*, during the first months of the conflict Republican governments tolerated them or at least did not halt them. For example, about half of the clergymen killed were executed in the first six weeks of the war.[21] Potential victims tried to hide their identity by going underground or disguising themselves by wearing "proletarian" clothes.

Militants of the Popular Front who prevented the military rebellion from triumphing in half of Spain intensified the social revolution that the rebellious officers were trying to halt. The activists – Socialists, Communists, and libertarians – collectivized numerous farms and most factories in the Republican zone. The anarchists and anarcho-syndicalists of the CNT (Confederación Nacional del Trabajo) demonstrated their desire to defend the new-born revolution by abandoning their anti-statism and joining governments for the first time in history. Their participation in the Generalitat in September and the national government in November reinforced the Republic's radical reputation. Anarchist armed squads imposed "class justice" in Barcelona by eliminating the local bourgeoisie and confiscating their property, especially private cars which they drove joyfully, if recklessly, around the city. Urban anarchists also requisitioned supplies from the peasantry, exacerbating urban-rural tensions.

Although Communists attempted to downplay the revolutionary nature of the Republic in the civil war, their attitude toward the Spanish Revolution was more complex than is often stated. While they usually insisted that Spain must remain at the stage of bourgeois democracy, and eventually attempted to suppress both revolutionary "Trotskyites" of the POUM and anarchists of the CNT, Communists immediately supported revolutionary terror against both their "bourgeois" and even "proletarian" opponents. In fact, they contributed more to the killings than perhaps any other revolutionary organization.[22] Despite PCE rhetoric, the Republic surpassed the "bourgeois democratic" stage of the French Revolution of 1789. The Republican zone was hardly democratic in any usual sense because the entire Right had been eliminated – sometimes physically – and the parliament played little or no role during the war. Furthermore, the Spanish Revolution endangered many more types of private property than the seigneurial dues, Church, and émigré possessions confiscated during the French Revolution. Communist, Socialist, and anarchist goals sharply contrasted with those of French revolutionaries of 1789 who had declared private property a "sacred right of man" and planned to promote a free-market economy. Despite calming rhetoric meant to reassure both the domestic and foreign middle classes, Communist attitudes toward private property were hardly bourgeois. Instead, they were inspired by Lenin's New Economic Policy (NEP, 1921–28) to protect small property in order to win over the petty bourgeoisie. The Spanish Republic adopted a variation of the Soviet NEP where different forms of private and collective property coexisted.

Communists also advocated nationalization of large employers and participated with both Socialists and anarchists in the management of collectivized farms and factories. The PCE introduced a prototype of a "people's democracy" in which large-scale capitalism and "fascism" – that is, all conservative groups, whether democratic or not – would cease to exist. Their republic guaranteed private property only temporarily, as Communist and even Republican leaders admitted when speaking candidly.[23] A "popular revolution" – a concept formulated by the Italian Communists to promote a broad leftist coalition against Fascism – prefigured the people's democracies of postwar Eastern Europe.[24] In 1936, Palmiro Togliatti, the most important representative of the Comintern in Spain, defined the Spanish Republic as a "new democratic republic." At the same time, Georgi Dimitrov, the Comintern chief, reaffirmed his subordinate's judgment and called the anti-Fascist Republic "an authentic popular democracy . . . in which the truly left bourgeoisie collaborates."[25] Comintern officials believed that the Spanish Republic offered the opportunity to create a "democracy of a new type."[26] Although the theme of transition to Socialism was downplayed in order not to alarm Western democracies, the Comintern and the PCE planned the Communist absorption of Socialists in a political union which would eventually culminate in a "proletarian dictatorship."[27]

The USSR initially agreed not to intervene in Spain in the hope that non-intervention would redound to the benefit of the Republic. Like other major powers, the Soviets calculated that the Republic had much greater possibilities of victory than its enemies did. At the end of July, the Republican zone contained 60 percent of the population, controlled 90 percent of Spanish maritime traffic, and 80 percent of industrial production, although only 28 percent of the total agrarian product.[28] Furthermore, Soviet intervention would have alienated British and French conservative anti-Fascists whom Joseph Stalin was hoping would cooperate with his country to isolate the nascent Axis. Before Franco's troops conquered Toledo in September, Socialists, Communists, and others felt that the Republic would quickly defeat the rebels.[29] Even at the end of 1936, the powerful Comintern representative in Spain, Victorio Codovilla, estimated that Nationalist forces had exhausted themselves and that the Republican strength was bound to grow.[30] In other words, the outcome of the conflict remained contingent. Unlike Germany and Italy, which immediately assisted the Nationalists in July, the USSR would send aid to the Republic on a major scale only in the fall of 1936.

Communists, Socialists, anarchists, and their allied trade unionists assumed that wage earners would labor devotedly in their newly collectivized farms, factories, and workshops. The militants quickly became disappointed since workers resisted laboring under the revolutionary political and trade union leaderships that had instituted various forms of democratic workers' control. Many wage earners continued to demand more pay and persisted in their attempts to avoid the constraints of factory space and time. The anarcho-syndicalists of the CNT and the Socialists and Communists of UGT who ran the collectives in Barcelona, Spain's most important industrial area, opposed many of the workers' demands that they had supported before the revolution and civil war. Instead, the activists called for more effort and sacrifice. Rank-and-file workers frequently ignored these appeals and acted as though the union militants were the new ruling elite. Direct and indirect resistance to work became major points of conflict between rank-and-file workers and militants, just as they had been when the bourgeoisie controlled the productive forces. These new industrial managers were continually beseeching the rank-and-file not to request wage hikes during the difficult times of war and revolution, but their pleas were frequently ignored in various industrial sectors.

Indeed, the workers took advantage of the revolution to escape wage labor. On July 22, the Sindicato de Artes Blancas (bakers) reminded its members that they should go back to work.[31] They returned to their jobs at the end of July only "little by little."[32] Some militants decided to engage in morning labor only and use the afternoons to "stroll through Barcelona."[33] The unions were forced to confront major problems of absenteeism and lateness, phenomena that have existed in varying degrees throughout the history of labor. Skipping work indicated the rank-and-file's determined dislike of the factory, however democratic. Sickness multiplied the number of workdays missed. Tobacco breaks and alcohol abuse, subjects of reprobation in wartime Spanish Socialist realist poster propaganda, contributed to the loss of worktime. Sabotage and theft – which implied a great detachment from the libertarian or Communist principles of cooperation in production – continued. Despite the anarcho-syndicalist slogan, "whoever does not work is a Fascist," resistance to work became much more common than strikes, which would have been brutally suppressed as "counterrevolutionary."[34] Faced with these varied forms of working-class resistance to labor and workspace, the unions and the collectives cooperated to establish strict rules and regulations that equaled or surpassed the controls imposed by capitalist enterprises. Wage earners' refusal to work conflicted with the militants' urgent need to combat the Nationalists through greater production. To increase output and reduce resistances, the urban revolutionary elite implemented piecework, elimination of holidays, medical inspections, fines, and dismissals. Even so, its industrial collectives were unable to produce sufficient quantities of arms for its soldiers. The anarchist Eugenio Vallejo, head of the Comisión de Industrias de Guerra of Catalonia, admitted that the production of cartridges was only one-sixth of what had been promised to front-line fighters.[35]

The outbreak of revolution led to the formation of a multitude of committees that often became a cover for the satisfaction of individual needs. A member of the Comité de Guerra de Gijón declared: "The revolution was fabulous. In its first days committees spontaneously emerged in all the neighborhoods. They established collective kitchens, expropriated food, and distributed vouchers . . . The result was a bit chaotic."[36] The non-committed – undoubtedly a majority of the population – took measures to ensure that they possessed a union and party card, which they needed to keep their job, eat in a collective kitchen, and gain access to health care. In the countryside, many small holders felt compelled to join collectives, which provided education for their children and some medical care.

Proletarians and others used the revolution not only to win welfare benefits and reduce work hours, but also to evade paying taxes or rent. In a situation in which the unions had confiscated the property of numerous landlords who had fled, many workers refused to pay them at all.[37] Like the Bolsheviks during their civil war (1919–21), the Republican regime collected few taxes and funded itself through confiscations of property and printing paper money. Future prime minister Juan Negrín was said to have distrusted collectives because as finance minister in Francisco Largo Caballero governments from September 1936 to May 1937, he had found it impossible to collect taxes from them.[38] The lack of state revenues placed public servants in an increasingly precarious position.

Many Republican militias would take what they needed and glibly assure the owners – whether businessmen or local governments – that they would be reimbursed in the future. In Madrid, partisans confiscated almost every commodity, including radios, typewriters, watches, and even bras.[39] In certain stores, looters left only the vacant display tables which they had stripped of all items. By October 1936, the uncontrolled requisitioning of militia columns in Aragon threatened the "total ruin" of the region.[40] Pillaging must have frightened the swing group of small holders and tenant farmers who were torn between Nationalists and Republicans. If they were attracted to the Republic by its de facto abolition of rents owed to large landowners, they were also repelled by its inability to protect property and the quartering of its troops in their villages. Disrespect for property alienated small holders, renters, and sharecroppers, and negated the Republic's attempt to win them over by its October 7 decree, which guaranteed their inalienable right to farm the land they worked. Uncontrolled requisitioning might have worked if the Republic had been able to achieve a quick victory, but it was disastrous in a long war. In response to the early requisitions, the provinces surrounding Madrid soon refused to supply food to the capital.

The militias' neglect of logistics confirmed their amateurishness. The lack of food naturally demoralized soldiers and workers. In October 1936, an anarchist militiaman complained of his own and his fellow soldiers' skinniness "because we eat so little."[41] He continued to report entire days where soldiers of the Popular Army went unnourished.[42] On the Aragon front in early September 1936, Nationalists related that the enemy's paucity of regular meals for two days had caused its morale to falter.[43] The Battalion of Mieres (Asturias) griped about administrative disorder and the resulting scarcity of bread and meat.[44] The militias' irrational and egotistical use of resources would corrode the Republic and contribute greatly to its ultimate demise. As the Popular Army grew larger, so, too, did requisitions. The friction in the Republican zone between soldiers and peasants stood in contrast to the relative confidence that existed in Nationalist regions. Nationalists could generally be trusted to protect property. In Navarre, for example, during the first weeks of the conflict, "purchases were paid in cash," thereby encouraging production for the market.[45] "Requisitions were no longer allowed since we had enough money. Moreover, requisitions disturbed the agrarian economy." Spanish farmers welcomed Nationalist currency and rejected the Republican militias' vouchers. When Nationalists did requisition items, they usually provided indemnities. In addition, the *franquistas* seem to have depended on regular collection of taxes, thereby providing soldiers with steady pay rather than unpredictable plunder.

Violently rejecting the neo-traditionalist Catholicism of the Nationalists, the working-class parties and trade unions that dominated the Republican zone introduced a revolutionary culture. The widespread use of *camarada* instead of *señor* imposed a verbal unity. Men removed their ties, a supposed vestige of the bourgeoisie, and for the first time, large numbers of revolutionary women donned pants.[46] Their alleged transvestism outraged *franquistas.*[47] The workers' and militias' blue overalls became a glorified and combative symbol of the proletariat, and the Alianza de Intelectuales Antifascistas named one of the most prestigious Republican journals *El Mono Azul* (the blue overalls), whose first issue appeared in August.[48] In its pages and well behind the lines, the poet Rafael Alberti incited combativeness:

> ¡A la pista,
> Pistola ametrallador,
> Mono azul antifascista!
> ¡Mono azul!: salta, colea,
> prudente como imprudente,
> hasta morir en el frente
> y al frente de la pelea [49]

On the visual front, the Republic offered Socialist realist posters, resembling those of the USSR. Although the Spanish posters were more graceful and accomplished than their Soviet counterparts, like the latter they glorified the producer and the means of production while denigrating the bourgeois enemy and the lazy worker. The Republic also provided moviegoers with both Soviet and Hollywood movies. The latter proved much more popular than the former. In 1937, Azaña commented acidly:

> It does not do the President of the Republic any good to speak of democracy and liberalism if, at the same time, the films that our propagandists show in the movie houses always finish with portraits of Lenin and Stalin.[50]

For cultural and many other reasons, Hitler's and Mussolini's claims to be fighting "Communist revolution" in Spain seemed plausible to many on the right and even the center. In the first crucial months of the war, the Nationalists received the highly effective aid of both powers, which initiated what would become the Axis in response to Spanish revolutionary anti-Fascism. In July 1936, with indispensable foreign assistance, Franco originated the first major airlift in history, and by August 1936 had transported more than 10,000 soldiers from Morocco to the peninsula. Several months later, their numbers had risen to 14,000, along with hundreds of tons of equipment and arms. Moroccan mercenaries were among the elite of Franco's forces and were instrumental in rapidly conquering large swaths of southern and central Spain in the summer and early fall. The North Africans, whose numbers would reach 80,000, were joined by 72,000 Italian ground troops over the course of the war. Following the airlift, Nazi aid to the Nationalists was largely devoted to supporting the Condor Legion. This 5,000–6,000 men aircraft group, which was assembled in Spain in November 1936, would be Hitler's most notorious contribution to the Nationalist victory.

German and Italian assistance to Franco was timelier, more persistent, and more regular than Soviet aid to the Republic, which tried to narrow the foreign assistance gap by employing approximately 40,000 International Brigaders. The Internationals, largely recruited by Communist networks, proved more interested in ideology and less in booty than Franco's African mercenaries. The Internationals often developed into excellent and committed soldiers whose gung-ho initiatives contrasted with ordinary Spanish soldiers' desires to maintain live-and-let-live nonviolence on quiet fronts. The Internationals frequently felt themselves superior to their more passive Spanish Republican comrades. One committed Spaniard estimated an International Brigader to be worth many indigenous soldiers.[51]

Anti-Fascist volunteers from France, the UK, the US, and many other nations emphasized that their fight in Spain was in defense of democracy and Spanish independence against German and Italian "invaders." The anti-Fascist struggle morphed into a patriotic one. The conflation of patriotism and anti-Fascism – initiated during the Popular Front era – permitted easier recruitment in the democracies where volunteers and aid for the Republic vastly outnumbered those for the Nationalists. Aware of the need to appeal to democratic public opinion, many International Brigaders, including the nearly 3,000 Americans mostly grouped in what became known as the Abraham Lincoln Brigade, tried to mask their revolutionary commitment. When the Lincolns sang "The Internationale," they claimed for public consumption that it was "The

Star-Spangled Banner."[52] The name of their unit, officially the Abraham Lincoln Battalion, evoked a fight for democracy, not Socialism. As Communists, most Lincolns accepted a rapprochement with the capitalist West in the form of the Popular Front only as a temporary expedient. They regarded themselves as part of a "proletarian army," even if – like leftist militants in Spain – they had a very orthodox and unrealistic view of Spanish workers.

Like the Lincolns, other International Brigaders never lost their close links to the Communist Party. Following the Communist line, many British volunteers defined the Republic that they served as a "democratic and parliamentary republic of a new type." An Eastern European Jewish-Communist commissar, who had volunteered to fight in Spain, constantly referred to his "revolutionary" commitment and his colleagues' desire to "fight for the proletarian cause." Most of the famous (or infamous) figures who led the post-1945 Communist regimes were involved in the Spanish conflict, including the German Walter Ulbricht and the Czech Klement Gottwald. Josip Broz, the future Marshal Tito who became the head of the Federal People's Republic of Yugoslavia, organized International Brigade volunteers from the Balkans and central Europe. At the end of World War II in their "people's democracies," these men put into practice the Communist theory that the world wars had initiated an era of Socialist revolutions.[53]

The assassinations of clergy, military, and bourgeois accompanied by massive property confiscations in Spain convinced a broad range of public opinion across the Atlantic and beyond that the Spanish Republic had become a revolutionary state unable to impose order and discipline on its supporters. Many non-Communists refused to believe that members of the Comintern had ceased to be dedicated revolutionaries. Some Soviet officials – such as Foreign Minister Maxim Litvinov – saw a contradiction of their own policy, which aimed for broad anti-Fascist alliances with democratic moderates, yet supported a revolutionary republic. Despite the wishes of the Comintern, Litvinov opposed Russian involvement in Spain since he realized that the Spanish Revolution would hinder Soviet attempts to ally with the democratic West.[54] Although Stalin decided to intervene in Spain, he ultimately downplayed popular anti-Fascism and favored traditional diplomacy and alliances among states.

The Spanish Republicans' commitment to revolutionary anti-capitalism alienated powerful businessmen and diplomats. US Secretary of State Cordell Hull denounced the Barcelona workers' seizure of American corporate property, specifically the General Motors plant in that city. Thus, as one of the most prominent Lincoln Brigade veterans admitted, Communists were unable to alter US public opinion and convince in sufficient numbers "other democratic forces" to aid the Republic.[55] The same political ineffectiveness and inability to persuade democratic governments to assist it was repeated in the UK and France. The revolutionary anti-Fascism of Communists, Socialists, anarchists, and the POUM scared moderates, conservatives, and Catholics throughout the world. Western policies of non-intervention in the Spanish Civil War may not have stopped Fascism – as critics claimed Western intervention would have – but non-intervention prevented a deep division within and among the Atlantic democracies. The latter had large numbers of counterrevolutionary anti-Fascists on the moderate left and conservative right who rejected any form of Fascism in their own countries and were eventually willing – especially after the Spanish Civil War – to combat Fascist expansionism. Non-intervention distanced counterrevolutionary anti-Fascism from revolution and Communism and would help to make it respectable among moderate, conservative, and Catholic opinion.

France, the UK, and the US deplored German and Italian intervention in Spain on the side of Spanish counterrevolutionaries and Fascists. France and Britain would have preferred a quick Republican or even a Nationalist victory that preserved the European status quo. In August 1936, the French prime minister – the Socialist Léon Blum – proposed an official policy of non-intervention. Blum's proposal was designed to help the Republic by restraining the flow of German and Italian aid while preventing a wider European war, and Azaña and the Soviets initially supported it. The French government, whose commitment to appeasement had been demonstrated by its passive response to the German invasion of the Rhineland in March, hoped that the limitation on arms exports would force both sides to negotiate a settlement arranged by the Great Powers.[56] Ultimately, non-intervention was successful in limiting the war to Spain and preventing it from triggering a larger conflict, but it damaged the Spanish Republic, which would have remained nearly totally isolated without the intervention of the Soviet Union.[57]

Although non-intervention angered French Communists who were part of Blum's own Popular Front coalition, it won the support of Blum's other major coalition partner – the Radical Party. Despite its name, the latter was the French Third Republic's swing party and represented its center. Aiding revolutionary Spain would have alienated the Radicals and ruptured the tripartite coalition of the French Popular Front. This Popular Front was a non-revolutionary, center-left coalition, nominally similar but profoundly different from the Spanish Popular Front. Influential French Radicals suspected that Communists were attempting to enlarge the Spanish conflict into a general war in defense of Soviet interests. In general, the French Right, including some leading Radicals, insisted on altering the French Popular Front's electoral slogan, "Fascism means war" to "Communism equals war." The Right and even much of the center vowed complete neutrality since they held that Moscow controlled the Spanish Popular Front. The prominent right-wing deputy and journalist Henri de Kérillis, who would become a leading anti-Nazi by the end of 1936, strongly supported the Nationalists throughout the conflict. Kérillis detested Spanish "revolutionary convulsions . . . anarchy and murder," and feared that conservative Britain would abandon its French ally if the latter entered an anti-Fascist block with Republican Spain and the USSR. Kérillis, the editor of *L'Écho de Paris*, attempted to sabotage any French aid to the Republic by publishing sensationalist articles on secret arms traffic between France and Spain.[58]

Non-intervention reflected the distaste of the Atlantic establishment for the Spanish Revolution. In September, the French ambassador to Spain, Jean Herbette, who had been the first French envoy to the Soviet Union, judged that the radical Left dominated a Spanish Republic that was acting unconstitutionally, and advised Paris to follow the British policy of complete non-intervention. The majority of ambassadors – including the British and French – left Madrid for the tranquil territory of southern France. In vain, the Republican government sharply protested this nearly unprecedented exit. Foreign diplomats also estranged the Spanish Republic by attempting to aid approximately 7,000 persons who, rightly or wrongly, had been labeled Fascists, and were threatened by revolutionary violence. The envoys of many nations engaged in what was one of the most massive asylum and rescue efforts in the history of international diplomacy.[59]

Great Britain was central in the decisions concerning non-intervention since it was France's principal ally in the 1930s. Britain warned its continental partner to be cautious about aiding the Spanish Republic. At the end of July 1936, Prime Minister Stanley Baldwin told French President Albert Lebrun that the UK would remain neutral if the Spanish conflict led to war between France and the future Axis powers, Germany and Italy. British pressure on Blum to stop controlled and discreet arms shipments to Spain increased in early August. In the UK, even more than in France, official opinion viewed the Spanish Republic as unable to curb extremists and protect property. High-ranking British Foreign Service officers feared that the "Bolshevik" contagion that had begun in Spain in the summer of 1936 would soon infect Popular Front France. Conservative papers and the liberal *Manchester Guardian* criticized the Republic in July 1936 for failing to restrain its "extremists." British

Conservatives were either indifferent to the conflict or regarded the Republican coalition as encouraging revolutionary terror against their Spanish conservative counterparts. The killing of Spanish naval officers by Republican sailors provoked wide sympathy for the Nationalists in the Royal Navy. As in France, a number of Rightists who were pro-Franco were not necessarily pro-Hitler. Some – such as the prolific and best-selling author Major Geoffrey McNeill-Moss – praised the Nationalists but wanted to stop the Nazis.[60]

Like the French Right, the British Right's attitudes toward Communism and the Soviet Union hardened during the Spanish conflict. Hitler and Mussolini found a sympathetic audience throughout Europe when they invoked anti-Communism to justify their pro-Nationalist activities. Poles, Romanians, and Yugoslavs – allies of the French and friendly to Britain – were nonetheless supportive of the anti-Communist interventions of the Fascist powers, and their attitude weakened France's attempt to tighten its eastern European alliances.[61] As Litvinov had seen, Soviet aid to the Republic made conservatives uneasy about supporting it and discredited analysts who had regarded the USSR as too preoccupied with its own internal problems to promote revolution abroad.

The Spanish conflict divided the politically aware British public as had no other foreign question since the French Revolution, and this discord encouraged official policy to maintain a certain balance between the two sides. At the beginning of the war, the government restricted pro-Republican speakers from entering the country but provided facilities to Republican vessels in Gibraltar while restricting exports and communications from Nationalist Spain. Despite increasing pressure from *franquistas*, the government remained reluctant to grant belligerent rights to the Nationalists since this would allow them to blockade Republican ports. At the start of the conflict, the British Left – including the Labour Party, the trade unions, and the Communist Party of Great Britain – supported non-intervention since it believed – like Blum and the Soviets – that the balance of forces favored the Republic.[62]

By September these prognoses had proven erroneous. At that time, the revolutionary Socialist and trade union leader, Largo Caballero, replaced Giral as prime minister. Caballero's government of anti-Fascists included Socialists, Communists, Republicans, and both Catalan and Basque nationalists. This "government of victory" proved unable to reverse the Republic's deteriorating military and economic situation, and in November was enlarged to include, for the first time in history, four anarchists. The new minister of justice, the anarchist Juan García Oliver, had defended *paseos* as a form of "popular justice" which substituted for what he considered the failure of the rule of law.[63] In November, as Franco's forces approached the capital, the consequent siege mentality in Madrid provoked collective delusions characteristic of wars and revolutions.[64] In Paracuellos and vicinity, young Communists (and anarchists) who feared the backstabbing maneuvers of the Fascist Fifth Column in Madrid executed 2,500 prisoners. The Paracuellos assassins acted with the knowledge of many members of the Caballero coalition government. At the end of 1936, Communists extended their own campaign of terror to "Trotskyites," thus replicating on a much smaller scale the great Soviet purges begun in the same year.

At the same time, with the support of all major parties of the Popular Front, the anarchist justice minister initiated the Spanish version of Soviet work camps, which were designed to repress and re-educate enemies through labor.[65] Like the Soviet and German camps, their intimidating presence also disciplined "free workers" outside.[66] The Spanish camps also had their own propagandists – in this case, libertarians – who depicted them as humane institutions.[67] In some ways, their establishment was a response to the desires of the revolutionary base – some of whom worked as guards and administrators of the camps – who regarded the bourgeois and clerics as "parasites" who should be forced to produce.[68] In this context, it is logical that anarchists – like much of the entire Left – would be hostile to Gypsies. The Roma were not anti-Fascist and disinterested in either working or fighting for the cause. As George Orwell noted in December 1936, they continued to beg on the streets of Barcelona.[69]

The outbreak of the Spanish Civil War in 1936 provoked the eruption of revolutionary anti-Fascism. Historians and others – both Fascists and anti-Fascists – have erroneously argued that the civil war was the first stage of World War II. However, unlike the Spanish Civil War, World War II was not a revolutionary/counterrevolutionary struggle, until the Red Army conquered Eastern Europe in 1944–45. In contrast to Republican Spain where conservatives were suppressed or eliminated, conservatives elsewhere in Europe – Winston Churchill and Charles de Gaulle are among the most prominent – created in the Western democracies a counterrevolutionary anti-Fascism that launched a war of attrition that the Axis powers would eventually lose. The Soviet Union became a key part of their coalition and made the bloodiest sacrifices to defeat Fascism. Its conquests imposed on Eastern Europe "popular democracy," a model pioneered by revolutionary anti-Fascism in Spain in 1936. Both experiments shared an anti-Fascist ideology, increasing Communist influence, renewed versions of the NEP, anticlericalism, and terror, even if the Republic's political pluralism and military ineptitude prevented it from becoming a fully successful precursor of a "people's democracy."

The demise of the Soviet Union and the "popular democracies" of Eastern Europe has encouraged the return of the Popular Front's claim that Spanish anti-Fascists fought for democracy, not revolution. In fact, as in 1936, there has been a renewed attempt to camouflage the revolution and to portray Republican Spain as a parliamentary regime abandoned by its fellow democracies, its natural allies.[70] Some historians have transformed the leftist regime into an "imaginary Republic," but an examination of the political, social, diplomatic, and cultural history of 1936 reveals a revolutionary anti-Fascist regime, which alienated centrists, conservatives, and Catholics in Spain and abroad.[71]

Notes

1 Axel Schildt, Detlef Siegfried, and Karl Christian Lammers, eds., *Dynamische Zeiten: Die 60er Jahre in den beiden deutschen Gesellschaften* (Hamburg, Christians, 2000), 11.

2 Arthur Marwick, *The Sixties: Cultural Revolution in Britain, France, Italy, and the United States, c. 1958–c. 1974* (New York, Oxford University Press, 1998).

3 Émile Temime, *1936, La Guerre d'Espagne commence* (Brussels, Complexe, 2006); Enrique Moradiellos, *1936: Los mitos de la Guerra Civil* (Barcelona, Ediciones Península, 2004); Gabriele Ranzato, *La grande paura del 1936: Come la Spagna precipitò nella Guerra civile* (Rome-Bari, Laterza, 2011); Manuel Álvarez Tardío and Roberto Villa García, *1936: Fraude y violencia en las elecciones del Frente Popular* (Barcelona, Espasa, 2017).

4 Stanley G. Payne, *Civil War in Europe, 1905–1949* (New York, Cambridge University Press, 2011), 37.

5 Alfredo Muñiz, *Días de horca y cuchillo: Diario 16 de Febrero–15 de julio de 1936* (Sevilla, Ediciones Espuela de Plata, 2009), 72.

6 Eduardo González Calleja, *En nombre de la autoridad: La defensa del orden pública durante la Segunda República Española (1931–1936)* (Granada, Editorial Comares, 2014), 269–70; Muñiz, *Días de horca y cuchillo*, 69, 76, 79, 149, 200.

7 Julio de la Cueva Merino, "Revolución, guerra y violencia contra la religión," in *Políticas del odio: Violencia y crisis de la democracias en el mundo de entreguerras*, ed. Fernando del Rey and Manuel Álvarez Tardío (Madrid, Editorial Tecnos, 2017), 423.

8 Joan María Thomàs, *José Antonio: Realidad y mito* (Barcelona, Debate, 2017), 265; Muñiz, *Días de horca y cuchillo*, 97.

9 Muñiz, *Días de horca y cuchillo*, 305.

10 Juan Ortiz Villalba, *Sevilla 1936: del golpe militar a la guerra civil* (Seville, Vistalegre, 1998), 261; *La Provincia*, 12 June 1936.

11 Muñiz, *Días de horca y cuchillo*, 250, 261, 271, 277, 281, 296, 301. Oddly,

leftist historiography often de-emphasizes the reality of the class struggle following the election of the Popular Front.

12 Temime, *1936*, 21.

13 Hugo García, "De los soviets a las Cortes: Los comunistas ante la República," in *Palabras como puños: La intransigencia política en la Segunda República española*, ed. Fernando del Rey (Madrid, Editorial Tecnos, 2011), 147.

14 Thomàs, *José Antonio*, 264, 266; Antonio Elorza and Marta Bizcarrondo, *Queridos Camaradas: La Internacional Comunista y España* (Barcelona, Planeta, 1999), 279.

15 Muñiz, *Días de horca y cuchillo*, 177.

16 Thomàs, *José Antonio*, 263.

17 Stanley G. Payne, *Spain's First Democracy: The Second Republic, 1931–1936* (Madison, University of Wisconsin Press, 1993), 357.

18 José Manuel Martínez Bande, *La invasión de Aragón y el desembarco en Mallorca* (Madrid, Librería Editorial San Martín, 1970), 23.

19 Temime, *1936*, 27.

20 Eduardo Haro Tecglen, *Arde Madrid* (Madrid, Temas de Hoy, 2000), 92; José de Arteche, *El Abrazo de los muertos: Diario de la guerra civil 1936–1939* (Zarauz, Editorial Icharopena, 1970), 27.

21 Julio de la Cueva, "Religious Persecution, Anticlerical Tradition, and Revolution," *Journal of Contemporary History* 33, no. 3 (1998): 357.

22 Julius Ruiz, *El Terror rojo: Madrid 1936* (Barcelona, Espasa, 2012), 260–348; Francisco Alía Miranda, *La agonía de la República: El final de la guerra civil española (1938–1939)* (Barcelona, Crítica, 2015), 46, 65; Stanley G. Payne, *The Spanish Civil War, the Soviet Union, and Communism* (New Haven/London, Yale University Press, 2004), 117.

23 Tom Buchanan, "Anti-fascism and Democracy in the 1930s," *European History Quarterly* 32, no. 1 (2002): 43; Payne, *Spanish Civil War*, 150; Geoffrey Roberts, "Soviet Foreign Policy and the Spanish Civil War," in *Spain in an International Context, 1936–1939*, ed. Christian Leitz and David J. Dunthorn (New York/Oxford, Berghahn Books, 1999), 93–96; Fernando Hernández Sánchez, *Guerra o Revolución: El Partido Comunista de España en la guerra civil* (Barcelona, Crítica, 2010), 325–331, 373–374, 454, 471; Hugh Ragsdale, *The Soviets, the Munich Crisis, and the Coming of World War II* (New York, Cambridge University Press, 2004), 189; Lisa A. Kirschenbaum, *International Communism and the Spanish Civil War: Solidarity and Suspicion* (New York, Cambridge University Press, 2015), 78–79, 109–12, 120–25.

24 See José Luis Martín Ramos, *El Frente Popular: Victoria y derrota de la democracia en España* (Barcelona, Pasado & Presente, 2015), 9, 29, 228. However, the author does not consider this revolution to be a precursor of those that followed World War II in Eastern Europe.

25 Ibid., 229.

26 Elorza, *Queridos Camaradas*, 321.

27 Ibid., 234, 242, 250, 253, 430.

28 Joan Serrallonga, Manuel Santirso, and Just Casa, *Vivir en Guerra: La zona leal a la República (1936–1939)* (Barcelona, UAB, 2013), 164, 169.
29 Elorza, *Queridos Camaradas*, 308, 315, 317.
30 Ibid., 377.
31 Serrallonga, *Vivir en Guerra*, 42.
32 Joaquín Aisa Raluy, *Diario de un miliciano republicano (1936–1939)* (Barcelona, Editorial Base, 2010), 29.
33 Ibid., 30.
34 Moradiellos, *1936*, 127.
35 Martín Ramos, *El Frente Popular*, 223.
36 Cited in Serrallonga, *Vivir en Guerra*, 171.
37 Acta de la reunión, January 7, 1937, Madrid 991, Archivo Histórico Nacional-Sección Guerra Civil [hereafter AHN-SGC].
38 Ronald Fraser, *Blood of Spain: An Oral History of the Spanish Civil War* (New York, Pantheon, 1986), 450.
39 José Martín-Blázquez, *Guerre civile totale* (Paris, Denoël, 1938), 115–17, 231.
40 Burnett Bolloten, *The Spanish Civil War: Revolution and Counter-revolution* (Chapel Hill/London, University of North Carolina Press, 1991), 524.
41 Aisa Raluy, *Diario*, 55.
42 Ibid., 139, 145.
43 Martínez Bande, *La invasión de Aragón*, 260.
44 A los camaradas, December 6, 1936, Gijón F 89, AHN-SGC.
45 Bartolomé Aragón, *Con Intendencia militar de las Gloriosas Brigadas Navarras* (Madrid, Imprenta del Patronato de Huérfanos de Intendencia e Intervención Militares, 1940), 46.
46 Haro Tecglen, *Arde Madrid*, 150.
47 María de la Luz Majías Correa, *Así fue pasando el tiempo: Memorias de una miliciana extremeña* (Seville, Editorial Renacimiento, 2006), 126.
48 José-Carlos Mainer, *Años de Vísperas: La vida de la cultura en España (1931–1939)* (Pozuelo de Alacrón, Espasa, 2006), 187.
49 In position,
Machine gun,
Antifascist Blue Overalls!
Jump, Jump! Blue Overalls,
prudent as reckless,
until dying in the front
and in front of the fight
50 Cited in Moradiellos, *1936*, 141.
51 Manuel Tagüeña Lacorte, *Testimonio de dos guerras* (Barcelona, Planeta, 1978), 191; Ángel Lamas Arroyo, *Unos y Otros* (Barcelona, Luis de Caralt, 1972), 275; Elorza, *Queridos Camaradas*, 462.
52 Peter N. Carroll, *The Odyssey of the Abraham Lincoln Brigade: Americans in the Spanish Civil War* (Stanford, Stanford University Press, 1994), 199.
53 Tom Buchanan, *Britain and the Spanish Civil War* (New York, Cambridge University Press, 1997), 132; Sygmunt Stein, *Ma Guerre d'Espagne: Brigades*

internationales la fin d'un mythe, trans. Marina Alexeeva-Antipov (Paris, Seuil, 2012), 23–83.

54 Silvio Pons, "La diplomatie soviétique, l'antifascisme et la guerre civile espagnole," in Serge Wolikow and Annie Bleton-Ruger, eds., *Antifascisme et nation: les gauches européennes au temps du front populaire* (Dijon, Editions universitaires de Dijon, 1998), 63–66.

55 Carroll, *Lincoln Brigade*, 159.

56 Moradiellos, *1936*, 158.

57 Dominic Tierney, *FDR and the Spanish Civil War: Neutrality and Commitment in the Struggle That Divided America* (Durham, Duke University Press, 2007), 74; Glyn Stone, "The European Great Powers and the Spanish Civil War," in Robert Boyce and Esmonde M. Robertson, eds. *Paths to War: New Essays on the Origins of the Second World War* (New York, St. Martin's Press, 1989), 214; David Wingeate Pike, *Les français et la guerre d'Espagne* (Paris, Presses universitaires de France, 1975), 101.

58 Jean Vigreux, *Le front populaire, 1934–1938* (Paris, Presses universitaires de France, 2011), 38; Yves Denéchère, *Jean Herbette (1878–1960): Journaliste et ambassadeur* (Paris, PIE-Peter Lang, 2003), 302; Pike, *Les français*, 55, 174.

59 Antonio Manuel Moral Roncal, *Diplomacia, humanitarismo y espionaje en la Guerra Civil española* (Madrid, Biblioteca Nueva, 2008), 324, 330, 354; Javier Rubio, *Asilos y canjes durante la guerra civil española* (Barcelona, Planeta, 1979), 29–39, 87–95; Denéchère, *Herbette*, 269, 281.

60 Serge Berstein, *Léon Blum* (Paris, Fayard, 2006), 517; Martin Thomas, *Britain, France and Appeasement: Anglo-French Relations in the Popular Front Era* (Washington DC, Berg, 1996), 91; Buchanan, *Britain and the Spanish Civil War*, 45; Stone, "The European Great Powers," 214; Pike, *Les français*, 83, 195; Maurice Cowling, *The Impact of Hitler: British Politics and British Policy, 1933–1940* (Chicago, University of Chicago Press, 1977), 130–31; Tom Buchanan, *The Impact of the Spanish Civil War on Britain: War, Loss and Memory* (Portland, OR, Sussex Academic Press, 2007), 2, 13; Richard Griffiths, *Fellow Travellers of the Right: British Enthusiasts for Nazi Germany 1933–9* (London, Constable, 1980) 264.

61 Neville Thompson, *The Anti-Appeasers: Conservative Opposition to Appeasement in the 1930s* (Oxford, Clarendon Press, 1971), 124; Cowling, *Impact of Hitler*, 131, 135; Zara Steiner, *The Triumph of the Dark: European International History 1933–1939* (Oxford, Oxford University Press, 2011), 206.

62 Robert Graves and Alan Hodge, *The Long Week-End: A Social History of Great Britain 1918–1939* (New York, Norton, 1940), 337; K. W. Watkins, *Britain Divided: The Effect of the Spanish Civil War on British Political Opinion* (London, T. Nelson, 1963), 4, 77; Hugo García, *Mentiras necesarias: La batalla por la opinión británica durante la Guerra Civil* (Madrid, Biblioteca Nueva, 2008), 210; Buchanan, *Britain and the Spanish Civil War*, 51–59.

63 Francesc Badia, *Els camps de treball a Catalunya durant la guerra civil (1936–1939)* (Barcelona, Publicacions de l'Abadia de Monserrat, 2001), 25.

64 Ruiz, *El Terror Rojo*, 26.

65 Julius Ruiz, "'Work and Don't Lose Hope': Republican Forced Labour Camps during the Spanish Civil War," *Contemporary European History* 18, no. 4 (2009): 431; Anne Applebaum, *Gulag: A History* (New York, Doubleday, 2003), 6, 8, 12, 44, 67–71, 231–41.

66 Marcel van der Linden, "Forced Labour and Non-Capitalist Industrialization: The Case of Stalinism (c. 1929– c. 1956)," in *Free and Unfree Labor: The Debate Continues*, ed. Tom Brass and Marcel van der Linden (Berne, Peter Lang, 1997), 355.

67 Augustín Souchy Bauer, *With the Peasants of Aragon*, trans. Abe Bluestein (Sanday Orkney, Cienfuegos Press, 1982), 32–34.

68 Badia, *Els camps*, 82. The Bolsheviks had a similar attitude to their bourgeois enemies.

69 George Orwell, *Homage to Catalonia* (New York, Harcourt Brace Jovanovich, 1980), 6.

70 This contradiction between the supposed fight for democratic freedoms and the revolutionary nature of the Socialist and Communist militants can be found in Majías Correa, *Memorias*, 178–79.

71 Pedro Carlos González Cuevas, *El pensamiento político de la derecho española en el siglo XX: De la crisis de la Restauración (1898) a la crisis del Estado de partidos (2015)* (Madrid, Editorial Tecnos, 2016), 254; Fernando García de Cortázar, "La República imaginada," *ABC*, June 23, 2006; Gabriele Ranzato, "Es posible un auténtico debate historiográfico sobre la historia de la Segunda República y de la Guerra Civil?" *Historia del Presente.* 22, (2013): 151–64.

2

The Pioneers of International Defense of the Republic: The Athletes of Barcelona's Popular Olympiad

RAANAN REIN

Chaim Elkon arrived in Palestine in 1924 in the uniform of the legendary Hakoah Vienna football team to play against Maccabi Tel Aviv. When the squad returned to Europe, Elkon decided to stay behind. He was an active member of the outlawed Palestine Communist Party until he was deported by the Mandatory authorities.[1] In July 1936 he traveled to Barcelona to serve as a referee at the planned Peoples' Olympiad. But the games, which were supposed to begin on July 19, never took place. A few hours before the scheduled opening ceremony, with some 6,000 athletes and 20,000 visitors already in the city for the event, the military uprising against the elected government of the Second Spanish Republic broke out. The revolt, led by General Francisco Franco, soon devolved into a long and bloody civil war. Most of the athletes who had come to the capital of Catalonia departed hastily. Elkon was among those who decided to remain and help defend the Republic.

Budapest-born Imre Jacobi, one of the greatest football players in Mandatory Palestine in the 1930s, also arrived in Barcelona in July 1936. He, too, decided to remain in Spain and fight against the Nationalists. The Jewish team on which he had played in his youth, Hagibor Bratislava, had occasionally gone on tour outside Czechoslovakia in order to augment its coffers. After the team played in Palestine in 1927 he decided not to return home. Almost immediately he found work as a foreman in a road-building company that carried out projects for the Mandatory authorities. The harsh conditions to which both Arab and Jewish laborers were subjected led Jacoby to start organizing the workers of both groups in order to improve their situation. After a major strike by the road workers, the company management fired Jacoby, who by that time had joined the Palestine Communist Party. The British authorities arrested Jacoby during the May Day demonstrations in 1935. In subsequent months he was in and out of police stations, courts, and prisons.[2] When the British authorities expelled him from Palestine in 1936, Jacoby made his way to Spain. After he realized that the Peoples' Olympiad would not take place, he, too, decided to join the international volunteers fighting in Spain, anticipating by several weeks the formation of the International Brigades at the initiative of the Comintern.

This chapter seeks to shed light on the Peoples' Olympiad, planned as a response to the official Olympics, which were about to open in Berlin, and which had been hijacked to serve the ends of Nazi propaganda. It also hoped to highlight friendly sporting events as an ethical alternative to the competitive spirit of the Olympics.

Thousands of athletes came from various countries and from all over Spain to take part in the counter-Olympics organized by the government of Catalonia. As a result of the last-minute cancellation, however, the Peoples' Olympiad has received scant attention from historians. In addition, this chapter focuses on the delegation of athletes from the Yishuv (the Jewish community in Palestine) who planned to compete in Barcelona. The delegation, which consisted mainly of members of the Hapoel Sports Federation, was the first expression of the Yishuv's solidarity with the Spanish Republic and the anti-Fascist struggle.[3]

The Unsuccessful Campaign to Boycott the Berlin Olympics

In late April 1931, about two weeks after King Alfonso XIII left Spain and the Second Republic was proclaimed, the International Olympic Committee (IOC) convened in Barcelona to select the host city for the 1936 Summer Games. The two candidates were Berlin, which had been designated to host the 1916 games that were subsequently called off because of the First World War, and Barcelona itself, which had been a candidate in 1924.[4] Not all the members of the IOC came to Barcelona; some voted by mail. Although the transition from monarchy to republic in Spain had been quiet and without bloodshed, it had worried some delegates. The decision to prefer Berlin rather than Barcelona, however, reflected neither a conservative policy nor a soft approach toward Fascism. Despite the economic crisis, Weimar Germany was still democratic. By a huge majority, 43 against 16, Berlin was awarded the 1936 Summer Games.[5]

After the Nazis came to power, they quickly realized the immense propaganda potential of the Olympics as a display window for the National Socialist regime, its vision and achievements, and as an opportunity to demonstrate the athletic superiority of Aryans and the renaissance of Germany under Nazi rule.[6] In 1935, however, in reaction to the Nazis' exclusion of non-Aryans from various branches of sport and the militarization of German sporting organizations, an international campaign to boycott the 1936 games was launched. To dispel the calls for a boycott sounded in countries like the Netherlands and United States, the Nazi regime backtracked from its earlier statements that only Aryans could represent Germany at the games and that Jewish athletes from other countries would not be welcome in Berlin. In practice, though, very little if anything changed in German policy. The German representatives' promises soon proved to be worthless and Jewish athletes continued to be victims of discrimination. The international protest did not die down, either.[7] By a narrow majority of 61 to 57, the US Olympic Committee decided to participate in the Berlin Games and not support a counter-Olympics; the Soviet Union, however, did boycott the Berlin games. Republican Spain was represented by several athletes, including its hockey team. The Spanish government preferred not to make a sweeping decision and left it to each sports federation to decide whether it would participate. Most of them opted to boycott Berlin.

Sports and Regional Identity in Catalonia

In early 1936, the political map of southern Europe changed. In February, a new Popular Front government came to power in Madrid, and Catalonian governmental organs, suspended after the failed uprising in October 1934, were restored.[8] In mid-May, a Popular Front government was installed in Paris, too, under Léon Blum.[9] Given the political climate in the two countries, the decision by the government of Catalonia to organize a Peoples' Olympiad in July, two weeks before the start of the Berlin games, was welcomed widely, and in some circles enthusiastically. Nevertheless, the Blum government tried to appease both supporters and opponents by allocating 1.1 million francs for French participation in the Berlin games and about half that amount for participation in the Peoples' Olympiad in Barcelona. It goes without saying that this gesture hardly satisfied any of the political blocs.

Catalonia had a tradition of encouraging popular sports that were accessible to everyone, as well as a modern athletic infrastructure. Only a few years earlier a large new stadium, with 72,000 seats, had been constructed in Barcelona to host the International Exhibition (Expo) of 1929. Catalonia's regional identity was built on a strategy of culture planning, which included popular sports and physical activity in nonpartisan workers' associations.[10] Barcelona and the industrial belt around it were home to a large proletarian class, proud of its identity and experienced in labor, social, and political struggles.

During the dictatorship of Miguel Primo de Rivera (1923–30), when the Spanish state suppressed various expressions of Catalan regional identity, sports remained one of the channels where it was possible to bolster Catalan pride and distinctiveness. The motto above the masthead of the Barcelona daily *La Rambla*, launched at the start of 1930 at the initiative of Josep Sunyol i Garriga, who was also president of FC Barcelona, was "Sports and Citizenship" (*esport i ciutadania*). Hence, it is not surprising that alongside the regular sporting competitions at the Peoples' Olympiad in Barcelona, there were also plans for cultural events to celebrate cultural diversity and recognize the Other by means of music, theater, folklore, and folk dancing. The decision by the government of Catalonia to organize the counter-Olympics was largely an independent initiative and not another link in the series of Spartakiads, founded by the Comintern and supported by the Soviet Union (the first Spartakiad was held in Moscow in 1928). However, the opening of the Soviet archives has made it clear that Communist involvement in the organization of the anti-Fascist Olympics was much greater than previously believed.[11]

Lluís Companys, the president of the autonomous government of Catalonia, was the moving spirit behind the organizing committee of the Peoples' Olympiad and served as its honorary president. Esquerra Republicana Catalunya, the moderate left-wing party that was the dominant political force in the government of Catalonia, was established in 1931, with a membership and objectives very similar to those of the Popular Front, even before the Soviet Union began promoting the idea of an anti-Fascist alliance of all leftist parties.

A vast amount of organizational effort was required from the Catalans. Unlike the Berlin games, which were several years in the making, everything required to run a competition of similar scope in Barcelona was done within a few weeks (the organizing committee first met in late April 1936). The bulk of the funding came from four sources: the French government (600,000 francs);[12] and the Spanish government (300,000 pesetas),[13] the Generalitat (government) of Catalonia (100,000 pesetas), and the Barcelona municipality (100–200,000 pesetas), which, combined, was equivalent approximately to the French contribution.[14] The athletes were to compete in 16 different categories, including football, tennis, basketball, boxing, track and field, wrestling, the traditional

Basque sport of pelota, rugby, and chess (the last three were not recognized by the International Olympic Committee).[15] According to the British Trade Union Congress, "We feel this will be an effective answer to the continued violation and exploitation of the Olympic Spirit by the Hitler Government, and will be a strong counter to the Berlin Olympic Games."[16]

Rightwing circles in Spain and abroad were of course critical of the idea of the Peoples' Olympiad and presented it as a Communist affair.[17] Another element in the propaganda against the initiative was the claim that it was effectively the games of international Jewry. Several assertions were made to "prove" this charge: Jews were playing an important role in the international campaign to boycott the Berlin Olympics; the Barcelona games would include a delegation from Mandatory Palestine, consisting of Jewish athletes only, as well as a delegation of European Jewish exiles; and the Popular Front government in France, which was providing major financial support for the venture, was headed by a Jew, Léon Blum, about whom the rightwing newspaper *La Veu de Catalunya* wrote "[he] has such an un-French name as Blum and several prominent Semitic physical traits."[18]

But the most incriminating "evidence" of all was that the anthem chosen for the Olympiad ("March of the Peoples' Olympiad," written by the renowned Catalan poet Josep Maria de Sagarra) had been composed by Hans Eisler, son of a Jewish father and Lutheran mother, who had been forced to leave Germany because of his origins and Communist views.[19] Eisler's work included music he had written for the plays of his friend Bertolt Brecht. Brecht's "Song of Solidarity," set to Eisler's music, was sung at many working-class demonstrations and protests all over Europe in the first half of the 1930s. After the Second World War, Eisler composed the anthem for the new German Democratic Republic.

Competition with No Distinction of Class, Race, or Nationality

In France, the reaction to the Catalonian initiative was enthusiastic. The labor movement's sports and gymnastics federation, Fédération Sportive et Gymnique du Travail, (FSGT), which drew its members from both the Socialists and Communists – formerly bitter enemies – had long been waging a campaign "to save the Olympics," which had deteriorated into "hypocritical, chauvinistic, and commercialized bourgeois games."[20] In mid-May 1936, the Parisian *Sport* praised the decision to hold "the popular Olympic Games" in Barcelona as welcome news for all who believed in the fraternity of men and aspired to a better world. In addition, left-wing groups in France and Spain saw the event as an opportunity to improve the ties between the two Popular Front governments. It was not surprising, then, that Léo Lagrange, the French undersecretary of state for sports, promised readers of the Communist Party daily *L'Humanité* that he would do his utmost to ensure maximum participation by French athletes in the Barcelona games.[21]

Indeed, the French delegation was the largest of the 23 attending the Barcelona games, with some 1,300 athletes and support personnel. A total of some 6,000 persons came to take part in the Peoples' Olympiad, about half of whom represented Spain, the Galicia region of Spain, the Basque Country, and Catalonia. This means that about half of those from abroad were French.[22] As a result of the large number who registered for the games, the organizing committee decided to extend the scheduled period. The opening ceremony, originally planned for July 22, was advanced by three days.[23]

Somewhat surprisingly, although the Spanish Communist Party newspaper extolled Soviet sports policy and the superiority of Soviet athletes, and expressed its hope that the Soviet Union would take part in the Barcelona games,[24] no Soviet delegation turned up. This was in spite of the expectation of some members of the organizing committee that more than 100 Soviet athletes would be present – the country's first ever participation in a major competition in Western Europe. But the government of Catalonia was not interested in painting the games too "red" and was not excessively disappointed by the Soviets' failure to appear. Jaume Miravitlles, a former Communist cadre who joined the Republican Left in Catalonia in 1934, was a vice-president of the organizing committee of the Peoples' Olympiad. When the civil war broke out he became general secretary of the Catalonian Central Committee of Antifascist Militias. Some years later he recounted that one of the missions assigned to him by President Companys was to make sure that Soviet Communism did not exploit the Peoples' Olympiad to further its own political ends.[25]

Did the Soviets stay away because they did not want to cast a dark shadow on the Catalonian government and the Barcelona games? Or was their nonparticipation a manifestation of Stalin's policy, which preferred the Soviet Union's political interests over expressions of international solidarity? The Soviet dictator's hesitation at the start of the civil war, before he decided to provide practical assistance to the Spanish Republicans who were trying to put down the military uprising, suggests that the second option is more plausible.[26] The year before, the Soviet Union had begun making efforts to integrate into the international sports world and forged ties with international federations, such as FIFA and the IOC. It is possible that Moscow did not want to endanger these efforts by taking part in the Peoples' Olympiad in Barcelona.

The official emblem of the Peoples' Olympiad featured three stylized human figures, red, yellow, and brown (to represent the fraternity and equality of all races), each with a hand grasping the pole of the games' banner. The emblem symbolized the integrationist ethos of the Peoples' Olympiad, with no distinction of class, race, or nation. One of its posters gives prominent display to women. In fact, the Catalan Club Femenino y de Deporte (women's and sports Club) played a central role in organizing the Olympiad.[27] The inclusion of black athletes in the visual material distributed before the games was intended to transmit a message of an inclusive, progressive, and tolerant event in a world that was threatened by the polarization between Communism and Fascism.[28] The goal went beyond bringing together only elite athletes who would try to set new records; the hope was also to create a shared and unifying experience for sports lovers everywhere and for all those who engaged in physical activity.[29]

Protests against the Berlin Olympics in Mandatory Palestine

At the opposite end of the Mediterranean, the decision to hold a counter-Olympics in Barcelona stirred great interest, in which considerations of local and international politics were intermingled. Many articles were published in the Hebrew press about the international effort to thwart the Olympics in Germany.[30] The Histadrut daily *Davar* emphasized that sports and politics are intertwined, "whether we like it or not."

> And precisely for that reason it is not all one and the same for us where the Olympics are held and under what regime. This is why the enlightened and progressive public that has raised its voice against holding the Olympic Games in the Germany of Hitler and Goebbels is in the right. It is not a matter for athletes only, but for all progressive humanity.31

At the end of May, the Tel Aviv newspapers reported that "the Jewish Labor Committee in America has decided to support the workers' movement in several European countries to hold a special Olympic event of all the workers of the world in the Netherlands or Belgium as a protest against the international Olympics in Berlin."[32] Ultimately, the Jewish Labor Committee, in cooperation with the Amateur Athletic Union, organized a World Labor Athletic carnival in New York on August 15–16, 1936 – coinciding with the last two days of the Berlin Olympics – to protest both the holding of the Olympics in Nazi Germany and American participation in the games.[33]

The government of Catalonia's decision to hold a People's Olympiad was welcomed by the Hebrew press, and *Davar* published a number of articles on the subject:

> Whereas in Berlin only people who are pursuing records will meet, large numbers of athletes . . . will assemble for the Olympiad in Barcelona. According to the introduction to the program for the international gathering, "a Nazi spirit" will prevail in the Berlin Olympics, that of enslavement and racial hatred, whereas the Barcelona Olympiad will be marked by the pure Olympic spirit that makes all races equal and all nations equal and aspires to educate young people of all nations in an atmosphere of peace and fellowship.[34]

Soon after, the Hebrew press in Palestine began referring to the Barcelona games as a "model Olympiad."[35]

The Hapoel Sports Federation had no doubt that it must organize a delegation to Barcelona. Hapoel had sent athletes to the Workers' Games in Vienna in 1931 and in Prague in 1934. This time the games were particularly important because of the international campaign to boycott the Berlin Olympics and the desire to organize a left-wing alternative to the "Nazi Olympics." Local developments, too, and especially the outbreak of violent clashes between the emerging Palestinian national movement and the Yishuv, spurred a desire to wave the banner of Socialist Zionism at international forums. Supplementing this was a desire to provoke the Palestine Olympic Committee and the leadership of the Maccabi Movement, Hapoel's bitter rivals in the competition for primacy in the Zionist sports arena. Maccabi had seriously considered sending a delegation to the Berlin games and had excluded Hapoel representatives from the second Maccabiah Games, held in April 1935.[36]

So far as the leaders of Hapoel were concerned, Maccabi was a group of bourgeois capitalists who were reluctant to express active opposition to Fascism, antisemitism, and dictatorship; whereas they, the representatives of the working class, were making a strenuous effort to participate in the Barcelona Olympiad.[37] Shortly before departing for Barcelona, Israel Carmi, co-head of the Hapoel delegation, drafted "Hapoel's message to the anti-Nazi Olympiad in Barcelona":

> To the free workers of Spain, greetings! At the very time when the banners of freedom are waving over this Olympiad, an Olympics is taking place in Nazi Germany that symbolizes slavery, repression, and

> tyranny. Long live our Olympiad! May there emerge from this Olympiad an enthusiastic call to the workers of the world to unite forces for a war against war and for the realization of Socialism.
>
> Brothers and comrades! Our small country, which lay in waste for 2000 years, has revived since we began returning to it. We have come back to our desolate homeland with a sincere desire to build there, arm-in-arm with the Arab working class, a free homeland for members of both peoples . . . For three months now, brutal [Arab] terror has prevailed in the country, with assaults on [Jewish] children and women. But our young people – with their muscles and knowledge of war – know they must refrain from revenge and avoid spilling innocent blood.
>
> From here, from the Olympic platform, we proclaim to all peoples and workers of all the world: our path is toward cooperation and peace with the Arab people. And finally: Long live the anti-Nazi Olympiad! Long live freedom! Long live the brotherhood of nations! Long live Socialism! Long live free Spain! Long live the rebirth of the worker in the land of Israel![38]

Hapoel and the Delegation of Athletes from Palestine

The Hapoel federation put together a delegation of prominent athletes.[39] A document titled "The bill for arranging the delegation's trip to the Olympiad (in Barcelona)" includes the names of 21 athletes, for whom Hapoel would have to cover the expenses of one French visa and two British visas, passport renewals for four, and the return ticket to Palestine for one. The remaining expenses would be covered by the hosts in Catalonia.[40] Prominent among the sportsmen were football players, mainly from Hapoel Tel Aviv and Hapoel Haifa.

The Barcelona organizing committee welcomed the news of the expected arrival of a football team from Palestine, to compete against 15 other teams.[41] The Peoples' Olympiad press service emphasized the team's caliber: "Mention is particularly due to the participation of a first-class team from the Palestine Sporting Club Hapoel, which recently contested a match with the Hungarian Boskays, the match being drawn at 2:2. Their coach is the well-known Austrian Nemes Neufeld."[42]

Sándor Nemes, otherwise known as Alexander Neufeld, was a famous Hungarian Jewish football player and coach of that era. Born in 1899, his long and extensive career included stops in Hungary, Austria, Switzerland, the United States, and Yugoslavia. He played on the national teams for Hungary and Austria. In Austria he wore the uniform of Hakoah Vienna. He coached various European clubs in the 1930s, including Hapoel Haifa for several months in 1935–36. In 1950 he returned to Israel as manager of Hapoel Tel Aviv.

The Palestine delegation of 30 included athletes from other branches as well.[43] Notable among them was the wrestler Nikolaus (Micki) Hirschl, born in Vienna in 1908, a member of Hakoah Vienna. He was the Austrian champion for a decade as well as European champion in 1932. At the 1932 Los Angeles Olympics he won bronze medals in the heavyweight division in both freestyle and Greco-Roman wrestling. In 1936, Hirschl was living briefly in Palestine.

The most prominent woman on the delegation was Sonja Lewine-Szmukler. Born in Poland, she began her athletic career with Maccabi Wilno and excelled in the shot put, discus, and hammer throw. In the Polish track-and-field championships in 1930 she won the gold medal in the shot put. That same year she was ranked tenth in the world. At the second Maccabiah, in 1935, she won the silver medal, losing out to Lillian Copeland, the Olympic champion from the United States. After the Maccabiah she remained in Palestine with her family.[44]

In an interview before the Barcelona games opened, Haim Glowinsky, the other co-head (with Israel Carmi), of the Hapoel delegation to the Peoples' Olympiad, told the Spanish Communist daily *Mundo Obrero* that he was proud of the composition of the Hapoel delegation and the caliber of its members.[45]

The Long Journey to Barcelona

The French delegation to Barcelona was the largest of all.[46] Georges Revel, then a 19-year-old football player from the University Sports Club of the Labor Unions, and André Codreau, the 1200-meter French junior champion in 1931, preferred not to compete in Berlin for political and ideological reasons and were delighted to have the opportunity to participate in the Barcelona games. They were excited to see the large crowd that had gathered at the station to farewell the athletes when they boarded a special train on July 16.[47] The French athletes went to the Olimpico Hotel in Plaça Espanya, where they found large dormitories with many mattresses. Because of time and budget pressures, no Olympic village had been erected and the thousands of visiting athletes had to sleep in cheap hotels that were more like workers' hostels, four to eight in a room, or in apartment buildings scattered around the city.[48]

The athletes from Palestine had a more arduous journey than the French. They sailed from Haifa to Algiers and Tunis and then to Marseilles. From there they travelled by train to the border town of

Portbou in the Pyrenees, and were supposed to proceed onward to Barcelona. Two weeks before they left for Spain, Haim Glowinsky (who was also one of the founders of the Hapoel Federation[49]) made his way to Barcelona to prepare for the delegation's arrival. The Hapoel athletes waited in Haifa for his cable from Catalonia that everything had been arranged and they could board the *Patria* and set off.

On Saturday night, July 18, many athletes converged on the stadium at the top of Montjuïc, the hill overlooking Barcelona, to take a look at the venue for the games and mingle with those who had arrived from various places. Some wanted to practice before the competition began; many of the organizers decided to stay and sleep there. Cellist Pablo Casals, the conductor of the Barcelona Orchestra, led a dress rehearsal of Beethoven's Ninth Symphony, in preparation for the gala opening ceremony to be held the next day. But the concert did not take place and Casals never again conducted or performed on Spanish soil.

The Peoples' Olympiad was an attempt to present an alternative to sporting competitions based explicitly on citizenship or nationality. Representatives of countries under colonial rule participated as if they came from independent states, of equal standing with long-established ones. Such was the case of Mandatory Palestine, under the British, and of Morocco, then under French and Spanish control.[50] Jewish refugees from Nazi Germany and anti-Fascist exiles promised to compete, and there were also to be regional delegations from Alsace-Lorraine and the Spanish regions of the Basque country, Galicia, and Catalonia.[51] The willingness to accept multiple identities was exemplified by a women's football team representing the United Students of the World.

In the middle of the night, the athletes who were staying at the Olimpico Hotel were awakened by the sound of explosions. Only the next morning did they learn that units of the Spanish Army had revolted. Responding to orders from the headquarters in Pamplona, under General Emilio Mola, one of the leaders of the rebellion, some soldiers of the Barcelona garrison had left their barracks to take part in the coup. The visitors were forbidden to leave the hotel, while members of anarchist militias took up positions behind hastily erected barriers.[52] The British delegation, which numbered about 50 athletes, arrived in Barcelona on July 18, after a 57-hour train ride.[53] One of its members was the long-distance runner and boxer Tony Binet:

> I was awakened in the early hours of the morning by what I took to be the vigorous turning of football rattles . . . Peering over [the balcony] I saw a narrow street deserted except for six armed civilians, members of the Workers' Militia Night Patrol. From the end of the street opposite I

> saw a number of men and a woman firing from behind a hastily erected cobbled barricade, at a car which was being driven through the street at breakneck speed.[54]

On the afternoon of July 19, representatives of the organizing committee tried to calm the visitors. They explained that while it was true that some military units had rebelled against the Republic, so far as Barcelona, at least, was concerned there was no need for the athletes to fear for their safety; the Republic's control of the city was secure. But the speakers themselves were not relaxed, and the visitors understood that the situation had changed and the sports competitions would not go ahead as planned. There were broken windows in the streets, burned-out motor vehicles, and a few heavily damaged buildings. Some of the athletes hurried off to find the nearest post office in order to cable their friends and relatives back home and reassure them that their lives were not in danger.

The athletes from Palestine did not reach Portbou, on the Spanish side of the Pyrenees, until July 20. From there they planned to take the train to Barcelona. As Israel Carmi recalled:

> There was a long tunnel at Portbou through which the train had to pass. The soldiers who controlled the area told us that the road was blocked. Only then did we learn that the civil war had broken out the night before we reached Spain and that General Franco was trying to seize control of the country . . . We turned on the radio to find out what was happening . . . At the end of the announcements on military matters the broadcaster said that the organizing committee of the Workers' Olympiad had stated that, in light of the security situation, the games' opening had been postponed until further notice.[55]

Carmi instructed the members of the delegation to stay in the railcars, while he prepared to go to Barcelona:

> Before I left Portbou I listened to the radio, which was broadcasting instructions to the various sports delegations. Among others I heard the voice of our colleague Glowinsky in Hebrew: "Welcome! I'm in Barcelona, handling everything associated with your situation. I'm waiting here for Carmi . . . " On the way we were stopped by Republican soldiers, who warned us that Fascist snipers were shooting at cars on the highway. We took a side road, but nevertheless ran into a hail of bullets, which fortunately did not penetrate the vehicle . . . Several dozen meters ahead we heard exchanges of fire. Large objects were flying through the

> air from the roof of a church, and a large throng of residents of the town and the environs were crying "Viva la republica," and singing loudly. The soldiers there told us that they had discovered a squad of Franco's men in the church and that the crowd had killed them by hurling them off the roof of the church, about four stories up.[56]

The train from Portbou to Barcelona should have covered the 200 km in only three hours, but it took Carmi and his companions from 3:00 p.m. until noon the next day.[57] Carmi finally reached Plaça Catalunya in the heart of Barcelona, where he saw the results of the bloodbath that had taken place there a short time before:

> The whole place looked like a slaughterhouse, with dozens of corpses of soldiers and horses lying all over the place, some of them still twitching. The walls were [full of bullet holes] like a beehive . . . In fear and despair we arrived at the building of the Olympiad organizing committee, where I finally met up with Glowinsky. On the way to the hotel, escorted by soldiers, we could hear the radio announcing: "Attention, attention, residents of Barcelona, a speeding car with a Fascist squad is shooting in every direction." Before we managed to enter the hotel, we saw a crowd gathered around a military truck. Republican soldiers were setting it on fire with its occupants, who . . . had wounded a number of pedestrians in the city, locked inside.[58]

Glowinsky's widow reconstructed her husband's impressions when he found himself in the heart of the tumult in Barcelona:

> Imagine how it was! In the morning Haim woke up in the midst of a coup. It wasn't easy. He knew that the delegation would get stuck at the border, and the situation was even more complicated because there were no Israeli passports back then. Everyone carried a different passport . . . Here at home we didn't know what was happening to them, because there was no contact until I received a cable from him in which he said, "I'm in Barcelona and we're in control of the situation." He meant that the leftists were in control on the ground. All of us were hoping that Franco would be defeated.[59]

According to Carmi, by the evening hours of that day, all the bodies he saw when he arrived had been cleared from the plaza, where there was now a mass demonstration of leftist parties and supporters of the Republic. "In the evening, the Olympiad executive told us that they saw no possibility of holding the games as long as the war continued."

Farewell to Spain

The French diplomatic mission in Barcelona announced that the Navy would send two ships then anchored in Algiers to evacuate the athletes to Marseilles. A number of sportsmen promised to return and help the Republicans in their battle.[60] Others preferred not to leave at all, but to remain and join the fighting forces. In any event, a solidarity march of all the athletes from the town center to the stadium where the games were supposed to have taken place was hastily organized.[61] According to Binet:

> With our Scottish pipers at the head, we, with the teams of all other nations represented, marched in the procession, escorted by armed cars, to the sports stadium. Through huge crowds we marched, crowds above whose heads a sea of fists were raised, clenched in the anti-fascist salute. Never before have I experienced such a thrill of pride as this.[62]

The French ships arrived to pick up the athletes on July 22. Glowinsky and Carmi were able to arrange tickets from Marseilles to Haifa for the members of the delegation from Palestine. Despite the conflict raging there between Jews, Arabs, and the British, Palestine seemed like a safe haven in comparison to the inferno that had erupted in Spain. The leaders of the delegation from Palestine decided that Carmi would sail at once from Barcelona to Marseilles and continue on to Portbou to pick up the stranded Jewish athletes. Glowinsky would stay in Barcelona for two more days and then he, too, would proceed by ship to Marseilles.[63]

Three days later Carmi reached the French side of the Pyrenees, but could not pass through the tunnel to the Spanish side because it had been closed for security reasons:

> By chance I met a group of volunteers from Hungary, Poland, Germany, and Russia, who wanted . . . to fight for the Republicans. They were about 30 women and men, with a French guide . . . The French villagers pointed us to a trail through the Pyrenees, about a 10 km hike to Portbou. During this strenuous trek I spoke with the volunteers about their enlistment in the cause. "Every day," they replied, "we see how two madmen, Hitler and Mussolini, are leading Europe to destruction. It will lead to a terrible war. We have to stop this destructive process." After several kilometers I saw a group walking toward us, which included two members of our delegation. "Shalom, shalom," we called out in Hebrew, and embraced.[64]

According to Carmi, the athletes from Palestine were sorry to hear that the Olympiad had been canceled because of the military uprising, but were glad to hear that they would be home in a few days. When the French locomotive arrived to pick up the two railcars the delegation had lived in for seven days, the parting from the villagers was moving.

The First International Volunteers

It is estimated that about 200 athletes from various countries stayed behind in Spain to join the struggle to defend the Republic. They organized themselves into a unit and set out for the Zaragoza front.[65] The best known of this group was Clara Ensner-Thalmann, born in Basel, the daughter of a German Socialist who had fled to Switzerland during the Franco-Prussian war. Thalmann had joined the Communist Party in Switzerland in her youth. Later she moved to France, where she wrote for the Communist daily *L'Humanité*. In the late 1920s she adopted an anti-Soviet position, returned to Switzerland, and drew close to Trotskyite groups. She came to Barcelona as a representative of a workers' swimming club, the Arbeiterschwimmclubs.

When the Civil War broke out she joined the anarchist fighters (the Durruti Column) on the Aragon front, where she was joined by her husband, Paul Thalmann. As a result of the Communists' persecution of the anarchists, the couple went underground and then tried to flee Spain, but were caught and arrested. After several months in jail they were released and made their way to Paris. Like many others who had fought in the International Brigades, they were active in the French Resistance during the Second World War.[66]

Less known are two Jewish tailors from London, Communist party members and cycling comrades Sam Masters and Nat Cohen. They travelled to Barcelona to witness the People's Olympiad, and stayed in Spain to defend the Republic. Masters was killed in the Battle of Brunete in 1937. Cohen fought in Majorca and then returned to the Catalan capital, where he tried to organize British volunteers in the Tom Mann Centuria. Injured in battle, Cohen fell in love with a Spanish nurse and returned to England with her.[67]

Israel Carmi recalled that some members of the Palestine delegation wanted to stay in Spain and join the anti-Fascist struggle:

> I didn't let any of them enlist. I forced all of them to come back with me to Haifa. I had given my word to all the families that I would bring the gang back hale and hearty. That was one of the conditions for their going. Their mothers would have sued me, and rightly so.[68]

Three athletes from Palestine went to Spain on their own, rather than as part of the Hapoel delegation, and stayed on to join the Republican forces. Chaim Elkon, who, as noted at the outset, came to Barcelona to serve as a football referee, joined a group of German and Polish volunteers who arrived from France and later enlisted in the Thälmann Battalion, a unit of the International Brigades named for the German Communist leader Ernst Thälmann. Elkon fell in battle in August 1936 in the University Quarter of Madrid.[69] Nahum Weiss came to the Barcelona games along with Elkon. He, too, decided to stay and fight to defend the Republic, and was killed in the early weeks of the war. Weiss joined the Edgar André Battalion (named for another leader of the German Communist Party). Weiss was killed in November 1936.[70]

Imre Jacoby was the best known of the three.[71] After the Jewish team on which he played, Hagibor Bratislava, came to Palestine for a series of matches in 1927, he decided not to return to Europe. He played for a succession of teams in his first years in Palestine: Hapoel Allenby Tel Aviv, Hapoel Haifa, and Maccabi Haifa. In 1930 Jacoby joined Maccabi Tel Aviv, where he played left wing. Jacoby gained fame in June 1933 when he kicked the winning goal in the finals of the Palestine Cup match against Hapoel Tel Aviv.[72]

Jacoby's decision to join the Communist Party was triggered mainly by his apprehension after the Nazis came to power in Germany and the suppression of the working-class political parties in Vienna in 1934. In the autumn of 1935, the Yiddish-language Polish-Jewish daily *Haynt* reported that the Tel Aviv police suspected that Jacoby, a member of the Maccabi motorcycle team, was part of a Communist cell. When the police searched his home they found rubber stamps bearing the signatures of the high commissioner and the French consul. They also found chemicals and forged passports of Palestine, Poland, Hungary, and Czechoslovakia.[73]

In June 1936, Jacoby and Robert Aquist were expelled from Palestine and boarded a ship from Haifa en route to Spain. Both men joined the International Brigades there. Jacoby served in the Thälmann Battalion. In February 1937, while serving as a motorcycle courier bringing orders from headquarters to the troops on the Jarama front, he was seriously wounded, evidently by a mortar shell, and died in a field hospital near Madrid. According to a letter that his nephew, Haggai Jacobi, sent to Zalman Saltzman, the secretary of the Israel Union of International Brigade Fighters, in June 1986, he was buried in the suburbs of the Spanish capital.[74]

The Peoples' Olympiad, which General Franco, in rhetorical flight typical of the Nationalist camp in the 1930s, later denounced as "a broad campaign of internationalist, Masonic, and Jewish propaganda, intended to turn Spain into a bastion of Bolshevism," did not take place, but the memory of its challenge to the Berlin Olympics did not fade completely. Nor did the workers' sports movement expire in July 1936. A Peoples' Olympics was held the following year in Antwerp, in cooperation with the Socialist Sports Internationale and the Communist Sports Internationale. No fewer than 27,000 athletes from 17 countries participated. This time there was a Soviet delegation as well, in addition to one from Republican Spain, which was riven by a cruel war.

With regard to the Jewish volunteers from Palestine who travelled to Spain to defend the Republic, Elkon, Weiss, and Jacoby blazed the trail for dozens of young people, most of them with Communist views. A few, such as David Karon, were Zionist Socialists. They left the conflict between Jews, Arabs, and the British behind them and went off to fight in Spain, in the hope of stopping the ugly Fascist wave that was threatening to swamp Europe.

Acknowledgement

I would like to thank the Israel Institute of Washington DC for support of this research project.

Notes

1 According to Israel Centner, *From Madrid to Berlin* (Tel Aviv: self-published, 1966), and Dan Yahav, *They Too Were Heroes: Volunteer Fighters from Eretz Israel in the International Brigades in Spain* (Tel Aviv: Tcherikover, 2008) both in Hebrew, Elkon was deported in 1929. In fact, it seems that he was not deported before 1933. See press reports on the detention of Communist activists, including Elkon, *Davar*, July 7, 1933, and August 16, 1933.

2 *Doar Hayom*, August 22, 1935; *Davar*, May 22/30, 1936, and June 3, 1936.

3 Raanan Rein, "Echoes of the Spanish Civil War in Palestine: Zionists, Communists and the Contemporary Press," *Journal of Contemporary History* 43, no. 1 (2008): 9–23; Raanan Rein, "A Belated Inclusion: Jewish Volunteers in the Spanish Civil War and Their Place in the Israeli National Narrative," *Israel Studies* 17, no. 1 (Spring 2012): 24–49.

4 Gabriel Colomé, "La Olimpiada Popular de 1936: deporte y política," *Working Paper* no. 264, Institut de Ciencies Politiques I Socials, Barcelona, 2008, 5.

5 James E. Stout, "Breakaway Nations: The Use of Sport and Physical Culture to Create a Cross-Class Catalan Identity during the Second Republic" (unpublished PhD diss., University of California, 2016), chap. 7.

6 Richard D. Mandell, *The Nazi Olympics* (New York: Macmillan, 1971); Duff Hart-Davis, *Hitler's Games: The 1936 Olympics* (London: Olympic Marketing Corp., 1986); David Clay Large, *Nazi Games: The Olympic of 1936* (New York: W. W. Norton, 2007).

7 Allen Guttmann, "The 'Nazi Olympics' and the American Boycott Controversy," in *Sports and International Politics*, ed. Pierre Arnaud and James Riordan (London: E. & F. N. Spon, 1999), 31–50; Moshe Gottlieb, "The American Controversy over the Olympic Games," *American Jewish Historical Quarterly* LXI (March 1972): 200–9.

8 Adrian Shubert, *The Road to Revolution in Spain: The Coal Miners of Asturias, 1860–1934* (Urbana: University of Illinois Press, 1987), chap. 8; Paul Preston, "Spain's October Revolution and the Rightist Grasp for Power," *Journal of Contemporary History* 10, no. 4 (1975): 555–78.

9 Martin S. Alexander and Helen Graham, eds., *The French and Spanish Popular Front: Comparative Perspectives* (Cambridge: Cambridge University Press, 1989).

10 Stout, "Breakaway Nations."

11 André Gounot, "El Proyecto de la Olimpiada Popular en Barcelona (1936), entre comunismo internacional y republicanismo regional," *Cultura, Ciencia y Deporte* 1, no. 3 (2005): 115–23.

12 *La Vangurdia*, July 15, 1936, 12; Olimpiada Popular de Barcelona, Organization Committee, Press Service, *Bulletin* no. 7, 1936, 7.

13 *Mundo Deportivo*, June 18, 1936.

14 Colomé, "La Olimpiada Popular de 1936," 15. According to Andrés Martín, the Communist member of the organizing committee, official contributions came from Switzerland as well. See "El éxito de la Olimpiada Popular está asegurado," *Mundo Obrero*, June 29, 1936, 5.

15 Olimpiada Popular de Barcelona, Organization Committee, Press Service, *Bulletin* no. 6, 1936, 3.

16 British Workers' Sports Association, Archives of the Trades Union Congress, "Press Information: Barcelona Popular Olympiad," June 9, 1936. Accessible in Warwick University digital library, http://contentdm.warwick.ac.uk/cdm/compoundobject/collection/scw/id/2267/rec/4. See also Ray Physick, "The Olimpiada Popular: Barcelona 1936, Sport and Politics in an Age of War, Dictatorship and Revolution," *Sport in History* 37, no. 1 (2017): 51–75.

17 Andrés Martín, "La prensa reaccionaria miente a sabiendas cuando dice que es una Olimpiada roja," *Mundo Obrero*, June 29, 1936. On the Popular Olympiad in the contemporary press, see María Casado Hernández, "The Popular Olympiad (Barcelona 1936) in the Spanish Press," in *Comité Europeo de Historia del Deporte, Actas V Congreso de Historia del Deporte en Europa*, ed. Teresa González Aja (Madrid: Universidad Politecnica Madrid, 2002), 627–32.

18 *La Veu de Catalunya*, July 2, 1936.

19 Olimpiada Popular de Barcelona, Organization Committee, Press Service, *Bulletin* no. 7, 1936, 8.

20 Quoted in "The Forgotten Olympiad," *Haaretz* [Hebrew], July 31, 1992.

21 *L'Humanite,* 7 July, 1936.

22 William J. Murray, "The French Workers' Sports Movement and the Victory of the Popular Front in 1936," *International Journal of History of Sport* 19, no. 1 (1992): 29–49; David A. Steinberg, "Workers' Sport and the United Front, 1934–1936," *Arena Review* 4, no. 1 (1980): 1–6. Among the delegations, there were 12 athletes from the United States, half of them, as emphasized by the officials of the Popular Olympiad, blacks, as well as six Canadians. See A. S. Lipschitz, Labor Chest for the Relief and Liberation of Workers of Europe, to Walter Citrine, Labor Chest for the Relief and Liberation of Workers of Europe, Archives of the Trades Union Congress, "Letter: Delegation to the Barcelona People's Olympiad," July 1, 1936, http://contentdm.warwick.ac.uk/cdm/compoundobject/collection/scw/id/2261/rec/2; Bruce Kidd, "The Popular Front and the 1936 Olympics," *Canadian Journal of the History of Sport and Physical Education* XI (May 1980): 1–18.

23 Olimpiada Popular de Barcelona, Organization Committee, Press Service, *Bulletin* no. 6, 1936, 8.

24 "El éxito de la Olimpiada Popular está asegurado," *Mundo Obrero,* June 29, 1936, 5.

25 Rafael Pacuet and Enric Pujol, eds., *La revolució del bon gust. Jaume Miravitlles i el Comissariat de Propaganda de la Generalitat de Catalunya (1936–1939)* (Barcelona: Viena Edicions, 2007), 42–43.

26 Stanley G. Payne, *The Spanish Civil War, the Soviet Union, and Communism* (New Haven: Yale University Press, 2004); Daniel Kowalsky, *Stalin and the Spanish Civil War* (New York: Columbia University Press, 2004).

27 Olimpiada Popular de Barcelona, Organization Committee, Press Service, *Bulletin* no. 6, 1936, 7.

28 "El día pro Olimpiada Popular se celebrará el próximo día 3 y constituirá el máximo impulso a la campaña de preparación y propaganda," *Mundo Obrero,* June 1, 1936, 5.

29 Olimpiada Popular de Barcelona, Organization Committee, Press Service, *Bulletin* no. 7, 1936, 1; British Workers' Sports Association, Archives of the Trades Union Congress, "Press Information," June 24, 1936, http://contentdm.warwick.ac.uk/cdm/compoundobject/collection/scw/id/2270/rec/5.

30 See, for example, "Demand in Yugoslavia to Boycott the Olympic Games," *Doar Hayom,* April 17, 1936, 11.

31 "Olympiad, Sports, and Politics," *Davar,* June 23, 1936, 9.

32 "Olympiad vs. Olympiad," *Doar Hayom,* May 29, 1936; "Anti-Nazi Olympiad," *Davar,* June 1, 1936, 6.

33 Edward S. Shapiro, "The World Labor Athletic Carnival of 1936: An American Anti-Nazi Protest," *American Jewish History* 74, no. 3 (1985): 255 73.

34 "Olympic Spirit vs. Fascist Spirit in Sports," *Davar,* June 1, 1936, 3.

35 "An Ideal Olympiad," *Davar*, June 14, 1936, 2; "In the Jewish Diaspora," *Doar Hayom*, June 9, 1936, 7.

36 "Hapoel on Rejecting Its Participation in the Maccabiah Games," *Davar*, March 31, 1935; Haggai Harif, *Zionism of Muscles: The Political Functions of Representative Sport in Eretz Israel and in the State of Israel, 1898–1960* [Hebrew] (Jerusalem: Yad Ben-Zvi, 2011), chap. 5.

37 Bruce Kidd, "'Another World is Possible': Recapturing Alternative Olympic Histories, Imagining Different Games," in *Global Olympics: Historical and Sociological Studies of the Modern Games, Research in the Sociology of Sport* (special issue) 3 (2005): 143 58; David A. Steinberg, "The Workers' Sport Internationals, 1920–1928," *Journal of Contemporary History* 13 (1978): 233–51; Robert F. Wheeler, "Organized Sport and Organized Labour: The Workers' Sport Movement," *Journal of Contemporary History* 13 (1978): 191–210.

38 Yahav, *They Too Were Heroes*, 214. Similarly, see the organ of the Socialist Zionist Hashomer Hatzair movement: N. P., "Hapoel in the Anti-Fascist Olympiad of Barcelona," *Hashomer Hatzair*, no. 14, 1936, 14–15.

39 *Sport Haboker*, July 5, 1936, 4.

40 Labor Party Archive IV-244–55, "To the Hapoel Secretariat," July 11, 1936, Lavon Institute, Tel Aviv.

41 Already in mid-June the organizing committee stated that "[they had] entered into communication with the International Zionist Organization in London, seeking to obtain official participation of Zionism in the International Sport Week in Barcelona. The negotiations suggest a very favorable result," Olimpiada Popular de Barcelona, Organization Committee, Press Service, *Bulletin* no. 6, 1936, 6.

42 Olimpiada Popular de Barcelona, Organization Committee, Press Service, *Bulletin* no. 7, 1936, 3, http://contentdm.warwick.ac.uk/cdm/compoundobject/collection/scw/id/2292/rec/6.

43 Xavier Pujadas and Carles Santacana, *L'altra olimpíada. Barcelona '36* (Barcelona: Llibres de l'Índex, 2006), 193; Olimpiada Popular de Barcelona, Organization Committee, Press Service, *Bulletin* no. 7, 1936, 4.

44 Her 1937 record in shot put, registered in Jewish Palestine, was broken only 22 years later. See Eliezer Ro'i, "Athletes and Records in Sport," *Davar*, February 8, 1952.

45 "Opiniones de tres delegados internacionales sobre la Olimpiada," *Mundo Obrero*, July 18, 1936, 5.

46 "Deportistas franceses constituirán la más fuerte delegción extranjera en la Olimpiada Populer," *Mundo Obrero*, July 18, 1936, 6.

47 "Un tren especial desde Paris," *Mundo Deportivo*, July 6, 1936; *Ha'aretz*, July 31, 1992.

48 "Los atletas noruegas en la Olimpiada Popular. Enorme pedido de alojamientos en Barcelona," *Mundo Obrero*, July 11, 5; Olimpiada Popular de Barcelona, Organization Committee, Press Service, *Bulletin* no. 7, 1936, 5–6.

49 Israel Paz and Uriel Zimri, "Haim at the Age of 80: Friends on Haim Glowinsky" [Hebrew], Wingate Institute, 1982.
50 *Mundo Deportivo*, June 7, 1936.
51 In a letter to the Secretary of the British Trade Union Congress, Sir Walter Citrine, the organizers emphasized that "of particular interest to anti-Fascists are the Jewish sportsmen coming from Palestine, the teams of exiled German-Jews from Paris and Amsterdam, and the Negro sportsmen from U.S.A.[*sic*]," Organizing Committee, Olimpiada Popular de Barcelona, collection Archives of the Trades Union Congress, "Letter (copy); Letter," June 12, 1936, http://contentdm.warwick.ac.uk/cdm/compoundobject/collection/scw/id/2296/rec/1.
52 For the testimonies of the British delegation members, see Guy Walters, *Berlin Games. How the Nazis Stole the Olympic Dream* (New York: William Morrow, 2006), chap. 6; Stephen G. Jones, *Sport, Politics and the Working Class: Organized Labour and Sport in Inter-War Britain* (Manchester, Manchester University Press, 1988), 185–86.
53 On the British delegation, see British Workers' Sports Association, Archives of the Trades Union Congress, "Press Information," June 24, 1936, http://contentdm.warwick.ac.uk/cdm/compoundobject/collection/scw/id/2270/rec/2.
54 Quoted in Paul K. Martin, "Spain's Other Olympics," *History Today*, no. 42 (August 1992): 6–8.
55 Yahav, *They Too Were Heroes*, 214–15.
56 Ibid., 215.
57 "In Spain during the Days of the Rebellion: Hapoel Delegation Members Report on Facts and Impressions," *Davar*, August 10, 1936, 2–3.
58 Yahav, *They Too Were Heroes*, 215
59 Ibid.
60 This was the case, for example, of the coach of the American team to the Barcelona games, Alfred Chakin, a boxer from New York who returned to Spain in 1937 and joined the Abraham Lincoln Brigade.
61 *La Vanguardia*, July 24, 1936, 1.
62 Quoted in Martin, "Spain's Other Olympics," 6–8.
63 Glowinsy indeed boarded a British war vessel on its way to Marseilles. See "In Spain during the Days of the Rebellion: Hapoel Delegation Members Report on Facts and Impressions," *Davar*, August 10, 1936, 2–3
64 Yahav, *They Too Were Heroes*, 216.
65 "Muchos de las Representaciones extrnajeras de atletismo se han alistado en las milicias," *La Vanguardia*, July 24, 1936; Dan Richardson, *Comintern Army: The International Brigades and the Spanish Civil War* (Lexington, KY: University Press of Kentucky, 1982), 24, note 35; Max Wullschleger, ed., *Schweizer Kampfen in Spanien* (Zurich: Buchhandlung Stauffacher, 1939), 78.
66 See the memoirs of Clara und Paul Thalmann, Revolution für die Freihei, 1974, at http://www.kommunismus.narod.ru/knigi/pdf/Clara_und_Paul_

Thalmann - Revolution fuer die Freiheit.pdf; 17-year old Marina Ginestá, an athlete from France who went to Barcelona for the games, also joined the militias after the war broke out. See *Independent*, January 22, 2014.

67 Robert Philpot, "The Jews of the Spanish Civil War: A Forgotten Story," *Jewish Chronicle*, July 13, 2016.

68 Yahav, *They Too Were Heroes*, 216.

69 "In Memoriam: Palestinian Volunteers who Died in the Holy War for Human Freedom on Spanish Soil," *Kol Ha'am*, July 18, 1947, 3; "In Memoriam: Palestinian Volunteers . . . ," *Kol Ha-am*, July 15, 1949, 5; Yahav, *They Too Were Heroes*, 216.

70 "In Memoriam: Palestinian Volunteers . . . ," *Kol Ha'am*, July 18, 1947, 3; "In Memoriam: Palestinian Volunteers . . . ," *Kol Ha-am*, July 15, 1949, 5.

71 "Imre Jacobi: 20 Years after His Death on the Spanish Front," *Kol Ha'am*, February 1957.

72 Asher Goldberg and Dani Dvorin, *Maccabi Tel Aviv: The First 100 Years* (Media Publishing , 2006), 59.

73 *Haynt*, September 23, 1935, 3; "Arrest Warrant for the Heads of a Communist Cell," *Doar Hayom*, August 22, 1935, 8.

74 Haggai Jacobi to Zalman Saltzman, June 1986. I would like to thank Eran Torbiner for sharing this document with me.

3

The Political Evolution of the Nationalist Zone in 1936: The Construction of the Francoist State

JOAN MARIA THOMÀS

> Since the "state of war" in its fullest sense implies the subordination of all instruments to the principal objective, it was clear that the adoption of a unified command would not be limited to the army, but would instead encompass the state in its entirety, a step so much easier and more necessary when the "state-army" relationship took a form that was the inverse of the normal one, given that it was no longer a case of a state making war by militarizing itself, but of an army which, breaking with the pre-existing state, had to invent a new state for its own ends.
> Ramón Serrano Suñer, *Entre el silencio y la propaganda. La Historia como fue* (Barcelona: Planeta, 1977), 158

These words, written by the man who was Franco's principal political advisor from 1937 to 1941, shed light on the beginnings of the construction of the Francoist State. The failure of the coup d'état of July 17–19, 1936 prevented the immediate installation of a junta, made up of generals and civilian advisors, aimed at seizing the powers of the state and controlling its entire apparatus. This meant that from this point onward the coupists had to act politically in the midst of a civil war, controlling only part of the country a part which, furthermore, did not include the capital, Madrid, where essential institutions and resources were concentrated. This initial failure was immediately followed by the accidental death of the man who was to have the led the junta after the coup, General José Sanjurjo.

Without having defeated the state, and without the leader they had agreed upon, the coupist generals formed another junta, this one wholly military, so that it could take command of the territory in their hands, that is, by the part of the army that had revolted. Not only was this all of the army, but it did not include the majority of the high command – the divisional generals – nor those generals, chiefs, and officers who had remained loyal to the Republic to which they had previously sworn fidelity.

While the seizure of power was expected to be difficult but inevitable, with hostilities lasting days or even weeks, the death in a plane accident on Monday July 20, 1936 when there was still fighting in the streets in various cities around the country to effect the coup d'état – of the man who was supposed to lead the "movement to save Spain" created a vacuum that would take months to fill. Undoubtedly, Sanjurjo was the most charismatic of the rebel generals, as well as having the purest anti-Republican pedigree of them all. As such, he had led the first – abortive – coup attempt against the Republican regime, in August 1932, as a result of which he was forced into exile in Portugal. Although pardoned, it was from Portugal that he set out in the light aircraft in which he met his death. Before the Republican period, he had worked closely with dictator General Primo de Rivera, 1923–30, serving also as the executive commander of the Alhucemas landing of 1925, the military operation that pacified the Spanish Protectorate of Morocco, winning him prestige among his fellow officers.

Thus, at the very beginning of the configuration of power in the so-called Nationalist zone (*zona nacional*, the name tellingly adopted by the pro-coup faction, as if the Spanish Republicans were not Spanish nationals but dangerous international revolutionaries), the army was distinctly present. Specifically, the so-called (again tellingly, as if the nation had to be defended from the Republic and the revolution) Junta de Defensa Nacional de España (Spain's national defense board) presided over, following the death of Sanjurjo and in accordance with military custom, by the highest ranking officer, Divisional General Guillermo Cabanellas.[1] Cabanellas was hardly representative of the coupists, given his Republicanism and his apparent past involvement in Freemasonry, rendering him untrustworthy for at least some of the other generals. From the outset, the junta included Divisional General Andrés Saliquet, brigadier generals Miguel Ponte, Emilio Mola, and Fidel Dávila, and colonels of the general staff Federico Montaner and Fernando Moreno.[2] Over the following days and weeks, these members would be joined by Navy captain Francisco Moreno Fernández, commander of the rebel fleet[3] (on July 30); Divisional General Francisco Franco[4] (on August 3); Divisional General Germán Gil[5] (on August 18); and Divisional General Gonzalo Queipo de Llano and Brigadier General Luis Orgaz (on September 19).[6] The commander of the rebel air force, Brigadier General

Alfredo Kindelán,[7] was also a member of the unta, although the date of his incorporation does not appear in the official record.

The insurrectionists' first act was to declare a "state of war" in the provinces in which they had been victorious, and then, on July 28, in "the entire national territory": in other words, the area they expected to conquer in the following weeks or months in a very short campaign. This "state of war" was a situation foreseen in the Republican public order law of July 28, 1933, which granted the army extraordinary powers to suppress opposition and re-establish order in extreme cases of public unrest those that the civilian authorities could not control by their own means. It granted these powers only after the declaration of the aforementioned "state of war" by the government or civilian authorities, a condition the coupists flagrantly flouted. The law also conferred on the military the power to try, in military tribunals, prisoners accused of "crimes of rebellion, sedition, and related offenses, terrorist attack, resistance to and disobedience of the Authorities and their Agents, as well as those crimes classified in the civil penal code as crimes against public order."[8]

The rebel generals' interpretation of this classification of offenses, as applied to members of the armed forces who had not joined the uprising and/or those who had resisted it, was to charge them with rebellion and sedition. This was part of the massive repression they then set in motion and which followed two parallel courses: first via formal means, with emergency military trials (*consejos de guerra sumarísimos* – summary courts martial or military tribunals) of soldiers and civilians; and second, repression of a completely irregular kind, specifically, murder by firing squad, without trial, of large numbers of civilians who were considered *chusma* (riffraff) because they were leftists or simply Republicans, among them both those who had resisted the coup and others, including many prisoners of war. Later, legal, formal repression – that of the courts martial – would be generalized, although extrajudicial executions continued throughout the entire period of the war, albeit to a lesser extent compared to those carried out officially.

The reality of the repression carried out by the rebel army went far beyond that outlined in Confidential Instruction Number 1 prepared before the coup by its leader General Emilio Mola, who stated:

> The action will need to be extremely violent to bring down the enemy, who is strong and well organized, as soon as possible . . . All leaders of political parties, societies, or unions that are not sympathetic with the Movement will be imprisoned, and exemplary punishments will be administered to those individuals, to stifle strikes or rebellions.[9]

In fact, this repression would end – in the words of an individual who would hold high office in the first stages of Franco's regime – with,

> the physical destruction of the cadres of the Popular Front, of the trade unions, and the Masonic organizations, without forgetting the more moderate democratic parties and the independent personalities who, in intellectual or professional circles, enjoy a reputation for being leftists or decidedly liberal . . . One can and must speak of a perfect operation to extirpate the political forces that sponsored and supported the Republic and represented advanced social trends or simply movements of democratic or liberal thought.[10]

It is worth recalling, furthermore, that the "state of war" would remain in force until as late as 1948.

As successors in an era of authoritarian *pronunciamientos* – military uprisings – which began in Spain in 1923 with the dictatorship of Primo Rivera, the coupists felt from the outset that it was perfectly legitimate to rebel against the constitutional Republican regime, convinced as they were that they represented the true Spain. They had no qualms about twisting the law, so that, according to their interpretation, the real rebels, seditionaries, and traitors, those who had betrayed their oaths, were not themselves but those who had not rebelled. It was, as Serrano Suñer, former interior and foreign affairs minister would put it forty years later (accurately, but also somewhat cynically, as if he had had nothing to do with it) "justice turned on its head."[11] But the rebel generals and their political associates must not have felt their consciences were clear with regard to their own, real, rebellion and sedition, because in late 1938 Franco ordered the creation of a commission of legal experts headed by the president of the Supreme Court, Ildefonso Bellón,[12] with the aim of "proving beyond doubt the illegitimacy of the public authorities in the Spanish Republic of July 18, 1936," and of making clear – ostensibly, of course – that the "National Movement" had in no sense been an act of rebellion. The commission performed the task it had been set with zeal.

In the weeks following the beginning of the uprising, the Junta de Defensa Nacional adopted far-reaching political measures, such as a ban on all the parties and trade unions of the Popular Front, as well as other groups that had opposed the coup, the confiscation of all their property, both assets and real estate, including all paperwork; a purge, with the possibility of punishment, of those public servants who had resisted the coup; and also the confiscation – by judicial means – of the property of private individuals who had been against it.[13] The justification offered for this last measure is striking: instead of being based on ideological or political considerations, it was enacted on the basis that the suppressed entities were "satisfying personal ambition to the detriment of the common good" and had "poisoned the populace by offering the lure of supposed social benefits so that they would follow their leaders, who exploited them to prosper at their expense."[14] Another measure, with limited practical effect, prohibited any political activity, including that of unions or employers within the Nationalist zone during the war, while at the same time announcing that "the day will come when the government that rules the destiny of Spain will be able to institute the only politics and unionization possible in any well-organized Nation: a politics and unionization that is ruled and controlled by the leaders of the state, as repositories of the trust of the people."[15] It was also decreed that the rebel flag would be that of the monarchy, "the red and yellow bicolor," a move, it was recognized, that granted "official status to what in fact already obtains throughout the liberated territory";[16] in other words, the Republican tricolor would be banned.

But, although the Junta de Defensa Nacional held power throughout the Nationalist zone, as soon as the coup attempt failed, it was clear that a different kind of power, far more effective, resided in the three generals with operational military forces. Among them, due to the size of the contingent under his command, the most important had always been Franco. Franco had rebelled in the Canary Islands and flown to Tetuán – the capital of the Protectorate of Morocco – to take charge of the troops stationed there, the best trained and equipped in the Spanish army, including mercenaries – the Legión, or Tercio de Extranjeros – and Moroccan regulars. Moreover, he immediately and personally ensured increased recruitment of colonial troops, dedicating plentiful funds to this end and decorating the Grand Vizir Sidi del Majzen, Sidi Ahmed Ben Hach Abd el Krim Ganmia, with the Great Laureate Cross of Saint Ferdinand, Spain's highest military award for gallantry, for having put down an attempted rebellion in Tetuán.[17] The Junta had named Franco "general commander of the Army of Morocco and of southern Spain," while Mola was named general commander of the "Army of the North,"[18] and Queipo de Llano of the forces operating in Andalusia,[19] but these were no more than ex post facto formalizations. In fact, it was Mola himself who had had the idea of creating the junta and of naming Cabanellas as its president. At that time all eyes were on the conduct of military operations by the three generals in command of operational forces, and who, after consolidating control over their own territory, came together to advance on Madrid, seeking a swift end to the war.

The dichotomy between the effective military power held by Franco, Mola, and Queipo de Llano, on the one hand, and the Junta de Defensa

Nacional, endowed with political and administrative powers, on the other, represented the first political characteristic of Nationalist Spain and would persist for just over two months until, at a meeting held on September 28, 1936, the junta named Franco "Head of the State Government of Spain . . . , Generalísimo of the Nationalist forces of land, sea, and air and . . . General Commander of the Field Armies."[20] Various factors contributed to this move. First was the need felt by some members of the junta to create a unified command, vested in a single person, of the Nationalist armies for the duration of the war, in order to ensure their victory; a command that should include, at a subordinate level, civilian powers – an idea that was not shared by all. Second were Franco's military successes, which were far greater than those of Mola and Queipo, and for which he was accruing far more prestige as director of operations; these marked him as having the greatest capacity to achieve the ultimate victory. Third, it was Franco who was the principal recipient of the military aid – both material and human – sent by Nazi Germany and Fascist Italy, which contributed to his operational feats. Finally, pro-Franco generals and Franco's own inner circle were instrumental in pushinghim as a candidate for supreme commander and were confident that he would accept the role.[21]

However, the generals who elected him as supreme commander on September 28 did so thinking of him as a temporary leader, his tenure limited to the duration of the war. And those who were key to his candidacy – Kindelán and Orgaz, in particular – acted while trusting both in Franco's (putative, as would become clear) pro-Alfonsine monarchism, and a subsequent speedy restoration of the kingship of Alfonso XIII (once the war was over). That Franco did not do this, either in the person of the king, or in that of his successor from 1941 onward, Juan de Borbón y Battenberg, was later – during the Second World War – the source of conspiracies and tensions within the upper echelons of Franco's regime.

The designation of Franco as sole military and civilian commander of Nationalist Spain entailed the continued supremacy of the military, as well as the creation of a subordinate structure of a political/administrative nature, known as the Junta Técnica del Estado (state technical council; JTE), headed by another general appointed by Franco himself, Fidel Dávila, who was also chief of the General Staff.[22] In his first law, the new generalissimo (who in the first official state gazette, "Boletín Oficial del Estado," which he launched at that time, no longer appears as "Head of the State Government" but as "Head of State," a not insignificant detail that apparently cost the diplomat José Yanguas Messía his post for not having given him this title "from the start"[23]), defined the JTE as a non-permanent forerunner "of a permanent junta, to be established once the entirenational territory is subject to control." This intention was never acted upon, because just over a year later, in early 1938, Franco passed another law which, abandoning the structure of the junta, established a formal government with ministries. What he did maintain were his self-assigned powers to enact laws, an aspect in which he outdid his predecessor, General Primo de Rivera, who despite being an autocrat, had never broken radically with the regime under which his dictatorship had arisen, and which had abided by the Constitution of 1876.

In the law that constituted it, the JTE was defined as a consultative body divided into committees whose function was to study and prepare, as well to propose regulations on questions related to the areas for which each was responsible, and which would subsequently be approved, or not, by the generalissimo and head of state. Eight such committees were created, namely "Revenue, Justice, Industry, Commerce and Supplies, Agriculture and Agricultural Labor, Labor, Culture and Education, and Public Works and Communications."[24] At the same time, the new Francoist political and administrative structure was supplemented by other posts and bodies. These included the position of governor general, which was appointed a general who was responsible for inspecting the life of the Nationalist provinces; he was superior to the civilian and military provincial authorities and worked closely with the JTE. There was also the Secretariat of War, headed by another general, which dealt with administrative and internal issues relating to the army; the Secretariat of Foreign Affairs, headed by a career diplomat (Francisco Serrat Bonastre, an ambassador), which was responsible for consular and diplomatic relations[25]; the Press and Propaganda Section, under the command of the head of the Corps of Wounded Veterans, José Millán-Astray, founder of the Legion, and with Ernesto Giménez Caballero, one of the founders of Spanish Fascism, as his assistant.[26] But a group of positions were also created for members of Franco's inner circle, in whom, alongside Franco himself, genuine power truly resided: the General Secretariat of the Head of State, which was required to include "staff specialized in matters that are that concern the different sections of the Technical Junta, as well as a prominent member of the Department of Foreign Relations," and whose configuration involved a certain degree of duplication with the JTE. This secretariat would become indispensable to General Franco, who placed it under the control of his elder brother, Nicolás, a lieutenant colonel of the navy engineers.[27] There was a similar duplication – in this case with the Secretariat of Foreign Affairs – with the establishment of the Diplomatic and Protocolary Office attached to the generalissimo, headed by a career diplomat who enjoyed his confidence, José Antonio Sangróniz, who replaced the disgraced and deposed Yanguas.

In fact, the appointment of his brother as secretary marked the beginning of a tendency that Franco would not forego until five years later: that of keeping a relative at his side as his senior political adviser, beginning with Nicolás and ending with his brother-in-law Ramón Serrano Suñer. The former would leave the post on the formation of Franco's first government, when he was sent to Portugal as ambassador, while the second lost it in 194142, as he was gradually replaced as Franco's most trusted political ally by a figure from outside the family, Luis Carrero Blanco, a Navy officer. However, it is worth bearing in mind that at another, lower, level, there would always remain – that is, until the dictator's death in 1975 – another relative, the generalissimo's private secretary and cousin Francisco Franco Salgado-Araujo, a career officer who reached the rank of lieutenant general.

The concentration of political power in the hands of the head of state, with the support of those closest to him (including his family) constitutes the second fundamental characteristic of the configuration of power in the period under study. And the fact that the duplication mentioned above worked in favor of Franco and the official bodies closest to him is evident if we take into account that of the 170 orders published in the official state gazette from the generalissimo's accession to power until the end of 1936, some 100 emanated directly from Franco himself.[28]

Among the rest, of those generated by the JTE, the most noteworthy were those relating to the counter-stamping of paper money (*estampillado*, the use of a distinctive stamp to differentiate banknotes, in pesetas, from those in circulation in Republican territory); the collection of gold and valuables destined for the National treasury; the creation of the Foreign Money Committee; the imposition of the *día del Plato Único*, "single course day," an indirect tax on businesses such as restaurants, bars, hotels, and lodging houses, revenue deriving from which was channeled to pay for care in orphanages and hospices, among others); the re-establishment of the special tribunals (*tribunales de honor*) in the army and the avy (suppressed some years earlier under the Republic); a prohibition on presenting legal appeals against the sentences of summary military tribunals; regulation of the purges of civil servants in all public offices; the promotion of divisional generals Orgaz, Mola, Ponte, Valdés, and López Pinto, and the permanent discharge from the army of others who had remained loyal to the Republic (some of whom, such as Batet, were held by Franco's forces and would eventually be executed by firing squad). Others were more unusual, such as the prohibition of *recomendaciones* (the use of connections to obtain favors) in the army.

In addition, during November and the first weeks of December, the JTE prepared orders relating to what was then believed to be the imminent occupation of the city of Madrid, mainly arrangements for repressive measures that were expected to be massive, given that eight military tribunals[29] were created. There was also the formation of a "specialist psychiatric team for the days following the liberation of Madrid, led by the Most Illustrious Sr. Antonio Vallejo Nágera, health adviser and director of the San José de Ciempozuelos Psychiatric [military] Clinic."[30]Later, and beyond the period that concerns us here, Vallejo would be named "head of the Army Psychiatric Services and director of Psychological Investigation for the Inspectorate of Concentration Camps," and would enter history, among other reasons, for his experiments on "red" women in the defeated city of Málaga.[31] The purchase of one hundred trucks for Madrid's city council was also ordered.[32] The failure of successive attacks on the capital during this period would prevent any of these measures from being applied to the population of Madrid for over two years.

The only political domain not subject to the absolute power acquired by Franco from the moment of his "exaltation" (his appointment, in the regime's baroque rhetoric) to the role of head of state was party power, that is,direct power over the political parties that were active in the Nationalist zone. This constitutes the third characteristic of the political configuration of Franco's regime during the first five years of its existence. Despite the ban decreed by the Junta de Defensa Nacional on September 25, they had continued to function politically, although their principal focus was on participation in the war. There were two main forces, the Fascist Falange Española de las JONS and the Carlist Comunión Tradicionalista; there were also small groups of Alfonsine monarchists such as Renovación Española as well as citizen militias of the Juventudes de Acción Popular (the youth wing of CEDA [Spanish Confederation of Autonomous Right-Wing Groups]) and Acción Popular – CEDA.

The Fascists and the Carlists turned out to be absolutely essential to the recruitment of volunteer militiamen for the front, at a time when the process of conscription was just beginning. The army needed the volunteers enlisted in these militia groups – the Falangists and the Carlists (whose militiamen were known as *requetés,* formed into units called *tercios*) – and thus permitted the parties that were recruiting them to continue to act as such. Moreover, it handed over to them a large proportion of the premises, newspapers, and other property confiscated from the parties of the Popular Front, while tolerating the enlistment of women, young people, children, and adults over military age, given that many of their activities also contributed to the war effort. There were units such as the *lavaderos del frente* (front line laundries) of the Falangist

Women's Section, as well as nurses and women who sewed winter clothing for the combatants. Carlist enlistment of women, for its part, included the Margaritas (the Carlist women's service) and the Front lines and hospitals section, among others.

But the Falangist and Carlist parties also had a role in the rearguard, through the creation of bodies such as Winter Aid, later Social Aid by the FE de las JONS, in late October 1936, "second line" militias which assisted in internal security duties in the cities, and would play a prominent part in the repression. They also assumed functions relating to the press and propaganda, to a far greater extent than in the pre-war period, after having been handed control of newspapers, printing presses, and radio transmitters confiscated from the Reds, as noted above.

By the second half of 1936, the Falange had become the more important of these two forces, to a surprising degree. Before the war the party had been relatively marginal, in terms of activist numbers, and was certainly smaller than the Comunión Tradicionalista. Nonetheless, it had first expanded significantly after the elections of February 1936, when it was still an underground organization, and it now underwent another unprecedented phase of growth. The Falange was the party that attracted most new members who were joining political parties in the Nationalist zone. Their enlistment was an expression of enthusiasm and interest in contributing in some way to the war effort on the part of the pro-coupist sector of the population, which had previously been affiliated to other parties of the right, or to the extreme right, or, perhaps to an even greater extent were unaffiliated to any party.[33] In far lower numbers they stemmed from the left. Those who came from the latter group found, in a party that proclaimed that its "arms [were] open to the worker and the peasant farmer," a means to protect themselves from repression. The presence of some ex-leftists in the Falange was known and remarked upon by other sectors among the pro-coup faction, who contemptuously and pointedly nicknamed it FAI-lange (referring to the FAI, the Iberian Anarchist Federation, a section of the anarcho-syndicalist Confederación Nacional de Trabajo [national confederation of labor], an essential constituent of the separatist Red enemy). The Falange accepted ex-leftists – as long as they were not former militiamen or well-known activists – in accordance with their reunifying Fascist ideology, while at the same time playing a central role in the anti-leftist repression.

The FE de las JONS was also the party that sent most militiamen to the various fronts, ahead of the Comunión Tradicionalista, which sent its *tercios de requetés* – as the battalions of Carlist militiamen were known – especially to Navarra and parts of the Basque Country. The proportion of volunteer combatants enlisted in both organizations was weighted heavily toward the Falangist side.[34]

Of course, the two parties did not limit their activity to the front lines, or to supporting them, but also concerned themselves with increasing their relative influence and preparing for the accession to power, which they regarded as the ultimate reason for their participation in the war. In the case of the Fascists, they hoped to establish a Fascist regime in Spain, headed by their leader José Antonio Primo de Rivera, once he had been freed from the prison in Alicante in which he was held within the Republican zone. In the case of the Carlists, they anticipated the coronation of their king, Alfonso Carlos I de Borbón y Austria-Este, until his accidental death in Vienna on September 29, 1936, after which they looked to his regent and successor, Javier de Borbón-Parma, who was resident first in Portugal and later in France. Both parties preserved their command structures – the Provisional Command Council in the case of the Falange, and the National Carlist Council of War in that of the Comunión Tradicionalista – and a certain degree of autonomy at a military level. But above all, their ambition, as noted, was to see the establishment in the country of one of the two regimes described above at the end of the conflict. News of the execution by firing squad of Primo de Rivera on November 20 did not alter the Falangists' aspirations, and they decided to keep the loss of their national leader secret, presumably so as not to demoralize their members. Nor did the exile of Fal Conde alter the aspirations of the Carlists, as will be seen below.

However, there were also differences within the upper echelons of both parties in regard to their final strategy. The Carlists were divided between those who wanted what they called the "fourth Carlist war" to end inexorably in the establishment of their monarchy – this was the position of the delegated leader Manuel Fal Conde; and others who were in favor of greater flexibility and cooperation with Franco, based on the role he played as a bastion against the reviled and heretical Republic and its pernicious anti-Catholic laws, and thus as a defense against Communist revolution, and regarded the restoration of the Carlist monarchy as a matter of secondary importance. Furthermore, some of the latter faction expressed an openness to a dynastic reconciliation with the other Bourbon line, that of Alfonso XIII. An important representative of this group was the count of Rodezno, a former delegated leader and the principal Carlist leader in Navarra. Meanwhile, within the Falangist Command Council tensions soon arose between those who favored a more collaborative attitude towards Franco in political matters without renouncing their ultimate aim – such as Manuel Hedilla, head of the council; and others – such as Primo de Rivera's family members and those closest to them – who advocated greater inflexibility.

The main conflict that arose between these two parties and Franco in the period under consideration was that caused by the Carlists and the (ultimately abortive) formation of their *requeté* officer training school, following an order signed by Fal Conde in the name of Don Javier and published in the "Boletín de Orientación Tradicionalista" (traditionalist gazette) on December 8. The creation of what was officially titled Royal Military Academy of Requetés – one of whose colleges was to be called Prince Regent came in response to the real need to train officers for the *tercios* and was not indicative of any intention to provoke Franco or to defy his power. It was an expression of the autonomy that the Carlists – like the Falangists – had until then enjoyed within the context of the insurrection. The order also included a regulation on promotions for merit in combat for *requetés.* The problem was that all this was utterly unacceptable to Franco, who, in a private conversation with Rodezno, described the actions of Fal Conde as "a coup d'état, a crime of treason . . . the behavior of an anarchist, not a man attached to the Movement,"[35] and as a challenge to his supreme commandership. He immediately had the president of the JTE, General Dávila, summon Fal, and offered him the alternatives of trial by military tribunal or exile to Portugal, of which he chose the latter. The dictator had interpreted the order as a questioning of his authority, and had probably been even more offended by the attempt to bypass his leadership in strictly military matters, such as officer training and promotions.

In the case of the Falangists, tensions with Franco would eventually become even more significant, but these would not emerge until the early months of 1937. They would culminate in the so-called Sucesos de Salamanca and an internecine struggle for power, before the forcible unification, by official decree, of the Falange and Comunión Tradicionalista into a single party whose national leader would be the generalissimo.[36]

As a result of the conflict over the Carlist military academy, the day after Dávila's interview with Fal Conde, December 20, 1936, Franco enacted a decree that has entered history as the "militariation of the militias." By virtue thereof, they were all subject to the Military Code of Justice; they were placed under the command of the army authorities; all their officers had to come from the army; they were limited to infantry or cavalry forces and not permitted to include artillery or engineers; all those acting in the rearguard were obliged to obey all the regulations laid down in the Cartilla de la Guardia Civil, the code of conduct for civil guard officers, in regard to detentions or incidents in which they were involved; and a set number of places were reserved in the military academies for the training of *alféreces de campaña* – later known as *alféreces provisionales* (temporary second lieutenants) – so that those Falangist militiamen or *requetés* who fulfilled admission requirements, and were selected, could enter them and become regular army officers.

In short, the decree marked the end of the relative autonomy the political parties' military forces had enjoyed, and integrated them into the regular military system. The conflict over the academy had hastened a measure that logically would have ended up being adopted anyway, if only on the grounds of military efficiency, but which constituted the first step toward what would finally come about on April 19 the following year, the unification by decree, under the generalissimo's command, of the two principal political forces active in Nationalist Spain, and with it the absolute consolidation of his rule, which now encompassed all spheres of political power. The beginning of these measures toward the unification and expropriation of the Falange and Carlism by Franco constitutes the fourth characteristic of the configuration of the regime during the first five months of the war.

In fact, by this stage, in late 1936, the generalissimo and head of state had already begun to consider the idea of creating some kind of single party or political force. The question had probably arisen due to the failure of the assault on Madrid, at the end of November, when it had become clear that the war would not be as short as had been expected. This fact must have convinced him of the need to provide his incipient state with a political structure during the war itself. He must have had in mind the experience of Primo de Rivera's dictatorship, and his Patriotic Union party, although probably more as an example to extend and improve upon. His regime, as he told Rodezno, would be "definitive"; it would be based on the elements that would reunite the rebels, would avoid giving an impression of disunity to the outside world, and would integrate "the working-class element."[37]

Shortly afterward, in 1937, a decision was made to draw on the two genuinely active mass organizations – FE de las JONS and Comunión Tradicionalista – to form his party, unifying them, placing them under his own control, and giving priority, in terms of structure and ideology, to the first, which must have seemed more modern than the second, more open to the working-class element, and more closely resembling parties in allied countries which were Fascist like the Falange. His allies, for their part, did not conceal their own interest not only in seeing the Francoist state, after their diplomatic recognition of it in November 1936, organized more formally than the motley assortment of bodies it had comprised up until this point,[38] but also in its having political characteristics comparable to their own; in other words, a single-party, Fascist regime. In February 1937 a personal envoy from Mussolini, leading Fascist politician Roberto Farinacci, discussed with Franco the need to form a government and to create "a Spanish National Party clearly oriented toward the working classes,"[39] which may have influenced the generalissimo – as might have the conversations to this effect with the Italian ambassador, Roberto Cantalupo, or otherssuch as Guglielmo Danzi, head of the Fascist propaganda office in Nationalist Spain (see below).

Elsewhere, the idea that it was necessary to unify all the Nationalist parties had been appearing in the press in the Nationalist zone, proposed by such well-known writers as the Fascist Ernesto Giménez Caballero or the Carlist Román Oyarzun, among others. It was also an idea that had been mentioned in a speech by the Falangist general Juan Yagüe. It had its detractors, such as the Falangist propagandist and priest Fermín Yzurdiaga.[40] But it was a powerful idea, given its congruency with the anti-democratic ideals that informed the doctrine of all the coupists. Putting it into effect, however, was a different matter, and, as would become clear during the first months of 1937, both Falangists and Carlists were open to the possibility – as long as their party was predominant in the resulting fusion.

By the end of 1936, in the generalissimo's immediate entourage, Nicolás Franco was considering the formation of a Francoist party, and probably at that time or in the months that immediately followed, Franco had personally noted the statutes of the FE de las JONS and compared the speeches of José Antonio Primo with those of Carlist Víctor Pradera[41] – both of whom had died some months earlier in the Republican-held zone. Of course, both the execution by firing squad of Primo and the forced exile of Fal Conde simplified matters, depriving the parties of their best-known leaders, although it would appear the effect was limited.

As noted, the specific steps taken toward planning unification in the form it would actually take belong to the period after the one dealt with in this chapter, from mid-February to mid-April 1937. A series of factors played a fundamental role in this process, among which it is worth highlighting, first, the arrival of Franco's brother-in-law, Ramón Serrano Suñer, in Salamanca after he had fled from Republican Spain. As a result of unification, he would become Franco's principal political advisor on questions relating to the design of the single party and the "new state." Serrano was an old friend of José Antonio Primo de Rivera's, and maintained good relations with his family circle, which was based in Salamanca. Second, there was the influence exerted by a thoroughly Falangist model when it came to creating the party, to the extent that the result was a clone of the former Falange, even down to its name, *Falange Española Tradicionalista y de las JONS*, instead of the previous *Falange Española de las JONS*. This option also brought the form of the state closer to that of Spain's allies, which was exactly what Farinacci, Cantalupo, and Danzi[42] (who had discussed the matter with Franco in January 1937) had been trying to achieve. Third, the fact that Manuel Hedilla, leader of the FE de las JONS, had a more positive attitude to unification (as long as it was – as it ultimately would be – based on the Falangist model) than the other leaders, allowed him to work more closely with Franco, although the relationship would take a turn for the worse, and the Falangist leader would end up in prison.[43]

In contrast to the situation during the months immediately before unification, in early 1937, when both the Italian Fascists, as described above, and ambassador Faupel[44] were attempting to sway internal Spanish politics (whether through Franco or through the leadership of the Falange), during the earlier period that is the subject of this chapter, their influence was much more decisive, and even crucial, for the future of the Francoist regime. Reference is to the way their respective country's military aid was channeled toward Franco and not to the other two generals with effective command of operating forces; this was seen as one of the factors that would ultimately contribute to his elevation to supreme commander. And while during the first days of the coup both Franco and Mola had sent emissaries to Rome and to Berlin to negotiate the purchase and shipment of military supplies, it was the former who was the beneficiary.

In the Italian capital, Mussolini had overcome his initial reluctance to grant the aid requested after being informed that France was considering sending aid to the Republic: he ordered the immediate shipment of the twelve bombers that Franco had requested. As for Berlin, at the same time as he was requesting transport planes through diplomatic channels, Franco had used more direct means of reaching Hitler: via the Nazi party. One of his agents in Tetuán, Johannes Bernhardt, had convinced the leader of the NSDAP's in the protectorate to travel to Germany, securing interviews first with Rudolf Hess and then with Hitler in Bayreuth (Bavaria).[45] It was there that the Führer made the decision to send aid, owing to his anti-Communist convictions, but probably even more to the thought that a speedy victory for Franco would provide him with an ally south of the border with France. – which he would face as an enemy in the future since he would be in debt to him.

To camouflage the aid, Hitler had ordered the formation of two pseudo-private companies – HISMA and ROWAK – and entrusted the coordination of operations with the Italians to the head of German military secret services (Abwehr) himself, Admiral Wilhelm Canaris; Canaris worked with General Mario Roatta, head of Italian military secret services. Both decided that the exclusive recipient of their respective aid shipments should be Franco. In fact, their aid was essential from the very beginning, both in transporting part of the army from Africa to Spain – in German Junkers Ju-52 aircraft – and in protecting the convoys of warships and militarized merchant ships involved in the same task.

However, Franco's military relations with the allies were far from cordial. His use of the material supplies and manpower they provided would induce a growing sense of alarm and provoke a wave of criticism among them. Germany and Italy would continue to negotiate jointly the conditions and quantities of the provisions they would continue to send the Nationalists, with whom they had associated themselves from the outset. Their efforts were more or less coordinated, although it finally became clear that Italy would involve itself to a higher degree, and more openly, than Nazi Germany, which was concerned that greater externalization of its participation could end with it being obliged to give up its rearmament program, or even in an outbreak of hostilities with France, for which it was not ready. Nevertheless, it was a phase in which the two countries grew closer, and during which Mussolini began to refer to the "Rome–Berlin Axis."[46]

In the months immediately following the period considered here, the Francoist state would take a fundamental step in regard to its political structure: it would become a single, Fascist party state. Later, in 1938, it would create a real government, as well as a labor charter (*fuero del trabajo*) copied from the Italian Fascists' Carta del Lavoro of 1927; and, after the war, it would take yet further steps to become, if not a Fascist regime in the strictest sense, then a "fascitized" one[47]; in other words, one with a Fascist component that coexisted alongside others, all of them within an authoritarian coalition. It would maintain this characteristic until its demise in 1977, the single party not being dissolved until that year, specifically two months before the first democratic elections of June 15. It was a long-lived state surviving 41 years – and despite undergoing several partial processes intended to strip it of its Fascist characteristics, it never shed this component represented by the party created in 1937.

Notes

1 *Jefatura del Estado*, Archivo de Presidencia del Gobierno (Madrid).

2 Decree of July 24, 1936, "Boletín de la Junta de Defensa Nacional de España," July 25, 1936.

3 "Boletín de la Junta de Defensa Nacional de España," July 30, 1936.

4 Ibid., August 4, 1936.
5 Ibid., August 18, 1936.
6 Ibid., September 19, 1936.
7 Ibid., July 30, 1936.
8 Public Order Law, July 28, 1933.
9 Santos Juliá, "Víctimas del terror y de la represión," in *Economía y economistas españoles durante la Guerra Civil,* vol. II, ed. and coord. Enrique Fuentes Quintana and Francisco Comín (Madrid: Real Academia de Ciencias Morales y Políticas & Galaxia Gutenberg/Círculo de Lectores, 2008), 385–410.
10 Dionisio Ridruejo, *Escrito en España* (Madrid: G. del Toro Editor, 1976), 121.
11 Ramón Serrano Suñer, *Entre el silencio y la propaganda. La Historia como fue* (Barcelona: Planeta, 1977), 245.
12 *El Movimiento Nacional ante el Derecho y la Justicia* (Santander: Real Academia de las Ciencias Morales y Políticas, 1938); *Dictamen de la Comisión sobre ilegitimidad de poderes actuantes el 18 de Julio de 1936* (Barcelona: Ministerio de Gobernación, Editora Nacional, 1939); Ignacio Tébar Rubio Manzanares, "El 'derecho penal del enemigo': de la teoría actual a la práctica represiva del 'Nuevo Estado' franquista," *Pasado y Memoria. Revista de Historia Contemporánea,* no. 13 (2014): 227–50.
13 Decree no. 108 of September 13, 1936, Boletín de la Junta de Defensa Nacional de España," September 16, 1936.
14 Ibid.
15 Decree no.31 of September 25 1936, "Boletín de la Junta de Defensa Nacional de España," September 28, 1936.
16 Decree of August 29 1936, "Boletín de la Junta de Defensa Nacional de España," August 30, 1936.
17 After the Republican bombardment of Tetuán on July 18, which hit two mosques and the medina, causing 15 casualties among the local population. Decree no.92 of September 2 1936, "Boletín de la Junta de Defensa Nacional de España," September 5, 1936.
18 Decree nos.2 and 3 of July 24 1936, "Boletín de la Junta de Defensa Nacional de España," July 25, 1936.
19 Decree no.68 of August 26 1936, "Boletín de la Junta de Defensa Nacional de España, August 27, 1936.
20 Decree no. 38 of September 29 1936, "Boletín de la Junta de Defensa Nacional de España," September 30, 1936.
21 See Javier Tusell, *Franco en la Guerra Civil. Una biografía política* (Barcelona: Tusquets, 1992); Paul Preston, *Franco: "Caudillo de España"* (Barcelona: Grijalbo, 1994); Alfredo Kindelán Duany, *Mis cuadernos de guerra,* 2nd ed. (Barcelona: Planeta, 1982; the 1st, censored, edition appeared in Madrid in 1945, published by Plus Ultra).
22 Decree no. 3 of October 1 1936, "Boletín Oficial del Estado," October 2, 1936.

23 Yanguas was made to pay for this mistake, according to the diary of Ambassador Francisco Serrat Bonastre: Ángel Viñas, ed., *Salamanca 1936. Memorias del primer "ministro" de Asuntos Exteriores de Franco Francisco Serrat Bonastre* (Barcelona: Crítica, 2014), 60.

24 An analysis of the staff on these committees can be found in José Luis Orella, *La formación del Estado Nacional durante la Guerra Civil española* (Madrid: Actas, 2001).

25 Decree no. 13 of October 4 1936, "Boletín Oficial del Estado," October 6, 1936. On this period in Serrat's life and its turbulent end, see Viñas, *Salamanca 1936.*

26 Ernesto Giménez Caballero, *Memorias de un dictador* (Barcelona: Planeta, 1979); Eugenio Vegas Latapié, *Los caminos del desengaño. Memorias políticas, II (1936–1938)* (Madrid: Tebas, 1987).

27 Ibid.

28 Tusell, *Franco en la guerra civil,* 61.

29 "Boletín Oficial del Estado," November 5, 1936.

30 "Boletín Oficial del Estado," November 16, 1936.

31 The first published work about this individual was by Antonio Nadal Sánchez, "Experiencias psíquicas sobre mujeres marxistas malagueñas. Málaga, 1939," *Baética: Estudios de Arte, Geografía e Historia* 10 (1987): 365–84. See also, among other works by the same author, Paul Preston, *The Spanish Civil War: Reaction, Revolution and Revenge* (London: Harper Perennial, 2006).

32 "Boletín Oficial del Estado," December 15, 1936.

33 Alfonso Lazo Díaz, *Retrato de fascismo rural en Sevilla* (Seville: Universidad de Sevilla, 1998); José Antonio Parejo Fernández, *La Falange en la Sierra Norte de Sevilla (1934–1956)* (Seville: Universidad de Sevilla, 2007).

34 There are still no exact figures for troop numbers originating from each political party for this period.

35 Personal diary of the Count of Rodezno, cited in Tusell, *Franco en la guerra civil,* 72.

36 Joan Maria Thomàs, *El gran golpe: El "caso Hedilla" o cómo Franco se quedó con Falange* (Barcelona: Debate, 2014).

37 Rodezno's personal diary, January 17, 1937, cited in Tusell, *Franco en la guerra civil,* 98–99.

38 Ramón Serrano Suñer, *Entre Hendaya y Gibraltar* (Barcelona: Nauta, 1973), 55, n. 11.

39 Letters from Farinacci to Mussolini from March and April 1937, cited in Tusell, *Franco en la guerra civil,* 110–14.

40 Joan Maria Thomàs, *Lo que fue la Falange. La Falange y los falangistas de José Antonio: Hedilla y la Unificación. Franco y el fin de la Falange Española de las JONS* (Barcelona: Plaza y Janés, 1999), 137.

41 Serrano, *Entre Hendaya y Gibraltar,* 56.

42 An updated account of Italian–Spanish relations during the civil war can be found in Javier Rodrigo, *La guerra fascista: Italia en la Guerra Civil española*

1936–1939 (Madrid: Alianza Editorial, 2016), a study that pays little attention to internecine political conflicts within the Nationalist zone.

43 Thomàs, *El Gran Golpe.*

44 Cantalupo, *Fu la Spagna. Ambasciatta presso Franco. Febbraio–Aprile 1937* (Milan: A. Mondadori, 1948), 164–66, 1969.

45 Paul Preston, *Franco, "Caudillo de España"* (Barcelona: Grijalbo, 1994), 2004.

46 Ibid., 257.

47 Joan Maria Thomàs, *La Falange de Franco: Fascismo y fascistización en el régimen franquista, 1937–1945* (Barcelona: Plaza & Janés, 2001).

4

Spanish Fascists and Nazi Germany, 1931–1940: From Fascination to Intervention

Xosé M. Núñez Seixas

The influence of National Socialism on the initial steps of Spanish Fascism was minor. The first groups that associated themselves with Fascism in Madrid and Barcelona in the 1920s were attracted by the shining image of Mussolini's Fascism, particularly the audacity of the March on Rome (October 1922), the removal of liberal political elites, and the mixture of revolutionary appeal, avant-garde aesthetics, and charismatic leadership.[1] This was particularly the case with the prolific intellectual Ernesto Giménez Caballero and his journal, *La Gaceta Literaria* (1927–32), after 1928. The common appeal to the heritage of the Roman Empire also enabled Spanish Fascists to feel that they were participating in a resurgence of classic, Catholic-impregnated Mediterranean Europe, the cradle of civilization.[2]

However, the founders of the first Fascist action groups in the 1930s, Ramiro Ledesma Ramos and Onésimo Redondo Ortega, belonged to a younger generation. To them, the March on Rome was an adolescent memory, while the rise of the NSDAP in Germany from 1929 had a decisive impact on their political views. Moreover, they were quite well acquainted with German culture. Ledesma, a pupil of the philosopher Ortega y Gasset, spent four months in Heidelberg in 1930; a self-made intellectual, he was influenced by the doctrines of Nietzsche, Nicolai Hartmann, Heidegger, and Spengler.[3] Redondo also spent an academic year (1928–29) as a tutor for Spansih language at the Commercial High School in Mannheim, where he devoted himself to an analysis of the political strategies set in motion by the Zentrum Party. A young Catholic himself, he regarded Hitler as a defender of Christianity in the face of Marxism, and advocated an alliance of the Nazi party with the

Zentrum Party in order to confront the rise of German Communism.

From the first issue of his new weekly, *La Conquista del Estado* (March 1931), Ledesma paid increasing attention to the path followed by German National Socialism.[4] Nevertheless, the Juntas de Ofensiva Nacional Sindicalista (JONS), founded by himself in October that year, were heavily inspired by Mussolini's social corporatism. Like many other radical right intellectuals and Fascist groups from the beginning of the decade, Redondo and his followers in the Castilian town of Valladolid, where he edited the weekly organ *Libertad*, were also strongly influenced by the model of social corporatism that they saw in Italy.[5] Redondo's group (Juntas Castellanas de Acción Hispánica, which later merged with the JONS) had a more Catholic imprint than Ledesma's one, but from the very beginning they voiced anti-Semitic slogans. Yet, the content of that anti-Semitism usually remained within the limits of Catholic anti-Jewish prejudice, overlaid with a violent rhetoric.[6]

In the eyes of Spanish Fascists, National Socialism emerged as a spectacular model of national resurgence, based on the hypnotizing charisma of a leader who had sprung from the heart of the people, as well as on his capacity to gain votes from both the Left and the Right of the political spectrum.[7] Several excerpts from *Mein Kampf* were first translated in *Libertad*, which was especially interested in Nazi agitation strategies.[8] Ledesma particularly admired Hitler for being a clever improviser, but also for being able to interpret what "the nation" wanted at every moment.[9]

Once the Nazis seized power in January 1933, admiration for Hitler went on to be shared by the entire spectrum of the Spanish anti-Republican right wing, from Catholics to monarchists. They saw in the new German chancellor the standard-bearer of a united anti-Marxist and nationalist front that clearly extended beyond party lines. The orchestration of national solidarity around a charismatic leader was perhaps the trait that most appealed to Spanish Fascists, who also dreamed of becoming a mass movement. But they also admired Hitler's boldness at imposing his political will and breaching the constraints of international law.[10] Germany's rebirth appeared to be an example for a decadent Spain, which was still lamenting the loss of its overseas empire.[11]

To many Spanish Fascists and traditionalists, however, Nazi racism and "paganism" posed a real problem. While detaching themselves from biological anti-Semitism, some attempted to develop a metaphysical theory of national-socialist racism, equated with the cultural and historical foundations of nationality and, therefore, also exportable to other countries.[12] Yet, they claimed that Spaniards did not like the Jews either, and expressed their understanding of the German interpretation of a universal *problem*, which in Spain was manifested as a religious, confessional issue. They displayed a benevolent attitude toward the first segregationist measures against the Jews adopted by the Nazi regime, and minimized the nature and extent of the new German "paganism."[13] The German Führer's anti-Communism redeemed him from his pagan error, asserted the journal *Libertad* in 1934:

> Since we all agree that the Hitlerian fact is a strong barrier against the Communist hell: Isn't it enough to find in every Christian chest embers of sympathy toward him? Let us Catholics advocate that Protestant or pagan National Socialism converts itself, but not that it collapses![14]

Spanish travelers to Nazi Germany propagated similar views, but also attempted to present a more moderate face of National Socialism regarding its treatment of religion. This was the case with the conservative writer and university professor Vicente Gay, a former Germanophile in 1914–18, who visited Germany in 1933. He mistrusted biological racism and expressed his preference for a "milder" authoritarianism; yet he also justified the establishment of the first concentration camps to "re-educate" "bad" Germans. One year later, the legal expert Juan Beneyto called for "delimiting" the influence of Jews and Catholics in public affairs as a strategy to "nationalize politics"; yet, the agreement reached by Hitler with the Christian churches was presented as proof of lack of Nazi animosity toward religion. In his view, Nazi anti-Semitism distinguished clearly between non-Zionists and Zionists, the latter being the object of control measures. Summing up the main points of the Nazi doctrine, the journalist César González Ruano, a press correspondent in Berlin of the monarchist newspaper *ABC*, presented the Jews as an "anti-national," stateless people by nature, who were intrinsically traitors to Germany and to all other nations.[15] Other visitors to the Third Reich before 1936 also agreed on that point. The young student Ramón de Rato regarded National Socialism as holding great promise for the future of European youth, which was besieged by Marxism and revolutionary threats. He also showed a great understanding of racism, as an expression of German nationalism. The filmmaker and writer Adelardo Fernández Arias also considered the "extermination" of the Jewish influence as necessary in Germany, and vehemently advocated the emergence in Spain of someone like the German Führer: "Spaniards! Let's recite every night this prayer: My God! Rescue Spain! Give us a man like Hitler."[16]

As of January 1933, the right-wing, anti-Republican press was no less sympathetic toward Hitler, although some groups, inspired by Social Catholicism, kept their distance from German racial materialism, regarding it as a threat to the autonomy of the Catholic Church.[17] However, monarchists, proto-Fascists, and traditionalists around the journal *Acción Española* were proof of the former attitude. Many had sympathized with Germany during World War I, and adopted the anti-rationalist reinterpretation of the foundations of the liberal state of Oswald Spengler and Carl Schmitt. German "national rebirth" and the modernity of the mass performances of the Nazis also fascinated them, as well as the priority the Nazis gave to the national community over other values and, of course, their resolute anti-Communism. The intellectual leader of the group, Ramiro de Maeztu, expected in May 1932 that Hitler would proclaim a program of anti-Communist national unity under a strong leadership.[18] However, most radical Spanish conservatives held some reservations regarding the Nazis' "paganism" and anti-capitalist rhetoric. They also disliked the NSDAP's strategy of running in democratic elections, and coming to power through the ballot box. Spanish anti-Republicans preferred a coup d'état.[19]

Nonetheless, the Italian model of Fascism was still regarded as the most appropriate one for a southern European and Catholic country. This preference went hand in hand with the conscious efforts of Italian Fascists to export their model between 1934 and 1935. A good example was the leader of the Falange Española (FE) from October 1933, José Antonio Primo de Rivera. Invited to visit Germany in the spring of 1934, José Antonio met some Nazi leaders, though only very briefly. Alfred Rosenberg recalled two years later that the young Spanish Fascist had appeared to be "clever and clear-minded; Catholic, not clerical; nationalist, not dynastic," but also that he had avoided making any comments on the Jewish question.[20] Indeed, on his return to Spain, the young Fascist leader barely referred to Germany in his speeches and writings.[21] This also meant that the attraction of Nazism was not inescapable. Some Spanish Fascists and radical conservatives also made an about-turn from their initial admiration for National Socialism. The journalist and economist Antonio Bermúdez-Cañete, who had studied in Munich in the mid-1920s and was attracted by the Nazi movement, later joined the Fascist group around the journal *La Conquista del Estado*, and subsequently adhered for some months to the JONS. He was the first to translate some chapters of *Mein Kampf*, which were intended for publication in Spanish, with the title *Mi batalla*. Bermúdez-Cañete also embraced anti-Semitic tenets. Yet, during the time he spent in Berlin (from October 1932 to February 1935) as press correspondent for the Catholic-oriented newspaper *El Debate*, he ended up repudiating Nazism, atheism, and the "socialist" tendencies of German National Socialism, which he proceeded to label systematically as a "racist party."

He denounced Hitler's economic policy, and particularly disliked his pagan tendencies. As consequence of his criticism of the Nazi regime, he was forced to leave Germany, and in February 1936 became a deputy of the Catholic CEDA party.[22]

Other Falangist writers, such as the poet Federico de Urrutia, worked as journalists for the newspaper *Informaciones* which, as of 1934, received subsidies from Berlin and propagated pro-Nazi propaganda articles.[23] Some German consulates, too, distributed Nazi leaflets and books in Spanish to local Falangist groups.[24] Strong links also existed between Falangist groups and local delegations of the foreign arm of the NSDAP (Auslandsorganisation, AO). The presence of German citizens in the Falangist groups was not unusual.[25] Yet, the fact was that German diplomacy was hardly in direct touch with Falangist leaders. Both the Falange and the new party, FE-JONS (February 1934), looked to Rome rather than to Berlin, particularly when they needed external financing During the spring of 1936, the Reich's diplomats in Spain were ignorant of ongoing conspiracies to overthrow the government. On the eve of the military uprising, the German ambassador stated that the Spanish Fascist movement bore the heavy burden of the aristocratic origin of some of its leaders, and was not in a position to threaten the Republican regime.[26] On the other hand, both the military conspiracy and several monarchist and traditionalist leaders received generous donations of money and weapons from Mussolini, while groups of Carlist militiamen were given military training by the Italians.

Seduced by the Third Reich

The outbreak of the Spanish Civil War marked a turning point in this process. As is well known, thanks to their contacts in Spanish Morocco with some German merchants, such as Johannes Bernhardt and Friedhelm Bohle, who were linked to the AO of the NSDAP, the military rebels were able to deliver their demand for help to Hitler directly in Bayreuth by July 25, 1936, while the contacts established through diplomatic channels were fruitless. As a result of the seemingly spontaneous decision made by Hitler there, Germany dispatched the first airplanes, military supplies, and an expeditionary corps, the Condor Legion, mostly composed of pilots and support land personnel. The German Führer's interest in Spain had been so far almost non-existent. But he now saw an opportunity to weaken France through the removal of the Popular Front government in Spain. Economic interests seemed to have played a secondary role at the beginning of the German intervention. However, thanks to the growing influence of Air Minister Hermann Göring on Spanish affairs, economics came to occupy an ever-increasing place in Germany's support for Nationalist Spain.[27] German propaganda vehemently underlined "anti-Bolshevism" and the need to counteract Soviet expansion in southern Europe as the main reason for authorizing the presence of German troops on Spanish soil. Yet, this was just a secondary argument, which was never regarded as one of the main motives of the Third Reich's elites to support the rebel side in the Spanish Civil War.[28]

In November 1936, Hitler sent both a military and a civil representative to the General Staff of Franco in Salamanca. While the former was tasked with having a voice in the planning of military operations, the latter had representative and political functions. Yet, both spheres clashed frequently, due partly to the strong personality of Hitler's civil envoy, the former military adviser in Peru and Argentina Wilhelm Faupel, who had been director of the Berlin-based Iberoamerikanisches Institut, in charge of Nazi influence on the Ibero-American countries. A committed Nazi —though he joined the NSDAP only a few months later— Faupel's appointment was a sign of the priority given by the Nazi party to establishing links with the Falange, a party that was rapidly increasing its influence in the Francoist rear. In February 1937, he was raised to the rank of ambassador. In fact, he was preferred over the Foreign Ministry's candidate, Eberhard von Stohrer, who had been nominated to the post before the outbreak of the war. Faupel had been instructed to avoid political intrigues, as the objective was not to export National Socialism but to pursue German strategic and economic interests by preventing a French-Spanish populist bloc from being formed. However, he and his collaborators – whose activities often clashed with other German offices – clearly disobeyed orders and intervened frequently in the political disputes of the insurgent rear and, where possible, in the planning of war operations.[29]

Faupel openly disdained Spanish traditionalists and the military, and eventually came to regard the Falange as authentic revolutionary Fascists. Thus, he lent some support to their aspirations to power. Faupel also outlined an ambitious project of cultural exchange between the "new" Spain and Nazi Germany, which included frequent visits to the Reich of Falangist leaders and young men and women members of the Falange, as well as a far-reaching program of German-Spanish cooperation in the field of cinema, which strove to extend German influence over Latin American countries using Spain as an appropriate bridgehead.[30] His purpose was to fascistize the Spanish rear and to compete with Italian Fascist influence, gaining the sympathy of the Falangists and other political groupings as part of German geostrategic interests. Thus, the German ambassador openly endorsed supporters of the dissident Falangist leader Manuel Hedilla, and opposed the Unification Decree of April 1937, which sanctioned the birth of the new FET de las JONS as a state party combining various political groups and tendencies. Moreover, his continued meddling in military affairs, which he felt entitled to do as a military officer, advising Berlin and Franco's headquarters on these issues, contributed to his removal by Hitler in August 1937, on Franco's insistence. Like many other Nazis, Faupel concluded that General Franco favored restoration of the influence of the Catholic Church and traditional elites, and viewed as erroneous the systematic repression of peasants and workers, instead of implementing proactive strategies to tempt broader sectors of the popular classes to join the national movement. The former ambassador returned to Berlin and took with him some Falangist assistants, who were given jobs at the Iberoamerikanisches Institut and stayed in Berlin over the following years.[31]

The period 1938–42 marked the finest hour of Nazi influence on Spanish Fascism, which was accompanied by increased economic, cultural, and diplomatic cooperation between the "new" Spain and Germany. The Germans viewed this close relationship in strategic rather than ideological terms. Hitler and his ministers sought to include Spain in the economic New European Order under the guidance of Germany, integrating the country in their strategy of "war in the periphery," whose objective was to force Great Britain to surrender and to build a continental empire. Culture and ideology played for the Germans a minor, though not irrelevant role. Thus, exchanges continued and expanded. As of 1937, dozens of Falangist leaders travelled to Germany, both as representatives of the state or as party delegates committed to reinforcing links with the NSDAP. Heinrich Himmler also visited Spain in 1940. The press and propaganda, youth and women's sections of the NSDAP were adopted as models by Falangist leaders to found, for instance, the Youth Front (Frente de Juventudes) in 1940, and the relief organization Auxilio Social was greatly inspired by the German Winterhilfe. Female Falangist leaders looked to the German Bund Deutscher Mädel to enhance and enlarge the power of the women's section of the Falange.[32]

In addition, there were frequent contacts at the grass-roots level, which went beyond the exchanges promoted by the Spanish and German party leaderships. Local Falangist leaders joined German consuls and local groups of the NSDAP on specific dates and holidays. The German banner, alongside the Italian and the Portuguese flags, could be found on posters and bullfighting arenas. Intellectual exchanges multiplied until 1944: Berlin became a routine destination for young Spanish academics from various fields, and Spanish health experts, medical students, and technicians spent long periods in Berlin, Munich, or Vienna.[33] The Nazi state also attempted to increase its influence on Spanish public opinion by means of generous subsidies to Spanish press organs, newspapers, and radio stations. Hundreds of leaflets were distributed, depicting Hitler not only as the savior of Europe against Bolshevism, but also as a new Christian knight devoted to protecting Western civilization.[34] Strong links were forged with Francoist cultural institutions, relying largely on the cooperation platforms and associations that already existed before 1930, such as the Deutsch-spanische Gesellschaft. The Instituto de Estudios Políticos, founded in 1939, functioned as a channel for Nazi theories in the fields of political theory, social sciences and the philosophy of law developed by Nazi law experts. The latter went beyond a revision of the individualist and positivist foundations of law, in order to craft a communitarian theory of law, a *Volksrecht*. This doctrine exerted a significant and particularly enduring influence on several writers and intellectuals who laid the theoretical foundations of the new Francoist state, such as legal expert Luis Legaz Lacambra and the sociologist Francisco J. Conde.[35]

Strategic cooperation and ideological agreement meant that a part of the Francoist politico-intellectual elites were in tune with Nazi Germany. This did not necessarily signify full-fledged identification with German strategic interests. However, from September 1939 on, and particularly from June 1940, total military commitment in World War II on the side of the Axis was certainly the preferred option for most Falangists. This would facilitate their mid-term objective of imposing their hegemony. Many members of the military, monarchists, and traditionalists were also in favor of joining the German war effort. Franco held the view that Spain would take part in the war in exchange for territorial concessions in Morocco and Northern Africa, as well as gasoline, food, and military supplies. Lack of interest by Hitler and his General Staff in the North African area of operations and the Mediterranean, until 1943 a secondary war theater, prevented Spain from entering the conflict. The Third Reich prioritized Spain's role as supplier of strategic raw materials for the German war effort, by integrating the country into an economic empire that was still in the making.[36]

For thousands of supporters of the Franco regime, Germanophile attitudes were not a synonym for National Socialism. Certainly, sympathy for Germany had roots among some sectors of the social elites, the military, and the Catholic Right dating back to World War I. Now, this traditional sympathy was reinforced by the admiration that most of them felt for Hitler, and by fascination with the Wehrmacht.[37] These feelings were not free of contradictions. In September 1939, many Falangists and traditionalists were shocked by the signing of the Molotov-Ribbentrop pact, and expressed their disapproval of the Nazi invasion of Catholic Poland, whose regime had expressed open sympathy for the Francoist side three years previously.[38] However, those reservations vanished quickly after the German conquest of France in June 1940. The Wehrmacht now fascinated both Falangists and members of the military. In fact, many anti-Falangist army officers yearned to enter the war on the side of the Axis.[39] Numerous traditionalists, monarchists, and anti-Communists regarded Hitler as the ultimate guardian of Christian European civilization, its gatekeeper against the Communist threat. A similar view was shared by thousands of so-called "provisory" lieutenants and ensigns, poorly trained NCOs, and officers who had fought in the Francoist army during the civil war and formed a solid basis of support for the Franco regime. They were astonished by Germany's "national resurgence" and its military might, now directed against France and Great Britain, the "historical enemies" of traditionalist Spain. Devoid of any sophisticated ideological convictions, most "war Francoists" adhered to basic values such as tradition, social order, religion, and hierarchy.[40] This was enough for most of them to support the Third Reich.

Falangist propaganda between 1940 and 1942 further extolled National Socialism and Hitler, now regarded as a clever, clairvoyant strategist. Anti-Semitic tones were not absent from these texts.[41] Several writers believed the time had come for the New Order, and endorsed the tenets disseminated by Nazi propaganda, whose tentacles subsidized Spanish newspapers, novels, and books.[42] The Cuban-Spanish Catholic writer Carmen Velacoracho published two biographies on Hitler in Spanish, portraying him again as a defender of Christian civilization in the face of the Antichrist, Freemasonry, and the Jews. Federico de Urrutia edited a book devoted to "eternal Germany," in which several poets praised the Third Reich and Hitler, seen as the restorer of Germania, heir to the Nibelungs, and champion of the Holy Cross against Jews, Freemasons, capitalists and Communists: an amalgam of Siegfried and Charlemagne.[43] Some groups of radical Falangists approached German consulates and institutions in search of political support. Thus, the clandestine Junta Política of Falange, led by Colonel Emilio Rodríguez Tarduchy, established some contacts with agents related to the NSDAP and German information services. Likewise, several groups of Falangists adopted Nazi symbols, constituted "secret" associations, and launched boycotts against British citizens or British interests. In some cases, they set up associations of support for a "Greater Germany," as at the beginning of 1941 in Valencia, where some

Falangists formed an underground group with links to the consulate, the German embassy and the local NSDAP. With the telling name Sección de Asalto, they disseminated some propaganda and attempted to develop a network of similar organizations throughout the rest of Spain.[44] Four months later, a rival "Group of Sympathizers of Greater German" emerged around the provincial chief Adolfo Rincón de Arellano.[45] However, both the local NSDAP group and the German consulate ceased to cooperate with any of the groups as late as June 1941, in order to avoid diplomatic problems.[46]

By the beginning of the 1940s, there were few Spanish National Socialists who went so far as to question the mainstream tenets of Catholic Fascism. Their rejection of Jews was based on traditional confessional grounds, though the anti-Semitism in Falangist propaganda increased. Certainly, some authors embraced biological racism, too, and managed to merge biopsychology with eugenic theories. This was the case with military psychiatrist Antonio Vallejo-Nágera, who sought to demonstrate the Semitic origins of the Spanish Left and to reconcile his biologicism with a "Hispanity" concept based on culture.[47] On the other hand, as good Fascists, radical Falangists were nationalists, and therefore reluctant to serve as an instrument of German interests. Even those who, in vain, approached the Third Reich's polyarchy in search of explicit political support hardly dared question Franco's leadership and insisted on preserving the Christian character of Spanish Fascism.[48]

Hitler, the Avenging Angel

Alfred Rosenberg noted that his agents in Spain told him that "Hitler is a myth; everything is expected from Germany." Yet, he also wrote that Spanish Fascists preferred to learn from the Nazis rather than from the Italians.[49] The perceptions of Italian representatives were just the opposite: they saw in the New Spain that emerged in the Francoist rear a copy of Mussolini's regime.[50] In 1939, many "ordinary Spaniards" from different social and political backgrounds openly sympathized with the Third Reich, regarding Hitler as a bulwark against Communism. On their own initiative, dozens of them sent greetings to the German embassy in Madrid on the occasion of the Führer's birthday (April 20) in 1940, and again in 1941. Many more epistles letters arrived at the embassy after the German conquest of France. These moments coincided with Spanish declarations of non-belligerency, and were linked to the Falangist offensive to increase their power within the regime. More letters were received after June 22, 1941, when Germany invaded the Soviet Union.[51]

Who were the writers? Their social background was middle or lower-middle class: liberal professionals, civil servants, and employees, as well as blue-collar workers. Many of them were war veterans of the Francoist army during the civil war, as well as former victims of "Red repression." They all saw in Hitler their avenging angel. Two officials of the German consulates in Madrid and Valencia reported that the demand for German propaganda material had much increased, thanks to the Wehrmacht's victories. Who asked for it? According to them, "surgeons, lawyers, and shopkeepers."[52] Such expressions of pro-German enthusiasm were made prior to Operation Barbarossa, and suggested that the efforts deployed by German propaganda machinery were effective not only among radical Falangists but also among the rank-and-file.[53] In July 1940, a Galician priest greeted Adolf Hitler "with the deepest feelings of my soul," while a Catalan merchant encouraged the German Führer to defeat England and thus facilitate the "return of Gibraltar to Spanish unity." Similar arguments were voiced by a shopkeeper from Extremadura, a factory owner from Seville —who considered Hitler to be a "God-given human being sent to impose justice and peace in Europe" – and a Valencian owner of a canning factory.[54] Others applauded the defeat of "decadent" liberal democracies, and longed for the imminent fall of Britain.[55]

Certainly, the letters were part of the general climate of skepticism towards liberal democracy, admiration for German power, and the confused expectations of authoritarian regeneration, which spread across continental Europe in the summer and autumn of 1940.[56] In non-belligerent Spain, the wave of pro-German feeling also had specific ingredients. Some were grateful for German support during the Spanish conflict. Others appreciated that the Third Reich was about to defeat Spain's main "historical enemies." A number regarded the German Führer as the architect of a European New Order whose characteristics were blurred, but which would supposedly be enriched by the Catholic imprint given by Spain. To all of them, Hitler's victory "is also ours." A family from Málaga were eclectic: "Although we are very Spanish, we also are very *hitlerianos*."[57] Many also adhered to the fight against liberal democracy and "Judaism," equated with international capitalism. Several members of the Falange in Córdoba expected that Hitler would soon achieve "victory over our common enemy, Jewish capitalism and the so-called democratic countries." Eighteen Falangists who embraced the "New European Order" expressed similar sentiments. An office worker from Madrid compared Hitler with Charles the Fifth and urged him to visit Spain in order to "check your theories and practices and accommodate them to the psychological, ethnic, and demographic requisites of the Spanish people."[58]

As often occurred in Germany, religious motivations often merged with *Führerprinzip*.[59] A devout woman wrote that she prayed for Hitler every day.[60] A priest from Valladolid also considered that the Führer was an "extraordinary man," sent by God to govern Europe so that it would be in a position to avenge the offenses inflicted in the past by Britain to the Spanish Empire.[61] There also was increasing interest in obtaining "mementos of the Führer," particularly signed portraits.[62]

The beginning of Operation Barbarossa marked the peak of popular Spanish Hitlerism, which German diplomats experienced on the streets. The vice-consul in Monforte de Lemos pointed out that even parish priests who had never approached him were now enthusiastically pro-German.[63] However, the motivations of Germanophiles before and after 1940 had hardly changed. Spanish Fascists continued their earlier admiration for Hitler. Radical Falangists still expected that joining the German war effort could boost their aspirations to achieve "absolute power" within the regime. Catholics, traditionalists, and some monarchists believed that the Wehrmacht was a God-given instrument to annihilate the reincarnation of Lucifer and to deliver a hard lesson to Britain. They also hoped that Nazi Germany would redeem its sin, its pagan character, thanks to its fight against the Antichrist. Once the 'beast" had been smashed, the Third Reich would experience a Christian conversion.[64] By doing this, Hitler would also humiliate the old internal and external adversaries of Spanish traditionalism, epitomized by the Soviet Union. A shopkeeper from Cuenca considered that "English imperialism" had always been an ally of the "Red hordes" and the "Judeo-Bolshevik Freemasonry."[65]

Carlist traditionalists, who had been most reluctant to adopt Nazi atheism, also shared Germanophile enthusiasm. While their leader in exile Manuel Fal Conde expressed his mistrust of National Socialism, some officers of the former *requeté* militia wished to join the rest of the "Christian world" in "annihilating Communism." To them, the Spanish Civil War was now experiencing a second chapter on the Eastern Front, and a similar alliance of anti-Communist forces should be reproduced.[66] The world war represented a fight between democracy, from which Communism had emerged thanks to the cooperation of Jews and Freemasons, and those nations "aware of their historical destiny."[67] Many Carlists were Germanophile, yet they distanced themselves from the main tenets of Nazi ideology, and saw in the Third Reich the appropriate successor of the Wilhelmine Empire, and therefore a potential ally of Catholic traditionalists, as the Kaiser had been.[68] Not all Germanophiles were Fascists or para-Fascists. Yet, in 1940–41, Fascists or not, they all looked to the Third Reich and supported it.

Notes

1 Giulia Albanese, "Alla scuola del fascismo: La Spagna dei primi anni venti e la marcia su Roma," in *Pensare la nazione: Silvio Lanaro e l'Italia contemporánea*, ed. Mario Isnenghi (Rome: Donzelli, 2012), 111–22.

2 Ernesto Giménez Caballero, *La nueva Catolicidad: Teoría general sobre el fascismo en Europa, en España* (Madrid: La Gaceta Literaria, 1933). For further details, see Xosé M. Núñez Seixas, "Falangismo, nacionalsocialismo y el mito de Hitler en España (1931–1945)," *Revista de Estudios Políticos* 169 (2015): 13–43.

3 See Ferran Gallego, *Ramiro Ledesma Ramos y el fascismo español* (Madrid: Síntesis, 2005), 50–55. Ledesma, in fact, translated Heidegger's essay *Was ist Metaphysik?* in *La Gaceta Literaria* (1930).

4 Thus, the journal translated an article by Hitler which disavowed the outdated nature of old liberal party politics, and advocated adapting to mass politics in order to successfully compete with Marxism. See Adolf Hitler, "La mecánica de los viejos partidos parlamentarios," *La Conquista del Estado* 12 (May 30, 1931).

5 Matteo Pasetti, *L'Europa corporativa. Una storia transnazionale tra le due guerre mondiali* (Bologna: Bologna UP, 2016), 212–20.

6 Matteo Tomasoni, "Onésimo Redondo Ortega: Vida, obra y pensamiento de un sindicalista nacional (1905–1936)" (PhD diss., University of Valladolid, 2014), 71–90, 543–88.

7 See, for example, L. Puértolas, "Un libro: Czech-Jochberg: Hitler, un movimiento alemán," *La Conquista del Estado* 16 (June, 27, 1931); R. Bader, "El triunfo nacional socialista de Hamburgo," *La Conquista del Estado* 21 (October 10, 1931).

8 R. L[edesma] R[amos], "El nacional-socialismo alemán: El partido de Hitler," *La Conquista del Estado*, 2 (March 21, 1931); "La liberación antimarxista. Episodios del nacional-socialismo alemán," *Libertad* 19 (October 19, 1931); "En torno al nacional-socialismo," *Libertad* 22 (November 9, 1931).

9 J. F. Pastor, "Crónicas de Alemania: Nacional-socialismo y comunismo," *La Conquista del Estado* 1 (March 14, 1931); R. Ledesma Ramos, "La supuesta derrota del nacional-socialismo," *La Conquista del Estado* 5 (April 11, 1931). See also C. Fernández-Cuenca, "Adolf Hitler y el nacional-socialismo," *Libertad*, March 21, 1932); "La recia figura de Adolfo Hitler: El muchacho con alma de artista," *El Fascio* 1 (March, 16, 1933).

10 "Alemania," *FE* 1 (December 7, 1933); "El gesto de Alemania y la Sociedad de Naciones," *Arriba*, March 21, 1935; "Ventana al mundo," *Arriba*, May, 16, and 30, 1935; June 6 and 13, 1935.

11 César González Ruano, *Seis meses con los nazis* (Madrid: La Nación, 1933), 18; E. Gutiérrez-Palma, "Italia, Alemania, España," *Libertad*, September 24, 1934.

12 F. García Márquez, "La raza: Fundamento de la comunidad," *JONS* 11 (August 1934).

13 "Alemania: Nazis y judíos," *FE* 2 (January 11, 1934); Gonzalo Álvarez Chillida, *El antisemitismo en España: La imagen del judío, 1812–2002* (Madrid: Marcial Pons, 2002), 302–3, 342–43.

14 O. Redondo, "Religión y política. Defensa de Hitler," *Libertad*, August 6, 1934.

15 Vicente Gay, *La revolución nacionalsocialista* (Barcelona: Bosch, 1934); Juan Beneyto Pérez, *Nacionalsocialismo* (Barcelona: Labor, 1934), 43–46, 113–18, 148–50; González Ruano, *Seis meses*. See also Ingrid Schulze-Schneider, "La propaganda alemana en la Segunda República Española," *Historia y Comunicación Social* 4 (1999): 183–97.

16 Ramón de Rato, *Vagabundo bajo la luna: Rápida visión de Europa y sus problemas* (Madrid: EPC, 1935); idem, *Una generación a la intemperie: Perfil juvenil de Europa* (Madrid: ABF, 1936), 119–23; Adelardo Fernández Arias, *Hitler: El salvador de Alemania* (Madrid: Fénix, 1935), 60–71, 79.

17 T. Serra, "Lecturas comentadas: Adolfo Hitler, el canciller," *Contemporánea* 10 (October 1933).

18 See Ramiro de Maeztu, "Hitler: Su triunfo y su programa," *Acción Española*, May 16, 1932.

19 Raul Morodo, *Los orígenes ideológicos del franquismo: Acción Española* (Madrid: Alianza, 1985), 114–24; Ferran Gallego, *El evangelio fascista. La formación de la cultura política del franquismo (1930–1950)* (Barcelona: Crítica, 2014), 165–67; J. Vigón, "Actualidad internacional," *Acción Española*, February 1 and 16, 1933.

20 Rosenberg's diaries, entry of August 23, 1936, in Jürgen Matthäus and Frank Bajohr, eds., *Alfred Rosenberg: Die Tagebücher von 1934 bis 1944* (Frankfurt a. M.: Fischer, 2015), 200.

21 Stanley G. Payne, *Franco y José Antonio: El extraño caso del fascismo español* (Barcelona: Planeta, 1997), 261–67; Ángel Viñas, *Franco, Hitler y el estallido de la guerra civil: Antecedentes y consecuencias* (Madrid: Alianza. 2001), 160–64, 186–87.

22 For an exhaustive compilation of texts, see Juan Velarde Fuertes, et al., *Antonio Bermúdez Cañete: Periodista, economista y politico* (Madrid: Actas, 2008).

23 Manfred Böcker, *Antisemitismus ohne Juden: Die Zweite Republik, die antirepublikanische Rechte und die Juden: Spanien 1931 bis 1936* (Frankfurt a. M.: Peter Lang, 2000), 200, 230, 289–90; Álvarez Chillida, *El antisemitismo*, 312–14.

24 Viñas, *Franco*, 187–88; reports from the German consuls in A Coruña, May 11, 1934, and Vigo, April 26, 1933, Politisches Archiv des Auswärtigen Amtes, Berlin [PAAA], Deutsche Botschaft Spanien-Generalkonsulat Barcelona, PRT 10/2.

25 See, for instance, Marco Claas, *Der Aufstieg der Falange Española: Faschistische Kultur und Gewalt im Nordwesten Spaniens 1933–1937* (Göttingen: V&R Unipress, 2016).

26 Viñas, *Franco*, 287–95.

27 Manfred Merkes, *Die deutsche Politik gegenüber dem spanischen Bürgerkrieg 1936–1939* (Bonn: Röhrscheid, 1961), 230–64; Angel Viñas and Carlos Collado-Seidel, "Franco's Request to the Third Reich for Military Assistance," *Contemporary European History* 11, no. 2 (2002): 191–210; W. Bernecker, "Das nationalsozialistische Spanienbild und Hitlers Eingreifen in den spanischen Bürgerkrieg," in *De Rebus Hispaniae Memorandia/1*, ed. Spanisches Kulturinstitut (Munich: Spanisches Kulturinstitut, 1998), 1–48. The later account by Bernhardt is not particularly reliable, although some historians disagree with this judgment. See Hans-Henning Abendroth, *Mittelsmann zwischen Hitler und Franco: Johannes Bernhardt erinnert 1936* (Marktheidenfeld: W. Schleunung, 1978); also idem, "Die deutsche Intervention im spanischen Bürgerkrieg: Ein Diskussionsbeitrag," *Vierteljahrshefte für Zeitgeschichte* 1 (1982): 117–29, and idem, *Hitler in der spanischen Arena: Die deutsch-spanischen Beziehungen im Spannungsfeld der europäischen Interessenpolitik vom Ausbruch des Bürgerkrieges bis zum Ausbruch des Weltkrieges 1936–1939* (Paderborn: Schöningh, 1973).

28 See Jörg Schmitt-Sasse, " . . . Gefallen ist die Stadt Madrid! Der spanische Bürgerkrieg im 'Völkischen Beobachter' und anderen reichsdeutschen Medien," *Communications* 15, no. 3 (1990): 275–90; Antonio Peter, *Das Spanienbild in den Massenmedien des Dritten Reiches 1936–1939* (Bern: Peter Lang, 1992); Peter Monteath and Elke Nicolai, *Zur Spanienkriegsliteratur. Die Literatur des Dritten Reiches zum spanischen Bürgerkrieg. Mit einer Bibliographie zur internationalen Spanienkriegsliteratur* (Bern: Peter Lang, 1986).

29 On Faupel's biography, see Oliver Gliech, "Wilhelm Faupel. Generalstaboffizier, Militärberater, Präsident des Ibero-Amerikanischen-Instituts," in *Ein Institut und sein General. Wilhelm Faupel und das Ibero-Amerikanische Institut in der Zeit des Nationalsozialismus*, ed. Reinhard Liehr, Günther Maihold, and Günther Vollmer (Frankfurt a. M.: Vervuert, 2003), 131–279. On the Condor Legion, see Stefanie Schüler-Springorum, *Krieg und fliegen: Die Legion Kondor im spanischen Bürgerkrieg* (Paderborn: Schöningh, 2010), 156–57. See also the memoirs of later ambassador Adolf von Moltke, quoted by Emilio Sáenz Francés, *Entre la antorcha y la esvástica: Franco en la encrucijada de la Segunda Guerra Mundial* (Madrid: Actas, 2009), 124–26.

30 For an in-depth look at this, see Manuel Nicolás Meseguer, *La intervencion velada: El apoyo cinematográfico alemán al bando franquista (1936–1939)* (Murcia: Universidad de Murcia, 2004).

31 See Robert H. Whealey, *Hitler and Spain: The Nazi Role and the Spanish Civil War 1936–1939* (Lexington: University Press of Kentucky, 1989), 44–71; Payne, *Franco y José Antonio*, 412–14, 447–48; Joan María Thomàs, *El "Caso Hedilla," o cómo Franco se quedó con la Falange* (Barcelona: Debate, 2014).

32 Miguel Ángel Ruiz Carnicer, *El Sindicato Español Universitario (SEU), 1939–1965: La socialización política de la juventud universitaria en el franquismo* (Madrid: Siglo XXI, 1996), 156–61; Toni Morant i Ariño, "Mujeres para una

'Nueva Europa': Las relaciones y visitas entre la Sección Femenina de Falange y las organizaciones femeninas nazis, 1936–1945" (PhD diss., University of Valencia, 2013).

33 See David Brydan, "Franco's Internationalists: Spanish Health and Welfare Experts on the World Stage, 1939–1959" (PhD diss., University of London, 2016).

34 Ingrid Schulze-Schneider, "Alemania y la guerra civil española: Información y propaganda," *Spagna Contemporanea* 26 (2004): 57–84.

35 See Manuel Ros Agudo, *La guerra secreta de Franco* (Barcelona: Crítica, 2002), 271–314, Mariciò Janué, "Un instrumento de los intereses nacionalsocialistas durante la Guerra Civil española: El papel de la Sociedad Germano-Española de Berlín," *Iberoamericana* 31 (2008): 27–44, and Nicolas Sesma Landrín, "Importando el Nuevo Orden: El Instituto de Estudios Políticos y la recepción de la cultura fascista y nacionalsocialista en España (1939–1943)," in *Rebeldes y reaccionarios. Intelectuales, fascismo y derecha radical en Europa*, ed. Ferran Gallego and Francisco Morente (Mataró: El Viejo Topo, 2011), 243–79. On the influence of Nazi law doctrines in Spain, see José Antonio López García, *Estado y Derecho en el franquismo: El nacionalsindicalismo: F. J. Conde y Luis Legaz Lacambra* (Madrid: CEPC, 1996), 131–53; Benjamín Rivaya García, *Filosofía del Derecho y primer franquismo* (Madrid: CEPC, 1998), 49–82, and Gallego, *El evangelio*, 510–16 and 740–47.

36 See Ch. Leitz, "Hermann Göring and Nazi Germany's Economic Exploitation of Nationalist Spain, 1936–1939," *German History* 14, no. 1 (1996): 21–37. Despite its abundant mistakes, see also Pierpaolo Barbieri, *Hitler's Shadow Empire: Nazi Economics and the Spanish Civil War* (Cambridge, MA.: Harvard UP, 2015).

37 See Maximiliano Fuentes Codera, *España en la Primera Guerra Mundial: Una movilización cultural* (Madrid: Akal, 2014), 100–12.

38 Wayne H. Bowen, "Spain and the Nazi Occupation of Poland, 1939–44," *International Social Science Review* 8, nos. 3–4 (2007): 135–48; Bartosz Kaczorowski, "España ante la invasión alemana y soviética de Polonia en septiembre de 1939," *Cuadernos de Historia Contemporánea* 35 (2013): 177–92.

39 See the information gathered by the German vice-consul in Badajoz among local members of the military: Reports from August 16, 17, and 20, 1940, PAAA, Akten Deutsche Botschaft Madrid [ADBM], Reg. Pol. Allg. [RPA] 558/2, Box 767.

40 Ángel Alcalde, *Los excombatientes franquistas: la cultura de guerra del fascismo español y la Delegación Nacional de Excombatientes (1936–1965)* (Zaragoza: PUZ, 2014), 83–111.

41 See, for example, "El hombre y su estilo," *Arriba*, July 20, 1940. Jewish refugees in Lisbon were described as the "dross of Europe" and were blamed for the outbreak of the war. See "El lastre de Europa," *Arriba*, November 12, 1940.

42 Some Falangist writers acted as full-fledged propagandists of the Third Reich. See Federico de Urrutia, *La paz que quiere Hitler* (Madrid: Blass, 1939); also idem [J. J. Estrada pseudonym], *Cuando Inglaterra quedó sola* (Madrid: Rubiños, 1940), and idem, *Por qué lucha Alemania (cómo Hitler ha sido empujado a la guerra)* (Madrid: Rubiños, 1940).

43 Carmen Velacoracho de Lara, *Un caudillo,* (Madrid: n. ed.,1940); idem, *Dos hombres: Mussolini, Hitler* (Madrid: Aspiraciones, 1943); Federico de Urrutia, ed., *Poemas de la Alemania eterna* (Madrid: Imprenta de Ernesto Giménez, 1940).

44 Reports by Löschner and Paul Winzer, Valencia, April 28 and May 5, 1941, PAAA, ADBM, RPA 557/2, Box 766.

45 Reports dated May 14, 20 and 30, 1941, PAAA, ADBM, RPA 557/2, Box 766.

46 Letters from Hans Thomsen (*Landesgruppenleiter* in Spain of the AO) to local NSDAP group in Valencia, June 10, 1941; Heyden-Rynsch June 39, 1941, and German consul, in Valencia, July 9, 1941, PAAA, ADBM, RPA 557/2, Caja 766.

47 Michael Richards, "Antonio Vallejo Nágera: Heritage, Psychiatry and War," in *Right-Wing Spain in the Civil War Era: Soldiers of God and Apostles of the Fatherland, 1914–1945,* ed. Miguel Ángel del Arco Blanco and Alejandro Quiroga Fernández (London: Continuum, 2012), 195–224.

48 This is illustrated by a a group of so-called 'Crusaders against Russia' and 'Parents of Crusaders', who sent a memorandum in July 1941 to the German ambassador in Madrid, asking for Nazi help to imprint on the state and the army the "imperial style of the Falange." Letter to the German ambassador in Madrid, July 13, 1941, PAAA, ADBM, RPA 557/2, Box 766.

49 Entry of September 26, 1936, in Matthäus and Bajohr, *Alfred Rosenberg,* 208–10.

50 Javier Rodrigo, *La guerra fascista: Italia en la guerra civil española, 1936–1939* (Madrid: Alianza, 2016), 177–203.

51 Joan Maria Thomàs, *La Falange de Franco. Fascismo y fascistización en el régimen franquista (1937–1945)* (Barcelona: Plaza & Janés, 2001), 264–76.

52 Reports by Löschner and Paul Winzer, April 28, 1941, PAAA, ADBM, RPA. 557/2, Box 766.

53 Report by Eberhard von Stohrer, Madrid, July 17, 1942, PAAA, R-29744; Ingrid Schulze-Schneider, "La propaganda alemana en España 1942–1944," *Espacio, Tiempo y Forma. Serie V, Historia Contemporánea* 7 (1994): 371–86.

54 Letters from priest Manuel Rodríguez, Regodeixón, July 11, 1940, PAAA, ADBM, RPA 555/1, Box 764; José Basiana, Manresa, July 1940; Mateo Rodríguez, San Martín de Trevejo, June 1940, and Marquis of Solanda, n.d.; José Puyana, Sevilla, June 27, 1940; Eugenio Ruiz, Valencia, June 14, 1940, PAAA, RPA 555/1, Box 763.

55 Letters from Ángel Pretel, Madrid, June 10, 1940; Martín Marco Teixidor, Girona, May 16, 1940; Manuel Valién Poblador, Caspe, June 26, 1940, PAAA, RPA 558/2, Box 767.

56 See Mark Mazower, *La Europa negra* (Barcelona: Ediciones B, 2000), 210–13.

57 Letters from Maria Dolores Rius, and Conchita Copa, Barcelona, June 17, 1940, PAAA, ADBM, RPA 558/2, Box 767, and Zurita family, Antequera, April 22, 1941, PAAA, ADBM, Box 796, Geheimakten, 6/9.

58 Letters from Cristóbal Sánchez, Víctor Díaz, and Asunción Gracia, Córdoba, April 8, 1941; Luis Martínez Pinto and seventeen more Falangists, Córdoba, June 22, 1940; Antonio Carreño, Madrid, April 30, 1941, PAAA, ADBM, RPA 555/1, Box 764.

59 Ian Kershaw, *The Hitler Myth: Image and Reality in the Third Reich* (Oxford: Oxford UP, 1987), 105–22.

60 Letter from María García Robles, Barcelona, April 20, 1941, PAAA, ADBM, Box 796, Geheimakten, 6/9.

61 Letter from priest Nazario del Campo, Valladolid, June 1941, PAAA, ADBM, Box 796, Geheimakten, 6/9.

62 Letters from José Martínez, Huesca, August 5, 1941, and German consul, Bilbao, June 22, 1941, PAAA, ADBM, RPA 557/2, Box 766; Socorro Lanzas, Antequera, July 16, 1941, PAAA, ADBM, RPA 555/1, Box 766.

63 Reports from German consuls, Bilbao, June 23, 1941, and Alicante, June 27, 1941; vice-consul in Monforte de Lemos, June 24, 1941, and consul in Santa Cruz de Tenerife, July 2, 1941, PAAA, ADBM, Box 796, Geheimakten, 6/9.

64 Alfonso Lazo, *La Iglesia, la Falange y el fascismo (un estudio sobre la prensa española de posguerra)* (Seville: Universidad de Sevilla, 1998), 165–75.

65 Letters from José Peñarrubia, Iniesta, July, 5 and 17, 1941, PAAA, ADBM, RPA 555/1, Box 766.

66 Report from German consul in Bilbao, July 1, 1941, and letter signed by six *requeté* officers, June 29, 1941, PAAA, ADBM, Box 796, Geheimakten, 6/9.

67 *Landesgruppenleiter* of NSDAP in Spain, Hans Thomsen, to German ambassador, Madrid, July 2, 1941, accompanied by a letter (June 1941) signed by the Navarrese *requeté* leaders Amadeo Marco, Cesáreo Sanz Orrio, Antonio Lizarza, Juan Villanueva, and Mario Ozcoidi, PAAA, ADBM, Box 796, Geheimakten, 6/9.

68. Anonymous letter, July 25, 1941, PAAA, ADBM, Box 796, Geheimakten, 6/9.

5

Women and the Spanish Civil War: The Radical Months

INBAL OFER

> Those of the war were extremely open women [*abiertisimas*]. Open because they lived through a truly revolutionary period. Do you think that in 1936–1937 women could go out and drive a car as they did? Like Pilar [Primo de Rivera] and Dora [Maqueda] all over the country? . . . We walked through the doors which they had opened for us.
>
> Women today claim with more insistence than ever before . . . the right to uphold their position in the struggle against barbarism. The claim regarding women's unpreparedness for certain tasks is of no relevance here. . . . Did all of our [male] comrades know how to use a weapon prior to July 18? No! Nonetheless, they headed for the front. With time, they acquired the skills necessary in order to advance the popular struggle. The same should be true for women, no matter what role is assigned to them.

The above citations are excerpts from an interview conducted with Consuelo Valcarcel Burgos[1] and an article written by Astrea Barrios,[2] respectively. Consuelo Valcarcel was a long-time member of the women's section of the Spanish Falange, Sección Femenina de la FET (SF), where she headed the Department for Professional Training for Women and Youth within the Falange's Students' Syndicate (SEU) and was the women's section representative within the Ministry of Education. Although a young child during the civil war, in an interview conducted with her in 2003, she reflected on the uniqueness of the SF's civil war generation. Astrea Barrios was a member of the Spanish Socialist Party in Bilbao and a founding member of the Association of Antifascist Women (Agrupación de Mujeres Antifascistas; AMA). The testimonies of these two women (the latter written in 1937 and the former over 60 years later) point to ways in which the civil war was experienced and remembered by Spanish women on both sides of the political divide.

The civil war was experienced and portrayed by both Republican and Nationalist women as a moment of rapture but also of despair: rapture in the narratives of social progress, but also of moral and ideological degeneration associated with the years of the Second Republic; personal rapture, a time when families and friends were torn apart; and a period when spatial, generational, and even gender divisions were temporarily suspended. This is especially true for the early months of the war between, July and October 1936, a stage which historian Sofía Rodríguez López called the Militia Period (*el periodo meliciano*).[3]

Those months were characterized by extreme violence throughout Spain due to the attempts to gain rapid control over territory and the state apparatus, and to bring to an end what was still considered by many as no more than a partially successful coup d'état. By September 1936 the military uprising had triumphed in Galicia, Leon, and parts of Andalusia. Madrid, Valencia, and Barcelona remained under Republican control, as well as the cities of Malaga and Bilbao. The experiences of women during the war were conditioned first and foremost by their physical location at any given moment. However, as historian Santos Juliá rightly noted, even within the Republican zone the very experience of citizenship, of negotiating one's position vis-à-vis social and state institutions, changed profoundly:

> The variety of situations produced by the rebellion and the revolution led to a phenomenon which is essential to our understanding of a war with so many victims not only at the front – the disappearance of the state and of state institutions.[4]

This was doubly true in the case of the Nationalist zone where many state and local institutions had to be reshaped and at times even reinvented. Political disarray and the need to forge new alliances affected both zones during the initial months of the war. At the end of July, after much hesitation, the Republican government decided to hand out arms to the newly created popular militias. In Barcelona, the Central Committee of Antifascist Militias was founded. On the Nationalist side, the rebellious forces formed a council of national defense in the town of Burgos. In October, General Francisco Franco was elected head of government and supreme commander of the armed forces and the navy. In between these dates testimonies exist of fervent activism on the part of an array of popular entities. As will be seen, during this period new organizational initiatives for women flourished and new patterns of public activism were encouraged by both sides.

An analysis of the activism of women during the Spanish Civil War must take into consideration that the political, professional, and military opportunities open before them were conditioned simultaneously by the strive to construct a new social order and by the need to maintain political and ideological control. As local studies make abundantly clear, the cultural profile of different communities and the socio-economic status of women determined their war experiences. On both sides, the space of everyday life was transformed and boundaries were forever shifting: homes were damaged and even destroyed and the families residing within them were torn apart; the function of communal spaces (such as churches, schools, markets, or those dedicated to leisure activities) was often modified or designated for other purposes, and the communities that were eligible to enjoy these spaces were redefined; political spaces changed hands, were destroyed, reconstructed, and diffused with changing symbolic meanings; finally, new spaces such as battlefields and frontlines emerged. This reality, coupled with the totalizing nature of civil mobilization, had profound gender implications.

Against this background, the current chapter focuses on several questions: How was the activism of Republican and Nationalist women regulated during the early months of the civil war? What organizational, professional, and spatial opportunities were opened before them on the home front and the frontlines? How were these opportunities legitimized and explained? In order to answer these questions, the first section analyzes briefly the structure and nature of some of the leading women's organizations that were active on both sides from July to December 1936. The second section explores the roles that were taken on by women and the ways in which they were represented and legitimized by the press and by prominent female activists on both sides. The concluding section attempts to evaluate the nature and long-term effects of the change in gender relations during the second half of 1936.

Historian Mary Nash identified three main themes related to the activism of Republican women during the Spanish Civil War. According to her:

> The collective responses of women to the war were greatly influenced by their previous historical apprenticeship . . . The social mobilization of women in order to ensure everyday survival prompted them to identify priorities that did not always go hand in hand with the definition of feminism . . . At the same time the civil war was a catalyst for women's mobilization. It generated changes in the ways in which women were viewed by society . . . The initial period of the war saw the construction of a new discourse regarding women's role and capacities. Unlike in pre-

> vious years, all of the political parties and syndicates now launched a call for their full mobilization . . . The traditional rules of the game changed with the active presence of women in the struggle against fascism.[5]

Great differences clearly existed between the Republican and Nationalist rhetoric regarding the role of women in the new social order to be forged following the war. At the same time, it is contended here that there were many similarities in the experiences and the roles assigned to Republican and Nationalist women during the war itself. With few exceptions (mostly of those who enlisted as *milicianas* [militiawomen], or those who took part in subversive activities of the nationalist Fifth Column in the heart of enemy territory), most Spanish women mobilized within all-women's organizations during the war. Almost all of these organizations had a clear ideological and political background. Quite a few of them were founded during the time of the Republic and reflected the significant increase in the importance of Spanish women as political actors. At the same time, most existing women's organizations entered the civil war with conflicting messages regarding their members' role in a future Spain: on the one hand, a clear call for their social and political mobilization, and on the other, a commitment to the preservation of differentiated gender roles. Left-wing organizations clearly stated that women were as fit as men to exercise their political rights, but so did some right-wing women activists, such as María Urraca Pator and Rosario Pereda. However, with the exception of the anarchist organization Mujeres Libres, most other entities had no clear understanding of how exactly the rights of women would be prioritized if they came into conflict with those of men within the family, the workplace, or society at large. At the same time, and while much research is still needed in this field, it is clear that one can hardly refer to a paradigmatic experience of either Republican or Nationalist women. War experiences (much like those of women during the years of the Second Republic and of the Franco regime) depended on a variety of factors: the socio-economic profile of a community; the differences between urban and rural settings; class, educational, and professional background; and different stages in the evolution of the war itself.

From Uprising to Total War: Popular Mobilization and the Creation of Organizational Structures

The everyday lives of Republican and Nationalist women were greatly transformed with the eruption of war. Women's organizations in both zones underwent changes in size as well as in function. At the same time, it is important to bear in mind that the attempts to mobilize women in the tense months following the October 1934 uprising in Asturias and during the February 1936 elections had laid the ground for the formation of most of the major groups which operated during the war itself. The early months of the civil war saw the rapid growth of some existing organizations and the shrinking of others, depending on the new political circumstances. All, however, faced the challenge of creating new platforms for mobilization in line with the particular needs of war in each territory.

In the Nationalist zone the oldest and one of the most prominent organizations was Margaritas. The ultra-traditionalist women were headed by María Rosa Urraca Pastor. The term "Margaritas" was coined during the Third Carlist War and referred to the followers of Doña Margarita, the wife of Carlos VII. The first formal female section of the Comunión Tradicionalista was founded in 1919 in Navarra. The organization increased in size following the granting of voting rights to women (1931) and the reform of the Comunión under the leadership of Manuel Fal Conde (1934). In 1936, its members founded the Socorro Blanco, a network intended to provide spiritual and material assistance to Carlist activists and their families arrested by the Republican authorities.

A survey conducted in early 1936 indicated that the number of registered Margaritas was 23,238. The areas in which the organization was most prominent prior to the war were Navarra, Vizcaya, Valencia, and Barcelona.[6] In view of the tense political situation, in February 1936 the national secretary of the Margaritas sent a communication calling for the opening of a clandestine nursing course wherever sympathetic doctors could be recruited. Against this background, it is perhaps not surprising that from the outset of war the Margaritas played a crucial role in providing auxiliary medical services throughout the Nationalist zone. In April 1937, following the publication of the Decree of Unification (which merged all of the political forces of Nationalist Spain into the Falange Española Tradicionalista y de las JONS, and transferred control over all militia forces to the Nationalist army), the Margaritas were put in charge of an organization called Frentes y Hospitales, which grouped thousands of nurses, liaison women, and frontline laundry workers.

Another Nationalist organization which existed prior to 1936 was the women's section of the Spanish Falange, Sección Femenina de la FET (SF). The SF was founded in June 1934. Throughout its 43 years of existence, it was led by Pilar Primo de Rivera (daughter of the former Spanish dictator Miguel Primo de Rivera and sister of Falange founder José Antonio Primo de Rivera). Prior to the war the SF was small, numbering only some 2,500 members, mostly relatives of prominent Falangist activists. During the early months of the civil war the organization expanded, reaching in 1939 a membership of over 600,000. During the war, the SF founded its own press service and took control over the Social Service for Women and the girls' section of the Falange Youth Movement. Through these bodies it consolidated its position as the administrator of political indoctrination and professional training schemes for women (such as nurses, youth instructors, and social workers).[7]

During the initial months of the war several other sections were added. The Auxilio de Invierno, or Auxilio Social (AS), was founded in July 1936 by Mercedes Sanz Bachiller (provincial head of the SF in Valladolid and wife of Falangist leader Onésimo Redondo). During the war the AS controlled most social aid schemes in the Nationalist zone and operated soup kitchens and children's homes, among other projects. Their first kitchen was set up in Valladolid in late October 1936 and eventually extended to the entire province, as well as to Seville and Navarra.

Large urban centers that fell into the hands of the Nationalist forces early in the war also saw the creation of women's committees (Comités Femeninos). The committees were formed under the auspices of the military authorities in response to urgent economic needs. The central role of these committees was to ensure the availability of supplies for the soldiers, militia forces, and the civilian population.[8] Historians Adoración Martín Barrio and Eduardo Martín González, who analyzed the workings of these committees in the city of Zamora, noted that while they were all headed by men, their membership consisted of the wives, daughters, and sisters of leading political activists, as well as members of the lay Catholic organization Acción Católica.

Another important framework for the mobilization of Nationalist women formed within Republican territory. During the war the ability to dominate space was equated with victory. Spatial mobility, however, was greatly constrained by the construction of new borders, the emergence of frontlines, and damage to transport infrastructure. At the same time, movement across space was often the only possible response in the face of life-threatening situations that did not distinguish between men and women. For Nationalist women who found themselves in Republican territory the distinction between the home front and the frontline was less meaningful than for those in the Nationalist zone. The streets of Madrid could be just as dangerous as the frontline that emerged along the Ciudad Universitaria.

However, except for a few well-known figures such as Pilar Primo de Rivera, Nationalist women who remained in Republican territory could move more freely than their male counterparts. This situation, and the absence of a direct line of communication with the SF's national leadership, created a situation in which women mobilized according to the needs of the hour. The best example of this could can be seen in the formation of Auxilio Azul in Madrid. This organization, headed by 19-year-old María Paz Martínez Unciti, was tasked with sheltering and smuggling Falangist activists and churchmen out of the capital. Its members also accompanied priests to clandestine Mass; infiltrated the Republican military intelligence service, SIM, thereby revealing the names of numerous Republican agents who were active in the rebel zone; and created a network of 289 nurses who attended the sick or wounded.[9] The Auxilio Azul only recruited individuals based on kinship and friendship ties and its members helped or worked with people who they already knew. Unknown applicants were not accepted, thus making infiltration unlikely. According to Javier Cervera:

> The organization was based on independent cells each composed of three women. All women were assigned numbers, and only one member in each cell knew the names of the other members. The system proved highly effective when a member was arrested since she could hardly provide the names of the others.[10]

Despite these measures María Paz Unciti herself was arrested in November 1936 while she accompanied a member of the Falange to the Finish embassy in Madrid. She was executed a week later and received the highest wartime decoration awarded to SF members – Y de Oro.

Organizations like the Auxilio Azul in Madrid also operated in Almeria and Granada. In Almeria, the organization was headed by Carmen Góngora López from August 1936 until her arrest in December 1938. She and other Catholic women protected political activists and members of the clergy from persecution. According to Sofía Rodríguez López, in Almeria too, personal ties became the criterion for recruitment in the network, which extended to several towns and villages in the province. In the province of Granada the predominance of women among Fifth Column activists was most notable in rural areas. The women passed information on the movement of troops, hid fugitives, and helped them to cross into the Nationalist zone.

As seen, the mobilization of women within the Nationalist zone took place almost exclusively within all-women's organizations and was channeled mostly via bodies affiliated with existing political parties or movements. The only network that formed spontaneously "from below" was the Auxilio Azul which, due to the conditions under which it operated, depended on individual initiatives and on the relative isolation of its members from one another. In the Republican zone, too, the mobilization of women took place almost exclusively within all-women's organizations. An outstanding exception was the *milicianas*, who enlisted independently in frontline units. As will be seen in the following section, from October 1936 and onward the patterns of activism promoted by most Republican women's organizations were similar to those in the Nationalist zone. The major difference between the two zones was in relation to the positive references which women's spontaneous mobilization, especially that of the militiawomen, elicited within Republican rhetoric.

The role and image of the militiawomen was widely discussed during the war. The exact number of Republican women who served in frontline units is unknown. They are estimated at 1,000 in total, but the impact of their activism was great. As Mary Nash noted, some militiawomen were integrated directly into combat units. A prominent example is Rosario La Dinamitera, who volunteered to go to the front with the popular militias and was trained to handle explosives. Fifí, Fidela Fernández de Velas Pérez, was schooled in using weapons and was a skilled driver of an evacuation lorry. Julia Manzano, known as Chico, was the political commissar of the Madrid battalion. She served at the front in an educational capacity, providing reading, writing, and political orientation classes to the soldiers. Lina Odena was a member of the United Socialist Youth (JSU) and general secretary of the national committee of the AMA. She fought at the Granada front and committed suicide in September 1936 as she was about to be captured by General Franco's foreign legionnaires.[11]

However, the presence of these women on the battlefield did not last long. In September 1936, Largo Caballero laid down recruitment criteria for the Republican Army, including the requirement that all soldiers be men between the ages of 20 and 45. In December, the Republic's representatives overseas (especially in Paris and Marseilles where recruitment centers of the International Brigades operated) were instructed not to enlist women for frontline positions in Spain. Finally, in May 1937 the government of Juan Negrín officially ordered the evacuation of all women from frontline positions.

Like their Nationalist counterparts, the majority of Republican women who contributed to the war effort at the home front did so within all-women frameworks. Political parties (such as the PSOE, POUM, and the PC-JSU) and workers' unions (such as the UGT) all formed women's sections (Secretariados Femeninos) during the summer and fall of 1936. The oldest and most established women's organization in Republican

Spain, however, was the pro-Communist Association of Antifascist Women. The AMA was founded by Dolores Ibárurri in 1934. During the final years of the Republic the organization included Republican, Socialist, and Communist members, among them Irene Falcón, Matilde Huici, Constancia de la Mora, Maragarita Nelken, and Victoria Kent. During the war the AMA expanded, enlisting through its Catalan and youth sections over 60,000 members.[12] Despite its Communist background, the goal of the AMA was to incorporate Spanish women into a broad anti-Fascist front. However, the diverse background of its members and leaders meant that it did not have any strong political backing and therefore had difficulties in integrating its members into official institutions.

Perhaps the most significant women's organization in political terms was the anarchist Mujeres Libres. Founded in April 1936, its declared goal was to free women "from their state of triple enslavement: the enslavement of ignorance, their enslavement as women, and [their enslavement] as members of the working class."[13] During the first year of the civil war, the organization expanded to include over 20,000 members. An article published in the journal *Mujeres Libres* immediately following the Nationalist uprising emphasized the unique position of anarchist women in relation to what they termed the "double war":

> The revolutionary man, who today struggles for his freedom, only has an exterior war to carry out: a war against a world that hinders his struggle for freedom and for social equality. The revolutionary woman, on the other hand, has to struggle on two fronts. She struggles for her external freedom, a struggle in which man is her ally. But women also have to fight for their interior freedom, the type of freedom that man enjoyed for many centuries now. And in that struggle she stands alone.[14]

Mujeres Libres was unique in its insistence that the struggle for gender equality not be sacrificed in the name of class struggle or the struggle against Fascism. Theirs was an integral vision of society where revolutionary change could take place only on all fronts at the same time, or it would be terminated on all fronts.

Apart from this singular group, most other women's organizations across Spain spent the first months of the civil war struggling against what was clearly a double standard in moral and political terms: on the one hand, a call for total mobilization in the name of a future society in which the values dear to them would be respected and protected; on the other, continious warnings against the potentially destabilizing effects which mobilization on all fronts and at all times might have on their status as mothers and wives.

Function and Rhetoric: Between the Home Front and the Frontline

During the war the most important spatial distinction was that which existed between the home front and the frontline. With the outbreak of war the home front acquired special importance not only as the focal point of supplies and manpower but also as a space of social experimentation, one where various constellations of power relations were tested: between men and women, between the young and the elderly, between the victors and the vanquished. On both the Republican and Nationalist home fronts the socio-economic structures that defined the routine of everyday lives underwent processes of militarization. This was especially apparent in relation to patterns of provisioning, social welfare, work, and professional training. With the enlistment of men, the home front was converted into a "world of women" within which members where assessed according to their capacity for survival and for self-sacrifice for the sake of the general cause.

Both Nationalist and Republican rhetoric referred to the home front, and specifically to the home itself, as women's stronghold. However, the reality of war was such that many women who resided in territories that remained in enemy hands, or in those that constituted a frontline, had lost all control over their so-called stronghold. Ana María de Fronda, a SF member who arrived in the Nationalist zone in September 1938, wrote about the experience of losing her home, her own private space, and consequently her place in the world:

> As we women came out of the state of stupor that enveloped us, the first thing that hit us deep in our souls was the lack of home. Those of you who had the unimaginable luck of remaining since the first days of the war in Nationalist territory . . . imagine this all too feminine pain: the sense that our material world was ripped out of our hands and left behind in the "Red zone." A home can be recreated, but what if all I ever have is a room in a hotel, or in the house of my in-laws?[15]

The reality of managing one's home was also radically transformed, especially in certain urban areas controlled by Republicans, where chronic lack of supplies forced the authorities to introduce rationing. This happened in Barcelona in early October 1936 and in Madrid in April

1937. According to historian Rafael Abella, in the Nationalist zone the economic situation varied. In Seville, for example, cinemas, restaurants, and shops functioned almost normally and the city experienced an economic boom as supplier of beer, ice-cream, paper products, and pharmaceutics to the Nationalist forces. Granada, on the other hand suffered due to its proximity to the front, as did Zaragoza, which was affected by air raids early in the war.[16]

In urban centers all over the country women's daily routines had to incorporate queuing for food and other supplies, alongside new forms of paid work. On both sides women entered the labor market in massive numbers during the war. On the eve of the war women constituted a small segment of the qualified labor market in Spain. Most working women were young and unmarried and their pay levels were much lower than those of their male counterparts.[17] The information we possess regarding changes in women's work patterns and professional training during the civil war is fragmented and partial at best. While historians have noted some of the more outstanding organized initiatives in this respect, much work is still needed. According to historian Mary Nash, in Madrid, for example, representatives of the anarchist Mujeres Libres organized work brigades (*secciones de trabajo*) in many sectors of the city. The brigades provided aid in the fields of transport, health, the clothing industry, metallurgy, and public services.[18] We do not know, however, how many women took part in this initiative, nor do we possess information regarding the involvement of women who were not identified with a specific political organization in these occupations. What can be said with certainty is that in the Republican zone women were actively encouraged to enlist and fill the place of missing male laborers in a variety of fields. In November 1936, the Communist journal *Mundo Obrero* expressed a position common to all political organizations in the Republican zone:

> The battlefields are colored with the blood of brave women who enrolled in the militias and pulled their weight as part of the struggle against the enemy. These women fulfilled their obligation, but now they must return to the home front and dedicate themselves to work in the factories, in commerce, and in the offices. The nation's life must not be halted due to the lack of male working-hands . . . Our workforce will be supplemented by women. All women to work! This is your battle post now![19]

In the Nationalist zone the SF also encouraged women to enter new and less acceptable professional spheres, all in order to fill the vacuum left by men who had departed for the front. Writer and poet Alfredo

Marquerie Mompín stated in the SF journal *Y, Revista para la mujer nacional sindicalista*:

> Women fill all sorts of posts at the home front: harvest in the countryside, office work, reporting to work in the factories and workshops in the cities. The strong arms of men are indeed missing. Instead of them, and in order not to disturb the rhythm of work, women are forever on guard – blue women, serious, and laborious.[20]

Such messages, however, stood in stark contrast to other calls which urged Nationalist women to retire from the factory floor due to the possible harmful effects of female labor on the reproductive capacities of the nation.[21] While no specific statistics exist regarding women's work in the Nationalist zone, it is clear that the greatest difference between the two zones lay in the way in which women's labor was presented. While Republican society viewed women's work both as an individual right and a collective duty, Nationalist society regarded women's work (essential as it was during the war) as a clear threat to the stability of the family and the existing gender order.

One profession that was clearly considered suitable for women in both zones was nursing. Indeed, the number of nurses and female auxiliary medical personal increased drastically due to the conditions of war and especially after the founding of new hospitals. During the early months of the war many volunteers were accepted as temporary auxiliary nurses, but their lack of professional training affected the quality of medical care. In the Nationalist zone a decree published in November 1936 stated that all nurses would henceforth have to possess an official certificate issued by a faculty of medicine or by the Red Cross. Mercedes Milá y Nolla, general inspector of the Women's Section of Hospitals and of Sanitary Services in Nationalist Spain, struggled to keep out too young and insufficiently prepared volunteers. Well into the war she wrote:

> They send me a young girl fresh out of the course for auxiliary nurses. The norm is that they have to be at least 20-years-old and she is only 16. It is crazy that these girls should be passing their days in hospitals instead of in school. These girls cannot go on night duty, for example . . . If they were 18-years-old we might have had some leeway, but not at the age of [16].[22]

Milá y Nolla and national delegates of the SF and Margaritas were all concerned about the destabilizing effects of war on young nurses. An extract from the novel *Porque lo quiso Dios*, by Francisca Cristina Sáenz de Tejada y Orti (under her penname Gracían Quijano) published in *Y. Revista para la mujer nacional sindicalista* provides a reflection on changes in the everyday life of volunteer nurses engendered by the war. The novel tells the story of Marisa, a young, middle-class woman in San Sebastian. The war interrupted her pharmacy studies and she opted to volunteer in one of the city's hospitals:

> The life of that 22-year-old [woman] – full up to that point with movies, tennis, swimming, and concerts – suffered what one might call a "revolution by war." Her current life is oriented towards continuous attempts to alleviate the hardships of war suffered by those who are fighting for the defense of the fatherland.

In the hospital Marisa meets and falls in love with a wounded soldier. When she assists him back to his room following Mass one day, she realizes that he is actually a Republican soldier. Within the church the two are equals; upon exiting it Marisa is stopped:

> A friend comes to meet and accompany Juan Manuel at the door and she is left standing there, torn between prohibition and her rigorous duty. "What are you doing Marisa?" asks Fernanda from afar. "It's just that no one talked to us about this ward. And I want to go in, if not now, then another day. I just want to bring them some tobacco as I did with the others. It's Christmas after all. They won't let me though. Do you know that ward?"[23]

This excerpt reflects the supposedly destabilizing effects of war even on women who mobilized within traditionally "appropriate" female spaces, especially due to interactions with unknown men, some politically suspect. However, it is worth noting that Marisa, who the author presents as a positive model for other young women (due to her religious devoutness, her enlistment as a volunteer nurse's aide, and her participation in SF activities), was not deterred by the spatial barrier (the forbidden ward of war prisoners) or by ideological ones. In the story (published in mid-1938), she ends up leaving her fiancé and continuing an intimate relationship with Juan Manuel.

Of all the roles fulfilled by women during the civil war those associated with the use of arms elicited the most complex responses in moral and cultural terms. In both zones the presence of women on the battlefield was perceived as contradictory to their "innate" role as mothers and nurturers. In the Nationalist zone, Carlist women and SF members alike had to deal with this contradiction in their capacity as nurses, members of the Axulio Azul, or as frontline laundrywomen. However, there was never an explicit discussion concerning the desirability of women's presence at the front. Although the number of Nationalist women who served in auxiliary posts alongside the troops probably did not vary significantly from that of Republican women, it was always assumed that their role was a transitory and undesired consequence of war.

Nationalist women were never photographed carrying arms. However, as Toni Morant indicates, the relationship of Falangist women to arms was far from a straightforward one.[24] Pilar Primo de Rivera herself referred to the experience of smuggling arms. It was a necessary auxiliary action upon which the women prided themselves, and yet:

> What tensions these young women had to deal with carrying pistols under their coats or within their boots, not knowing if the slightest movement might disengage the security handle. They did not even dare sit down in the metro on their way to a meeting place for fear that someone might notice what they were carrying.[25]

Felipe Ximenez de Sandoval, a leading Falangist ideologist, portrayed the proximity of women to arms and blood as an unfortunate, yet natural consequence of the war itself. In his eulogy for Pilar Carrillo de Albornoz, who mobilized as a laundry- and liaison-woman on the Madrid front, he wrote:

> Pili, perhaps is the most well-known figure on the Madrid front . . . Pili is a laundrywoman of the front, she is part of the [Carlist] delegation of Frentes y Hospitales. But she is neither a nurse nor a laundrywomen. Pili is a liaison officer. Her car is always full of bedsheets stained with the blood and sweat of the wounded . . . Pili goes in and out, visiting all the surgical teams. There is probably no other young woman in Spain who spends more time in Ciudad University. And only a few men have a permanent permit, as she does, to circulate within that glorious and terrible sector.[26]

As the above citations make clear, Nationalist women did not find their way to the front subversively and in opposition to the spatial practices imposed on them. They were encouraged to do so by the organizations that mobilized them. The distinction between committed service to the *patria* and inappropriate behavior did not emerge due to their willingness to carry arms or in relation to the spaces they occupied, but rather in regard to the function they fulfilled and the way in which they conducted themselves. In this respect uniforms played an important role. Unlike the Republican militiawomen, Nationalist nurses, as well as laundry- and liaison women were all required to wear uniform. These helped identify the organizations to which the volunteers belonged and could hold them accountable for any misconduct. The uniforms, which were regulated according to details such as length of the skirts and the way in which members could wear their hair, also minimized criticism regarding the possible "masculinization" of women.[27]

In the case of Republican militiawomen, it is clear that during the first months of the war their presence at the front (carrying arms and dressed as they were like their male counterparts) was celebrated as a revolutionary act of self-sacrifice. Republican propaganda materials depicted them as young, confidant, and attractive women. Indeed, the volunteers who joined their male comrades in the battlefield during the initial months of the war were mostly young, unmarried, urban women. The majority of them had prior political socialization and they arrived for the most part from an anarchist or a Communist background. However, as Mary Nash rightly notes, the proud and combative image of the militiawoman was not employed mainly in order to mobilize women; it was aimed principally at Republican men and used in order to encourage them to go out and fulfill their "proper" role in the struggle against the Fascist enemy so that women *would not* have to do that in their place.

The testimonies left by some of the militiawomen reflect the difficult reality of their everyday lives at the front. Those who managed to establish their reputation as good soldiers often did so at the expense of articulating themselves as women. They had to minimize any expressions of femininity out of fear of attracting criticism or feelings of discomfort. They had become quite literally "sexless women." Women who hid their bodies behind manly attire, and struggled in order to find moments of privacy in which they could change their clothes, bathe, or even use the toilet.[28] María de la Luz Mejías Correa, a member of the United Socialist Youth in Extremadura, who had joined the battalion of Pedro Rubio in defending the city of Badajoz, reflected in her memoirs on the struggle to find a place for herself in an exclusively male environment:

> There were those who accused us of prostitution, women who slept around and carried diseases. Some were that way, a few, but that was outright slander in the case of the majority of brave women who fought at the front. I joined the militia out of ideological conviction but, first and foremost, in order to follow my father, my brothers, and my husband. Like many others, I remained there in order not to be left all alone on the other side of the [home] front. If there were infectious sexual diseases it was just as much the fault of men as of women, mostly on the

home front. But they only blamed us, because men were chauvinists and they were afraid that all women would step out of the kitchen in order to join the militia.[29]

According to Mary Nash:

If, for men, putting on the blue attire of the working class represented a symbol of political identification, for women, putting on trousers or a blue overall had a much deeper significance . . . For women putting on the uniform of the revolution meant outwardly identifying themselves with the process of social revolution, as well as challenging the traditional [division] of gender [roles].

As the following citation from the official diary of the Antifascist Committee of Barcelona makes clear, however, it was precisely this challenge that worried the Republican authorities. On October 3, 1936, the committee stated:

The women who appear wearing blue overalls at the center of the city are confusing the war with some kind of a carnival. One must show more responsibility and put an end to the publication of photos of women carrying a gun, women who never in their lives fired a weapon.[30]

From December 1936, and in response to such concerns, the Republican authorities took advantage of the process by which all militia forces were incorporated into regular units of the Republican Army in order to withdraw most of the militiawomen from the front.

However, the image of the militiawomen continued to live in popular memory and culture and was often employed by the Nationalist authorities as a powerful propaganda tool. The militiawomen were used as testimony to illustrate the moral weakness of the Republic which, according to the Nationalist press, had to rely on the presence of women on the battlefield. In October 1936, the Carlist leader María Rosa Urraca Pastor referred to this issue precisely:

The "Reds" bring to the front hordes of women, undoubtedly because they are lacking [soldiers]. Here we have more than enough men to carry arms. [Luckily] our help is not needed in this respect and furthermore it is improper for our delicate sex.[31]

Such references constituted a clear manipulation of reality, as Urraca Pastor, who herself served in the sanitary unit attached to the column led by Colonel García Escámez at the Navarra front, well knew. However, they attest to the importance of the phenomenon that went well beyond the numbers and the actual war experiences of the militiawomen themselves.

Conclusions

The Spanish Civil War brought in its wake a transformation of existing private and public spaces, and the creation of new ones. Despite the horrors of the war this process sometimes provided new opportunities for public activism for both Republican and Nationalist women. On both sides of the political divide the distinction between the home front and the frontline emerged as central both in spatial and propaganda terms. While the home front was presented as the domain of women and of men unfit for active military service, the frontline was portrayed as the realm of men. In reality, however, this distinction was less meaningful than might have been expected, especially for young, unmarried women who were often encouraged, and even forced, to enlist in an array of frontline services.

Reflecting on the ways in which different political groups fashioned their discourse regarding the desirability and scope of women's wartime mobilization is important and contributes to our understanding of the interplay between gender, class, and ideological identification. This level of analysis, however, is limited and runs the risk of missing the particularities of women's activism "on the ground." The realities of the home front within both zones were a far cry from the "feminine haven" portrayed by the press and dreamed of by frontline soldiers. Bombardments, supply shortages, and political repression gravely affected the lives of most civilians. During the war new forms of social control and of political indoctrination emerged on the home front. Tactics of surveillance, coercion, and forced re-education usually took place within specific public spaces (such as the school, the workplace, and even the street), but also affected the private realm of the home. Since it focuses solely on the year 1936, this chapter does not refer to the role played by women in later stages of the war in maintaining the mechanisms of social repression and ideological indoctrination. It should be noted, however, that women on both sides played an important role in this respect within their homes, their local communities, the workplace, and the prison system.

The main contention of this chapter is that women's wartime mobilization on both sides did not differ significantly. The final citation by

María Urraca Pastor reflects the similarities and differences between the experiences of women in both zones. On both sides political organizations, as well as individual men and women, feared the destabilizing effects of war on the existing social order. The majority of women's organizations – both Republican and Nationalists – were willing to put their specific agendas aside for the time of the war in order to create large-scale coalitions within their respective camps. The anarchist women constituted a singular exception to this rule. Of all of the women's organizations that operated within the Republican zone the anarchist Mujeres Libres was the one entity that consistently struggled on all fronts throughout the civil war. Using their journal, also titled *Mujeres Libres*, anarchist women advocated a policy according to which no role was beneath anyone if they were called upon to fulfill it. According to them, "teachers should be peeling potatoes, nurses should be washing the floor . . . die-hard feminists should care for children, a seamstresses should hold a gun."[32] Refusing to join the Communist-led AMA, anarchist women criticized the notion that the women's revolution had to await the defeat of the Fascist enemy. In December 1936, they wrote in anger and disappointment:

> In the majority of the syndicates in the countryside, while our comrades discuss and resolve issues of importance, women are faced with the same mentality which in their homes led them to assume "feminine" functions such as cooking and washing. Since the outbreak of war we have travelled the villages of anti-Fascist Spain and – except in those syndicates that accepted good-looking middle-class typists – we have seen nothing but simple women struggling as always under the same weight of servitude.[33]

Nevertheless, the months between July and December 1936 were a period of radicalized activism for both Spanish men and women. Prior to the consolidation of formal military and administrative structures on both sides, popular mobilization took place in accordance with the most pressing needs of the hour and some generational and gender distinctions were momentarily overlooked. However, for most Spanish women (as anarchist activists noted), 1936 was not Year Zero. While new organizations were formed during the early months of the war, the majority of Spanish women were mobilized along the same ideological lines that divided Spanish society throughout the years of the Spanish Republic. The largest and most important women's organizations already existed prior to July 1936. And while the number of women mobilized on behalf of the nation increased, the war itself did not signify rupture in terms of established power relations.

Would it be correct to say that no differences existed between the patterns of mobilization and wartime experiences of Nationalist and Republican women throughout 1936? One must be careful in reaching such a conclusion. Just as in other times, differences existed between the experiences of women who lived in large urban communities and those that resided in small towns and rural communities. Women also differed depending on their marital status, their education, and their professional training. However, during the first months of the war the greatest difference between the two zones had less to do with patterns of women's activism and more with its rhetorical justifications.

Republican women legitimized their wartime interventions within all spheres of life by referring not only to their role in the struggle against the Fascist enemy but also to their rights as individuals, especially the right to work and the right to bear arms in order to protect themselves and their community. Nationalist women, on the other hand, rationalized their decision to take advantage of the political and professional opportunities offered to them by the realities of a total war through a different discourse. This was a gender one that employed the concepts of "order" and "function." It had clear Catholic overtones, but at the same time stepped well beyond the traditional debate on the role of women within society. Consequently many Margaritas and SF members were free to act everywhere in the name of the nation (including the front) so long as they adhered to the social status and functions assigned to them. Under the Franco dictatorship the more radical aspects of women's public activism during the civil war were erased from collective memory. However, as the opening citations of this chapter demonstrate, these experiences left their trace on women both explicitly and implicitly throughout their lives.

Acknowledgement

The author is a member of the project HAR2015-63624-P (MINECO/FEDER).

Notes

1 Interview with Consuelo Valcarcel Burgos, Madrid, March 25, 2003.
2 Astrea Barrios, "¡Hombres a la vanguardia! ¡Mujeres en la retaguardia!" *Mujeres* (Bilbao ed.), April 17, 1937, in Mary Nash, *Rojas: las mujeres republicanas en la Guerra Civil* (Madrid: Taurus, 2000), 88.
3 Sofía Rodríguez López, "La presencia de las mujeres en la prensa Almeriense de la Guerra Civil," *La Mujer. Actas del III Congreso de Historia de Andalucía*, vol. I (Cordoba: CajaSur, 2002), 157–72.

4 Juliá, De Santos, "Guerra contra el invasor" a "guerra fratricida," in *Victimas de la guerra civil*, ed. Juliá Santos (Madrid: Temas de Hoy, 1999), 17.
5 Mary Nash, *Las Mujeres Republicanas* (Barcelona: Taurus, 1999), 18, 62.
6 María Dolores Andrés Prieto, *La Mujer en la Política de la Memoria: María Rosa Urraca Pastor, una estrella fugaz* (MA diss., University of Salamanca, 2012), 72.
7 Inbal Ofer, *Señoritas in Blue: The Making of a Female Political Elite in Franco's Spain. The National Leadership of the Sección Femenina de la Falange (1936–1977)* (Brighton: Sussex University Press, 2009).
8 Adoración Martín Barrio and Eduardo Martín González, "Las mujeres de la retaguardia: Los comités femeninos de apoyo a la guerra (Zamora, de agosto de 1936 a abril de 1937)," in A los 70 años de la Guerra Civil española*: Actas del encuentro celebrado en Zamora,* ed. Juan Andrés Blanco Rodríguez (Zamora: UNED, 2006), 465.
9 Sofía Rodríguez López and Antonio Cazorla Sánchez, "Blue Angels: Female Fascist Resisters, Spies and Intelligence Officials in the Spanish Civil War, 1936–9," *Journal of Contemporary History*, DOI: 10.1177/0022009416668039 (first published December 22, 2016), 10.
10 Javier Cervera, *Madrid en Guerra: La Ciudad Clandestina, 1936–1939* (Madrid: Alianza Editorial, 2006), 277–88.
11 María López Vallecillo, "Presencia social e imagen pública de las enfermeras en el siglo XX (1915–1940)," (PhD diss., University of Valladolid, 2016), http://uvadoc.uva.es/handle/10324/16513, 192.
12 Ángela Cenarro, "Movilización femenina para la guerra total (1936–1939): Un ejercicio comparativo," Historia y política: Ideas, procesos y movimientos sociales 16 (2006): 163.
13 Nash, *Rojas*, 99.
14 Ilse, "La doble lucha de la mujer," *Mujeres Libres*, VIII Mes de la Revolución.
15 *Y Revista para la mujer nacional sindicalista*, July 1938, 11.
16 Rafael Abella, La vida cotidiana durante la guerra civil: la España nacional (Madrid: Planeta, 1974).
17 See for example, Alexise Véronique Ikossie Seibo épse Kouakou, "La mujer salmantina en el trabajo durante la Segunda República (1931–1936)," No es país para *jóvenes*, ed. Alejandra Ibarra Aguirregabiria (Instituto Valentín Foronda, 2012), https://dialnet.unirioja.es/servlet/oaiart?codigo=4715088 ; Olga Paz Torres, "Aspiraciones y oportunidades de las mujeres en la Segunda República Española: El acceso a la inspección de trabajo," *IUSLabor*, no. 1-2015 (January 2015), 1–15.
18 Nash, *Mujeres Libres*, 63.
19 *Mundo Obrero*, November 8, 1936, in Noelia García Castilla, "La imagen femenina en la publicidad durante la Guerra Civil española: Análisis de contenido aplicado a la publicidad gráfica" (PhD diss., Complutense University, Madrid, 2015), 102.
20 Alfredo Marquerie Mompín, *Y Revista para la mujer nacional sindicalista*, March 1938, 70.

21 In this regard, see for example, Dr. Juan Bosch Martín, "El fuero de trabajo y la mujer," *Y Revista para la mujer nacional sindicalista*, April 1938, 7.

22 Mercedes Milá y Nolla, in María López Vallecillo, "Relevancia de la mujer en el bando nacional de la Guerra Civil española: las enfermeras," *Memoria y Civilización* 19 (2016): 426.

23 Gracían Quijano, "Porque lo quiso Dios," *Y Revista para la mujer nacional sindicalista*, May 1938, 29.

24 Antonio Morant i Ariño, "Para influir en la vida del estado futuro": Discurso-y práctica- falangista sobre el papel de la mujer y la feminidad, 1933–1945," *Historia y política: Ideas, procesos y movimientos sociales* 27 (2012): 121–22.

25 Pilar Primo de Rivera, "Historia de la Sección Femenina," *Y Revista para la mujer nacional sindicalista*, May 1938, 32–33.

26 Felipe Ximenez de Sandoval, *Y Revista para la mujer nacional sindicalista*, June 1938, 19.

27 Dionisio Ridruejo, "Historia del Primer Consejo de la Sección Femenina," *Y Revista para la mujer nacional sindicalista*, February 1938, 5.

28 See, for example, Vallecillo, "Presencia social e imagen pública de las enfermeras," 196–200.

29 María de la Luz Mejías Correa, *Así fue pasando el tiempo: Memorias de una miliciana extremeña* (Seville: Renacimiento, 2006), 88.

30 "De Solidaridad Obrera: La frivolidad en los frentes y la retaguardia. La guerra es una cosa más seria," *Diari oficial del Comité Antifeixista i de Salut Pública de Badalona*, October 3, 1936, cited in Nash, *Rojas*, 69.

31 María Rosa Urraca Pastor, October 1936, cited in Antonio Manuel Moral Roncal, "Auge y caída de una líder carlista en el franquismo: María Rosa Urraca Pastor", *APORTES* 81 (2013), 81.

32 "Las mujeres en los primeros días de la lucha," *Mujeres Libres*, no. 10 (July 1937).

33 Editorial, "Mujeres en la transformación revolucionaria," *Tierra y Libertad*, December 1936, cited in Nash, *Rojas*, 94.

6

Taking Sides: Salazar's *Estado Novo*, the Nationalist Uprising and the Spanish Civil War

PEDRO AIRES OLIVEIRA

Throughout its history, Portugal's relations with neighboring Spain have always been complex. If the study of nationalism shows us that the choice of an external enemy is usually a key feature in the process of binding a community, then Spain (or Castile) has performed that role in shaping Portuguese collective identity, especially since the late nineteenth century, when a nationalist historiography helped crystalize an account of the country's history in which this adversary was always present. But it is also noteworthy that this "vilification" of Spain had also co-existed with a body of opinion favorable toward a close rapport, or even a federal arrangement, between the two countries. This school included several politicians and intellectuals who, throughout the nineteenth century, thought that an Iberian union could be the appropriate answer to the diminishing geopolitical importance of the two states after the loss of their respective empires in Latin America.[1] This kind of speculation, however, lost much of its allure in the years of the First Portuguese Republic (1910 26), when the relationship between the two countries came under great strain because of Madrid's discreet support for the opponents of the fledgling Portuguese regime – an attitude that fed the suspicions of politicians in Lisbon as to the alleged hegemonic designs of King Alfonso XIII. After a period of denouement in the late 1920s, coinciding with Primo de Rivera's government and the establishment of a right-wing military dictatorship in Lisbon in 1926, relations again became strained when a "radical" republic was inaugurated in Spain in April 1931 and Portugal was in the process of consolidating an authoritarian, corporatist regime under the aegis of a Catholic law professor, António de Oliveira Salazar (1889–1970).

This chapter will examine the reasons that led the Portuguese premier to perceive a victory of the Popular Front government against the Nationalist uprising in July 1936 as an existential threat to his own regime, encouraging him to pursue a policy of outright support for the Nationalist (afterward Francoist) camp in the civil war. It will also chart some of the tensions that arose from this orientation within the Anglo-Portuguese alliance, Lisbon's most valued foreign policy asset, as well as its continuing suspicions concerning Spain's hegemonic ambitions, embodied by some of the more imperialist-minded elements of the Falange. It will conclude by taking stock of some of the arguments advanced by recent revisionist literature on the foreign policy of the *Estado Novo*, the New State, in the period up to 1945, in an attempt to see how they stand in the light of Salazar's political behavior vis-à-vis the Spanish conflict.

The Coming of the Second Republic

Salazar's decision to take the side of the Nationalist uprising in the summer of 1936 is best explained by the fears and apprehensions sustained since the first victory of the Left in Spain five years earlier.[2]

The proclamation of the Second Republic had given the Portuguese oppositionists – the *Reviralho* (a term which described the constellation of radical Republicans who repeatedly tried to topple the military dictatorship in successive, but ultimately fruitless coups) – an important basis to prepare and launch political activities against a regime that was still in the process of finding a constitutional formula that would be acceptable to the various components of the coalition which had brought it into being. The new Republican government in Madrid, though, did not limit itself to providing shelter to Portuguese émigrés. Manuel Azaña, minister of war and later head of government, encouraged, financed, and armed those same elements, either for political solidarity (most likely cemented by Masonic connections), or for the ill-defined ambition of allowing the new Spanish regime to become an irradiating center of democratic and Republican values across the Iberian Peninsula and the Hispanic world.[3] If we add to this the federalist component of the Second Republic's constitutional project (or the inclusion of an article in the constitutional text allowing the acquisition of dual nationality by any Portuguese citizen settled in Spanish territory), it is easier to understand the heightened fears of Portuguese diplomats in Spain who, in the following years, would nurture Lisbon's anxieties concerning the inclusion of Portugal in a federation of Iberian nationalities, possibly with Soviet encouragement,[4] as well as the near-hysterical attitude of the Portuguese right-wing press vis-à-vis the new Spanish regime.

With highly conservative, ultra-Catholic elements of the dictatorship gaining the upper hand in Portugal, the prospect of a democratic, socially progressive, anti-clerical Spain was a disturbing development, an unwelcome reminder that the replacement of parliamentary regimes by authoritarian ones in Europe might not be a "historical inevitability" after all.[5] One of the key arguments put forward by the right-wing ideologues of what would become the Portuguese corporatist regime of 1933 (one also frequently used by conservative observers from European democracies[6]) was, it should be recalled, the notion that the liberal tradition in the Iberian Peninsula was synonymous with irresponsibility, insecurity, and chaos. For some time, every event that seemed to validate the image of a lawless (and godless) Spain – strikes, assaults against churches and convents, incidents involving the land reform program – was exploited in deeply Manichean terms by the pro-government press, which at times even went to the point of suggesting a possible pact between Madrid and Moscow (mediated by "international Masonry") to destabilize the situation in Portugal.

Relations relaxed somewhat after the electoral victory of the center-right in Spain in November 1933, but more markedly after the entry of the CEDA (Confederacion Española de Derechas Autónomas) in the government and the heavy-handed handling of the Asturian miners' strike of 1934[7] – an event that persuaded the New State's authorities that their counterparts in Madrid now had a different understanding of the use of state power and what it took to maintain order in the streets. Another development was the opening of a parliamentary inquiry into the sale of arms to Portuguese émigrés in Spain, a case that implicated high profile politicians such as Manuel Azaña and Indalecio Prieto, as well as the Basque industrialist Horacio Echevarrieta, and led to the detention of several Portuguese exiles.[8]

The new Spanish government seemed eager to make the best of the political thaw brought about by these events. The two regimes soon found ways to cooperate in the League of Nations (namely in the context of the Abyssinian crisis, in which Portugal was called to play a relevant diplomatic role[9]); a high profile visit of Spanish intellectuals to Portugal was organized with the help of the Secretariat for National Propaganda (SPN); and in May 1935 the Spanish premier, Alejandro Lerroux, approached Salazar with a proposal to sign a trade agreement (the last one had been concluded in 1893), the corollary of which would be the signing of a "pact of non-aggression, friendship, and good neighborliness." For about a year, the foreign ministries of both countries discussed these two proposals extensively, but were unable to bring them to a conclusion.

The main obstacles came from the Portuguese side and were of two kinds. First, Lisbon was all too aware that the political situation in Spain was volatile and therefore unlikely to provide the foundations for a sound, long-term bilateral relationship. As long as there was a chance that political power in Madrid would return to the hands of the "radical" Left, any commitment would always look provisional. But no less relevant were the geopolitical and historical suspicions that haunted the minds of Portuguese decision makers. In their "mental maps,"[10] the Iberian neighbor remained a potential threat to Portugal's integrity and independence; the Spanish elites could never be entirely trusted because, deep in their hearts, they had never reconciled themselves to the idea of another independent entity in the peninsula. (In 1940, Franco's foreign minister, Serrano Suñer, would articulate this mind-set when he confided to Ribbentrop that "geographically-speaking Portugal has no right to exist."[11]) In a memorandum addressed to the Portuguese foreign affairs minister from February 1935, the most senior Portuguese diplomat of the time, Ambassador Luiz Teixeira de Sampayo (a man known for being Salazar's *éminence grise* in the Necessidades Palace[12]), cautioned against the sympathetic approaches of the Spanish center-right government. According to Sampayo, a man who had earned a reputation largely due to his command of Portugal's diplomatic history, it was unlikely that Spain would try to achieve its expansionist goals militarily; its elites were now keener to pursue a subtler course of action, namely, one that involved modalities of cultural and economic penetration, as well as a well-targeted flattering of Portugal's intelligentsia. Even if a friendship pact might render Portugal some gains in terms of good neighborhood policy, Sampayo thought that such dividends would hardly countervail the risks that greater intimacy with Spain could bring about.[13]

The impact of Sampayo's views on Salazar's foreign policy thinking had become discernible first in the extensive interviews given by the Portuguese premier to the journalist António Ferro (later his chief propaganda adviser as head of SPN) in 1932,[14] and, later, in September 1935, in a long "official note" in which Salazar articulated his foreign policy doctrine for the first time. Portugal was conceived as an essentially Atlantic country, with the bulk of its interests located overseas, and therefore only marginally interested in the politics of continental Europe. The Anglo-Portuguese alliance was singled out as the cornerstone of the country's foreign and security policy (the ultimate guarantee of its independence in Europe and of its overseas possessions), even though Salazar expressed a desire to obtain greater leverage in his dealings with London. As to Spain, he reiterated Portugal's desire to maintain a friendly and cordial relationship with its neighbor, but only as long as Portugal's independence was a "fundamental axiom" in Madrid's foreign policy.[15]

Red Scare: The Victory of the Popular Front

Unsurprisingly, the triumph of the Popular Front in the general election of February 16, 1936, again with Azaña as prime-minister and for the first time with Communist and Anarchist support for the government, raised the level of anxiety of the New State's authorities, as well as of Portuguese Catholic circles, to new heights. Having once described Communism as "the great heresy of our time,"[16] Salazar gradually came to perceive the new situation created by the elections in Spain as an existential threat to his regime. Although he insisted that he should not be seen as a representative of the Church in the profane world of politics, and made sure that this idea was well understood by his old Christian Democrat companions from Coimbra University, it is unquestionable that Salazar's worldview was deeply marked by the writings of some of the figures associated with "integral Catholicism" of the turn of the century.[17] Accordingly, he believed that "Portugal's soul" was inseparable from the Catholic faith, the key ingredient of the nation's collective identity, and the driving force behind its overseas expansion. The reason for the country's troubles – or even decadence – throughout the nineteenth and early twentieth centuries had been, to a large extent, the corrosive effect of secular ideologies (Liberalism, Socialism, radical Republicanism) – a trend he hoped to reverse through a "re-Christianization" of Portuguese society, including a prominent role awarded to the Church in the "spiritual" realm (namely, education), and the revival (or invention) of old corporatist concepts and institutions. By the beginning of 1936, this program was well under way – the constitutional foundations of the New State had been laid down in 1933 34 and Salazar had been able to overcome successive challenges to his authority, both from the Left (the crushing of several Republican revolts in 1931, the dismantling of the last bulwarks of free trade unionism in 1934), and from the Right (the neutralization of the openly Fascist Blue Shirts movement in that same year). Therefore, the emergence of a coalition of anti-clerical Republicans, Socialists, and Communists across the border – in a context of mounting international uncertainty – was an event that might well merit a reappraisal of some of the traditional tenets of Portugal's foreign policy. In his 1935 memorandum, Sampayo insisted that in light of history Portugal had nothing to gain from interfering in the domestic affairs of its neighbor, even if it might bring about a regime hostile to Britain (thus conferring greater strategic value to the Anglo-Portuguese alliance). Sampayo also cautioned against a scenario involving the "Balkanization' of Spain," since such territorial dismemberment would most likely be accompanied by social upheavals, with significant risks of a "revolutionary contagion" spreading to Portugal. Even if the Popular Front's program could in many ways be considered a relatively moderate one, perceptions – even if distorted by ideology – counted as much as a more fact-based appreciation of what was happening in Spain. Reports sent by Portuguese representatives fed all sorts of fears. Socialist leader Largo Caballero, for instance, was credited by the Riba Tâmega viscount, Portugal's representative in Madrid, as having called for the creation of a republic modelled on the Soviet Union, a "Confederation of Iberian Nationalities" that would "give battle to Fascist Portugal."[18] For Salazar – and some of the firebrands in his circle, such as Minister of Trade and Industry Pedro Teotónio Pereira, Spain was living through an ideological conflict akin to a "religious war," with a high potential for a transnational spillover, and thus to remain neutral would hardly be an option for the New State.

With the concept of collective security seriously undermined by successive setbacks experienced by the League of Nations – most notably, the Abyssinian crisis and Hitler's direct challenges to the Versailles Treaty (such as the remilitarization of the Rhine in March 1936) – the Portuguese authorities became more aware of the need to make appropriate adjustments in their foreign and security policy. In several cabinet meetings held in January and February 1936, and then again at the Higher National Defence Council of 21 April, the main threat to Portuguese integrity was thought to be a Spanish attack (motivated by the "expansionist drive" of an "extremist regime").[19] The paramountcy of such a threat had already been identified before the electoral victory of the Left (on account of the old historical ambitions of the Spanish elites), but afterward it was perceived as even more likely to materialize, since the new Popular Front government might feel tempted to wage a war against Portugal as a way of reasserting "Spain's internal unity."[20]

Salazar convinced himself that he would have to run some risks and act on his own, after having sounded out the British to see if London would be willing to exert pressure on the Spanish government to contain the "extremist elements of the local Left" who had direct links to Portuguese subversive groups and were allegedly encouraging them to fight for a "federal Socialist republic in the Iberian Peninsula."[21] Approached by his Portuguese counterpart, British Foreign Secretary Anthony Eden replied in vague and noncommittal terms, in part because the British ambassador in Madrid downplayed the influence of the Communists in Azaña's government. This response seems to have led Salazar to turn a blind eye to the conspiracy (or maybe even more than that[22]) which prominent right-wing Spanish exiles, headed by General José Sanjurjo, had set in motion to prepare the overthrow of the Second Republic.[23]

Backing Franco without Qualms

When the military uprising began to unravel in July 1936, the Portuguese regime would go further than merely providing encouragement or token facilities to the rebels. While treating the Spanish conflict as a "domestic problem," Salazar was more than keen to mobilize the resources of the state, as well as the goodwill of private individuals, banks, and businesses to make sure that the right-wing generals would enjoy safe sanctuary in Portugal. By doing so he was deliberately tying the fate of his regime to the outcome of the struggle in Spain, a daring move that allowed him to take over the key government portfolios of finance, war, and foreign affairs in the last months of 1936.[24]

The New State's support for the Nationalist *alzamiento* was a multi-faceted one, consistent with the idea that this was a total conflict in which the classic boundaries between civilian and military, and regular and irregular combatants had become blurred and the achievement of victory was seen as justifying the use of all means deemed necessary – a rationale that underlined an "action plan" to assist the uprising put forward by Pedro Teotónio Pereira to Salazar in the last days of July 1936.[25]

The logistical and material assistance provided from the outbreak of the rebellion was undoubtedly a key feature of Portugal's involvement, and probably helped the Nationalists to secure control of the full extent of the border with Portugal in a relatively short period of time (in August 1936, with the fall of Badajoz), as well as to conquer the important provincial capital of Seville. Portuguese roads and aerodromes (and improvised airfields on farms close to the border) were used to transport arms, munitions, fuel, food, clothes, medical equipment, and supplies, among other items, at a stage of the conflict when the insurgents were still struggling to unite their troops from the North and the South, and some Portuguese ports were used to unload military supplies from Germany (such as disassembled airplanes and light armored vehicles), which were then taken in special road convoys to the areas controlled by the Nationalists. Portuguese firms played a role as intermediaries for the acquisition of such supplies and Portuguese banks (including the Bank of Portugal and the state-controlled Caixa Geral dos Depósitos) and wealthy businessmen, such as the founder of Companhia de União Fabril, the industrialist Alfredo da Silva, provided the necessary credit.[26]

Cooperation in the security field was also extremely close, with the authorities of the New State, particularly its gendarmerie, the National Republican Guard, the Fiscal Guard, and the Political Police, handing hundreds of Republican refugees over to the Nationalists (including many of those who had managed to escape the Badajoz massacre of August 14, 1936), knowing in advance that many of them would face summary trials or even a firing squad. Members of the Spanish community expatriated in Portugal known for their Republican proclivities were put under close surveillance, and the Spanish ambassador, Claudio Sánchez-Albornoz, had to endure all sorts of minor indignities before Salazar finally decided to break off relations with the Madrid government, on October 23, 1936. Official contacts were still maintained with Sánchez-Albornoz, a so-called Black embassy – staffed by a runaway diplomat and several right-wing expatriates, such as the marquises of Quintanar and Contadero, and the Count of Peña Castillo – which began to deal directly with the Portuguese authorities.[27]

Given the highly charged ideological dimension of the conflict, it was to be expected that the press and propaganda institutions of the regime would also be mobilized, and this was certainly the case between 1936 and 1939. The SPN, for instance, employed a team of newspapermen completely devoted to the task of writing articles and "reporting" on the progress of the war in Spain, either for the purpose of praising the military feats of the Nationalists, or for denouncing the atrocities allegedly perpetrated by the Reds in areas under their control, particularly those which targeted churches, monasteries, and charitable institutions. This sort of coverage – fed also by a Catholic press staunchly aligned with Salazar – allowed the creation of an "emotional atmosphere" that formed the ideal background for the government's pro-Franco intervention.[28]

The most relevant feature of this propaganda offensive was, undoubtedly, the use of Rádio Clube Português (RCP), a private radio station run by a long-time supporter of Salazar, retired army captain Jorge Botelho Moniz, as a propaganda tool at the service of the Nationalists. This was made possible thanks to the potent transmitters of the RCP, which allowed it to broadcast into Spanish territory, reaching areas where the Nationalists had no equivalent instrument to influence the population. Besides organizing charity campaigns aimed at providing humanitarian relief to the areas under the control of the rebels, the RCP also took great pride in its alleged role in the "heroic" resistance of the besieged Nationalist forces in the Alcazar of Toledo; according to Moniz, it was the RCP's casual interception of a speech by a Communist MP, indicating that the Republicans had not yet succeeded in taking control of the city, that encouraged a military unit led by General Varela to make a detour from their march toward Madrid and provide crucial support to those were defending the stronghold in Toledo.[29]

Moniz also became a pivotal figure in the recruitment of Portuguese volunteers – the Viriatos (named after the Lusitanian chief who put up resistance against the Roman legions in the second century BC) – who fought alongside the Francoist forces. Their recruitment normally took place through the so-called *Banderínes de Enganche*, first in Portuguese territory – under the benevolent watch of the authorities – and then in Spain, which directed them to various army corps and militias. They never formed an autonomous fighting unit, but instead were distributed by the Spanish Foreign Legion, the militias of the Falange and the *requetés*, the regular army units, or the Army Health Services. An accurate estimate of their numbers has never been possible to establish up to this day, in part because many chose to enlist under false identities, or simply because their Portuguese surnames were rendered into the Spanish form (Lopes into López, Rodrigues into Rodríguez, for instance), but César Oliveira, the foremost historian of Portugal's involvement in the civil war, suggests a "conservative" estimate of 3,000 4,000 men (or boys, since a not insignificant number of them enlisted as minors).[30]

Selling Franco to the British

If the contribution of these adventurers and right-wing idealists was certainly negligible to the outcome of the struggle in Spain, the same cannot be said of Portugal's diplomatic involvement with the Francoist cause. Here Salazar possessed an unquestionably valuable asset: his privileged relationship with Britain, the power which, along with France, had been the sponsor of the multilateral Non-Intervention Agreement in Spain, and later the host of its ill-famed Permanent Committee. Ever since he became noted in the late 1920s as the only member of the Portuguese military dictatorship who could be said to possess statesman-like qualities, Salazar was extremely well regarded by British representatives in Lisbon and high ranking Whitehall officials. At times he was perceived as "difficult," and "high-minded," but overall he represented an immense improvement over the Republican politicians dismissed from power in 1926.[31]

All too aware that a lax application of the agreement would play into the hands of Franco, Salazar exercised a dilatory diplomacy that allowed the Nationalists to escape more rigorous scrutiny from the powers that supported the non-intervention policy in (relatively) good faith. By dragging their feet when the British government was pressing them to adhere to the agreement, in the first weeks of August 1936, the Portuguese were free to allow the transit of supplies to the rebels through their territory, as already seen. It was one matter to have a written commitment but another to have the proper machinery to ensure its enforcement (something that would never come to pass), and here again Portuguese procrastination in the early days of September perfectly suited the needs of the insurgents and their powerful – but all too conspicuous – backers, Nazi Germany and Fascist Italy.[32] For weeks, Anglo-Portuguese relations underwent some of their tensest moments in recent years, causing the Anglophile Armindo Monteiro to submit his resignation to Salazar because he thought the impasse created by the Portuguese premier was endangering the alliance. When in September Portugal finally agreed to take part in the committee's sessions, and was therefore liable to answer the charges pressed by Ivan Maisky, the Soviet representative, Salazar made sure that he would be represented by Monteiro, an appointment that was to be read as a sign that Portugal's alignment with the totalitarian powers in the Spanish conflict did not constitute a deviation from its commitments toward Great Britain.[33]

In London, Monteiro, who quickly established a close rapport with the Duke of Alba, Franco's unofficial representative in the British capital, pursued such a dogged defense of Franco's positions that the Germans and the Italians felt at times compelled to alert Salazar to the counterproductive effects of such a posture. One of the most flagrant examples of Portuguese tactics – which were occasionally out of touch with the military realities on the ground – occurred in the early months of 1937 when Lisbon insisted that it would not cooperate in an Anglo-French plan to supervise Spanish maritime and land frontiers. Salazar's procrastination, however, was more prolonged than was advisable since it was now the Republic which had more to lose from strict enforcement of the non-intervention agreement, just when significant supplies originating from the Soviet Union were beginning to reach its Mediterranean ports.

Although a marginal diplomatic arena with regard to the situation in Spain, the League of Nations was also a place where Portugal rendered some services to the insurgents, either by boycotting every attempt to convey a special General Assembly session on the "Spanish question," or by portraying a number of initiatives concerning possible mediation, or the provision of humanitarian relief, as an "indirect" form of interference on behalf of the Republic. When the Spanish crisis was finally discussed during the 18th General Assembly of the League, between September 18 and 20, 1937, the Portuguese delegate, José Caeiro da Matta, replied to the accusations of the Republic's foreign minister, Juan Negrín, by asserting the New State's position in very blunt terms: "It is true that we desire, with all our hearts – today more than ever – the triumph of Spanish Nationalism, and for the simple reason that we all know that the absorption of Portugal by Spain is one of the aspirations of Iberian Communism."[34] After the debate in the plenary sessions, Negrin's dramatic appeal for the approval of a resolution demanding the repatriation of all "non-Spanish combatants" would be defeated by the abstentions of 14 member states, and the negative votes of Albania and Portugal.

But perhaps the single most decisive diplomatic maneuver to be credited to Salazar on Franco's behalf was his mediating role with the British. Once the stalemate in Spain began to look more favorable to the Nationalist side, by mid-1937, Salazar patiently began to build a line of reasoning to justify Britain's approach to the Francoist camp, even if London was not yet ready to sever its diplomatic ties with the Republican authorities. Needless to say, Salazar was all too aware of Spain's strategic significance to Britain. First and foremost, what was at stake was the security of the Gibraltar Mediterranean route: the Baleares and the Canary Islands could not be allowed to fall into enemy hands, and the Strait of Gibraltar should preferably be controlled by a weak but friendly Spain. Above all, Britain could not run the risk of watching Spain becoming the pawn of a hostile coalition of powers.[35] All these premises soon became threatened by Franco's massive reliance on the backing of Germany and Italy, two likely adversaries of the UK in a future European conflagration. Portugal saw here an opportunity to exploit British strategic anxieties and persuade London that Franco's supreme desire was to be "rescued" from the Nazi-Fascist "embrace" (knowing full well that, for the moment, this was far from the truth). At a time when the appeasement doctrine was about to reach its peak, with the appointment of Neville Chamberlain as prime minister in May 1937, there were indeed some sympathetic ears in the Foreign Office to this line of thinking. In fact, it is now clear that since the early months of the conflict there was already a current of opinion in Whitehall that believed that Franco did not represent a threat to British interests; in fact, most likely he would be a factor of stability and, moreover, someone who could bring significant political and financial benefits to Britain.[36] On October 22, 1937, after the conclusion of the "Northern campaign" by Nationalist forces, the British Cabinet decided to designate a "special agent", the diplomat Robert Hodgson, to be in close contact with General Franco, a step suggesting that de facto recognition of the Burgos junta was about to take place. The British move was a sign that

Salazar needed to proceed in the same direction. He again chose a high-profile emissary, Teotónio Pereira – who in the meantime had also become involved in the creation of the Portuguese Legion, a paramilitary organization roughly modelled after the Italian MVSN (Black Shirts), which reinforced the Fascist outlook of the New State – to be his eyes and ears in Franco's Spain, a post he would held until 1944.

The Hubris of the Falange

Interestingly, it was Teotónio Pereira who gradually became deeply suspicious of the true intentions harbored by certain sectors of the Spanish Falange toward Portugal.[37] This sense of unease regarding the closeness between the Francoist camp and the totalitarian powers and its potential threat to Portugal's integrity had been discernible among Portuguese military circles, particularly those of a more Anglophile inclination, since 1937. Spain would emerge from the conflict physically and economically exhausted, but with a strong army – whereas Portugal was still in the process of modernizing its own appallingly inefficient and underequipped forces. Portugal's consul in Salamanca, for instance, could not help noticing the "mystique of exalted imperialism and the openly declared cult of violence" which permeated the leadership of the Falange. And to add a "graphic" dimension to his warnings, Vasco da Cunha thought it important to mention the circulation of a Falange newspaper in San Sebastian with a map of the Iberian Peninsula devoid of political frontiers and headed by the word *Unidad*, "the innocent title of the newspaper."[38] More expressions of worry were voiced in the ensuing months by several observers of the situation in Spain, including diplomats, journalists, and members of the Portuguese Military Observation Mission with the Francoist forces.[39] Nazi Germany's presence, for instance, was considered by the journalist Armando Boaventura a nefarious influence which threatened to undermine the "traditional affection" of the Spanish people toward the Portuguese.[40] The rising star of Serrano Suñer, Franco's brother-in-law, to the detriment of more moderate elements, such as the traditional Monarchists, was another disquieting development noted by the Portuguese. "Franco's victory will give imperialist wings to his followers and will resurrect the old ambitions of an Iberian union," telegraphed Monteiro from London on April 1938, noting on another occasion that Portugal's contribution to the Nationalist side was now in the process of being "effaced," with Berlin and Rome claiming all the credit for the success of the uprising.[41] Gradually, Salazar was forced to realize that the black-

and-white, Manichean picture of the conflict, presenting the Republic as the sole threat to Portugal's security, was no longer a credible frame for making sense of what was going on Spain. Therefore, in the speech in which he announced the imminent de jure recognition of Franco's government, on April 28, 1938, Salazar decided to allude to some "deviations" in what he considered should be the "healthy" orientation of Nationalist Spain. Those elements should be in no doubt as to the "irreducible fact of the peninsula's duality, against which the federalist traditions of the two republics, as well as the imperialist tradition of Philip II, were impotent."[42]

The "hubristic" state of mind which Salazar and other observers feared was prevailing in Burgos made him hesitate when Franco approached him in October 1938, at the height of the Sudeten crisis, to propose the building of a "common neutrality policy, with the guarantee of common frontiers": namely, a non-aggression pact. From London, his ambassador advised him to proceed with caution, arguing that such a pact could give the impression that all Franco wanted was to secure his rearguard in order to have his hands free to attack France, due to his long-standing ambitions regarding the French empire in North Africa. Monteiro thought it dangerous for Portugal to commit itself to such an agreement at an extremely volatile juncture in Europe, and his warnings were taken into consideration by Salazar, who decided to postpone his reply to the Spanish foreign minister, the Count of Jordana. He was also adamant that Portugal's alliance with Britain be mentioned in the text, where an allusion was made to the "non-alteration of previous relationships."[43] On March 17, 1939, a few days before the end of the conflict, the two governments finally signed the Treaty of Friendship and Non-Aggression. They made a pledge "to respect each other's frontiers and territories"; to abstain from "committing acts of aggression" against one another; to "refrain from assisting a third aggressor," or "entering into a pact or alliance against the other party"; and to always safeguard "the compromises defined in the pact" in any future commitments with third parties.[44] In the "Darwinist" setting of international politics of the late 1930s, such agreements had, of course, a limited value – its announcement coincided with the disintegration of what was left of Czechoslovakia and the occupation of Bohemia and Moravia by Germany (not to mention Franco's decision to join the Anti-Comintern Pact on March 27, 1939, which he kept secret from Salazar until its public disclosure a few days later).[45] Until 1942, at least, Franco would lean dangerously toward the Axis in order to see if he could take advantage of France's enfeeblement and claim territorial gains in Morocco, or even in Portugal, in a scenario of a war with Britain.[46] For his part, Salazar would employ all his diplomatic skills to make sure that, at least, Franco could find in Portugal a trustworthy friend which would allow him to reconnect with Britain and distance himself from the Fascist powers. When the civil war came to a close, with Franco's triumphant entry into Madrid, on April 1, 1939, Salazar delivered a speech in which he also claimed his share of the victory, but in a tone that was significantly less assured than his pronouncements on the Spanish question made three years previously (and issued instructions that the participation of the Portuguese Viriatos in the victory parade be as discreet as possible).

Conclusions

Over the last few years, a revisionist literature has attempted to reinterpret Salazarist foreign policy in the period 1936 45 in a way that gives greater weight to the role of ideology, and questions some of the classic assumptions on the New State's neutrality policy in the Second World War. According to this school of thought, far from being a mere Catholic reactionary, imbued with classic notions of raison d'état, Salazar was in fact much closer to other modern autocrats than his post-1945 propaganda, or even some contemporary historians, would like to concede. For authors such as Manuel Loff, Salazarist Portugal was every bit as Fascist – or even as totalitarian – as Mussolini's Italy or Francoist Spain. The Spanish Civil War played a role in bringing about radicalization of the regime, as evidenced by the creation of Fascist-type militias such as the Mocidade Portuguesa (Portuguese youth), the Legião Portuguesa (Portuguese legion), and the Obra das Mães para a Educação Nacional (mother's work for national education); the encouragement given to the creation of "corporatist" trade unions (*sindicatos nacionais*); and the hardening of the repressive apparatus of the state, with the opening of the first concentration camp for political prisoners.[47] This "Fascist impetus" would go on well into the Second World War and manifest itself not only in the complicity between Salazar and the Axis powers at key junctures of the war (particularly in the domain of economic warfare), but also in the enthusiasm with which Hitler's plans for a "New European Order" (as well as Germany's assault on the USSR in 1941), were allegedly greeted by Salazar and other high-ranking officials and ideologues, at least until the fortunes of the war turned against Nazi Germany.[48]

Although some of these points may ring true for some, the gist of the argument is not, in my view, entirely convincing. In many of its facets, the New State could hardly be reduced to the condition of being merely a repressive illiberal regime; rather it can be said to have pursued a "total" project for the transformation of society along nationalist/ Catholic/ traditionalist lines, and it proved that it could be ruthlessly efficient in its "preventive" use of state violence.[49]

A close study of Salazar's conduct throughout the Spanish Civil War makes quite clear that this was a crisis that helped the Portuguese premier to reconsider some of his certainties with regard to the benefits that could be derived from any sort of "Fascist fraternity" in the peninsula. While his virulent anti-Communism and scorn for liberal democracy were never seriously shaken – they remained part and parcel of his core ideological beliefs right up to the end of his life – Salazar became much more acutely aware of the menaces that could emerge from a European continent dominated by the totalitarian powers and their apparently insatiable appetite for conquest. As the leader of a country who had no irredentist or expansionist designs, either in Europe or in Africa, he was an essentially pro-status quo statesman, a believer in the virtues of the balance of power and the rights and freedoms of small European states. This – and the fact that Portugal's domestic economy and overseas empire were highly dependent on British trade, investment, and military protection – made him a politician naturally inclined to favor Britain's lead in European and world affairs. With its broadly elitist profile, honest commercial ethos and love of tradition, Britain in the 1930s was a liberal great power with which Salazar could do business (as opposed to the French Republic, for instance). He was a great admirer of many of the achievements of Fascist Italy (starting with its corporatist legislation, an important source of inspiration for the New State) and was ready to accept that Germany should be treated on an equal footing by Britain and France, not least because it constituted a formidable bulwark against Russian Bolshevism (according to Salazar, Germany was the "frontiersman" who guarded Europe against the "Slav invader"). But in many other respects, he seemed genuinely taken aback by some of the emblematic features of the right-wing totalitarian regimes of interwar Europe, both in domestic and international terms ("to live habitually," was his favorite slogan, in contrast with Mussolini's motto, "to live dangerously").[50] Hence, by 1939 he seemed to have acquired a more sober view of international politics: as well as being an ideological contest between the forces of "order" and "revolution," it was also one of power politics, of old geopolitical ambitions reasserting themselves under new guises. Therefore, Portuguese foreign policy should be guided by the "permanent" factors that had allowed the country to retain its independence throughout most of its history, and this required a very fine balance between its alliance with Britain and its relationship with Spain and other continental powers. Salazarist Portugal and Francoist Spain would undoubtedly form a singular partnership up until the mid-1970s – cemented by the so-called Iberian or Peninsular Pact of 1939 (slightly expanded in 1940) – but the Portuguese made sure that, geopolitically, they remained oriented toward the Atlantic, "with their backs turned against Spain."

Notes

1 See Hermínio Martins, "O federalismo no pensamento político português," *Penélope*, no. 18 (1998): 13–49.

2 On Portuguese reactions to the institution of the Second Republic, see César Oliveira, *Portugal e a II República de Espanha 1931–1936* (Lisbon: Perspectivas & Realidades, 1985), and Hipolito de la Torre Goméz, *A Relação Peninsular na Antecâmara da Guerra Civil de Espanha 1931–1936* (Lisbon: Ed. Cosmos, 1998). For a broader time frame, see César Oliveira, *Cem Anos nas Relações Luso-Espanholas* (Lisbon: Cosmos, 1995), and José Miguel Sardica, *Iberia. A Relação Peninsular no Século XX* (Lisboa: Aletheia, 2013).

3 Hipolito de la Torre Gómez, "La conspiración iberista de Manuel Azaña," in *Portugal e a Guerra Civil de Espanha*, ed. Fernando Rosas (Lisbon: Colibri, 1998), 213.

4 Luís Farinha, "1931: A Ditadura face ao 'perigo espanhol'," *História* (December 1995): 4–13.

5 Even so, in 1932 Salazar felt confident enough to declare that "the process of parliamentary democracy is concluded; its crisis is universal; . . . an era has come to an end, irrevocably." Quoted by Bernardo Futscher Pereira, *A Diplomacia de Salazar* (Lisbon: Dom Quixote, 2012), 26.

6 See, for instance, some of the comments made by British diplomats in the 1920s, stressing the necessity of a "strong man" in Portugal, in Glyn Stone, "No Way to Treat an Ancient Ally: Britain and the Portuguese Connection, 1919–1933," in *Peacemaking, Peacemakers and Diplomacy 1880–1939: Essays in Honour of Professor Alan Sharp*, ed. Gaynor Johnson (Newcastle-upon-Tyne: Cambridge Scholars Publications, 2010), 223–52.

7 The suppression of the Asturian rebellion (4–19 October) was ordered by Alejandro Lerroux's government, and ruthlessly carried out by General Franco, provoking high casualities among the miners (conservative estimates mention 1 000 lost lives and at least 15 000 prisoners). See, among others, Antony Beevor, *The Battle for Spain. The Spanish Civil War 1936–1939* (London: Penguin Books, 2006): 30–32.

8 César Oliveira, *Salazar e a Guerra Civil de Espanha*, 2nd ed. (Lisbon: Ed. O Jornal, 1988).

9 Pedro Aires Oliveira, "Portugal e a Crise Italo-Abissina," *Ler História*, no. 42 (2002): 5–28.

10 For the concept of "mental map," see Steven Casey and Jonathan Wright, eds., *Mental Maps in the Era of Two World Wars* (Basingstoke: Palgrave-Macmillan, 2008).

11 Paul Preston, *Franco: A Biography* (London: Harper Collins, 1993), 375.
12 The Necessidades Palace is the building where the Ministry of Foreign Affairs is located in Lisbon.
13 Arquivo Histórico-Diplomático do MNE (AHD–MNE), Armário de Ferro, "Guerra Civil e Outros Assuntos de Espanha. Parecer "confidencialíssimo" de Luiz Teixeira de Sampayo," February 7, 1935.
14 António Ferro, *Entrevistas de António Ferro a Salazar* (Lisbon: Parceria A. M. Pereira, 2003).
15 António Oliveira Salazar, *Discursos e Notas Políticas 1935–1937*, 2nd ed. (Coimbra: Coimbra Ed., 1945), 80–81.
16 Quoted by Valentim Alexandre, *O Roubo das Almas: Salazar, a Igreja e os Totalitarismos 1930–1939* (Lisbon: Dom Quixote, 2006), 52.
17 For an introduction to Salazar's early trajectory and ideological education, see Filipe Ribeiro de Menezes, *Salazar: A Political Biography* (New York: Enigma Books, 2009); also Alexandre, *O Roubo das Almas*, chap. 1.
18 Sardica, *Iberia*, 116.
19 AHD–MNE, 2º P, A 47, M 70. "Statement (*parecer*) read by Armindo Monteiro at a Cabinet Meeting," January 1936.
20 Ibid.
21 See Monteiro's account in *Dez Anos de Política Externa*, vol. 3. doc. 2, 5–6. For Eden's own account, see his dispatch to Ambassador Charles Wingfield, March 21, 1936, The National Archives (TNA) FO 453 413 (confidential print).
22 The Spanish ambassador, Claudio Sanchez-Albornoz, reported to Madrid that Salazar might have influenced the facilitation of a loan of 2,800,000 escudos from Bank Fonsecas & Viana to Gil Robles in order to finance the military coup against the republic. See Sardica, *Iberia*, 126.
23 On the conspiracy to overthrow the republic and its Portuguese ramifications, see Francisco Alia Miranda, *Julio de 1936: Conspiración y alzamiento contra la Segunda República* (Barcelona: Crítica, 2011), and Angel Viñas, *La Conspiración del General Franco*, rev. ed. (Barcelona: Crítica, 2012).
24 The standard account of Salazar's involvement in the conflict remains César Oliveira, *Salazar e a Guerra Civil de Espanha*. See also the pioneering work by Iva Delgado, *Portugal e a Guerra Civil de Espanha* (Mem Martins: Europa-América, 1980).
25 See Comissão sobre o Livro Negro do Regime Fascista, *Correspondência de Pedro Teotónio Pereira para Oliveira Salazar*, vol. 1, doc. 27 (Lisbon: CLSRF, 1987), 54–56.
26 See César Oliveira, *Salazar e a Guerra Civil de Espanha*, 140–55, and José Ángel Sánchez Asiaín, *La Financiación de la Guerra Civil Española: Una aproximación histórica* (Barcelona: Crítica, 2012).
27 See António Pedro Vicente, "O Cerco à embaixada da República Espanhola em Lisboa (Maio a Outubro de 1936)," in *Portugal e a Guerra Civil de Espanha*, ed. Fernando Rosas (Lisbon: Colibri, 1998), 3–105; and, more recently, Alberto Pena Rodríguez, *Salazar y Franco:La alianza del fascismo*

ibérico contra la España republicana: diplomacia, prensa y propaganda (Gijón: Trea, 2017), chap. 9.

28 See Alberto Pena Rodríguez, *Salazar, a Imprensa e a Guerra Civil de Espanha* (Coimbra: Minerva Ed., 2007), and *O Que Parece É. Salazar, Franco e a Propaganda contra a Espanha Democrática* (Lisbon: Tinta da China, 2009).

29 See Nelson Ribeiro, "Using a New Medium for Propaganda: The Role of Transborder Broadcasts during the Spanish Civil War," *Media, War & Conflict* 71, no. 1 (2014): 37–50.

30 César Oliveira, *Salazar e a Guerra Civil de Espanha*, 243–55. A doctoral dissertation on the topic is currently being carried out at the Institute of Contemporary History in Lisbon, by Rui Aballe Vieira.

31 See Fernando Rosas, *O Salazarismo e a Aliança Luso-Britânica* (Lisbon: Fragmentos, 1988), and Glyn Stone, *The Oldest Ally: Britain and the Portuguese Connection, 1936–1941* (Woodbridge, Suffolk: Boydell, 1994).

32 See Pedro Aires Oliveira, *Armindo Monteiro: Uma Biografia Política* (Venda Nova: Bertrand, 2000), 156–65.

33 For Monteiro's performance in the Non-Intervention Committee, see Pedro Aires Oliveira, *Armindo Monteiro*, 171–77, and Luís Soares de Oliveira, *Guerra Civil de Espanha. Intervenção e Não Intervenção Europeia: Uma Análise*, 2nd ed. (Lisbon: Instituto Diplomático, 2013).

34 Rosas, *O Salazarismo*, 95.

35 Michael Alpert, *A New International History of the Spanish Civil War*, 2nd ed. (Basingstoke: Macmillan, 2004), 16. See also Enrique Moradiellos, "La politica británica ante la guerra civil española," *Espacio, Tempo y Forma*, no. 5 (1992): 185–210, who stresses the relevance of a "preventive anti-revolutionary" predisposition in the behavior of Conservative governments in Whitehall before the outbreak of the civil war.

36 Alpert, *A New International History*, 196. See also Peter Day, *Franco's Friends: How British Intelligence Helped Bring Franco to Power in Spain* (London: Biteback, 2011).

37 César Oliveira, *Salazar e a Guerra Civil de Espanha*, 261–62.

38 Alexandre, *O Roubo das Almas*, 308.

39 See Rui Aballe Vieira, *Tomar o Pulso ao Tigre: Missões Militares Portuguesas em Espanha, entre a vigilância e a cooperação 1934–1939* (MA dissertation, FCSH-UNL, 2011), 103–4.

40 Ibid., 326.

41 Pedro Aires Oliveira, *Armindo Monteiro*, 175.

42 António Oliveira Salazar, *Discursos e Notas Políticas 1938–1945*, vol. III, 83.

43 See Pedro Aires Oliveira, *Armindo Monteiro*, 175–77.

44 On the pact and its context, see César Oliveira, *Salazar e a Guerra Civil de Espanha*, 349–66.

45 Pereira, *A Diplomacia de Salazar*, 182.

46 This was a possibility contemplated in an invasion plan approved by Franco, "Plan de Campaña número – I – (34)," on December 18, 1940, as revealed in Manuel Ros Agudo, *La Gran Tentatción: Franco, el Imperio Colonial y los*

planes de intervención en la Segunda Guerra Mundial (Madrid: Styria, 2008), 271–72.

47 The Tarrafal Camp in Cape Verde, opened in 1936 with the incarceration of Portuguese Community Party militants and sailors who had mutinied aboard three warships in Lisbon on September 8, 1936, as a gesture of solidarity with the Spanish Republic. See Gisela Oliveira, *A Revolta dos Marinheiros de 1936* (Venda Nova: Comissão de Homenagem à Revolta dos Marinheiros de 8 de Setembro de 1936, 2009).

48 See Manuel Loff, *O Nosso Século É Fascista! O Mundo Visto por Salazar e Franco 1936–1945* (Porto: Campo das Letras, 2008). For a critical appraisal of his views, see Bruno C. Reis, "Este século não foi fascista. Salazar, Franco e a efémera nova ordem internacional nazi-fascista," *Relações Internacionais*, no. 27 (2010): 129–38.

49 See Rosas, "O Salazarismo e o homem novo," 1031–54.

50 A good discussion of Salazarism in the context of European authoritarianism and Fascism can be found in António Costa Pinto, *The Salazar's Dictatorship and European Fascism* (New York: SSM–Columbia University Press, 1995).

7

Italy 1936: From Consensus to First Doubts about the Regime

Luciano Casali

> In the current social organization, public approval is crucial for any major project. So a movement, though worthy of all praise, may fail if it does not imprint its image in the public mind. The use of propaganda, carefully adjusted to the mentality of the masses, constitutes an essential complement to political life.
>
> (Edward Bernays, 1928)

Proclamation of the Empire

There were two "spontaneous" manifestations (but, in fact, they were carefully prepared) that were intended to highlight, both for Italians and for foreign policy purposes, that Fascism had performed a remarkable leap of quality and could now be presented to Europe as one of the world's greatest powers, and as such, it now had to be taken into consideration. On the eve of May 9, 1936 (specifically, at 10:30 p.m.), Mussolini spoke from the central balcony of Palazzo Venezia to Rome, delivering a live theatrical-like performance, thanks to its careful orchestration, including the use of lights projected up to the balcony and into the crowd. Thus, the effect of the speech was accentuated. Even the words Mussolini pronounced had been carefully chosen:[1] the new Fascist Italy was back on the *colli fatali* [fatal hills] of ancient Rome; Ethiopia had been conquered, and the Roman Empire was reborn.

A few days earlier, on May 5, the Duce declared that that same day, at 4:00 p.m., Marshal Pietro Badoglio, "head of the victorious troops," had entered Addis Ababa. After seven months the war in East Africa was over and Ethiopia had become Italian[2]: "Italian in reality, because it is occupied by our glorious armed forces; Italian by law because with the *sword of Rome* it is civilization that triumphs over barbarism, justice that triumphs over unlawful cruelty, the redemption of the weak that triumphs over millennial slavery." Mussolini reminded them of his efforts – when he had begun the war – to ensure that "an African conflict would not expand into a European war. I have kept that commitment, and I am more than ever convinced that disturbing Europe's peace means to bring Europe down." The head of the Italian government could thus announce to "the Black Shirts of the Revolution" and to "the men and women of Italy" that "a step in their journey" had been made. Now he would continue "to march in peace, for the tasks that are awaiting us tomorrow that we will face with our courage, our faith, and our will."[3]

In reality, if examined carefully, these were not calming words, especially if one bears in mind what Mussolini had said a few weeks before, on March 23, at Campidoglio during the National Assembly of Corporations:

> Safe within its borders, thanks to the mass of its weapons and the spirit of its fighters, equipped with political and social instruments that are increasingly adapted to the conditions of life and to the evolution of times in advance of all the countries of the world, the Italian people today, thanks to Fascism, have unleashed the road to an ever-increasing power.[4]

And they appear even less soothing if we re-read the words that would be pronounced once again from a balcony, in this case, from the town hall in the City of Bologna on October 24, that same year, overlooking a square packed with a cheering crowd. Mussolini had not visited that city for a long time.. His last visit to Emilia's capital dated back to October 31, 1926, when he had been the target of an attack, after which he no longer wished to return):[5]

> It is therefore a great olive branch that I raise at the end of the year xiv [the Fascist era] and at the beginning of the year xv.
> Warning! This olive tree stands out in an immense forest: it is the forest of eight million bayonets, well sharpened and clutched by young intrepid hearts![6]

Nevertheless, May 9 was a particularly exciting date because on that solemn occasion the "Fascist Empire" was proclaimed, and the King of Italy, Vittorio Emanuele III, was declared emperor.

It is worth transcribing part of the speech Mussolini made then:

> All ties were cut off by our shining sword and the African victory remained in the history of the homeland, pure and whole, as the fallen and surviving legionaries had dreamed and desired. Italy finally has its empire. Fascist Empire, because it carries the indestructible signs of the will and power of the Roman Symbol, because this is the goal which for fourteen years the overwhelming and disciplined energy of young, vigorous Italian generations have striven to achieve. Empire of peace, because Italy wants peace for itself and for all and chooses war only when it is forced by the imperious, insuppressible necessities of life; empire of civility and humanity for all the people of Ethiopia . . .
>
> The Italian people created the empire with their blood. They will fertilize it with dedication and defend it against anyone with its weapons.
>
> In this supreme certainty, stand up, oh legionnaires, insignias, iron, and hearts, to greet, after fifteen centuries, the reappearance of the empire on the fatal hills of Rome.
>
> Will you be worthy of it? [The crowd erupts with a tremendous "Yes!"].
>
> This cry is like a sacred oath, which binds you before God and before men, for life and for death![7]

Among the great nations of Europe, Italy's colonial possessions were of shorter duration (from 1882 to 1944) and the country itself was territorially smaller – as well as economically less productive. The resonance of the 1936 conquest undoubtedly subtracted the country from an "inferiority complex vis-à-vis the great colonizers of Europe;"[8] but the fact that Italy, with these new achievements, declared that it possessed an "empire" also meant that Fascist occupation was distinct from previous territorial acquisitions and conferred on the country a particular "dignity and prestige."[9] Fascist propaganda led to the belief that the colonial conquest, presented ideally as a continuation of the Roman past, was almost an entitlement for Italy, precisely because it had its roots in imperial Rome, in the magnificent domains of *Roma caput mundi.* It was this sign of power and greatness that was offered to the Italians. At the two *adunate oceaniche* (enormous rallies) of May 1936, Mussolini, "doubling the oratorical fervor with the theatricality of his presentation, reached the peak of his potential and probably the success he sought with the crowds."[10] These speeches were composed of "a perfectly orchestrated set of voices, with monotonous and threatening tones, inflections, pauses, screams, gestures, and glares." His "spectacular speeches" succeeded in exploiting "with fine expertise, all that could touch and excite the imagination"[11] of the public. The conquest of Ethiopia and the proclamation of the empire were an appropriate moment of propaganda that undoubtedly characterized the "years of consensus." As Renzo De Felice wrote, "the Duce's prestige had never been so high and would never be in the years to come,"[12] In part, this was because numerous Italians, convinced by his words, would seek their fortune in the newborn empire. No doubt these were many more than the regime wanted; the latter planned to permit emigration only to "Italians filtered through a selection process."[13] Mussolini and the regime were aware that it was far more difficult to maintain a consensus thousands of miles from Rome. Therefore, in order to avoid the spread of dissatisfaction, it would be best if those who went to Africa be committed Fascists, who above all were trustworthy. On the other hand, from the second half of the 1930s, even in Italy, with the rise of economic hardship and the regime's failure to maintain its promise of full employment, which would provide well-being in exchange for consensus, discontent became increasingly more evident. As of 1936, since emigration to Ethiopia was therefore an opportunity (and a hope) to overcome economic difficulties, it was not easy to curb departures for those lands and to that empire, described by propaganda as rich and full of prospects for everyone.[14] The possibility of work and well-being were at the center of propaganda: "There were those who departed imbued with imperial fervor, those who followed a desire for adventure, those who wanted to change their lives and start from scratch, and those who set off in an attempt to escape . . . unemployment and poverty."[15]

Yet the lands conquered for the empire were far from rich and what they offered was insufficient to overcome the economic difficulties that prevailed in the peninsula.

Shape New Italians; Give Weapons Back to the *Miles Romanus*[16]

"The character of the Italians must be created in the fight," Mussolini had declared to Foreign Minister Galeazzo Ciano on November 13, 1937.[17] This statement was repeated countless times in different ways, perfectly placed within a will to give life to a "new man" and in which found – as Emilio Gentile reminds us – in the "soldier citizen" his accomplishment.[18] This "soldier citizen" had to be constructed through "information" transmitted to him in the form of a vision of a heroic and "fighting Italy"; moreover, he would have had to distance himself from the "narrow boundaries" which resulted with the conclusion of World War I.

"Constructing the news" thus became the priority task of journalists during the Fascist era. It was not just about reporting the (obligatory) evolution of events, "often at the expense of the credibility of the action and the decisions taken."[19] On the other hand, Mussolini had been a journalist and editor of newspapers from when he began to dabble in politics. As a result of his mentality and attitude toward the Italians, who he believed could be shaped precisely through journalism, he continued to highlight the press as the main tool for propaganda and the construction of the mind-set of the masses. Above all, with this device, he thought it possible to "impress upon the country a 'national' and Fascist spirit with which every citizen would have had to identify."[20] Thus, not only did the problem of censoring unwanted news exist – an issue that was dealt with comprehensively by the Duce himself – but it was crucial to know exactly what to say and how to say it, when opting for a line of action or information: to decide and direct when to release information, what to hide, and what – when necessary – to invent completely. In fact, it was necessary *to build the news*, because in this way Mussolini thought it was possible *to build Italians*; or rather, the new Italians who would constitute the Fascist Empire.

In other words, the regime "used ideas 'ideologically', without any regard to whether they were true or not, and it knew how to manipulate public opinion to the point that it was a 'publicized' opinion, or rather a 'prefabricated' one."[21]

Many journalists, even leading ones who had written important articles, accepted or pleaded to receive money or favors, placing themselves in the position of being corrupted by the regime's offices or directly by Mussolini himself, volunteering to distribute and manipulate provisions, agendas, and news of all kinds, or agreeing not to disclose unwelcome news.[22] Often, there was no need for direct censorship, as "good journalists" understood themselves what should be divulged to readers and how to convey news.

In order to construct a general line of information for circulation, so-called *veline* [press orders originally copied on tissue paper], printed orders that the Ministry of Folk Culture (Minculpop) had been issuing since the early 1930s, were of great importance. The image of Fascist Italy emerging from these press releases is that of a country that did not exist: geared solely to the Fascist cause, driven by constant enthusiasm for Mussolini, his statements and his agenda, untroubled in any way by problems, ready for military mobilization and war.[23] All this enabled a genuine "efficiency in the system from the point of view of the regime's requirements and aspirations"[24] and the application of systematic procedures to the construction of imperial Italians.

Reconstructing the ways in which propaganda was created in order to build an enthusiastic consensus on the Ethiopian war, Enrica Bricchetto shows how imperial Fascist policy became more explicit in the 1930s, underlining the "necessity" to revitalize an army that would be capable of reproducing, for those "fatal hills," that empire that ancient Rome had already attained. As was the case two thousand years before, all Italians had to be able to take up weapons, and the "Fascist militia" had to become *miles romanus* again.[25] After 1932, according to Esmonde Robertson, Fascist Italy was "no longer on the defense, it was now ready to revive the myth of imperial Rome."[26] Many decisions took place on this basis, even if not explicitly. When, for example, on March 31, 1934, Mussolini and Italo Balbo, the famous aviator, met with Spanish traditionalists visiting Rome, they signed a protocol of political and military assistance. This was not simply due to their liking of Spanish right-wing anti-Republicans, as much as a step further in Fascism's strategy of "expanding its ideological bases even before the military ones."[27] This was a new stage for the Italians in imperial politics within the authoritarian and "Fascist" trend that was advancing in Europe.[28] It could almost be argued that Mussolini and Ciano were not particularly attentive to the requests that the Spaniards made to them, since they were concerned merely with the construction of "alliances" and contacts in accordance with the imperialist policies of Fascist Italy.[29] Two years after that meeting, Italy's participation in the Spanish Civil War was not simply – as opposed to the arguments of John Coverdale and Renzo De Felice[30] – a geostrategic intervention for the control of the western Mediterranean, almost an incidental thing; many scholars are now convinced that the Italian intervention in Spain occurred only as a consequence, and was almost an imitation, of the aid Hitler's Germany had sent to Francisco Franco.

It should, however, be understood that Fascist foreign policy since the institution of Mussolini's government, had immediately been imperialistic and aggressive, "hiding" behind the slogan of a "mutilated victory" after World War I (historical slogan referring to the inadequate compensation of territories even though Italy had won). A quick look at the Fascist government's foreign policy reveals a series of such episodes: reconciliation with Libya, aggressiveness toward Tunisia, "attention" to Yugoslavia (with the financing and training of the Ustaša), the claiming of Corsica, Nice, and Savoy, the occupation of Rijeka and Corfu (the latter already in 1923), the progressive control of Albania until its conquest, and its policy toward Bulgaria with the marriage of Giovanna di Savoia and Czar Boris III, as well as its "friendship" with Romania.

As can be seen, Mussolini's imperialist attention was not only directed toward the Mediterranean and Africa, but also toward central-eastern Europe and the Middle East. Most importantly, it should be kept in mind that Mussolini was not willing to recognize the validity of the balance of power that had been established since World War I in Balkan-Danubian Europe, at the cost of destroying the difficult and delicate equilibrium that had been achieved[31].

It was therefore a crucial part of national policy that Italians become warriors, as they had been two thousand years earlier, and to sacrifice themselves, because "sacrifice was necessary if you want to create a bold and strong soul."[32] What was needed were Italians who were deeply convinced of the Fascist regime, its superiority, and its ideologies.

Consensus, Fascism, and Volunteering in the Spanish Civil War

The proclamation of the empire was at the heart of the intense propaganda that was widespread in a detailed manner: the Italians, having re-conquered an empire, had returned to being invincible fighters and had to continue to fight in order to make the nation greater and stronger. From a strategic point of view, Italy had the potential to progress from the status of "first-class European power" to world power.[33] Due to its greater importance since (as of June 1936) its occupation of the islands of the Aegean Sea (Rhodes became a base for eventual bombing operations throughout the entire eastern Mediterranean basin[34]), it was faced with a possible war against Great Britain, and also a possible Mediterranean war against France, which would thus involve the great western islands (Corsica, Sardinia, Sicily, and Pantelleria, as well as Tunisia).[35] Special attention to the Balearics was therefore understandable, since they constituted an actual "bridge" between mainland France and Tunisia. It was no coincidence, then, that in September 1936 Mussolini was planning an "ambitious large-scale military intervention" in Majorca, where Arconovaldo Bonacorsi and other Fascists had been sent to oversee the activity of the Falange,[36] and on September 3, Great Britain warned that maintaining the status quo in the western Mediterranean was one of its major concerns.[37] In 1937, Hitler himself urged Mussolini to "never abandon Majorca again, a new formidable pawn in our Mediterranean game."[38]

As Morten Heiberg states, the main feature of Mussolini's foreign policy was continuing aggression, and intervention in Spain constituted an excellent occasion to prove this strategy by upsetting the balance of power in Europe; the birth of a third Fascist regime would have been perfect alongside Italy and Germany.[39]

Just a few months after the war in East Africa officially ended, talk began about the possibility of intervening in Spain, where a civil war had broken out in July after a failed coup, and its commander, General Francisco Franco, asked for help from Hitler and Mussolini. It is therefore appropriate to ask the following questions: Were the Italians ready to help Franco in order to support Mussolini's power policy? Were they "enthusiastic" about participating in a new conflict, as urged by Fascist propaganda? If the answers to the above questions were positive, we might ask how deep and widespread this consensus was?

Irene Di Jorio, who carried out a detailed study of the mass media of the Fascist-type state organized by Marshal Pétain in France, pointed out that probably in no other case was so much money invested, nor were so many specialists involved in the organization of propaganda, as there were in Vichy France. Complex instruments were applied in all fields: from radio to cinema, to printed publicity, and to demonstrations of all kinds. Yet Pétain and his men experienced complete failure and were unable to convince the majority of the French of the importance of fighting alongside the Germans. The clandestine leaflets of the anti-Fascist resistance, ugly, and badly printed and illustrated, were much more appreciated and sought after than the glossy Vichy magazines, full of beautiful photos and occasional articles by famous writers.[40]

Reading what might be considered the "official story" of the Italian participation in the Spanish Civil War (we can consider it "official," because it was published by the Ufficio storico dello Stato maggiore dell'Esercito italiano),[41] it may be concluded that the Italians were completely in agreement with the Fascist call to fight in Spain. Reconstructing the military events there, generals Alberto Rovighi and Filippo Stefani praised the participation of Italians who volunteered to fight alongside Francisco Franco.

Although quite lengthy, it is worth reproducing the entire quote:

> The documented truth is the absolute free will of the those in combat . . .
>
> The great majority of Italians were on the Spanish insurrectionists' side from the beginning. On the other hand, the way it was presented, propounded, and supported by the regime's press and radio, as Italy fighting to defend itself against Communism and anarchy, could not in that moment and in that situation fail to obtain the consent of most Italians who considered intervention a means to safeguard those traditional ideals that the majority recognized. This consensus concurred with the regime's propaganda, the reduced accessibility of other sources of information, the trust and prestige acquired by Mussolini after the conquest of the empire, and the discreet but clear support of the Catholic Church . . .

> In such a national atmosphere, it should not be surprising that there were many applications to fight in Spain and that part of them were motivated by idealism . . . In fact, the requests exceeded the number of recruits needed for the OMS [Oltre Mare Spagna; Overseas Spain].[42]

This differs little from the observations penned a few years later by Massimiliano Griner, who, "based essentially on the memoirs of a number of convinced Fascists,"[43] argued that most of the participants "were in Spain only by choice," demonstrating "concrete and direct proof of [their] faith in Fascism."[44]

The determination and lack of doubt with which Rovighi and Stefani claimed that it would be sufficient to do a careful archival search (as did D'Alessandro) in order to disprove that "the volunteer formula was adopted in a pretentious and instrumental way by Italy and Germany, with the support of European democratic powers, solely in order to bypass the commitment of 'non-intervention'," [45] was thus not surprising. In any event, the propaganda was very intense and precise: from mid-1936 to the end of the war Italian newspapers dedicated thousands of background articles, items, and commentaries on that theme.[46] Voluntary enlistment and conviction were present, although not among everyone; nor were they limited or superficial. As Fortunato Minniti noted, among the 78,846 Italian fighters in Spain "on Franco's side" deserters numbered a mere 336 (0.43 per cent, an insignificant figure) and only 30 of them had fled due to "political rejection of the war" and 31 out of fear during combat.[47]

Were those who went to Spain really "committed Fascists"?

The documentation that we have is not voluminous. The memoirs left by soldiers themselves – as Javier Rodrigo notes – are few, if journalistic reports that in themselves were intended for propaganda and not information purposes are excluded. The memoirs of soldiers, written during the war or immediately afterward, were generally also written for propaganda purposes, sometimes "sweetened, in other cases exaggerated." Undoubtedly, "most of these books were written by those we could identify as committed Fascists."[48]

Of particular interest is the case of Davide Lajolo, who wrote two books about his Spanish war: in 1939 he published *Bocche di donne e di fucili*,[49] and in 1963, *Il "Voltagabbana."*[50] In the latter, he admitted that in the older book he had been "forced" to "distort the reality, to give epic and heroic tones to facts that had instead been sad and full of contradictions and fear."[51] Yet, what might have seemed exaggerated in the first book was the true spirit with which Lajolo had fought that war, as was also apparent in most of the pages written in 1963, which often convey a similar tone because that was "more generally the attitude of 'young people' along the Fascist trajectory.[52]" Why was Lajolo, who went to Spain as a volunteer, but was persuaded to leave for Africa, not a simple member of the National Fascist Party?

> He was an enthusiastic Fascist . . . He was a propagandist of Fascism, an intellectual militant, and part of the "staff." His Fascist activism began in 1938–39, when others began to distance themselves from Fascism.[53]

Thus, was the Spanish Civil War an element that contributed to the radicalization of Italians? To their complete fascisization? To the formation of soldiers who would continue the imperial enterprises of *milites romani*? Was the war in Spain able to fashion, in the midst of battle, a new species of Fascists, like "prophets, apostles, evangelists, soldiers of religion, of the homeland purified by the fire of war."[54]?

Undoubtedly,

> as fervid believers of the "Mussolinian faith" or convinced of the evangelizing capabilities of the war, for all of them the fighting and sacrifice in Spain was the fight and sacrifice for Italy, for the nation identified by a Fascism that was far more than a mere political faction: it was Italy.[55]

All this makes clear that if we confront the central themes of propaganda used for the recently concluded African war, we are faced with a radical change. If the popular motivation (and propaganda aimed at the masses) that had flourished in Africa was the conquest of a "place in the sun," which meant fields to cultivate, industries and businesses to launch, an occupation through which to overcome unemployment and hunger (even though working in the empire proved to be neither easy nor profitable),[56] in the new Spanish conflict there were no lands to be subjugated for unemployed farmers. "The main theme around which Fascism constructed the public discourse to justify military intervention was that of the anti-Bolshevik crusade," a war for the "defense of civilization,[57] against "Red Spain," and of course, in defense of religion, as sustained by a part of the Catholic Church, and also as a consequence of persecutions endured by many Catholics.[58]

It was therefore direct political propaganda, centered on the will to export Fascist ideals, Fascist doctrine, and Fascist organization. Franco was represented as a Spanish "expansion" of Fascism: D'Alessandro notes the headline of *La Stampa*," October 3, 1936: "The Spanish State Organized by Franco Is Totalitarian,"[59] while Paola Lo Cascio highlights how Italian public opinion saw a complete affinity between the

Caudillo's political project and that of the Italian regime,[60] among them, its external aspects, such as adoption of the Roman salute by the Spanish Falangists.

Hence, propaganda and attempts to convince Italian fighters were exclusively political, as is evident in Lajolo's memoirs, and above all were consistent with the process of "building a Fascist Europe, as a part of the progressive, authoritarian, and Fascist trend of the continent."[61] It should be recalled that the men who Mussolini began to send to Spain from December 18, 1936, had not been requested by Franco. On the contrary, the Caudillo protested against the arrival of those soldiers, who were not welcome, but Mussolini wanted to fight, regardless of Franco, "to achieve a victory for the glory of Italy."[62]

An in-depth study has yet to be completed about the extent and depth of the consensus among the Italian volunteers. Undoubtedly, Minniti's figures are of great interest regarding the prosecution of Italian deserters in Spain. However, other considerations that we know of only in part should also be analyzed. According to Rovighi and Stefani, in the long Battle of Guadalajara, from March 8 to the 24, 1937, 496 soldiers of the volunteer corps troops (CTV) were taken prisoner, many more than were usually taken in battle. Without explicitly saying so, they therefore seem to suggest that the "Fascist volunteers" put up little resistance to surrendering to the Italians who fought in the International Brigades: they were "not very motivated" to make war, or were "lacking consistent, moral motivation"; many factors had a "negative impact on them and on the will to fight as part of the CTV."[63]

Had the will to fight with which volunteers had left been quickly exhausted? This is the claim made by Luigi Barzini on March 18, 1937, in his letter to the editor of *Il Popolo d'Italia*. They "went into fire disoriented, with good spirits but were almost surprised that they would shoot seriously"; nonetheless, acts of heroism did take place.[64] According to Giuseppe Bottai, on April 10, 1937, Mussolini had stated, during a meeting of the Council of Ministers in which the battle of Guadalajara was discussed, that the behavior of CTV men was understandable, since it was not at all easy to manage a "war of doctrines" and build "a military conscience," without "the immediate element of territorial defense, of the land, of the country, of the home, and of the family."[65] In other words, Fascist volunteers lacked motivation. Even Galeazzo Ciano could see only the widespread "fatigue" of participating in that war.[66] We may therefore ask ourselves whether and to what extent the "watchwords", which were the basis of the propaganda with which the regime tried to construct an Italian consensus for participating in the Spanish Civil War, were correct or mistaken. We may furthermore wonder how broad was the consensus that supposedly prevailed in Italy at the end of 1936, just six months after the enthusiastic proclamation of the empire.

It is important to remember the significance of propaganda in society during those years, during which the ease and complexity of communication, in addition to the extraordinary speed of dissemination, could not lean on fragile foundations – although this seemed to be the case. As pointed out by the chief of propaganda in Catalonia during the civil war, Jaume Miravitlles, the propaganda services of a state in wartime

> are coessential to the very life of the war and, most importantly, to its success . . . [b]ecause war, an open field to passions, creates complex atmospheres, confusing and complicated areas, and. unthinkable and urgent needs which must be either destroyed or molded, depending on convenience.[67]

In such a situation, therefore, it was important to create the best terms for propaganda, to eliminate all possible doubts, to channel the exhilaration in order to inspire the most valiant fighters, to reinforce morale using the right words. It was not just the defeat at Guadalajara that became a source of perplexity; even the inability to offer concrete and palpable goals carried considerable weight. Nor should the climate within Italy, where doubts arose about the legitimacy of that intervention, be underestimated.

A Fractured Consensus

"We are still unemployed, without subsidies, in rags, poor beggars along the streets." These words can be found in a letter that an anonymous citizen of Carpi (Modena) addressed in December 1936 to the editorial office of *L'Humanité*. Since it was directed to a foreign, and furthermore Communist newspaper, it was blocked by censorship, and on December 14 the prefect of Modena conveyed it to the interior minister.[68] Did this (and many other similar letters that can be read in that archive) constitute a real barometer of popular thought that was being formed, gradually, at least in some parts of Italy?

Another episode that occurred a few months later may shed more light on the situation. Tullio Ughetti, a 44-year-old laborer entered the Stella Cafe in Reggio Emilia and saw a black-shirted Fascist conversing among a large group of friends. Immediately, Ughetti approached him and, to the astonishment of those present, who did not intervene, attacked him with insults, punches, and kicks until the dumbfounded Black Shirt fled precipitously. Afterward the aggressor explained his behavior: "Today, that is how it's done in Valencia." Then, as if he had acted in perfectly normal fashion, he calmly left the cafe.[69]

When, between October and November 1936, the assemblies of the various sections of the Fascist party were called to the province of Ravenna to urge younger members to volunteer to fight in Spain against the Second Republic, there were rumors that, clearly in opposition, these young men declared: "Absolutely not: I will never go to fight against the Republic." In fact, many members of the Fascist party had been involved in the old Republican Party until 1922, and, evidently, their Mazzinian spirit had survived the end of that party and affiliation, more or less forced, to the winning Fascism.[70] Similar episodes were reported in many localities of that province: San Pietro in Vincoli, Voltana, Fusignano; further, some people were arrested and taken into police custody.[71]

These and many other similar episodes cannot be connected directly to real anti-Fascism or to a radical rejection of Fascism. However, as D'Alessandro points out, "the objectives of the regime to permeate society completely induce the significance of 'opposition', although temporary and limited, to deviations from the norm," which were probably articulated as "simple conscientious objection."[72] In any event, there was difficulty in recruiting volunteers in almost all of the cities where designated offices had been set up, so in many cases it can be said they were "forced volunteers."[73]

Generals Rovighi and Stefani, however, believed that all those who left for Spain were committed "volunteers" and that the presence of soldiers who were forced to serve was a legend or fallacy invented by anti-Fascists after World War II:

> There is no serious validity to the opposing allegations made by some of the veterans in reference to that campaign, after the end of World War II, when they claimed that being a volunteer in the Spanish Civil War on the Nationalists' side [Francoists] was considered almost a crime.[74]

This last statement is questionable since (apart from the episodes of dissidence mentioned above), documents – such as military records – exist demonstrating how not all those drafted were volunteers: some (we do not know how many and we hope that this issue will be carefully researched) were drafted or re-drafted and sent to Spain as early as the end of 1936. For example, the military records of Luigi Bonfanti, from Colorno (Parma), show that he was released from the Guardia di Finanza (where he did his compulsory military service) on October 8, 1936, and re-drafted to the Carroccio Battalion on November 23, after which he was shipped from Gaeta to Spain on December 18.[75] According to Rovighi and Stefani,[76] on December 18, three thousand *volunteer* Black Shirts departed from Gaeta.

There are numerous clues indicating that most of those who were sent to fight in Spain were not simply volunteers without real training, but carefully selected, prepared, and even specialized troops. Among the many examples: on February 23, 1939, General Gastone Gambara asked for a "division of alpine artillery" – definitely not a patched-together contingent – to be sent to him and he received it immediately.[77]

In any event, doubts began to circulate in Italy about the veracity of the news that the regime spread about Spain, which were reinforced by Spanish radio broadcasts in Italian. On January 12, 1937, the chief of the Ministry of Communications assured the chief of police that three ministries (War, Navy, and Communications, as well as the Directorate of Propaganda) were engaged in interfering in the reception of radio transmissions from Spain to Italy.[78] On the other hand, they did not just try to block Radio Barcelona. As Bottai wrote: "We've smashed some heads and several radios, everything is in order.[79] Regardless of the joint actions carried out in several parts of Italy, this was a matter of great concern to the police, as can be seen in the telegram that Arturo Bocchini sent to all of prefects on March 23, 1937:

> It has been discovered that many radio listeners try to listen to the unfair and false radio propaganda from Barcelona and from other Spanish stations, as well as from Moscow. For this purpose, they also try to gather . . . at radio transmission points in homes, offices, and local public buildings. This phenomenon is particularly visible among laborers, farmers, small bourgeoisie. It is essential to intervene promptly and energetically with preventive and repressive action, starting with police intervention, and the closure of public places where listening takes place, and the confiscation of radio devices in the event of violation. EE. LL. (to the Prefects) will require special services to be used for this purpose and where necessary including fiduciary services. Nothing should be left unattempt in suppressing this morbid phenomenon.[80]

Towards the End of Fascism?

Did 1936 represent the "year zero" of Italian Fascism? This year undoubtedly witnessed the height of consensus, with the conquest of the empire, and was then followed by the beginnings of significant dissent. This would lead – a few years later – to the expansion of a genuine anti-

Fascism, in light of Mussolini's choice to continue involving Italy in wars causing economic crisis and the furtherance of tragedy and grief within the country.

It is probably a moment that has not been studied enough, but which – we are convinced – will be worth the effort.

Translation by Diana V. Lippi

Notes

1 Although the speeches were delivered at night, the texts were transmitted to the press so that newspapers could publish them the following morning.
2 In reality, a "complete" conquest of Ethiopia was never achieved and the country was riven by a continuous and widespread guerrilla war, against which even chemical weapons were used. Indeed, continuation of the belligerence made demobilization of the Italian troops impossible, and it was necessary to dig heavily into the state's finances. See the diary entries of then foreign minister Galeazzo Ciano, for example, from over a year later, in September 1937: Galeazzo Ciano, *Diario 1937–1943,* ed. Renzo De Felice (Milan: Rizzoli, 1980), entries September 17 and 23, 1937, 38, 40. On the entire Ethiopian event, see Angelo Del Boca, *Gli Italiani in Africa Orientale. 2: La conquista dell'Impero* (Rome-Bari: Laterza, 1986) and idem, *I gas di Mussolini: Il fascismo e la guerra d'Etiopia* (Rome: Editori Riuniti, 2007).
3 *Il Popolo d'Italia,* May 6, 1936.
4 Benito Mussolini, *Opera omnia,* ed. Edoardo and Duilio Susmel, vol. XXVII, *Dall'inaugurazione della Provincia di Littoria alla Proclamazione dell'Impero (December 19, 1934–May 9, 1936)* (Florence: La Fenice, 1959), 257.
5 See especially Brunella Dalla Casa, *Attentato al duce. Le molte storie del caso Zamboni* (Bologna: Il Mulino, 2000).
6 *Il Popolo d'Italia,* October 25, 1936.
7 Ibid., May 10, 1936.
8 Laura Ricci, *La lingua dell'impero: Comunicazione, letteratura e propaganda nell'età del colonialismo italiano* (Rome: Carocci, 2005), 10.
9 Emanuele Ertola, *In terra d'Africa: Gli italiani che colonizzarono l'impero* (Rome-Bari: Laterza, 2017), VIII.
10 Ricci, *La lingua dell'impero,* 51.
11 Paola Desideri, *Teoria e prassi del discorso politico: Strategie discorsive e percorsi comunicativi* (Rome: Bulzoni, 1984), 86.
12 Renzo De Felice, *Mussolini il Duce: Gli anni del consenso 1929–1936* (Turin. Einaudi, 1974), 758.
Nonetheless, this same De Felice specifies (p. 778) that "the enthusiasm and the exhilaration . . . were brief and not such to determine a new type of consensus among the popular classes."
13 Ertola, *In terra d'Africa,* 30.

14 Paul Corner, *The Fascist Party and Popular Opinion in Mussolini's Italy* (Oxford: Oxford UP, 2012); Paul Corner, "L'opinione popolare e il fascismo negli ultimi anni trenta," *Storia e problemi contemporanei*, no. 46 (2007).
15 Nicola Labanca, *Posti al sole: Diario e memorie di vita e di lavoro delle colonie d'Africa* (Rovereto: Museo storico italiano della guerra, 2001); Ertola, *In terra d'Africa*, 210.
16 Some of the considerations contained in this paragraph appear in Luciano Casali, "A proposito dell'imperialismo fascista," *Storia e problemi contemporanei*, no. 73 (2016 [published in April 2017]).
17 Ciano, *Diario*, 56.
18 Emilio Gentile, *Fascismo. Storia e interpretazioni* (Rome-Bari: Laterza, 2002), 235–64.
19 Guido Bonsaver, *Mussolini censore: Storie di letteratura, dissenso e ipocrisia* Rome-Bari: Laterza, 2013), VIII.
20 Mauro Forno, *La stampa del Ventennio: Strutture e trasformazioni nello stato totalitario* (Soveria Mannelli: Rubbettino, 2005), VII. Still important is the survey in Philip V. Cannistraro, *La fabbrica del consenso: Fascismo e mass media* (Rome-Bari: Laterza, 1975).
21 Karl Dietrich Bracher, *Il Novecento secolo delle ideologie* (Rome-Bari: Laterza, 1984; orig. ed. Stuttgart, 1982), 6.
22 Pierluigi Allotti, *Giornalisti di regime: La stampa italiana tra fascismo e antifascismo 1922–1948* (Rome: Carocci, 2012), 27–55.
23 Nicola Tranfaglia, *La stampa del regime 1932–1943: Le veline del Minculpop per orientare l'informazione* (Milan: Bompiani, 2005).
24 Forno, *La stampa del Ventennio*, XI.
25 Enrica Bricchetto, *La verità della propaganda: Il Corriere della sera e la guerra d'Etiopia* (Milan: Unicopli, 2004).
26 Esmonde Manning Robertson, *Mussolini as Empire-builder* (London/New York: Macmillan, 1977), 10.
27 Enzo Collotti, Nicola Labanca, and Teodoro Sala, *Fascismo e politica di potenza: Politica estera 1922–1939* (Milan: RCS-La Nuova Italia, 2000), 287. Antonio Goicoechea and General Emilio Barrera's visit to Rome is mentioned in all of the publications relating to the history of Spain. See, for example, Paul Preston, *Franco: A Biography* (London: HarperCollins, 1993), 30.
28 Luciano Casali, "Europa 1939: Fascismo, nazionalismo, autoritarismo," *Storia e problemi contemporanei*, no. 52 (2009): 131–57; idem, *Dictaduras meridionales: Italia*, in *Civilización o barbarie. El totalitarismo y la construcción de la Europa moderna*, ed. Gutmaro Gómez Bravo (Madrid: Editorial Pablo Iglesias, 2016), 103–22.
29 Morten Heiberg, *Emperadores del Mediterráneo: Franco, Mussolini y la guerra civil española* (Barcelona: Crítica, 2004), 57.
30 John F. Coverdale, *Italian intervention in the Spanish Civil War* (Princeton, NJ: Princeton UP, 1975); Renzo De Felice, *Mussolini il duce*, II*: Lo Stato totalitario 1936–1940* (Turin: Einaudi, 1981).

31 Luciano Casali, "Europa 1939: Las Derechas," in *Europa 1939: El año de las catástrofes*, ed. Francesc Vilanova i Vila-Abadal and Pere Ysàs i Solanes (València: Universitat de València, 2010), 109–27.

32 Ciano, *Diario*, October 29, 1937, 50–51.

33 Fortunato Minniti, *Fino alla guerra. Strategie e conflitto nella politica di potenza di Mussolini. 1923–1940* (Naples: Edizioni Scientifiche Italiane, 2000), 140.

34 In September 1936, the Italian troops were attributed the function of a "large-scale operation toward the Orient", ibid., 141. For a general survey, see Williamson Murray, *The Change in the European Balance of Power, 1938–1939: The Path to Ruin* (Princeton: Princeton UP, 1984).

35 Minniti, *Fino alla guerra*, 148.

36 Heiberg, *Emperadores del Mediterráneo*, 87–88. For a study of the presence of Italy in Majorca and the activity of Mussolini's messenger, Arconovaldo Bonacorsi, see especially Josep Massot i Muntaner, *Vida i miracles del "conde Rossi": Mallorca, agost-desembre 1936; Màlaga, gener-febrer 1937* (Barcelona: Abadia de Montserrat, 1988); also Georges Bernanos, *Les grands cimitières sous la lune* (Paris: Plon, 1938).

37 Coverdale, *Italian Intervention*, 148–49.

38 Ciano, *Diario*, October 24, 1937, 49.

39 Morten Heiberg, "La intervenció militar feixista a la guerra civil espanyola," in *Fu la Spagna! La mirada feixista sobre la Guerra civil espanyol* (Barcelona: Museu d'Història de Catalunya, 2016), 24.

40 Irene Di Jorio, *Tecniche di propaganda politica: Vichy e la Légion française des combattants. 1940–1944* (Rome, Carocci, 2006).

41 Four lengthy volumes published between 1992 and 1993 by two generals, Alberto Rovighi and Filippo Stefani, *La partecipazione italiana alla Guerra civile spagnola (1936–1939)*, which include numerous maps and images.

42 Ibid., vol. I, 169–71. It should be pointed out that the paychecks were quite high, with soldiers earning 20 liras and 150 pesetas a day. Coverdale, *Italian Intervention*, 107–71.

43 Leonardo Pompeo D'Alessandro, *Guadalajara 1937: I volontari italiani fascisti e antifascisti nella guerra di Spagna* (Rome: Carocci, 2017), 22.

44 Massimiliano Griner, *I ragazzi del '36: L'avventura dei fascisti italiani nella guerra civile spagnola* (Milan: Rizzoli, 2006), 177, 179.

45 D'Alessandro, *Guadalajara 1937*, 107.

46 Ibid., 41.

47 Fortunato Minniti, "Italiani in Spagna. I disertori del Corpo Truppe Volontarie," in *Fascismo e franchismo. Relazioni, immagini, rappresentazioni*, by Giuliana di Febo and Renato Moro (Soveria Mannelli: Rubbettino, 2005), 61, 69. Similar figures appear in Pedro Corral, *Desertores* (Barcelona: Debate, 2006).

48 Javier Rodrigo, *La guerra fascista: Italia en la Guerra Civil española, 1936–1939* (Madrid: Alianza Editorial, 2016), 247.

49 Davide Lajolo, *Bocche di donne e di fucili* (Osimo: Barulli, 1939).

50 Idem, *Il "Voltagabbana"* (Milan: Il Saggiatore, 1963).
51 Ibid., 132.
52 Dianella Gagliani, "La fascinazione del fascismo," in *I filari del mondo. Davide Lajolo: politica, giornalismo, letteratura*, ed. Laurana Lajolo (Alessandria: Edizioni dell'Orso, 2005), 2–5.
53 Ibid., 13.
54 Rodrigo, *La guerra fascista*, 329.
55 Ibid., 325.
56 Regarding the complex bureaucracy and the obstacles of every kind that made beginning any work project extremely difficult in Italian East Africa, see E. Ertola, *In terra d'Africa*, 31–86.
57 D'Alessandro, *Guadalajara 1937*, 41.
58 Luciano Casali, "L'ultima crociata," in *Dai cantieri della storia: Liber amicorum per Paolo Prodi* (Bologna: Clueb, 2007). It tackles a theme that even today still finds supporters who, without offering any documentation, describe horrendous blood baths to which the Republic submitted secular and religious Catholics. It is worth remembering at least one of these books which, unfortunately, readers and editors continue to encounter: Mario Arturo Iannaccone, *Persecuzione: La repressione della Chiesa spagnola tra Seconda Repubblica e Guerra Civile (1931–1939)* (Turin: Lindau, 2015) (613 pp.!).
59 D'Alessandro, *Guadalajara 1937*, 43.
60 Paola Lo Cascio, *La guerra civile spagnola: Una guerra del Novecento* (Rome: Carocci, 2013), 214–15. The hypothesis regarding supporters of the theory that Italian intervention in Spain was determined only by the will of Mussolini to "play the last card of collaboration with Germany all the way till the end, is unacceptable . . . and also, there never was a real imperialistic plan of intervention, nor even the will for ideological expansion." Xavier Tusell and Genoveva García Queipo de Llano, *Franco y Mussolini: La política española durante la segunda guerra mundial* (Barcelona: Editorial Planeta, 1985), 14.
61 Rodrigo, *La guerra fascista*, 41; Casali, *Dictaduras meridionales.*
62 Gabriel Cardona, "Il Corpo truppe volontarie nella guerra di Spagna," in *Legionari: Un sudtirolese alla guerra di Spagna: Ein Südtiroler im Spanischen Bürgerkrieg (1936–1939)*, ed. Andrea Di Michele, Marina Miquel, and Margarida Sala (Rovereto: Nicolodi, [2007]) 35.
63 Rovighi and Stefani, *La partecipazione italiana*, vol. I, 313, 295, 315.
64 The letter is cited in D'Alessandro, *Guadalajara 1937*, 171.
65 Giuseppe Bottai, *Vent'anni e un giorno: 24 luglio 1943* (Milan: Rizzoli, 1949), 131.
66 Ciano, *Diario*, October 17, 1937, 47.
67 Jaume Miravitlles, *La propaganda en la guerra*, January–February 1938; cited in Xavier Domènech and Laura Zenobi, *Quan plovien bombes: Els bombardeigs i la ciutat de Barcelona durant la Guerra civil* (Barcelona: Ajuntament de Barcelona/Museu d'Història de Catalunya, 2007), 31–32.

68 Central State Archive, Rome, Ministry of Internal Affairs, General Directorate of Public Security, General and reserved affairs [henceforth, ACS], 1936, cat. K1B, b. 28, fasc. Modena.

69 Luciano Casali, "La guerra civile spagnola e l'incrinatura del consenso al fascismo in Emilia-Romagna," in *Immagini nemiche: La Guerra civile spagnola e le sue rappresentazioni (1936–1939)* (Bologna: Editrice Compositori, 1999), 129.

70 Luciano Casali, "'Chi sono i nemici del popolo': La guerra civile spagnola nella stampa antifascista," *Rassegna di storia*, no. 6 (1987).

71 Alessandro Luparini, ed., *Ravenna e provincia tra fascismo e antifascismo (1919–1945): Sintesi e ipotesi di ricerca* (Ravenna: Longo, 2006).

72 D'Alessandro, *Guadalajara 1937*, 129.

73 Ibid.,133, 134.

74 Rovighi and Stefani, *La partecipazione italiana*, vol. I, 171.

75 Giorgio Monti, *Se non ci conoscete . . . Verità negate della guerra di Spagna* (Imola: Editrice La Mandragora, 2017), 16.

76 Rovighi and Stefani, *La partecipazione italiana*, vol. I, 154.

77 Ciano, *Diario*, 256.

78 Casali, "'Chi sono i nemici del popolo'," 114; D'Alessandro, *Guadalajara 1937*, p. 209.

79 Bottai, *Vent'anni e un giorno*, 110.

80 ACS, 1937, cat. I4D ("Propaganda antifascista a mezzo radiodiffusione"), b. 38/B.

8

From Marginalization to Mobilization: The Soviet Union and the Spanish Republic

DANIEL KOWALSKY

On the last day of 1936, Soviet Defense Commissar Kliment Voroshilov sent a brief note to Chairman Joseph Stalin, informing him that a single payment of 25,000 rubles would be offered to each of the families of the 25 Soviet pilots and tank crew that had thus far perished in the Spanish Civil War.[1] The matter-of-fact tone of Voroshilov's dispatch reveals nothing of the remarkable series of events that had led the Soviet Union to become deeply involved in a struggle that was being waged on the opposite side of the Continent, 3,500 kilometers away. Indeed, at the beginning of 1936, no one foresaw that the destinies of the USSR and Spain would soon be intertwined. How did these two great states that had never been allies, and had few points of common contact in their long imperial histories, come to wage war side by side? What events during the year 1936 propelled Soviet Russia and the Spanish Republic toward their unprecedented diplomatic, cultural, and military alliance? This chapter explores the Soviet entry into the Spanish Civil War, one of the most improbable developments in modern history.

Prior to the July uprising, Spain and Russia had never actually been estranged, but they were not allies by any stretch, and in no realm were their relations active or robust. This was true in the cultural and military, as well as the diplomatic spheres. In fact, diplomatic relations may be the most appropriate place to begin this account. Despite Vladimir Lenin's calls for a worldwide Socialist revolution and the avowed Bolshevik goal of the overthrow of the capitalist West, the Soviets early on made serious diplomatic attempts to curry favor with most European states, including Spain.[2] In February 1918, People's Commissariat for Foreign Affairs (NKID) Commissar Georgy Chicherin made an appeal to Spain for the resumption of cordial relations, but nothing of the sort would occur for another decade and a half.[3] With the declaration of the Second Spanish Republic on April 14, 1931, many Spaniards believed that relations with Moscow would be rapidly restored. This was logical, as the chief impediments to normal diplomacy with the Soviets were no longer there: the military strongman Miguel Primo de Rivera was dead and King Alfonso XIII had fled the country. Even before the monarchy fell, Spain's Republican leaders had met in August 1930 at San Sebastián to agree on the particulars of the soon-to-be established republic. Signers of the pact conceded that in the new Spain, which they described as a "workers' republic," relations with the Soviets must be established.[4] Bi-lateral recognition was duly achieved in July 1933, but the exchange of ambassadors was stalled, and would not occur until after the beginning of the civil war, three years later.[5]

Moscow's foreign relations were not limited to the official channels of diplomacy, nor were they necessarily incapacitated by the USSR's inability to win diplomatic recognition. Enter the Comintern, the clandestine shadow of the NKID, and a parallel institution that could advance Soviet interests in areas where normal relations were nonexistent, pending, or strained. Since Madrid was one of the last foreign governments to exchange ambassadors with the Soviet Union, the Comintern sought openings in Spain in the years leading up to 1936, even if it had few agents on the ground.

Indeed, since the early 1920s, both the Spanish Communist Party (PCE) and the Comintern had been active in Spain. Though founded in 1920, the PCE initially joined a crowded field of left-wing Spanish workers parties and union organizations that competed with the Spanish Socialist Workers Party (PSOE), its trade union, the Unión Géneral del Trabajo (UGT), the anarcho-syndicalist trade union, Confederación Nacional del Trabajo (CNT), and the closely linked anarchist federation, Federación Anarchist Ibérica (FAI). The decade of the 1920s was an era of obscurity, with the PCE reduced to a membership numbering in the hundreds, and its headquarters and conferences relocated to France. The coming of the Second Republic augured growth for the PCE, and by early 1932, the party had some 10,000 members and had established several newspapers, the most important of which was *Mundo Obrero*.[6] Initially, the Comintern lobbied for an immediate proletarian revolution in Spain; the PCE leaders, however, believed that cooperation with the democratic parties of the Republic was necessary. In October 1932, the anticipated purge finally took place, and Moscow expelled the old guard and replaced it with loyal cadres.[7] Yet months later, the Nazis were in power and Moscow's position began to evolve toward the Popular Front, a step that was finally made official at the Seventh Comintern Congress in summer 1935. National Communist parties like the PCE would now enter mainstream political life and cement anti-Fascist alliances with more moderate Socialist and republican parties. As a result, in January 1936, left-wing Republicans and Socialists, together with the PCE, agreed on an electoral platform, the most striking aspect of which was the lack of a revolutionary social or economic agenda. On February 16, the Spanish Popular Front won a narrow victory.[8]

The PCE now had Moscow's attention. The Comintern multiplied its efforts to shore up support for its party in Spain, and to disseminate Communist and Soviet propaganda. The Comintern Executive Committee (ECCI) began directing operatives to accelerate their propaganda efforts, and specifically to

> expand during the course of 1936 publication in the Spanish language of all varieties and forms of Communist and revolutionary-educational literature. Utilize to the greatest degree available legal avenues to achieve the rapid distribution of our literature in all of Spain, and assure its continuous circulation and availability in every corner of the country.[9]

The Soviet agency most effective in disseminating propaganda in Spain was the Society for Cultural Relations with Foreign Countries, known by its Russian acronym VOKS. Operating within the NKID, VOKS was established by the Soviet regime in 1923 to respond to individual, non-diplomatic foreign inquiries regarding the Soviet state.[10] One of VOKS's principal goals was to assist Spaniards in establishing chapters of Friends of the Soviet Union (Amigos de la Unión Soviética, or AUS), a well-organized Communist front organization dating from 1927. By 1936, on the eve of the civil war, AUS chapters had been established in more than 30 Spanish cities and towns.[11] That this propagandizing from Moscow resulted in a burgeoning cult of the USSR in Spain cannot be doubted. Unpublished archival material in Salamanca and Moscow bear witness to the wide interest Spaniards displayed for all things Soviet.[12] For example, on February 24, 1936, a certain José Rodríguez proposed a bicycle trip from his home in Seville to the Soviet Union. Once in Russia, he and a friend hoped to cycle around the country and "study . . . the great project being constructed by those true fighters, our Russian brothers."[13]

In the first months of 1936, Soviet policy in Spain was continually evolving. Communist front organizations such as the FSU were making greater inroads, and winning adherents, while the PCE saw its membership expanding, riding the wave of victory in the February elections. A turning point in Russian-Spanish relations now occurred in a place equidistant between the two countries. On March 7, 1936, the German Wehrmacht reoccupied the Rhineland. This was the most significant repudiation yet of the post-Versailles European order, and the best evidence thus far that the Soviet Union might soon confront a resurgent Germany. In response, the Comintern directed the PCE to make no further references to revolution. The ECCI specifically decreed that "the basic, urgent task of the Communist Party of Spain and the Spanish proletariat at the present moment is to secure the complete victory of democratic and revolutionary forces over Fascism and counter-revolution."[14]

The Popular Front had come to power in France and Spain; in both it was under siege by the forces of reaction. By spring of 1936, the Comintern recognized that a broadly conceived coalition against Fascism would likely first be tested in one of these two states. Though the July uprising was still some months away Moscow's position, should war come to the Iberian Peninsula, had already been cemented. Even while the enemies of the Spanish Republic circled and conspired, Madrid's unlikely eventual ally also lay in waiting, committed to its defense.

The Spanish Civil War, which broke out on July 18–19, 1936, nonetheless presented Moscow with a dilemma. Since 1917, the Bolsheviks had encouraged revolution and civil war among the Communist faithful. Now revolution and civil war had erupted in Spain, but for the party, as has been observed, 1936 was not 1917. The official Soviet strategy since 1935 was cooperation with non-revolutionary parties in Europe against the common threat of Fascism.[15] In the Republic, the onset of hostilities led to a power vacuum in the center, quickly filled by revolutionary parties. The popular revolution, centered in large cities still under Republican control, undertook property redistribution and widespread collectivization. Critically, that revolutionary fervor also supplied manpower and enthusiasm in the first pitched battles with the Nationalists.

For the Kremlin, it was never clear how Soviet aid to the Republic would not appear as support for revolution in Spain, and consequently Stalin responded with extreme caution.[16] Recently declassified documents from the Presidential Archive suggest a Kremlin riveted by the July uprising, but in no hurry to show its hand. As early as July 21, 1936, Comintern official Dimitri Manuelskii sent Stalin a first update from the field.[17] The following day, the Soviets agreed to sell discounted fuel to Madrid.[18] Then, on July 23, Comintern chief Georgii Dmitrov implored Stalin, in a hand-written note, to issue further orders in response to the evolving situation on the Iberian Peninsula.[19]

The impetus for the Soviet leader to eventually act more forcefully came from numerous quarters.[20] From the first days of the war, pressure from international Communism and the international Left, had been mobilized in favor of the Republic. For Moscow to ignore Spain would be to surrender a chance to champion this most popular of causes and risk alienating the global Left. This ideological justification for involvement was complemented by a geo-strategic imperative: Spain provided Moscow with an opening not only to confront Fascism but to test both the viability of collective security with Western powers and the popular front tactic adopted and made official in 1935 at the Seventh Party Congress. Finally, the financial incentive to the Soviets should not be ignored. The Republic was prepared to pay for foreign military assistance in gold, and the Bank of Spain possessed the fourth largest stock in the world. For Stalin, what lay in the balance, and what was eventually dispatched to Moscow, was 510 tons of gold valued in 1936 prices at 518 million dollars.[21]

The odd circumstances of the internationalization of the Spanish Civil War occurred in three phases. First, from late July, the rebels sought and received military support from Nazi Germany and Fascist Italy, catapulting General Francisco Franco into a position of pre-eminence, and allowing the Nationalist army to make rapid progress on the march toward Madrid. Second, in early August, the democratic West, led by France and Britain, adopted a position of neutrality, formalized in the Non-intervention Agreement. The signing of this agreement by 27 European states effectively cut off the Republic from any military assistance.[22] Finally, Stalin approved on September 14, 1936, a substantial military aid package, code-named Operation X, that rescued the Republic from early defeat.[23] The Spanish gold, which paid for military aid, was mobilized one day later, on September 15, but it did not reach Russian hands until November 6.[24]

The first forceful policy decision from the Kremlin came on August 2, 1936. The decree that opened up Soviet policy toward the Republic was intended not for the beleaguered Madrid government, but for a captive audience in the USSR. Stalin seized on the Nationalist uprising as an opportunity to rally domestic support for his regime and for its policy of a popular front against Fascism, that is, collective security. Moscow acted to convert events on the distant Iberian Peninsula into a cause for which the populace was compelled to noisily demonstrate its support and make sizable individual contributions for humanitarian aid. This solidarity campaign was highly coordinated, meticulously directed, and spared little expense.[25] Its initiation resulted, on August 3, in demonstrations of large numbers of workers in cities across the USSR, who issued calls for solidarity with the Spanish Republic. According to the Soviet press coverage, and confirmed by some foreign observers, these rallies attracted masses of workers, ranging from 10,000 in Tbilisi and 30,000 in Minsk, to 100,000 in Leningrad and 120,000 in Moscow.[26] In the weeks that followed, the campaign gained in strength; by 20 September the Politburo issued more detailed directives in the form of a 12-point protocol, entitled, "Conference on the Question of Developing a Campaign of Assistance to the Spanish People," which included the organization of further meetings, mobilization of trade unions and youth organs, voluntary pay deductions to raise humanitarian funds, and saturation coverage in the national and regional press.[27] By the end of 1936, donations totaled 115 million rubles (4,791,000 pounds sterling).[28] These funds were used to purchase massive quantities of food, clothing, medicine, and children's toys, which were shipped to Spain in Soviet vessels. During the first three months of the campaign alone – August–October 1936 – five separate shipments ferried humanitarian aid from Soviet ports to the Spanish Republic.[29]

Simultaneously, the Politburo authorized the dispatch of *Pravda* correspondent Mikhail Koltsov to begin covering the war directly from the Republican zone. Kolstov was followed by two additional Soviet print journalists: Ilya Ehrenberg of *Izvestiia* and Ovadii Savich, the TASS correspondent.[30] It was the task of the journalists to provide content and copy for the increasing amount of coverage of the Spanish Civil War afforded in the Soviet national press. One result of this press mobilization was that column space in *Izvestiia* devoted to Spain went from an already substantial 10 percent to 25 percent of the newspaper.[31]

Meanwhile, the Politburo sent two filmmakers to Spain: Roman Karmen and his assistant Boris Makaseev. Their heady baptism in war cinematography is indicative of the high value the Kremlin was already placing on the Spanish war and its potential for exploitation in the USSR.[32] The Politburo ordered the filmmakers to depart for Spain on August 18, 1936 – exactly one month after the uprising.[33] The pair traveled by air to Paris – passing directly over the Olympic stadium in Berlin where the famous games were taking place – then continued overland to the Spanish border, arriving in the Republican zone on August 23, where they immediately began shooting. Two days later, they sent 600 meters of exposed raw film back to Moscow. It was hastily processed and the first edited newsreel, entitled "On the Events in Spain," debuted in large Soviet cities on September 7, only three weeks after the Central Committee had approved funds for the filmmakers. Karmen and Makaseev stayed in Republican Spain for 11 months, where they shot footage for 20 newsreels, several documentaries, and the feature-length

Ispaniia, which appeared after the war's conclusion, in 1939.[34] By early September, Soviet citizens were reading daily front-page accounts of the Spanish war and viewing in movie theaters moving images of the conflict. Thus, between the solidarity campaigns and saturation coverage the Spanish war had indeed been converted into a cause of enormous ideological and emotional importance to the workers of the USSR.

The next stage of the Soviet Union's escalating involvement in Spanish affairs saw the Kremlin hasten to effect a diplomatic rapprochement with the Spanish Republic, thereafter promoting the Madrid government to an unusually privileged position of ally and friend.[35] On August 22, the Soviet government appointed Marcel Rosenberg as its ambassador to Madrid.[36] Rosenberg and his large staff, including economic and military attachés, arrived in Spain before the end of that month. It is worth noting that despite a concerted search, the Politburo sent to the Spanish embassy only one diplomat with any knowledge of Castillian. This was the chargé d'affaires, Leon Gaikis, who would later be promoted to ambassador.[37] It cannot be doubted that an important function of the Madrid appointments was to provide cover for Stalin's intelligence agents. One of these was People's Commissariat for Internal Affairs (NKVD) and senior representative to Spain, Alexander Orlov, who first reported to Ambassador Rosenberg on September 16, 1936.[38]

In Madrid, the Soviet entourage took up residence in the Palace Hotel, located at Plaza de las Cortes 7 – the political center of the Republic.[39] There the Soviet embassy remained for only eight weeks, before following the Loyalist government to Valencia on November 7, 1936, where it was installed at an address of equal prominence, the Hotel Metropol, directly across from the bullring.[40]

The appointment of the Soviet Union's first diplomatic mission to Spain, its heavy military advisory component, and its rapid dispatch, signaled a shift in Stalin's attitude toward events in Spain. Rosenberg's sudden appearance in the Spanish capital was accompanied by considerable enthusiasm, not for the man himself but for the widespread belief that improved relations with the Soviets could only help the Republic's flagging war effort.[41] Claude Bowers, then American ambassador in Madrid, took note of the "high state of excitement" that Rosenberg's arrival elicited among even ordinary Madrileños.[42] Rosenberg presented his credentials to President Manuel Azaña on August 29, 1936. At the ceremony, the new ambassador made a brief speech in which he assured the Republican government that its political ideas and institutions would be respected by his delegation. In retrospect, it is remarkable that at this early stage of Soviet involvement in the Republic's affairs Rosenberg precisely anticipated the chief source of friction between the two states, and the principal controversy that has raged to this day:

> I know perfectly well that the government of the Spanish Republic does not wish to have alien political or social ideas thrust upon its native ones. This desire fully corresponds to that of my government.[43]

In his own speech at the ceremony, Azaña avoided any acknowledgement that the political systems of the USSR and the Spanish Republic were highly dissimilar. But appreciating the potential salvation in an alliance with the Soviets, Azaña declared that the exchange of ambassadors was "one of the most important events" to grace his presidency.[44] Later, Rosenberg's actions would stand in stark contrast to his early promise of non-intervention. At the time, of course, the remarks made for good diplomacy with his hosts, and good copy in Russia, where, three days later, *Izvestiia* printed his speech in full.[45]

At the time of the new ambassador's reception in Madrid, Catalonia was still without an official Soviet representative. In the absence of an appointed Soviet consul, in September 1936 the *Izvestiia* correspondent Ilya Ehrenburg used his journalistic cover to supply reports to Rosenberg on the political and military situation in Barcelona. These dispatches, which included detailed notes of meetings with Catalan President Lluis Companys were considered important enough to forward in duplicate to the entire Soviet leadership. Of special importance are the installments of September 17 and 18, in which Ehrenburg alerted Rosenberg to two simultaneous crises developing, on the one hand between the Catalan regional government and the anarchist federation (FAI), and on the other, between the Loyalist seat in Madrid and the Catalan authorities. In Ehrenburg's version, the alleged intransigence of the anarchists threatened to weaken the overall war effort and delay the required military conversions in vital Catalan industries. The journalist also reported that Companys would welcome the establishment of a Soviet consulate in Barcelona.[46]

While it is impossible to determine precisely when Ehrenburg's letters on the Catalan question arrived in Moscow, it appears that they elicited an unusually hasty response. On September 21, the Politburo appointed Vladimir Antonov-Ovseenko, a revolutionary hero and leader of the assault on the Winter Palace, as consul general to Barcelona.[47] He departed immediately and arrived at his new post on October 1. It is evident that the precise time of the appointment and arrival of the consul is not trivial: Antonov-Ovseenko's mission to Spain was quite unlike Rosenberg's, for it is convincing evidence of Moscow's evolving perception of the potential Soviet role in the conflict, specifically the need to rectify the perceived problem of Catalan revolutionary anarcho-syndicalism and to oversee a Soviet-style centralized authority in a republic that had, since its founding in 1931, allowed Catalonia extensive regional autonomy.

On October 3, 1936, Antonov-Ovseenko presented his credentials to President Lluis Companys. As was the case with Rosenberg, the consul-general's activities were given glowing front-page coverage in Soviet newspapers.[48] These reliable old Bolsheviks brought to their posts an undeniable prestige and seriousness, underscoring the Soviet commitment to the Republic. Indeed, that commitment went a bit too far, for the ambassador and consul meddled excessively in both the war effort and internal Spanish politics. They were consequently poorly received by Republican officials, who often refused the Russians' advice and counsel, and accused them of attempting to rule Spain from their hastily organized embassy. In any event, these high-level postings were short in duration. By early spring 1937, both the ambassador and consul-general had been recalled to Moscow and executed, victims of the Stalinist terror that coincided with the war in Spain.[49] The final ambassadorial replacement kept his head low, and left nary a fingerprint.

There was still the question of the revival of the Spanish embassy in the Soviet Union, which had never been re-established, even after diplomatic relations resumed in 1933. That the Soviets were prepared to give Madrid's representatives strong support was a foregone conclusion, given the energetic solidarity campaign decreed on August 2, the mobilization of leading journalists and filmmakers to provide content for a transfixed Soviet audience, and the dispatch to Madrid of Moscow's most seasoned diplomats. By the end of August, all this suggested a sea change in official and indeed public Soviet attitudes toward the Republic, and augured well for the eventual effectiveness of a diplomatic mission. Despite the positive conditions now in place for bilateral rapprochement, and notwithstanding the perilous state of Madrid's defenses and the urgent need for international rescue, the Republican government of Largo Caballero was slow to respond to the Soviet opening. Only on September 16 did the premier approve the creation of a Moscow embassy, and it was not until September 21 – one month after Stalin had nominated Rosenberg – that the government announced the appointment of Marcelino Pascua, a physician and moderate Socialist, as the new ambassador to Moscow.[50]

Born in 1897, Pascua had no experience in diplomacy when the civil war began in the summer of 1936. A rising star in Spanish science, he had earlier pursued postgraduate studies in the United States and Britain, was the recipient of a Rockefeller Fellowship, and had led a scientific survey to South America.[51] In 1932, Pascua had visited the Soviet Union to observe the state of Soviet public health, an experience that opened his eyes to the Soviet experiment, while also motivating him to learn Russian.[52] Indeed, Pascua's Russian language skills made him a rare commodity among the Spanish governing elite; during the abortive attempt to exchange ambassadors in 1933, his name was already high on the list of potential choices. Though Pascua always diminished his own abilities in Russian, in summer 1936, he was asked to act as an interpreter between Rosenberg and the Spanish premier.[53]

Given the Republic's worsening military situation, the dispatch of Pascua's mission led to considerable hopes and expectations among both government officials and the military. Two days prior to Pascua's departure, the Socialist journalist Julian Zugazagoitia attended a dinner party hosted by the newly appointed ambassador. According to Zugazagoitia, the atmosphere in Madrid at that moment was pessimistic but, in the case of Pascua's mission, those present looked to "the aid that might come to us from the other end of Europe." "As soon as he arrives," his friend believed, Pascua, must send us victory, certified and urgent, in the form of immense shipments that will replenish, in the blink of an eye, all our civil and military needs."[54]

The paradox of the collective sense of high hopes for Pascua's mission to Moscow was that the question of military assistance had already been taken up and decided at the most senior levels in Moscow.[55] Thus, from the beginning of Soviet military involvement in the Spanish war, the planning stages and logistics were entirely removed from the diplomatic apparatus. That is not to say that the Soviets paid Pascua little interest. Indeed, in October 1936, the Soviet government prepared a lavish reception for the new Spanish ambassador. Optimistic, and hoping for genuinely warm relations, the Soviets gave Pascua VIP treatment in Moscow, according him unusual perks that included the lease of a well-appointed, centrally-located, free-standing house, the assignment of a state-owned limousine, the use of otherwise restricted communications and mail lines, and unfettered personal access not only to key Soviet ministries but to the leadership itself – to Molotov, Voroshilov and, on several occasions, even Stalin.[56] Though magnanimous in appearance, the exceptional conditions of Pascua's mission ultimately gave the Kremlin greater influence over the ambassador and the Republic's war effort. Indeed, Pascua's own notes from his private meetings with members of the Politburo reveal a remarkably unequal relationship – hardly what one would expect between sovereign states. In all discussions, Pascua was treated as the subordinate; he was reprimanded when his government did not comply with Soviet wishes, and policy was repeatedly dictated to him by officials from the Defense Commissariat.[57]

Meanwhile, despite the obvious opportunities that might have come through diplomatic cooperation with the Russians, the Republic paid scant attention to its Moscow embassy, first neglecting, then starving the mission of funds before eventually transferring Pascua to Paris in early 1938. The Republic sent no ambassadorial replacement to Moscow and thus for the balance of the war it had no ambassador in the one country that had come to its defense in 1936.[58] This decision would have severe consequences in spring 1939 when the collapse of the Republic left stranded in the USSR several thousand Spanish refugees without any diplomatic support.[59]

Even before ambassadors had been exchanged between Moscow and Madrid, Soviet diplomacy was brought to bear in London, at the Non-intervention Committee (NIC), organized in early August 1936 under the auspices of British and French leadership. The NIC's express purpose was to prevent the sale of weaponry to either side in the war and forestall its internationalization. Yet the committee was powerless to limit Fascist and Nazi support for the Nationalists. It could have fallen to the Soviet representative Ivan Maisky to advocate on the Republic's behalf, and, in fairness, he did issue protests against German and Italian violations of the neutrality agreement.[60] But, ultimately, Moscow was complicit in this diplomatic charade, legitimizing the NIC farce through its continued participation.[61] Nonetheless, on three separate occasions – October 7, 12, and 23, 1936 – Moscow reiterated that if NIC signatory states continued to supply arms to the rebels, the Soviet government would "consider itself free of the obligations" of the Non-intervention Agreement, or "would not consider itself bound" by the pact.[62] Strong words, but highly disingenuous; already in mid-September, the Kremlin had begun preparations for its own military assistance to the Republic, and it is to that aid that this discussion is now turned.

How best might Stalin's military support for the Republic's defense be summarized? The high point of this assistance took place during the ten months between October 1936 and July 1937, when regular shipments of Soviet military aid were sent to Spain; over one thousand Soviet tank crews and pilots and some 600 advisors were active on the side of the Republic, and the Comintern-sponsored International Brigades entered the fight alongside the newly organized Popular People's Army. This aid to the Republic, code-named Operation X, was the most logistically challenging military adventure launched by Soviet armed forces up to that point, to say nothing of the deepest penetration into Western Europe by any Russian military force in history. Using extremely secretive measures, the Soviet navy dispatched 64 shipments of hardware, including some 600,000 tons of war materiel, over a distance of some 3,500 km.[63]

The logistics of delivery, carried out entirely by sea, were complicated and dangerous, for they required the Soviets to negotiate patrolled and sometimes mined waters, facing at various times the German, Italian, British, and French navies.[64] Of course, just as Franco received nothing for free from the Fascist states, the dispatch of Soviet arms to the Republic was not an act of charity but carried out as a normal commercial transaction between sovereign states. As compensation for the weaponry, the Madrid government would transfer to the Soviet regime its remaining gold stocks, valued at 518 million dollars at 1936 prices.[65] It cannot be doubted that the Republic got good value for the gold. In late October 1936, the Red Air Force, through its use of advanced I-15 and I-16 fighters and SB bombers, allowed the Republic to regain the advantage in the skies it had lost several weeks into the war. Soviet-led mechanized units, operating the technologically superior T-26 tank, played an instrumental role in supporting Loyalist operations in most of the key battles of the war, not least the battle of Madrid, from October to December 1936, but also later, at Guadalajara, Brunete, Teruel, and the Ebro.[66] Due to Loyalist reliance on Moscow's arms, Soviet advisors were able to involve themselves in many aspects of the Republic's war effort. For the short-staffed, bottom-heavy Loyalist armed forces, Soviet advice was actively sought and sometimes followed, most notably in the organization of the Popular Army in October 1936, which took place through Soviet initiative and replicated the structure of the Red Army. More significantly, in the last three months of 1936, the defense of Madrid was to a great extent directed by the Soviet military attaché, Vladimir Gorev. In Loyalist waters, too, the Soviets held sway; the de facto commander of the embattled Republican navy was the Russian attaché Nikolai Kuznetsov.[67]

The positive results of Soviet assistance from the moment of its arrival can scarcely be exaggerated. The first major shipments of planes and tanks reached Cartagena in mid-October. Commanded by Soviet pilots and tankers, this materiel was immediately deployed to the central front, where the Nationalist forces were engaged in a punishing assault on Madrid. The most decisive action involving Soviet pilots came in the last days of October 1936. Prior to the appearance of Soviet planes, the rebel air force had free rein in the air and could bomb Madrid at low altitude and with complete impunity. By the second week of November, however, the skies belonged to Soviet pilots and the rebel offensive was halted on the outskirts of Madrid. Whereas Nationalist pilots had routinely flown over central Madrid at 500–700 meters – the ideal altitude for targeted bombing – after the Soviets gained control of the skies, rebel planes were forced to operate at the much less effective altitude of 800–2000 meters.[68] But Russian aerial prowess won the Republic more than a tactical dividend; equally decisive was the concomitant boost in civilian morale, a development remarked upon by many contemporary observers, and conveyed to Moscow by Soviet representatives in the field. Throughout the late fall of 1936, the balance of air power weighed heavily in the Republic's favor. The arrival of hundreds of skilled Soviet airmen and the voluminous deliveries of the most modern fighters, bombers, and attack planes led to the creation of a formidable Republican air force which, at this stage of the war, had no demonstrable weaknesses. The Soviet-dominated fleet soon eclipsed the Italian and German forces flying at the behest of the Nationalists.

The baptism of Soviet armor on the Iberian Peninsula was similarly decisive. On October 26, 1936, the first company was formed from fifteen tanks and a group of Soviet tank instructors and specialists, supported by Republican trainees. At Esquivias, Soviet and Italian tanks squared off against one another for the first time in the war. A detailed telegram sent from the central front to Voroshilov indicated that Soviet tankers had scored a substantial victory. According to the report, Republican tank forces destroyed 2 rebel tanks, 13 artillery guns, 2 artillery batteries, 2 supply vehicles bearing infantry, and 6 legionary vehicles carrying officers.[69]

Stalin authorized the dispatch of officers, pilots, tankers, and engineers, but he balked at sending the Red Army to Spain. Instead, manpower was provided by the International Brigades, organized, funded, and supplied by the Comintern. On September 18, 1936, the ECCI approved the "recruitment of volunteers having military experience among workers of all countries, with the purpose of sending them to Spain."[70] The focal point for the early recruitment of the Brigades was Paris, with the organizational aspects handled jointly by the French Communist Party (PCF) and the Italian Communist Party in exile (PCI).[71] The leadership was headed by André Marty, chief of the PCF, a representative in the Chamber of Deputies, and a member of the ECCI. His assistant was PCI stalwart Luigi Longo (aka Gallo), who had been active in Spain since shortly after the Nationalist uprising.[72] Numerous other foreign Communist nationals also took part in mobilizing international cadres, issuing recruitment quotas to national parties and cells throughout the world, and overseeing their transport to the Spanish border. Among the most active of the early organizers was the Yugoslav Josip Broz (aka Tito).

Though many Communist propagandists doggedly adhered to the notion that the International Brigades formed spontaneously, even during the war itself some Comintern members openly acknowledged the central role of the ECCI.[73] But it was not until the late 1960s that Moscow admitted that the ECCI had made a decision in September 1936 "to locate among the workers of various countries volunteers with military experience and send them to fight in Spain."[74] Of course, none of this contradicts the fact that in the first weeks of the war, long before the Comintern became involved, volunteers did appear spontaneously to fight with the Loyalists.[75] It was the Comintern, however, that would convert this unorganized trickle into a well-directed flood of new cadres, the engagement of whom would leave a strong imprint on key battles in the first year of the war.

The International Brigades' training base in Spain was established near the town of Albacete. It was here that the first 500 volunteers began their service on October 14, 1936. The date is significant – just two days after the Soviet vessel *Komsomol* arrived in Cartagena with fifty Soviet T-26 tanks and their operators.[76] Over the course of the war, as many as 35,000 foreigners would stream through the Albacete base on their way to the front.[77] These volunteers were overseen by Comintern agents operating under orders from Moscow, in a manner identical to that of the general Soviet advisory apparatus under Operation X. Soviet advisors assigned to various sections of the Republic's military structure invariably worked with the International Brigades as well.[78]

Soviet entry into the war in Spain had been piecemeal, rolled out in stages. First came the mobilization of the Soviet populace around solidarity campaigns and humanitarian fundraising. This occurred in tandem with the dispatch of print journalists and newsreel filmmakers. Diplomatic rapprochement followed, paving the way for military support, initiated mid-September, but only deployed on the Madrid front some six weeks later. The missing piece was the cultural offensive, soon to follow in the last months of 1936. The presence of official Soviet representation in the Republican zone transformed the local potential for the wide dissemination of Comintern and Bolshevik propaganda. From the first days of their arrival, Moscow's diplomatic personnel in the Republic served as active and effective facilitators for the importation and distribution of all manner of Soviet cultural and political materials. Embassy officials also made appearances at AUS-sponsored agit-prop events.[79]

Certainly, the cultural exchanges set in motion through the bilateral alliance worked both ways. In the Soviet Union, thanks to the active direction of state authorities, all things Spanish were soon the rage. A Spanish exhibit was hastily added to the venerated Museum of the Revolution, a required stop for schoolchildren to pay homage to the secular religion of Marxism-Leninism. Literary and theatrical events on Spanish themes dominated cultural circles throughout the major cities of the USSR.[80] But not all of the cultural exchanges were especially successful. The dissemination of Soviet literature in Spain, for example, was handicapped by a wholesale linguistic failure. Of the thousands of books, posters, films, and recordings the Soviets sent to the Republic, nearly all were in Russian, and thus not fit for agit-prop purposes.[81] At other times, supplies of materials from the USSR proved unreliable. At the end of October 1936, the Soviet head of propaganda activities in Barcelona grew desperate and beseeched Moscow: "The task before us is vast and possibly unrealizable. But please send us some material."[82]

More successful was the mobilization of Soviet cinema. In Spain, the Soviet film industry would be inextricably linked to the Kremlin's war mobilization. Moscow sent to the Republic feature-length films whose function was at once propagandistic and commercial. In the fall of 1936, a new company, Film Popular, was organized to oversee the production of propaganda newsreels and Spanish-language versions of Soviet films.[83] Film Popular's first widely distributed Soviet movie was Efim Dzigan's *We of Kronstadt* (1936), which premiered in Madrid's Cine Capital on October 18, 1936. The choice of *Kronstadt* to initiate the Soviet series was based on careful considerations of the film's value to the Republican war effort. Set during the Russian Civil War, it chronicles the transformation of an anarchistic band of marines into a disciplined Red Army unit. According to *Pravda* correspondent Mikhail Koltsov, the premiere was attended by the entire cabinet, leaders of various political parties, and many parliamentary deputies, who were greeted at the theater by a large crowd shouting "¡Viva Rusia!" A newsreel shot at the debut captures much of the excitement: advertisements for the film pasted all over town, and a long line of enthusiastic cinephiles queuing up to see it.[84]

Film Popular's next major presentation was Georgii and Sergei Vasiliev's *Chapayev* (1934), released in the USSR to commemorate the seventeenth anniversary of the Revolution. First screened in Madrid on November 2, 1936, *Chapayev*, like *Kronstadt*, was a war story that strongly resonated with Republican soldiers.[85] The movie recounts the life of Vasilii Chapayev, a mythic figure of the Russian Civil War who, in 1919, terrorized White troops in the Urals and inspired the peasants to defend the Revolution. In the film, Chapayev is promoted to commander, brilliantly leads his men in an offensive, and then heroically falls in battle.[86] *Chapayev* became the most frequently viewed film in the Spanish Republic; the Spanish Communist Party believed it held great pedagogical value, and many soldiers saw it repeatedly.[87]

If Soviet cinema had special resonance for the Republican audience, it was far from Moscow's only cultural export. More ambitious were the elaborately staged public celebrations of the anniversary of the Bolshevik Revolution, also rolled out in the war-torn Republic. The first such opportunity occurred around the nineteenth anniversary of the October Revolution. This was a propitious moment in the rapidly evolving relations between Moscow and Madrid. The first Soviet hardware had arrived only on October 12. 1936, barely three weeks before the anniversary date of November 7.[88] In the final days of October, mobilization around Madrid of the first Soviet T-26 tanks and I-15 fighters coincided with the arrival of the Comintern-sponsored International Brigades.[89] A narrative began to emerge that was picked up and augmented by the Loyalist press: 19 years after the Bolshevik Revolution, Soviet arms and Communist volunteer fighters, together with the citizens of Madrid, were saving the Spanish capital from counter-revolutionaries. Parallels with the Russian Civil War and the eventual Bolshevik victory over the Whites were made explicit.[90]

To conclude, we note the remarkable trajectory of Soviet–Spanish relations over the second half of 1936. In a year that began with scant Comintern mobilization in Spain, a stagnant Spanish Communist Party, no diplomatic ties, and only halting cultural exchanges, the onset of the civil war transformed the possibilities for a bi-lateral alliance, even for two states on the periphery of Europe. The components of this burgeoning friendship were far-flung, and touched countless lives in both the Spanish Republic and the USSR. Diplomatic rapprochement occurred surprisingly quickly, while the initiation of Soviet humanitarian campaigns to provide relief to the Republic was a great boost to morale in war-torn Spain. Moscow's military support, arriving at a key moment during the Battle of Madrid, breathed life into a republic that was nearing breaking point. And this captive audience, in turn, was exploited by the Soviets in a multifaceted cultural offensive.

Yet, the last months of 1936 also proved to be the high point of the Soviet-Republican project of cooperation. We now know that the fate of the Republic was determined in the opening months of the war: in July, August, and September 1936. The Fascist powers' commitment to General Franco, the signing of the Non-intervention Pact by the West, and Stalin's decision to tie Soviet military aid to the finite gold reserves of the Bank of Spain, meant that the outcome of the Spanish Civil War would be dependent on a set of international conditions that evolved little, even two and half years later. The Republic's fortunes may have hung in the balance through summer 1936, but Madrid's fate was sewn up just weeks into the initiation of Operation X. This was in part due to the difficult logistics of supply, but also to Moscow's refusal to expose itself more fully to the Republican cause. In a war that saw over one million men take up arms on both sides, Voroshilov's 1936 New Year's Eve tally of 25 dead Soviet servicemen is a stark reminder of the limits of Stalin's contribution to Republican Spain. In a long struggle of attrition, separated from its ally by 3,500 km, Moscow could win Spanish battles but never the Spanish Civil War.

Notes

1 Arkhiv Prezidenta Rossiiskoi Federatsii (Presidential Archive of the Russian Federation; APRF), f. 3, op. 53, d. 470, l. 109.

2 The key study on Soviet-Spanish relations for the period between the October Revolution and the declaration of the Second Spanish Republic is Juan Avilés Farré, *La fe que vino de Rusia: La revolución bolchevique y los españoles (1917–1931)* (Madrid: Biblioteca Nueva, 1999).

3 Chicherin to Spanish Embassy, January 29 (Febuary 11), 1918. *Dokumenty vneshnei politiki SSSR (DVP SSSR)*, vol. I, 102.

4 Marina Casanova, *La diplomacia española durante la guerra civil* (Madrid: Ministerio de Asuntos Exteriores, 1996), 67; Juan-Simeón Vidarte, *Las Cortes Constituyentes de 1931–1933: Testimonio del Primer Secretario del Congreso de Diputados* (Barcelona: Ediciones Grijalbo 1976), 565.

5 Recognition occurred through an exchange of telegrams between Mosocw and Madrid, reprinted in *DVP SSSR*, vol. XVI, 464–65. They were published in *Izvestiia* and *Pravda* on July 29, 1933.

6 On the Spanish Communist press in the early 1930s, see Rafael Cruz, *El Partido Comunista de España en la II República* (Madrid: Alianza, 1987), 67–70.

7 Tim Rees, "The Highpoint of Comintern Influence?" in *International Communism and the Communist International, 1919–1943*, ed. Tim Rees and Andrew Thorpe (Manchester: Manchester University Press, 1998), 145–47.

8 See Stanley G. Payne, *Spain's First Democracy: The Second Republic, 1931–1936* (Madison: University of Wisconsin Press, 1993).

9 "Resolution on the Development of Publication Activities in Spain." The decision was the eighth item on the agenda of the ECCI session of February 28, 1936, Protocol no. 30. Rossiiskii gosudarstvennyi arkhiv sotsial'no-politicheskoi istorii (Russian State Archive of Socio-Political History; RGASPI), f. 495, op. 18, del. 1078, ll. 317–24.

10 For the most complete history and analysis of VOKS, see Jean-François Fayet, *Voks: Le laboratoire helvétique: Histoire de la diplomatie culturelle soviétique l'entre-deux-guerres* (Georg: Chêne-Bourg, 2014).

11 Antonio San Román Sevillano, "Los amigos de la Unión Soviética: Propaganda política en España: 1933–1938" (PhD diss., Universidad de Salamanca, 1993), 35–38, 136.

12 See Daniel Kowalsky, *La Unión Soviética y la Guerra Civil Española* (Barcelona: Crítica, 2004), 131–52.
13 Archivo Histórico Nacional, Sección Guerra Civil (AHN SGC), PS Madrid, carp. 385, fol. 33–34.
14 "Decision on the Spanish Question," June 13, 1936. RGASPI, f. 495, op. 18, del. 1092, l. 51.
15 The now classic study on mid-1930s' collective security is Jonathan Haslam, *The Soviet Union and the Struggle for Collective Security in Europe, 1933–1939* (London: Macmillan, 1984).
16 Remarkably, the same conundrum that lay behind Stalin's reluctance to intervene in Spain would come to dominate the historiography of the war, indeed, for several generations of scholars. That Soviet policy in Spain was counter-revolutionary, advocating support of the capitalist, bourgeois Republic, did not prevent it from being condemned in much of the literature for attempting to "Sovietize" Spain – that is, to convert it into a peoples' democracy in the style of post-1945 Eastern Europe. On the other hand, the Troskyist reading of the war faulted the Soviets for destroying the revolution in Spain – and with it the Republic's most spirited defense. Meanwhile, the Republican mainstream and its supporters denounced the Soviets for providing insufficient aid: supplying only enough weaponry to keep the Republic alive, but not to win the war. The debate is well covered in Paul Corthorn, "Cold War Politics in Britain and the Contested Legacy of the Spanish Civil War," *European History Quarterly* 2014, no. 44: 678–702.
17 APRF, f. 3, op. 65, d. 221, l. 33.
18 Ángel Viñas, *La soledad de la República* (Barcelona: Crítica, 2006), 86.
19 APRF, f. 3, op. 65, d. 221, l. 34.
20 For a succinct presentation of Stalin's motives, see Ángel Viñas, "September 1936: Stalin's Decision to Support the Spanish Republic," in *Looking Back on the Spanish Civil War*, ed. Jim Jump (London: Lawrence & Wishart, 2010), 146–49.
21 Viñas, *La soledad de la República*, 373–98.
22 On the policy of non-intervention, see David Cattell, *Soviet Diplomacy and the Spanish Civil War* (Berkeley: University of California Press, 1957).
23 Declassified archival materials flesh out the initiation of military support: APFR, f. 3, op. 65, d. 221, l. 97–101. Decades earlier, a Soviet official publication had discussed key aspects of the dispatch of arms to Spain: *Istoriia vtoroi mirovoi voiny*, vol. II (Moscow: Voennoe izdat., 1974), 54, 137.
24 See Kowalsky, *La Unión Soviética*, 232–40.
25 APRF, f. 3, op. 65, d. 221, l. 44.
26 On the domestic campaigns, see Academy of Sciences of the USSR. *International Solidarity with the Spanish Republic, 1936–1939* (Moscow: Progreso, 1974), and Kowalsky, *La Unión Soviética*, 73–95.
27 RGASPI, f. 17, op. 120, del. 274, ll. 1–2.
28 Afanasii Arsen'tevich Komshukov, "Natsional'no-revoliutsionnaia voina ispanskogo naroda 1936–1939 gg. I sovetskaia obchshestvennost" (PhD diss., Kharkov, 1979), 179.

29 V.A. Tolmachaev, "Sovetskii Soiuz i Ispaniia: Opyt I uroki internatsional'noi pomoshchi (1936–1939)" (Ph.D. diss., Leningrad, 1991), 68–69.

30 On Ehrenburg's appointment, see APRF, f. 3, op. 65, d. 217, l. 17. All three Russian print journalists who travelled to Spain left memoirs of their experiences. In Spanish, see Mikhail Koltsov, *Diario de la guerra española* (Madrid: Akal Editor, 1978). and Ilya Ehrenburg, *Corresponsal en España* (Barcelona: Editorial Prensa Ibérica, 1998). In Russian only, see Ovadii Savich, *Dva goda v Ispanii, 1937–1939* (Moscow: Sovetskii Pisatel, 1981).

31 David Allen, "The Soviet Union and the Spanish Civil War" (Ph.D. diss., Stanford University, 1952), 437–38.

32 On the filmmakers' appointment, see APRF, f. 3, op. 65, d. 221, l. 66 The filmmakers, too, left memoirs, but neither has been translated from the Russian: Roman Karmen, *No Pasaran!* (Moscow: Sovetskaia Rossiia, 1972), and Boris Makaseev, "Iz khroniki geroicheskoi respubliki," in *My internatsionalisty: Vospominaniia sovetskikh dobrovol'tsev-uchastnikov natsional'no-revoliutsionnoi voiny v Ispanii,* 2nd ed. (Moscow: Izdat. Politicheskoi Literatury, 1986), 158–64.

33 Politburo Protocol from August 17, 1936. RGASPI, f. 17, op. 3, del. 980, l. 235.

34 For an overview of Russian newsreel production in the civil war, see Daniel Kowalsky, "The Soviet Cinematic Offensive in the Spanish Civil War," *Film History* 19, no. 1 (2007): 7–19, and "La ofensiva cinematográfica soviética en la guerra civil española," *Archivos de la Filmoteca*, nos. 60–61 (2008): 50–77.

35 Kowalsky, *La Unión Soviética*, 25–41.

36 APRF, f. 3, op. 65, d. 217, l. 22.

37 APRF, f. 3, op. 65, d. 217, l. 21.

38 Boris Volodarsky, *Stalin's Agent: The Life and Death of Alexander Orlov* (Oxford: Oxford University Press, 2015), 155.

39 Admiral Kuznetsov, the naval advisor who arrived just days after the ambassador, has written in some detail about the establishment of the Soviet HQ. See his *Memoirs of Wartime Minister of the Navy* (Moscow: Progreso, 1990), 54, and the same author's chapter, "Con los marinos españoles en su guerra nacional-revolucionaria," in *Bajo la bandera de la España republicana* (Moscow: Progreso, 1967), 133.

40 The Soviet delegation's various relocations in Madrid and Valencia, as well as a comparative discussion of the embassy's position vis-à-vis other foreign representatives, are discussed in Javier Cervera Gil, *Madrid en Guerra: La Ciudad Clandestina, 1936–1939* (Madrid: Alianza, 1998), 351–54.

41 For Rosenberg's generally upbeat reception in the Spanish press, see *Mundo Obrero,* August 28, and *Claridad,* August 28 and 29, 1936. In the secondary literature, only Soviet historians or their sympathizers make much of Rosenberg's arrival on the scene. See David Pritsker, *Podvig ispanskoi respubliki* (Moscow: Izdat. Sotsial'noekonomicheskoi literatury, 1962), 160; and Academy of Sciences of the USSR, *International Solidarity with the Spanish Republic, 1936–1939* (Moscow: Progreso, 1974), 308–9.

42 Claude G. Bowers, *My Mission to Spain: Watching the Rehearsal for World War II* (New York: Simon and Schuster, 1954), 317.
43 *DVP SSSR*, vol. XIX, 416.
44 Ibid., 417.
45 *Izvestiia*, September 1, 1936
46 The original Ehrenburg reports are located at RGVA, f. 33987, op. 3, del. 852, ll. 150–162. Translated versions are available in Mary Habeck and Ronald Radosh, *Spain Betrayed: The Soviet Union and the Spanish Civil War* (New Haven, CT: Yale University Press, 2001), 23–32.
47 On Antonov-Ovseenko's early career, see Isaac Deutscher, *The Prophet Armed* (London: Oxford University Press, 1954), 221, and idem, *The Prophet Unarmed* (London: Oxford University Press, 1959), 116–17, 160–61. On the consul's appointment, see Protocol of Politburo meeting of September 21, 1936, RGASPI, f. 17, op. 3, del. 981, l. 213.
48 *Izvestiia*, October, 3 and 4, 1936.
49 Kowalsky, *La Unión Soviética*, 36–41.
50 Ibid., 47–148.
51 AHN-Madrid. Diversos. M. Pascua, leg. 16, exp. 3. The source document is Pascua's curriculum vita dating from 1939. The same file reveals much about Pascua's life after the war. In the spring of 1939, the ambassador immigrated to the United States, where he took a teaching post in public health at Johns Hopkins University. He ended his career in Geneva, as a public health official with the UN. Pascua died in 1977.
52 Pascua wrote two favorable articles on Soviet medicine after returning from the USSR. See *El Socialista*, November, 11 and 12, 1932.
53 Ángel Viñas, *La Soledad de la República* (Barcelona: Crítica, 2006), 264.
54 Julián Zugazagoitia, *Guerra y vicisitudes de los Españoles*, vol. I (Paris: Librería Española, 1941), 170.
55 APRF, f. 3, op. 65, d. 221, l. 97–101.
56 The establishment of Pascua's embassy is covered in Kowalsky, *La Unión Soviética*, 42–67. Kowalsky used unpublished Politburo protocols housed in the former Party archive, together with the ambassador's personal papers at the Archivo Historico Nacional-Madrid. The decree granting Pascua the detached residence at number 18, Malaia Nikitskaia, appears in Politburo Protocol 128, October 23, 1936; RGASPI, f. 17, op. 3, d. 982.
57 Kowalsky, *La Unión Soviética*, 50–62.
58 Ibid., 42–67.
59 Ibid.
60 Maiskii wrote in detail about his time on the NIC twice, in the translated *Spanish Notebooks* and in a work that to date is available only in Russian: *Vospominaniia sovetskogo diplomata – 1925–1945* (Tashkent: Nauka 1980).
61 Now over a half century old, but not beyond its use-by date, the only account of the much-maligned Non-intervention Committee remains David Cattell, *Soviet Diplomacy and the Spanish Civil War* (Berkeley: University of California Press, 1957). Another useful account is Harald Geiss, "Das

'Internationale Komitee für die Anwendung des Abkommens über die Nichteinmischung in Spanien' als Instrument sowjetischer Außenpolitik 1936–1938" (PhD diss., Frankfurt-am-Main, 1977).

62 *DVP SSSR*, vol. XIX, 464–64, 470–71, 513–14.

63 *Istoriia vtoroi mirovoi voiny*, vol. II (Moscow: Voennoe izdat., 1974), 54, 137.

64 The military intervention is best covered in Iurii E. Ribalkin, *Operatsiia "X": Sovetskaia voennaia pomoshch' respublikanskoi Ispanii* (Moscow: "AIRO-XX, 2000).

65 The gold has been revisited many times by Angel Viñas. See his *El oro de Moscú* (Barcelona: Grijalbo, 1979), *El oro español en la guerra civil* (Madrid: Instituto de Estudios Fiscales, 1976), and "The financing of the Spanish Civil War," in *Revolution and War in Spain, 1931–1939*, ed. Paul Preston (London: Methuen, 1984), 266–83; and more recently and definitively, in *La Soledad de la República* (Barcelona: Critica, 2006), 373–98.

66 There is no specialized scholarship in any language on Soviet air power in the war. The most up-to-date account of Soviet armor in Spain is Steven J. Zaloga, *Spanish Civil War Tanks: The Proving Ground for Blitzkrieg* (Oxford: Osprey, 2010); See also, Yuri Rybalkin, Operatsiia 'X': Sovetskaia voennaia pomoshch' respublikanskoi Ispanii (1936–1939) (Moscow: AIRO-XX, 2000).

67 Kuznetsov's memoirs have rarely been incorporated into the non-Russian literature on the war, yet they have wide-ranging value, not least in clarifying the logistical problems faced by the Soviet navy in transporting hardware to Spain. See N.G. Kuznetsov, *Nakanune* (Moscow: Voenizdat, 1969); *Na dalekom meridiane*, 3rd ed. (Moscow: Nauka, 1988); and in English, *Memoirs of Wartime Minister of the Navy* (Moscow: Progress, 1990).

68 Kowalsky, *La Unión Soviética*, 290–306.

69 Ibid., 307–20.

70 Codavilla report to ECCI, September 22, 1936, RGASPI, f. 495, op. 2, del. 233, ll. 56–99.

71 The best introduction to the formation of the International Brigades is the work of Rémi Skoutelsky, including *Novedad en el Frente: Las Brigadas Internacionales en la guerra civil* (Madrid: Ediciones Temas de Hoy, 2006); "The Comintern and the International Brigades," in *The Volunteer* XXIV, no. 1 (March 2002): 9–13; and *L'espoir guidait leur pas: Les volontaires français dans les Brigades internationales, 1936–1939* (Paris: Bernard Grasset, 1998).

72 For Longo's version of the International Brigades, see Luigi Longo, *Las Brigadas internacionales en España* (Mexico City: Ediciones Era, 1966).

73 In September 1937, the CPUSA organ *Daily Worker* acknowledged that it had actively recruited cadres. See R. Dan Richardson, *Comintern Army: The International Brigades and the Spanish Civil War*, (Lexington: University of Kentucky Press, 1982), 32.

74 *Komunisticheskii Internatsional: Kratkii istoricheskii ocherk* (Moscow: Politizdat, 1969), 460.

75 See Skoutelsky, *L'espoir guidait leur pas*, 29–54.

76 For the arrival of the International Brigades, see Hugh G. Thomas, *The Spanish Civil War*, 3rd ed. (New York: Simon & Schuster), 456. On the establishment of the Albacete base, see Skoutelsky, L'*Espoir guidait leur pas*, 29–79, and *Novedad*, 76–84.

77 This is the relatively conservative though by no means final estimate of Thomas, *The Spanish Civil War*, 982–83. Declassified Soviet documents indicate as many as 50,000. See RGASPI, f. 495, op. 76, del. 33, l. 18. Cited in M.V. Novikov, *SSSR, Komintern i grazhdanskaia*, vol. II (Iaroslav: Iaroslavskii gosudarstvennyi pedagogicheskii universitet, 1995), 100.

78 Moscow's role in shaping and overseeing the International Brigades is the subject in part of Ronald Radosh, Mary R. Habeck, and Grigory Sevostianov, eds., *Spain Betrayed: The Soviet Union in the Spanish Civil War* (New Haven/London: Yale University Press, 2001), 233–60, 431–73.

79 For example, Arthur Stachevsky, the economic attaché who arrived in late August 1936 and participated in an AUS meeting in mid-December of that year. RGVA, f. 33987, op. 3, del. 853, l. 322.

80 Kowalsky, *La Unión Soviética*,180–90.

81 On the cultural exchanges between the two countries, see ibid., 133–90.

82 Sofiia Antonov-Ovseenko to VOKS, October 31, 1936, State Archive of the Russian Federation (GARF: Gosudarstvennyi arkhiv Rossiiskoi Federatsii), f. 5283, op. 7, del. 840, l. 180.

83 On the history of Film Popular, see Arturo Perucho, "Una organización cinematográfico nacido en la guerra," *Nuevo Cinema (*Barcelona) 2 (June 1938): 12–14.

84 See the ninth installment of *K sobytiiam v Ispanii* ("On the events in Spain"), preserved in the Filmoteca Española, Madrid.

85 *Heraldo de Madrid,* November 4, 1936.

86 The film's genesis, and its wide popularity within the Soviet Union, is described in Jay Leyda, *Kino: A History of the Russian and Soviet Film,* 3rd ed. (Princeton, NJ: Princeton University Press, 1983), 314–21.

87 Mikhail Koltsov, *Diario de la Guerra española* (Madrid: Akal, 1978), 123.

88 Kowalsky, *La Unión Soviética,* 212.

89 Daniel Kowalsky, "Operation X: Soviet Russia and the Spanish Civil War," *Bulletin of Spanish Studies: Hispanic Studies and Researches on Spain, Portugal and Latin America* 91, nos. 1–2 (2014): 168. On the arrival of the International Brigades, see Hugh G. Thomas, *The Spanish Civil War.* 3rd ed. rev. New York: Simon and Schuster, 1986, 456.

90 See *Mono Azul,* October 29, 1936. The journal was the principal mouthpiece of the Alianza de Intelectuales Antifascistas (Alliance of Antifascist Intellectuals). See also Carlos Fernandez Cuenca, *La Guerra de España y el Cine,* Vol. I (Madrid: Ed. Nacional, 1972), 297–324.

9

An Engagé in Spain: Commitment and Its Downside in Rafael Alberti's Philo-Sovietism

SILVINA SCHAMMAH GESSER AND ALEXANDRA CHEVELEVA DERGACHEVA

Rafael Alberti: Between Political Tourism and the Tradition of the Engagé

Rafael Alberti (1902–99), a maverick among Andalusian poets in the early 1920s and the civil war's most iconic Communist agitator, was a latecomer to the Spanish proletarian struggle. Radicalized at the end of Primo de Rivera's dictatorship, the poet's embrace of the Republican cause was undoubtedly tardy and his political consciousness a delayed "awakening" compared to other less spirited and histrionic figures in Madrid's intellectual and artistic circles.[1] Nonetheless, this did not diminish his role as a fellow traveler of ideological tourism in the early 1930s, or his public persona as a passionate celebrity of Soviet Communism in civil war Spain.

Indeed, because of Rafael Alberti's philo-Sovietism, which was largely shared by his wife, María Teresa León, they embarked on five journeys to the Soviet Union: in the winter of 1932–33; in August 1934; in March 1937; in 1964 (to receive the International V.I. Lenin Prize); and in 1976. Most intriguing was their visit in 1937, when the Albertis held a two-hour, face-to-face meeting with the highest Soviet leader and head of the Communist Party.

Widely referred to as the Iberian example of the engagé who experienced the Spanish Civil War as the epicenter of European turmoil, Rafael Alberti faced dilemmas that also troubled many other well-known fellow travelers, such as André Gide and Lion Feuchtwanger. In contrast to the widely studied visits of Gide and Feuchtwanger to the Soviet Union, the

Albertis' repeated sojourns there, and especially the clandestine issues involved in their 1937 trip, have received much less scholarly attention.[2] This chapter addresses the poet's third visit to Moscow at the peak of the civil war and raises pressing questions regarding Alberti's moral call as the voice of the proletariat, committed to the Republican cause, and his ability to read, interpret, and transmit the "Soviet experiment."

Indeed, nearly 100.000 foreign visitors hurried to the USSR in the interwar years in order to witness first-hand the "wonders" of the new Soviet era. Among them were thousands of writers, professionals, scholars, and artists, who constituted a highly-varied population in terms of countries of origin, occupation, motivation for travelling, political outlook, and biography. Many, among those who saw themselves as "friends of the Soviet Union," censored themselves when they related their experiences on their return. The gap between what they had encountered and what they later published only increases when we take into account documents and testimonies that have been declassified in the Russia. As scholars of Soviet history reveal, the reports and memoirs of many European intellectuals, Spaniards included, cannot be understood on the sole basis of their published texts, where elements of faith, political intrigue, self-interest, or fear for their lives overshadowed criticism. Undoubtedly, their stage in lifecycle, position in their country of origin, and recognition in international circles also played a major role in generating sympathy as much as in determining whether, when, and to what extent fellow-travelers were ready to risk and correct their philo-Sovietism and contest the given narratives of the host country.[3]

Be that as it may, the dimensions of the 1930s' Stalinist purges and repression – from the Show trials, secret persecutions and propagandistic arrangement of facts up to mass arrests and incarcerations – remained a shadow lurking over the political pilgrims who endlessly reinvented themselves as they either refrained from condemnation or suppressed doubts and disbelief about the Soviet reality in masterly fashion.[4] An astonishing dissonance seems to have especially persisted among those fellow travelers who viewed themselves as engagés.

The notion of engagé refers to the responsibility of intellectuals and artists who, facing drastic social and political change, utilize their cultural and symbolic capital to clearly state their views on pressing public issues according to their own set of values. The engagé as a modern social type had, in late nineteenth century France, a foundational moment. The Dreyfus affair that divided French society helped to establish the figure of the committed thinker in the intellectual field, which later evolved from the pioneer figure of Emile Zola through Julian Benda and Romain Rolland during World War I and André Gide in the interwar period, to

Jean-Paul Sartre after World War II. Despite differences, they all shared common premises that tied them to either the liberal Republic and/or the Left.[5]

In contrast to their French counterparts, young Republican Spaniards in the early 1930s counted among a very small cadre of outspoken left-wing intellectuals and artists capable of creating a significant mass of followers.[6] Likewise, in comparison to France or Germany, Spain had no institutional structures that could channel the Communist impetus and activities experienced in the French and German political landscape. The Spanish Communist Party's scarce presence and permanent state of crisis had led to a low level of attention on the part of the Comintern.[7]

This situation changed dramatically only when the USSR began to perceive that Spain's mobilization against dictatorship might advance the rehearsal for a future revolution. The entry of the Spanish Socialist Workers' Party (PSOE) to the 1931 coalition further increased Russian expectations, despite the fact that the Spanish Communist (PCE) Party remained small and isolated at the beginning of the Second Republic.

Diplomatic relations between Spain and the USSR were established in July 1933. It took another three years before they actually exchanged diplomatic representatives. Meanwhile, Moscow sought to strengthen the Comintern's direct influence on the internal politics of the Spanish Communist Party by deepening cultural bonds and propaganda channels.[8] Soviet sponsoring and financing of regular contacts initiated in 1931 reached a climax with the waning of the Republican-Socialist coalition, the reorganization of the Spanish right with its radical offshoots, and the prospects of German Nazism which, by 1933, prompted sympathizers of the Soviet Union in Madrid who were not members of the PCE to organize in anti-Fascist associations. The cases of the Asociación de Amigos de la Unión Soviética (promoted by the law professor Luis Jiménez de Asúa, and the politicians Victoria Kent and Juan Negrín) formed in April 1933; the Unión Internacional de Escritores Revolucionarios (gathering writers Joaquín Arderius, César Arconada, Ramón Sender, Antonio Espinas, César Vallejo, María Teresa León and Rafael Alberti, and sculptor Alberto Sanchéz) created in June; the Frente Único Antifascista (that included Ramón Sender, José Balbontín, Dolores Ibárruri, and César Falcón) launched in July; and the Asociación de Escritores y Artistas Revolucionarios, – an organization parallel to L'Association des Écrivains et Artistes Révolutionnaires, France's premiere left-wing cultural organization founded in 1932 by Henri Barbusse – was set up simultaneously in Madrid, Barcelona, and Seville.[9] These overlapping cells, as organs of pro-Soviet propaganda under Comintern tutelage, fostered unconditional support for Soviet national and international policy, and for its general secretary, Joseph Stalin.

It was at this crucial juncture that Rafael Alberti, together with María Teresa León and César Arconada, founded *Octubre*, a pioneering journal of propaganda and agitation, originally conceived in Moscow. Alberti's presence in *Octubre* (1933–34), was crucial in promoting the poet's pro-proletarian public persona.[10] Alberti's first visits to the USSR, in the winter of 1932–33, and in August 1934, also provided the poet with material for various articles in Spanish in the journal *Luz*, which published a series of them. While often superficial and imprecise, these texts made Alberti a "specialist" on the Soviet Union in the eyes of the Spanish public.[11] Soon, Alberti's new political popularity at the peak of the Black Biennium (1933–35) turned him into a spearhead of left-wing ideology.[12] The poet's pre-eminence as a left-wing sloganeer, who had risen during the rampant repression that followed the failure of the 1934 Asturian uprising led the Republican authorities to close *Octubre*, considered a dangerous platform of Communist agitation.

The events had a lasting impact on the poet and his wife's political trajectories. Already active in the international writers' circuits and public anti-Fascists events, the Albertis' who had attended the First Congress of Soviet Writers in Moscow from August 17 to September 1, 1934, could, under no circumstances, return to Spain. Forced to remain in Paris, they gathered testimonies and information about the Asturian events, which they heard from Spanish exiles and refugees who had managed to escape the turmoil. In so doing, they took a further step in international political involvement. Instructed by Palmiro Togliatti, a member of the Comintern and secretary of the Italian Communist Party, the Albertis sailed to North America to launch a public campaign to explain the plight of their Spanish comrades and raise funds for the Asturian victims. In 1935, a year of forced exile, the Albertis gained visibility as the Spanish representatives of pro-Soviet ideology visiting the United States, Central America, and the Caribbean, and two years later the couple engaged in diplomatic activity as loyal representatives of Republican Spain, meeting no less than Josef Stalin himself.

Spanish Poets, Soviet Interests, and the Politics of Reception

Initially, Alberti's rising fame as a spokesman of the Soviet worldview in Spain did not correspond with an equal interest in the poet's artistic output among Soviet literary circles. Rafael Alberti's first trips to the USSR, in 1932–33, and in 1934 went almost unnoticed in Soviet propaganda. Likewise, an analysis of Soviet magazines of the early 1930s reveals minimum recognition of Alberti's work in relation to other Hispanic writers, such as Ramón Sender, a popular figure of the time, many of whose works were translated into Russian between 1933 and 1937.[13]

In fact, the few poems by Rafael Alberti that were translated were those that emphasized *casticismo* and a strong racial image of a secular Spain.[14] Before 1937, only one poetry collection by Alberti had been published in the USSR. This was *Ispanskie krestyane,* a translation of his poetic cycle *Campesinos de España,* which included poems such as *Niños de Extremadura* and *Romance de los campesinos de Zorita.*[15] They evoke a picturesque landscape, where a poor and backward Spain coexisted with the first demands for revolutionary changes by the peasantry. Prioritizing the effects of their reception, the poems' allusions to Spanish politics in the original were reframed in Russian through mystic topoi and models of Soviet scenery.[16]

Clues to Alberti's as yet unclear status vis-à-vis the Soviets emerged during organization of the First Congress of Soviet Union Writers of 1934. Alberti was included only in the third version of the guest list. At the opening of the Congress, Maxim Gorki's speech consecrating "anti-Fascist foreign writers and poets," mentioned André Gide (though he was not present) and 18 out of 22 other foreign participants included on the list, but somehow omitted the names of Rafael Alberti and María Teresa León who were present at the event.[17] Yet, Alberti's interests and activities in the name of the Soviet Union, and his success in becoming a "living symbol" of pro-Communist tendencies in Spanish poetry and culture intensified, even if they did not have an impact on Soviet reception of his work and public persona, which by 1937 still remained limited.

As a rule, Soviet sympathy for one foreign author or another rested upon those who could best serve the regime's interests. Rather than the artistic value of their work, Stalinist propaganda tended to select figures that could be marketed as fighters for Communist ideals, saviors of the peasantry, or fatal victims of Fascist regimes. Thus, prior to the outbreak of the Spanish Civil War, interest in and knowledge of Spanish letters and poetry in Russian intellectual circles was slight.[18]

This situation changed drastically after the military coup of July 18, 1936, when the Soviet Union began to show a steady interest, albeit more propagandistic than intellectual or political, in Spanish literary production, figures, and events. Such was the case of Federico García Lorca who, until his tragic assassination, had remained unnoticed by Soviet critics.[19] On Lorca's execution, Mikhail Koltzov, *Pravda*'s correspondent in Spain, and one of the first reporters to confirm the news of his death on September 10, 1936, initiated a series of obituaries dedicated to the poet, which were followed by other important Hispanists of the time – Fyodor Kélyin, David Vigódskiy, and Nikolai Gabinskiy.[20] The obituaries provided a "Soviet myth of Lorca" which, in ideological terms, provided the perfect match: a victim of "Falangist executioners hired by the forces of international Fascism."[21]

Obviously, Lorca's wealthy family, flamboyant personality, and homosexuality, his journey to the United States, and his poetry anthology *Poet in New York*, which was strongly influenced by surrealism – aesthetics despised in official Soviet circles – were omitted.[22] Instead, Kélyin and Gabínskiy reported that Lorca had signed anti-Fascist manifestoes and was affiliated to revolutionary writers' circles, attributing to him publications that were nonexistent.[23] In other words, Lorca's inclusion in the mainstream of Soviet poetry took a clear direction: emphasis on "revolutionary" themes, the poet's "civic attitudes," and the folkloric roots of his creativity. His "Soviet" canonization focused for the most part on exploitation of the gypsy theme, and *Romancero Gitano* became Lorca's most translated piece as it clearly explored popular topoi and depicted the "lives of ordinary people," demonstrating not just the "correct" political orientation of Lorca but of all foreign writers and poets who adhered to the Soviet cause.[24]

Alberti's articles on the dead poet in 1937–39 further contributed to Lorca's entry into the pantheon of foreign figures accepted by Soviet censorship.[25] By the end of the 1930s, Lorca had become *the* Spanish reference for pro-Communist tendencies vis-à-vis Soviet culture, notwithstanding the fact that Lorca's Communist orientation remained, for the most part, an invention of Soviet propaganda.[26] Embracing Lorca's story was indeed part and parcel of the Soviet reception of the Spanish Civil War, which was deemed crucial due to its huge propaganda potential. In 1936–37, news from Spain occupied central space in Soviet newspapers such as *Pravda* and *Izvestia*, and even got to the point that it was given more visibility than national news, probably in an attempt to deflect attention away from pressing domestic problems. Articles by Mikhail Koltzov and Ilya Ehrenburg, Russian reporters of the Spanish Civil War, always written in very emotional and dramatic tones, were accompanied by various fund-raising campaigns published in Soviet newspapers to help the Spanish workers.[27] Even the New Year issue of *Pravda* on January 1, 1937, placed Spanish news on the second page, just after Stalin's New Year greetings, whereas page five of each number of this newspaper between 1936 and 1937 featured a column called "On the Fronts of Spain," which was dedicated almost completely to Spanish events.

As far as the Soviet public was concerned, Lorca's death and poetic talent embodied the suffering of the Spanish working class.[28] But, while Lorca became the dead poet enthroned in the USSR, it was Rafael Alberti, the living one, who efficiently capitalized on his position in the Spanish artistic field from 1936 to 1938. While a re-examination of the crucial and intensive activism that Alberti and María Teresa León displayed in Madrid during the civil war years demands a study that is beyond the limits of the present chapter, suffice to say that it included a series of key projects. Among them were the launching of *El Mono Azul* (1936–37); their advocacy for *teatro de urgencia*;[29] León's administrative responsibilities in protecting artistic patrimony and the evacuation of museum holdings; her pivotal role in the direction of the young theatre company *Nueva Escena*; Alberi's adaptation of Miguel de Cervantes's tragedy *Numancia* and its opulent representation at the Zarzuela Theater, as well as speeches on radio and at public meetings, to mention just some of their most well-known activities. They all affirm that throughout the civil war the Albertis' presence and activities in Republican Spain were paramount and omnipresent. Only once did the Albertis leave the country. That was in March 1937, when the poet and his partner returned to the USSR for the third time. Alberti himself published a few miscellanies on this journey. Always colored by superficial impressions, they included a laconic note, poorly translated, about his meeting with Stalin, whom he portrayed naively as a friendly character.[30] Similarly, very few publications appeared in the Spanish press.[31] It seems that Alberti and María Teresa León elegantly concealed any circumstances, events, and sensitive topics that could shed light on their mission.

If that is the case, then Rafael Alberti's close relations with Fyodor Kélyin, the couple's major contact in Moscow during their first three visits, and Rafael's persistent loyalty to Soviet Stalinism, which conceal crucial issues of translation, mediation, and financing, not to mention the 1933–38 purges and repression – need to be revisited. All in all, they highlight the tensions between Alberti's moral commitment as *la voz del proletariado*, on the one hand, and his position as a fellow-traveler who, far from maintaining a critical attitude, indulged in Soviet agitation and propaganda, playing the role of the shrewd diplomat, on the other.

Camarada Stalin! From Ideological Tourism to Secret Diplomacy?

As opposed to the Albertis' two previous visits, during the 1937 one they elbowed their way through to the top figures of the Soviet apparatus. The couple became a source of machinations among agents such as Georgi

Dimitrov, the high-ranking leader who acted as general secretary of the International Control Commission (IKKI) and since 1935 had been director of the Comintern (along with Dolores Ibarruri and Ernst Thälmann), and Nicolai Yehzov, the newly appointed head of the NKVD – the People's Commissariat for Internal Affairs which concentrated Soviet intelligence services – known posthumously as "Stalin's loyal executioner."[32]

This interest in the Spanish poet on the part of major figures such as Dimitrov and Yehzov reveals that the Albertis were considered not mere representatives of Spanish culture, but political figures. If that was the case, Alberti, assisted by María Teresa León, was employing a double standard that allowed him to be active simultaneously in multiple spheres of influence in Spain, in the USSR, and in the international circuit of anti-Fascist artists and intellectuals which the Albertis deemed as top priority. What do these various levels of activity and intriguing connections reveal about Rafael Alberti's modus operandi? A reconstruction of the couple's visit to Moscow might help shed some light on this yet untapped issue.

On March 1, 1937, the date of Rafael Alberti and María Teresa León's arrival in Moscow, *Pravda* announced their eight-day visit to the USSR. María Teresa León herself declared that they were making a short, touristic trip: "During these days we want to see everything new that has appeared in Moscow in the last years. And there are many new things. First, we will see your spectacular subway, the Lenin Museum, we will [also] visit the Pushkin exhibition."[33]

The Soviet press followed the Albertis' movements and reported daily on their visits to factories, exhibitions, and the like. Although the couple remained in Moscow after their planned date of return, March 8, no further updates appeared. News of their meeting with Stalin, on March, 20, came out in *Izvestia,* which reported telegraphically on March 21: "On March 20, Comrade STALIN received the Spanish writers Rafael Alberti and María Teresa León. The conversation lasted two hours."[34]

The initial secrecy of the meeting, timidly broken by *Izvestia,* is worth noting. *Izvestia* was less prestigious than *Pravda,* which was considered the first Bolshevik newspaper. As the platform of the government's official news, *Pravda* set the tone for other Soviet publications and traditionally published information on Stalin's meetings with foreign intellectuals. A day later, on March 22, both *Pravda* and *Izvestia* published an identical text "signed" by Rafael Alberti on the conversation with Stalin:

> Two hours spent with Comrade Stalin is too short a time to understand and explain, who and how this man is. During the first few minutes of

our conversation we were overwhelmed by our own excitement: we were speaking, so simply and cordially, to the leader of the great Soviet Union.

Comrade Stalin is even more friendly and more human than all that could be said about him. We were astonished at the correctness and clarity of his words and judgments on Spanish affairs. He told us very cordially about our heroes, our leaders, our peasants, and writers. With an affectionate smile, he spoke of his sympathy for our brave youth. Other writers who have visited him always emphasize his energy and firmness. We were impressed by his kindness, his knowledge of the people, [and] his desire to see them happy, as well as by the unique ability of Comrade Stalin to resolve in his mind these constant problems posed by the fate of his enormous country, and the fact that he finds in this mind a place for our country as well.[35]

On March 23, Rafael Alberti and María Teresa León visited *Izvestia*'s editorial offices and gave yet another interview about the meeting. The newspaper reported as follows:

> . . . in the talk yesterday María Teresa León and Rafael Alberti expressed their great satisfaction with their visit to the USSR and emphasized that what had given [them] the greatest joy and impressed them in an unforgettable way was their conversation with Comrade Stalin. Comrades León and Alberti also shared their plans to convene the International Congress of Antifascist Writers in Spain.[36]

If indeed the Albertis intended to obtain a personal appointment with Stalin in order to convince him to send a Soviet delegation to the Second International Congress of Antifascist Writers that was to be held in Valencia in late 1937, their proposal was a blessing in disguise.

According to recent Soviet scholarship, prior to the meeting with Alberti, Stalin had discarded the idea of Soviet writers participating in the Second International Congress as by then, the Soviet higher echelons were highly suspicious of their contacts with Western intellectuals.[37] The previous visits to the USSR by André Gide and Lion Feuchtwanger had raised serious doubts about the capacity of the Soviet secret services to completely monitor foreigners' whereabouts on their visits to the USSR and, even less, predict their public declarations on their return.

The researcher Natalia Kharitonova, who worked with restricted access reports kept in the National Archives in Moscow, contends that Soviet agents knew that Alberti wanted to meet with Stalin, and provided arguments to reverse the decision. According to Kharitonova, Alberti had spread rumors that the presence of a Soviet delegation in Valencia could help to combat both Trotskyist tendencies and the growing popularity of Gide's recent book *Retour de l'USSR.* Far from presenting a benevolent review of Soviet life, the book that soon became a bestseller, had come out in Spanish, translated by Sur, the publishing house headed by Victoria Ocampo in Buenos Aires, Argentina. This information appeared in Nicolai Yezhov's special report to Stalin from March 11, 1937. Yezhov sent the dictator yet another urgent communication, this time with a message from Kélyin, Alberti's closest contact in Moscow. As a member of the "foreign commission" of the Union of Soviet writers which monitored foreign visitors to the USSR, Kélyin had apparently obtained from Alberti new details about clandestine negotiations between Julio Álvarez del Vayo, one of the most visible faces of the Spanish Popular Front on the international scene, and the British secret service, behind the back of the Soviet Union.[38] If indeed Kélyin reported directly to Yezhov, then Kélyin's implications regarding the inner workings of the NKVD during the most active period of the Great Purge, 1937–38, was in itself highly significant.

In any event, Alberti arrived at Stalin's office in the afternoon of that very same day, March 20. Whether the clandestine negotiations of Álvarez del Vayo were a kind of "bait" to put pressure on the Soviet apparatus and attract Stalin's attention, or whether Alberti indeed had confidential information about it, the poet did behave with great care, worthy of a professional diplomat. Most probably, Alberti's mission on his 1937 trip was to get an appointment with Stalin. And, among the matters to be raised were a request for the presence of Soviet writers at the Second International Congress of Antifascist Writers in Valencia, as well as the possibility of shipping Spanish children as civil war refugees to the Soviet Union. María Teresa León's memoirs provide an alternative version of their conversation with the Soviet leader, by inferring that the meeting with Stalin was a "pleasant surprise" for the couple and that it took place "at Stalin's own initiative."

> One afternoon, Fedor Kélyin, a friend who never separated his friendship from ours, invited us to a new teahouse that had opened in Moscow. My friends, I believe that today will be a great day for you. Please tell us more. No, no. I cannot say anything. I figure it, only. And we kept insisting, and he kept rejecting our request, amused by our insistence. Some time passed. Kélyin, you're cheating on us. No, no. And he was not deceiving us. An officer approached the table and said: "Comrade Stalin is waiting for you."[39]

Her memoirs dismiss the idea that they were "expecting to meet a major figure" in Moscow, and that their stay would surpass by almost two weeks the planned duration of their visit.León devotes several pages of her book to the meeting. Despite detailed descriptions of the décor and furnishings of the office, and her personal opinion of Stalin – "we thought he looked thin and sad" – she says very little about the content of the conversation, except for two important details:

> Stalin approved the coming of the Soviet writers to Spain . . . We talked about the great difficulties we had to protect our children. Oh, if I said to the Soviet women: do you want to receive a Spanish child? All Russian mothers would open their arms! But what about the journey, and the frontiers?[40]

Despite her loose references, the fact that the members of the Soviet delegation included such figures as Mikhail Koltzov, Alexei Tolstoi, Alexander Fadeev, Vsevolod Vishnevski, Vladimir Stavski, Agnia Barto, Ivan Mikitenko, Viktor Fink, and Ilya Ehrenburg, and that the first shipment of 72 children from Madrid and Valencia left for the Soviet Union that same month, March 1937, suggest that Alberti managed to advance these goals.[41]

But there was more to it than that. An entry in the published diaries of Georgi Dimitrov, dated March 20, opens a Pandora's Box, in the absence of other, more substantial documents. The account provides highlights of the Albertis' meeting with Stalin as apparently reported to Dimitrov by the translator, Serafima Gopner, who took notes of the conversation.[42] Even though Dimitrov's entry provides no direct evidence of Josef Stalin's thoughts or questioning, nor would Gopner herself, as Stalin's translator, speak to Dimitrov about Comrade Stalin's exchange with Alberti, it might shed light on topics that were relevant from the Soviet perspective. Dimitrov's notes clearly state that the Spanish people were in no condition to bring about a proletarian revolution – the internal and, especially, the international situation did not favor such a development in comparison with 1917 Russia. They also confirm the Comintern's embrace of the Popular Front in the Spanish Civil War, restating that the Communist and Socialist parties had to join forces in order to sustain a democratic republic. The latter would strengthen the Popular Front and intimidate the anarchists. Dimitrov's reports also state that on a global scale Spain was the vanguard but there was a danger of it running ahead of events. The recommendation was that Francisco Largo Caballero be kept as head of government, given his resolute character and will to fight against Fascism but not as minister of war: the "general staff" [the pro-Republican military forces under his command] was depicted as inept and unreliable.[43] The entry finally warns against the surrender of Madrid, which would cause complete demoralization among the Republicans, and lead to final defeat. Paradoxically, the entry also implies a belief in the final victory of the Spanish Republic![44]

Indeed, the highlights jotted down by Dimitrov, as "reported" by Gopner, repeat topics that appear in another entry dating from March 14, when Dimitrov himself attended a meeting with Stalin, Vyacheslav Molotov, and Palmiro Togliattti at the Kremlin. There, the need not to eject Largo Caballero as head of government but to remove him as minister of war; the demand for greater participation of the Spanish Communist Party in government; the possibility of a forced retreat of foreign forces from Spain; and the need to disband the International Brigades, were also raised.

Whether or not Dimitrov's entries are questionable, one point is clear: besides Stalin, Dimitrov, Togliatti, and Molotov were also major figures. Yezhov, as head of NKVD was extremely dangerous. Kélyin, as an espionage agent, probably against his will, was also an unreliable pawn. The fact that Alberti made his way through such a decisive cadre of figures attests to his capabilities of negotiating with the upper Soviet echelons and of being anything but a naive. However, throughout the years, Rafael Alberti built a smokescreen around these issues, repeating over and over a story that presented him as either an innocent traveler to the USSR or as an infatuated, philo-Soviet street poet in Spain – an image that does not correspond with the facts, be they the circumstances of his journey, his intimate and enduring relationship with Kélyin, Yezhov's reports, or Dimitrov's memoirs. The smokescreen was maintained equally by both Alberti and the Soviet press. Nonetheless, much can be learnt about Alberti's silence, especially when the poet's 1937 journey is placed in the context of those of other fellow travelers who visited the USSR at about the same time.

Rafael Alberti vis-à-vis André Gide and Lion Feuchtwanger

André Gide visited the USSR in the summer of 1936, at the height of his prestige in French letters and in European intellectual circles. As one of the greatest assets of Soviet international cultural politics, Gide, an energetic and tireless voyager, then in his mid-sixties, spent nine weeks touring the Soviet Union. On his return, Gide published his best-selling travelogue, *Retour de l'USSR*. Gide's book, released in late 1936, months after the outbreak of the Spanish Civil War, proved to be a total fiasco for

Soviet propaganda abroad while Gide became notorious as one of the few celebrated fellow travelers to publically break with Stalin's Soviet Union. Overnight, the book became the most critical testimony of Soviet society ever published by an internationally famous former devotee. In methodical fashion, Gide's reflections warned readers against the dangers of post-revolutionary Soviet society, with its increasing re-stratification and differentiated lifestyles, the newly-born conformism, cultural decay, and ideological oppressiveness.[45] Gide's indignant comment as to whether in "any other country in the world, even in Hitler's Germany, thought was less free, more bowed down, more fearful (terrorized) or more enslaved" lost him many of the left-wing friends that his adherence to Communism had originally won him.

Even if we accept the assertion that an attentive reader of Gide's *Retour* will surely realize that the French intellectual knew full well the rules of the game of Soviet friendship and that, for quite a while, he was more than willing to play along, Gide's observations offer a challenging and thought-provoking portrait of Soviet society, as seen by a foreign and critical eye at the time.[46] His sagacious rhetoric, despite indulgence in overgeneralizations, could not but unsettle Western devotees of the Soviet creed, as he pondered:

> Are my fears exaggerated? I hope so. As far as that goes, the Soviet Union has already shown us that it was capable of abrupt reversals. But I do fear that in order to cut short these bourgeois tendencies that are now being approved and fostered by the rulers, a revulsion will soon appear necessary . . .
>
> What is known as "counterrevolutionary" in the USSR of today is not that at all. In fact, it is practically the opposite.
>
> The spirit which is today held to be counterrevolutionary is that same revolutionary spirit, that . . . first broke through the half-rotten dam of the old Tzarist world . . .
>
> But when the revolution was accomplished, triumphant, stabilized . . . the feelings which had animated the first revolutionaries . . . ceased to be useful.[47]

Many of Gide's assertions were directly critical:

> To say that Stalin is always in the right is tantamount to saying that Stalin always gets the best of it . . . We were promised a proletarian dictatorship. We are far from the mark. A dictatorship, yes, obviously; but the dictatorship of a man, not of the united workers, not of the Soviets. It is

> important not to deceive oneself . . . this is not what was desired . . . we should even say this is exactly what was not desired.[48]

In the same vein, the French writer argued that "to suppress the opposition in a State, to prevent it from declaring itself, in the light of day, is an invitation to terrorism." Actually, Gide – as opposed to Rafael Alberti and many other visitors who were carefully monitored by Soviet cultural officials inside the USSR – had relied on his own entourage, mostly a group of his acquaintances, which included French Communists and writers, and the Dutch ex-Trotskyist Jef Last, who knew Russian and had lived extensively in the USSR. It was this cadre of non-Soviet mediators who provided Gide with a measuring rod against which he could test the surroundings. In contrast to the Albertis' close intimacy with Fyodor Kélyin, who acted as a constant mediator between the couple and Soviet society and its interlocutors, Gide openly expressed complete distrust of the interpreter imposed on him, "the charming comrade [Bolya]" about whom he referred scathingly:

> Nothing indeed ever floors her, and she provides an answer to everything; the more ignorant she is of a subject, the more cocksure she becomes . . . Our charming guide is as obliging and devoted as it is possible to be. But there is this about her that is rather fatiguing – the information she gives us is never precise except when it is wrong.[49]

The scholar Ludmila Stern has meticulously uncovered the behind-the-scenes' operations of the guides, translators, and interpreters who worked for VOKS, the All-Union Society for Cultural Relations with Foreign Countries. Stern reconstructs VOKS' mechanisms of attraction and manipulation, in which Soviet employees, interpreters, and guides played a central role in seducing Western artists, intellectuals, and professionals. By planning, conducting, and monitoring foreigners' visits to the same socio-cultural institutions that promoted Soviet achievements (such as collective farms, the Central Park of Culture and Rest – the future Gorky Park – and the Moscow metro), VOKS's controlled hospitality, as Stern puts it, merged opulent banquets and heavy drinking holidays on the Black Sea with cynical, stage-managed displays of cultural excellence. The aim was clear: to have foreign visitors spread a positive image of the USSR in the West on their return.[50]

By the time the first Moscow trials had begun to cause consternation among the previously solid ranks of Western supporters, the Soviet authorities in Moscow strictly forbade visitors' deviations from arranged official tours and sites. An increased vigilance order issued by Yezhov himself in 1936 hit VOKS hard, leading members of the staff to spy on each other and even send letters of denunciation to the NKVD. The fact that Gide had travelled undisturbed, during the 1930s, was the exception to the rule according to which visitors were no longer allowed to wander off unsupervised as had been the case in the 1920s.[51]

By December 1936, following Gide's visit and shortly after the publication of his *Retour*, Mikhail Koltzov programmed the visit to Moscow of Lion Feuchtwanger, then a famous exiled German Jewish writer living in southern France. Koltzov had sought special approval for the invitation from the Central Committee and the Politburo. It was assumed that the visit might well prompt him not only to write a rebuttal of Gide's book but also reverse critical views of the Moscow trials.[52] Centainly, Feuchtwanger had condemned the 1936 trials of Zinoviev and Kamenev. Therefore, the German writer's visit was set to coincide with the second round of trials that included Pyatakov, Radek, and others, to be held in January 1937.[53]

As a "left-bourgeois writer" – *levoburzhuazny pisatel* – in VOKS's terminology, Feuchtwanger seems to have gone to Moscow, by his own account, as a sympathizer.[54] Although his travels in the Soviet Union are beyond the scope of this paper, it is worth noting that a report on his meeting with Stalin appeared the next day, January 9, on *Pravda*'s front page.[55] The transcription of their exchange has also been preserved at the State archives.[56] There is no access to any similar document on the meeting with the Albertis. Moreover, the transcription presents the main points that the German Jewish writer raised with the tyrant. Even if we assume that the resulting text was modified, Feuchtwanger touched on delicate issues: internal policy and the political regime that the Soviet Union was implementing; the cult of personality and the dangers of internal repression; the definition of the intelligentsia as an intellectual class and the possibility of criticism in Soviet literature; the plight of the Soviet people in their daily lives; and, last but not least, Stalin's own worldview and perception of society.[57] It is difficult to imagine that the exchange that took place between Stalin and the Albertis could have gone along similar lines, if only because the Albertis might not have been aware of the horrendous nature of the Stalinist regime. They were not in a position to voice a critical stance vis-à-vis Stalin and the regime he represented, given the dependence of Republican Spain on Soviet military and logistical assistance, whether real or imagined. Probably, the Albertis might have also been much more interested in discussing urgent issues of Spanish politics and the plight of their own people.

As opposed to Alberti, Lion Feuchtwanger, as was the case of Gide, did publish a book about his impressions of the trip upon his return. Despite the negative predictions of the Soviet secret agencies, the book offered a relatively benevolent appraisal, although it raised here and there cautious criticism.[58] Interestingly, in regard to the second round of public trials against Pyatakov, Radek, and a dozen other defendants hold in January 1937, the Russian translation of Feuchtwanger's book conceded that:

> . . . in Western Europe [the trials] looked one way . . . all the evidence was apparently obtained in very dubious ways. All the process seemed like a theater . . . in Moscow it looked another way. When I was present in Moscow during the second process, when I saw and heard Pyatakov, Radek, and their friends, my doubts were dissolved.[59]

Several sources cite the fact that Feuchtwanger was "subsidized" by the Soviet government and that the deputy director of the Council of People's Commissars, V.I Mezhlauk, published a document with a resolution to pay Feuchtwanger 5,000 US dollars. [60] As for the reception of Feuchtwanger's and Gide's books in the Soviet Union, it did not differ dramatically. In the case of Gide's *Retour de l'U.R.S.S.*, the response was the usual one for such texts in a foreign language: it was not translated, but various newspapers published highly critical articles, such as the one that appeared in *Pravda* at the end of 1936.[61] Like many other foreign books considered anti-Soviet, Gide's became a kind of apophasis: everyone knew about it; many specialists had read it; and everyone knew that others knew, but nobody confided this knowledge. Nonetheless, Mikhail Koltzov who was chair of the Foreign Commission of the Soviet Writers' Union and a well-known journalist in the USSR and the West, gave a highly negative report in Valencia of Gide's book and announced his decision to abandon the latter's status as "friend of the Soviet Union."[62] In the case of Feuchtwanger, the book was translated into Russian in 1937 and the short review articles that appeared in *Pravda* and *Literaturnaya Gazeta* discussed the text with only partial enthusiasm.[63]

Unlike Gide and Feuchtwanger, Alberti did not leave any significant document of his 1937 visit to the Soviet Union. In *La arboleda perdida*, Stalin is mentioned only once in the list of politicians who ruled the world, and, once again, in his "Resumen autobiográfico," published as part of the introduction to his *Obras Completas* (1988).[64] Both memoirs offer no details about his meeting with Stalin, except for his intention of seeing Stalin in order to ask him to enable Soviet delegates to attend the Second International Congress of Antifascist Writers.[65]

Alberti's silence is all the more intriguing given the complex contexts in which he operated. It is enough to mention that in the autumn of 1936, the Russian Hispanists Vadim Rakhmanov and David Vigódskiy were arrested and later died in concentration camps; members of the staff of *Sovetskaya Literatura,* such as Serguéi Sergueévich Dinámov and Serguéi Mijáilovich Tretiakov, the latter a friend of Alberti, fell in the purges, and Ilya Ehrenburg, the war correspondent for *Izvestia,* stayed in Spain until the end of the civil war and later fled to Paris. Among the important Hispanists of the time, only Fiodor Kélyin and Valentin Parnakh survived the repressions, probably at the cost of collaborating with the NKVD.

Gina Herrmann's study on Stalinist modes of self-fashioning among Spanish Communists reminds us that only a handful of Spanish Stalinists experienced first-hand the terror of Soviet persecution even when it permeated the rank and file of the Spanish Communist Party. Only later, claims Herrmann, would Spanish Communists become aware of the deportations and executions among their own ranks. If such an argument could partially justify Alberti's positioning in the mid- and late 1930s, when his own life was at risk and he felt obliged to stick to certain kinds of self-narratives from within the walls of the Party structure, this was less so when he published the autobiographical volumes of *La arboleda perdida,* which came out well after the 1956 Twentieth Congress of the Soviet Communist Party when Nikita Khrushchev exposed the crimes of the Stalinist era. Indeed, Alberti did no justice to the intricacies of the war years, as he himself declared at the end of the second tome of *La arboleda perdida.* His promise to review the conflict in a later volume never materialized.[66] Alberti's reticence to publically confront his Soviet past and connections continued in his Argentine exile.[67] Over the years, the public persona of Alberti of the war years as an extremely effective weapon of the Spanish Communist Party's cultural agenda faded away. The need to reinvent himself in the Argentine intellectual field led the poet to tame his pre-exile ideological zeal and activism. His contacts with the prominent pro-Republican figure who was highly critical of the Popular Front's policies, Victoria Ocampo, the first lady of Argentine letters, and *Sur,* the prestigious journal and publishing enterprise on the one hand, and the opportunities that Gonzalo Losada, the well-established Spanish entrepreneur and owner of a new publishing house that offered the growing community of Republican exiles in Buenos Aires an entry into the local editorial circuit, on the other, against the background of the establishment of Peronist rule, prompted Alberti to publically retreat into a poetic world where he returned to his pre-Republican lyricism and topics, against which he had so strongly rebelled in the 1930s.

Did Alberti internalize the ability to see and think one thing and with all sincerity say another, thus following what many Soviet actors deemed a necessary sacrifice for the future of Communism? George Orwell, one of the most lucid and committed intellectuals of the time, coined the concepts of doublethink and doublespeak to address the dilemmas faced by the intelligentsia and the intellectual class, albeit in totalitarian contexts. For Orwell, these notions meant the power of holding two contradictory beliefs in one's mind, simultaneously accepting both of them and having the capacity to deliberately tell lies while genuinely believing them. Doublethink and doublespeak also implied one's ability to be ready to forget any fact that had become inconvenient, and then, when it became necessary again, to retrieve it from oblivion for just as long as it was needed. This facility, to deny the existence of "objective" reality while taking into account the reality which one denies as indispensably necessary, is a complex doublethink exercise. Because, as Orwell put it: "if by tampering with reality while erasing such knowledge one can go on indefinitely, then the lie will always be one leap ahead of the truth."[68]

Notes

1 Cases in point are José Antonio Balbontín, José Díaz Fernández, Julián Zugazagoitia, Ramón Sender, Miguel Hernández, and the Peruvian César Vallejo.

2 A most important exception being Gina Herrmann, *Written in Red: The Communist Memoir in Spain* (Champaign, IL: University of Illinois Press, 2009). The impressive study of Lisa A. Kirschenbaum, *International Communism and the Spanish Civil War: Solidarity and Suspicion,* (New York: Cambridge University Press, 2015) mentions the Albertis'1937 visit very briefly focusing mainly on the figures of Dolores Ibarruri, Margarita Nelken and Juan Modesto.

3 See Michael David-Fox, "Opiate of the Intellectuals? Pilgrims, Partisans, and Political Tourists," *Kritika: Explorations in Russian and Eurasian History* (New Series) 12, no. 3 (Summer 2011): 721–38; Sheila Fitzpatrick, "Foreigners Observed: Moscow Visitors in the 1930s under the Gaze of Their Soviet Guides," *Russian History* 35, nos. 1/2, "'Festschrift' for Richard Hellie," part 2 (Spring–Summer 2008): 215–34.

4 From 1932 onward, Stalin and the top party elite agreed to destroy all dissidence through the staging of show trials, mass arrests, purges, and the prevention of any resistance to these "cleansings." In March 1936, the Soviet authorities published the ordinance "On Measures to Defend the USSR from the Penetration of Elements of Espionage, Terrorism and Sabotage." It specified "security measures" to control the activity of people who had contact with foreigners. See Lekha V. Zhukova and Leonid A. Kacva. *Istorija Rossii v datah. Spravochnik* (Moscow: Izdatelstvo Prospekt, 2014). By August-September, 1936, Stalin had launched "the Great Purge." The mechanisms of Stalin's purges, culminating in the Great Terror, made victims of millions of Russians between 1932 and 1939. See John Arch Getty, *The Road to Terror*

and the Self-Destruction of the Bolsheviks, 1932–1939, (New Haven/London: Yale University Press, 1999) and Hiroaki Kuromiya, *The Voices of the Dead: Stalin's Great Terror in the 1930s* (New Haven/London: Yale University Press, 2007).

5 Studies on the evolution of intellectual engagement in the context of early twentieth century European history that are relevant here are Alan Sheridan, *André Gide: A Life in the Present* (Cambridge, MA: Harvard University Press, 1999), and, David J. Fisher, *Romain Rolland and the Politics of Intellectual Engagement* (Berkeley, California University Press, 1988).

6 Rafael Osuna, *Las revistas españolas entre dos dictaduras: 1931–1939* (Valencia, Pre-textos, 1986), 126. A general assessment appears in Juan Avilés Farré, *La fe que vino de Rusia: La revolución bolchevique y los españoles (1917–1931),* (Madrid: Biblioteca Nueva, 1999).

7 Referred to as the Third International, the Comintern coordinated the USSR's interests with other national Communist parties. Active between 1919 and 1943, it integrated the various political networks into a general scheme to serve the directives of Soviet foreign policy. The organization's resolutions enforced the expansionist revolutionary ideology of Marxism-Leninism (a merger of Soviet messianic ethos and imperialism) that had determined Soviet policy since 1917 worldwide, Spain included. See Stanley G. Payne. *Unión Soviética, comunismo y revolución en España, (1931–1939)* (Barcelona: Plaza Janés, 2003), 8, and Antonio Elorza and Marta Bizcarrondo, *Queridos Camaradas. La Internacional Comunista y España, 1919–1939* (Barcelona: Planeta, 1999). On Soviet-Spanish diplomatic and cultural relations, see Daniel Kowalsky, *La Unión Soviética y la Guerra Civil Española* (Barcelona: Crítica, 2003).

8 See Kowalsky, *La Unión Soviética,* 153–94.

9 The Unión Internacional de Escritores Revolucionarios functioned as the Spanish Section of the International Union of Revolutionary Writers, known in Russia as MORP, with Fyodor Kélyin as director of its literary section. See Antonio San Román Sevillano, "Los Amigos de la Unión Soviética: Propaganda política en España, (1933–1938)," (PhD diss., Salamanca, 1994).

10 His poem "Un fantasma recorre Europa," published in a special issue completely devoted to the Soviet Union, moved the poet to the forefront as a popularizer of the Spanish Communist Party's slogans.

11 The articles are reprinted in Robert Marraste, ed., *Rafael Alberti: Prosas Encontradas* (Barcelona: Seix Barral, 2000), 110–51. For the Albertis' previous visits to the USSR and his embrace of Soviet ideology, see Silvina Schammah Gesser, *Madrid's Forgotten Avant-Garde: Between Essentialism and Modernity* (Brighton, Sussex Academic Press, 2015), 160–84.

12 It refers to the period of right wing rule during the Second Republic between the elections of November 1933 and February, 1936. It is generally discussed as a period of reaction to the policies of the Red Biennium that had proposed major reforms between 1931 and 1933.

13 See Natalia J. Kharitonova. "Izdatel'skaja sud'ba proizvedenij Ramona Sendera v SSSR: ot uspeha k zabveniju," *Novye rossijskie gumanitarnye issledovanija*, no. 9, (2014), http://www.nrgumis.ru/articles/298/ (accessed September 2, 2017).

14 *Casticismo* can be roughly defined is a literary, cultural and ideological stance, manifested in Spain since the eighteenth century in opposition to foreign influences, specially, the French Enlightenment. As a defensive claim of authentic cultural, religious and vital expressions, speech, and even political and social organization, the manifestations of *casticismo* are considered as markers of the Spanish national character.

15 Rafael Alberti, *Ispanskie krestyane: Perevod s ispanskogo i predislovie F. Kelyina* (Moscow, GIHL, 1934).

16 See Carlos Flores Pazos, "Amigo Kelyin: Ayúdennos. Rafael Alberti y la URSS, 1932–1934," in *Entre el clavel y la espada: Rafael Alberti en su siglo*, Museo Nacional Centro de Arte Reina Sofía (Madrid, 2003), 251–81.

17 See "Resolution of Politburo from May 9," RGASPI (Russian State Archive of Socio-Political History), f. 17, op. 163, d. 1022, l. 126, and Maxim Gorky. *Sobranie sochineniy v 30 tomah: Tom 27. Statji, dokladi, rechi, privetstviya (1933–1936)* (Moscow: GIHL, 1953), 51.

18 An exception was two reviews of Spanish literature published in 1934 in the journal *Internacionalnaya literatura* (International Literature), which presented a panoramic view of literary life in revolutionary Spain. The first focused mainly on Rafael Alberti and María Teresa León, while a second and shorter text was dedicated personally to the couple. See, Fyodor V. Kélyin, "Literaturnaja Ispaniya," *Internacionalnaya literatura*, No. 3–4 (1934): 267–79, and idem, "Rafael Alberti i Maria-Teresa Leon," *Internacionalnaya literatura*, No. 3–4 (1934): 239–45.

19 Olga Musaeva, who examined the Soviet reception of Lorca, affirms that the poet's name appears only once, in the list of members of the Association of Friends of the Soviet Union (AUS), published in the magazine *Socorro Rojo Internacional* in 1933. See, Olga I. Musaeva, "Federico Garcia Lorca v sovetskoj periodike 1930-h gg.: osobennosti recepcii," *Trudy po russkoj i slavjanskoj filologii. Literaturovedenie* (New Series) 7 (2009): 272–89. Also, the 1933 article dedicated to Spanish revolutionary writers by Fyodor Kélyin that mentions Ramón José Sender, Manuel Benavides, César Arconada, Joaquin Arderius, Isidoro Acevedo, and Rafael Alberti makes no reference to Lorca. Fyodor V. Kélyin, "Revoljucionnaja literatura Ispanii na pod'eme," *Internacional'naja literatura*, no. 4 (1933): 157–62.

20 Idem, "Federico Garcia Lorca," *Literaturnaya gazeta*, no. 52 (615); September 15). p. 4; David I. Vigodskiy, "Federico Garcia Lorca," *Literaturniy Leningrad*, no. 43 (1936): 2; Nikolai S. Gabinskiy, "Federico

Garcia Lorca," *Sovetskoe iskusstvo,* no. 45 (September 29, 1936): 2; idem, "Federico Garcia Lorca," *Knizhnye novosti,* no. 27 (1936): 6–7.

21 See Gabinskiy, "Federico Garcia Lorca."

22 Kélyin, "Federico Garcia Lorca."

23 See Olga I. Musaeva, "Recepcija tvorchestva Federico Garcia Lorki v russkoj kul'ture (1930–1960-e gg.)," (PhD diss.,Tartu University, 2011).

24 Unsurprisingly, in the Soviet *Encyclopedia of Literature,* published during the decade 1929–39, all Spanish literature was classified according to its folk (e.g., the 16th century novella *Lazarillo de Tormés*) or upper-class (Machado's poetry) themes and origin, whereas all "bourgeois" authors were automatically omitted. See Vladimir S. Uzin. "Ispanskaja literatura," *Literaturnaja enciklopedija, v 11 tomah*, Moscow, 1929–39, Vol. 4. (Moscow: Izd-vo Kom. Akad., 1930), 598–627.

25 Raphael Alberti, "K Federico," *Internacional'naja literatura,* no. 8 (1938): 128–29; Raphael Alberti. "Pamjati Garcii Lorki," Transl. by N. Ljubimov, *Literaturnyj kritik,* no. 3 (1939): 165–77.

26 Musaeva, "Federico García Lorca"; Maxim Gorky, *Sobranie sochineniy v 30 tomah: Tom 27. Statji, dokladi, rechi, privetstviya (1933–1936)* (Moscow: GIHL, 1953).

27 See José García, *Ispaniya Narodnogo Fronta* (Moscow: Izdatelstvo Akademii Nauk SSSR, 1957), 51–52.

28 Except for one short poem. Federico García Lorca. "Ballada o morskoj vode. Stihi," Transl. by D. Vygodsky. *Zvezda,* no. 9 (1937): 69, Lorca's first poetry collection in Russian was published much later, in 1939.

29 *El Mono Azul* was a magazine published in the Republican side during the Spanish Civil War under the auspices of the Alliance of Antifascist Intellectuals for the Defense of Culture. Among its collaborators were Miguel Hernández, Vicente Aleixandre, Rafael Alberti, Manuel Altolaguirre, José Bergamín, María Teresa León, Luis Cernuda, Antonio Machado and Ramón J. Sender; among the non-Spaniards, Pablo Neruda, Vicente Huidobro and André Malraux. See José Monleón, *"El Mono Azul". Teatro de urgencia y romancero de la guerra civil.*(Ayuyo: Madrid, 1979). For Rafael Alberti, *teatro de urgencia* meant a new type of theater to be staged at the trenches, hence a theater of guerrillas with formal and thematic constraints, its topics well raised and resolved had to produce the strongest impact. María Teresa León made a long-lasting contribution to this subgenre. Inspired by the Soviet agit-prop, she conceived it a weapon of combat to be fully exploited by the Republican dramatists. See Miguel Bilbatúa, *Teatro de agitación política 1933–1939.* (Edicusa: Madrid, 1976) and Nigel Dennis and Emilio Peral Vega (eds.), *Teatro de la Guerra Civil. El bando republicano.* (Fundamentos: Madrid, 2009).

30 *Pravda,* March 22, 1937 (no. 80), 6; "Rafael Alberti i Maria-Teresa Leon o besede s tovarishhem Stalinym," *Izvestia,* March 22, 1937 (no. 70; 6232), 1.

31 See, *AHORA*, March 6, March 23, April 18, and April 22, 1937.

32 As head of the NKVD, Nicolai Yezhov (1936–38) had followed in the foot-

steps of Genrikh Yagoda (1934–36). A devout Stalinist who was not a member of the organs of state security Yezhov conducted the prosecution of his mentor Yagoda, who was the first of many to die on Yezhov's orders. See Marc Jansen and Nikita Petrov, *Stalin's Loyal Executioner: People's Commissar Nikolai Ezhov, 1895–1940* (Stanford, CA: Hoover Institution Press, 2002).

33 "Ispanskie revoljucionnye pisateli v Moskve," *Pravda*, March 1, 1937 (no. 59), 6.

34 *Izvestia*, March 21, 1937 (no. 69), 1.

35 *Izvestia*, March 22, 1937 (no. 70), 1, and *Pravda*, March 22, 1937 (no. 80), 1.

36 *Izvestia*, March 23, 1937 (no. 71), 1.

37 Natalia Y. Kharitonova. "Rafael Alberti v Sovetskoj Rossii: poet, politika i politiki," *Liki XX veka. Literatura i ideologija* (Moscow: Izdatel'stvo MGU, 2016), 132–39.

38 RGANI (Russian State Archive of Modern History). F.3, Op. 34, D. 205, L. 9.

39 María Teresa León, *Memoria de la melancolía* (Barcelona: Galaxia Gutenberg, 1999), 95.

40 Ibid., 96.

41 On the Second International Congress of Antifascist Writers see Manuel Aznar Soler, *Materiales documentales del Segundo Congreso de Escritores para la Defensa de la Cultura. (Valencia-Madrid-Barcelona-París, 1937)*, (A Coruña: Edicios do Castro, 2009). See also Zafra Enrique, Rosalia Crego, and Carmen Heredia. *Los ninos espanoles evacuados a la URSS (1937)* (Madrid: Ediciones de la Torre, 1989), and Marie Jose Devillard, *Los ninos españoles en la URSS (1937–1997)*: *Narración y Memoria* (Barcelona: Ariel, 2001).

42 Serafima Ilinichna Gopner was a representative of the Ukranian CP section of the Comintern.

43 Georgi Dimitrov, *Annals of Communism: The Diary of Georgi Dimitrov*, (New Haven: Yale University Press, 2012), p. 60.

44 Ibid., p. 58.

45 See André Gide, *Return from the U.S.S.R.*, trans. Dorothy Bussy (New York: Knopf, 1937); idem, *Afterthoughts: A Sequel to Back from the U.S.S.R.*, 2nd ed., trans. Dorothy Bussy (London: Martin Secker and Warburg, 1938). See also the most complete study by Alan Sheridan, *André Gide: A Life in the Present* (Cambridge, MA: Harvard University Press, 1999),and Michael Lucey, *Gide's Bent, Sexuality, Politics, Writing (Ideologies of Desire)* (Oxford: Oxford University Press, 1995), especially 187–211.

46 David-Fox, "Opiate of the Intellectuals? ," 731.

47 Quoted from Gide, *Return from the U.S.S.R.*, 39–41, https://archive.org/details/returnfromtheuss010214mbp.

48 Ibid., 49.

49 Gide, *Afterthoughts*, reproduced in Ludmila Stern, "Moscow 1937: The

Interpreter's Story," *Australian Slavonic and East European Studies* 21, nos. 1–2 (2007), 79.

50 See Stern, "Moscow 1937," 73–96.

51 See for instance, Fernando de los Ríos *Mi viaje a la Rusia Soviética* (Madrid: R. Caro Raggio, 1921), and Walter Benjamin's *Moscow Diaries,* from 1927, reprinted in *October*, 35 (Winter 1985), 4–135.

52 On Feuchtwanger, see Anne Hartmann, "Un Anti-Gide Allemand: Lion Feuchtwanger," *Cahiers du Monde Russe* 52, no. 1 (January–March 2011): 115–32, and Stern, "Moscow 1937."

53 The second Moscow process was the trial of the "parallel anti-Soviet Trotskyite center", also known as the "trial of 17". It was the second of the so-called Moscow trials, a show trial of a group of former party leaders, participants of the opposition. The case was heard in the Military Collegium of the Supreme Court of the USSR from 23 to 30 January 1937. The main defendants were Georgy L. Pyatakov (former Chairman of Provisional Soviet Government of Ukraine), Karl .B. Radek (famous writer and journalist, coauthor of Soviet Constitution), and others.

54 Stern, "Moscow 1937," 82.

55 *Pravda,* January 9, 1937, (no. 10), 1.

56 Published in Leonid V. Maksimenkov. "Ocherki nomenklaturnoj istorii sovetskoj literatury, Zapadnye piligrimy u stalinskogo prestola (Fejhtvanger i drugie)." *Voprosy literatury,* no. 2 (2004): 257–60.

57 Ibid.

58 First edition in German: Lion Feuchtwanger, *Moscau 1937: Ein Reisebericht fur meine freunde* (Amsterdam: Verlag NV, 1937). The book was immediately translated into Russian: *Moskva 1937: Otchet o poezdke dlja moih druzej'* (Moscow: Izd-vo Hudozhestvennaja literatura, 1937), and to Spanish: *Moscow-1937: Mi visita descrita para mis amigos* (Santiago de Chile: Pax, 1937).

59 Quote of Lion Feuchtwanger, in Russian, in *Moskva Stalinskaya* (Moscow: Algoritm, 2015), 228.

60 Russian researcher Kirill Anderson in his book *Kremlevskij kinoteatr: 1928–1953. Dokumenty* (Moscow: ROSSP N, 2005), 334, reproduces the corresponding document note of July 22, 1936, issued by Mezhlauk.

61 "Smeh i slezy Andrje Zhida," *Pravda.* December 3, (no. 332), 1936, 4.

62 See Mikhail E. Koltzov. *Ispanskii dnevnik* (Moscow: Griphon, 2005), 416–24.

63 See Feuchtwanger, *Moskva 1937.*

64 See Rafael Alberti, *La arboleda perdida, 2. Tercer y cuarto libros (1931–1987)* (Madrid: Alianza, 1998), and *Obras Completas* Vol. 1. (Madrid: Aguilar, 1988).

65 Until 1937, Stalin had received many writers and poets, among them Bernard Shaw, Henri Barbusse, Emil Ludwig, Herbert George Wells, Romain Rolland, André Gide, and Lion Feuchtwanger. After the meeting with the Albertis, Stalin lost interest in this kind of encounter and no further

meetings with foreign intellectuals took place. Leonid V. Maksimenkov. "Ocherki nomenklaturnoj istorii sovetskoj literatury, Zapadnye piligrimy u stalinskogo prestola (Fejhtvanger i drugie)," *Voprosy literatury*, no. 2 (2004): 257–60; Zhores A. Medvedev and Roj A. Medvedev, *Neizvestnyj Stalin* (Moscow: Vremja, 2011), 174

66 Herrmann, *Written in Red*, 101.

67 On Rafael Alberti's exile in Argentina, see Raquel Macciuci, "Autonomía del arte y compromiso en la obra de tres escritores españoles exiliados en la Argentina: Ramón Gómez de la Serna, Francisco Ayala y Rafael Alberti," Universidad Nacional de La Plata, Facultad de Humanidades y Ciencias de la Educación, 2002, http://www.fuentesmemoria.fahce.unlp.edu.ar/tesis/te.127/te.127.pdf. See also Adriana Petra, "Cosmopolitismo y nación: Los intelectuales comunistas argentinos en tiempos de la Guerra Fría (1947–1956)," *Revista Contemporánea: Historia y problemas del siglo veinte* 1 (2010): 51–74, and Roberto F. Giusti, *Momentos de la cultura argentina*, (Buenos Aires: Raigal, 1954).

68 George Orwell, *Nineteen Eighty-Four* (London: Martin Secker & Warburg, 1949), 220.

10

Solidarity and Non-intervention: France and the Spanish Civil War

DAVID A. MESSENGER

With the outbreak of the civil war in Spain on July18, the Spanish Republican government wasted no time in seeking aid. A harried note from Prime Minister José Giral of the Spanish government asking for assistance on July 20 was followed on July 21 by a formal request for military aircraft and weapons from the French government and from Air Minister Pierre Cot; a more immediate request for 20 aircraft was made to the French ambassador in Madrid shortly thereafter, on July 24.[1] A first meeting on July 20 of France's Popular Front foreign policy leadership, headed by Premier Léon Blum, Foreign Minister Yvon Delbos, and the ministers responsible for military and defense matters had established that such aid would be possible and even desirable.[2]

By July 24, news of French aid had become public, sparking debate in the French press.[3] Concerns about French intervention were also raised in foreign capitals, such as Berlin.[4] Within the French Foreign Ministry at the Quai d'Orsay, debates about the implications of private businesses selling weapons compared with government sales, and the fear of sparking German or Italian intervention on the side of the rebels in Spain, revealed a deep hesitation about responding positively to the Spanish Republican government's request.[5] The secretary general of the Foreign Ministry, Alexis Léger, is credited with developing a non-intervention plan in the days immediately following the outbreak of war.[6] As a result, the French cabinet voted on July 25 to ban all sales of war materiel to Spain; unarmed commercial aircraft sold by private business to the Spanish government could be transferred to Spain, an important exception, but nonetheless the Quai had won the argument for the moment. Measures to disarm Spaniards in the south of France were ordered by the Interior Ministry and communicated to prefects in the border region.[7] France announced its decision by making a firm commitment not to intervene in the affairs of other states. However, it also made clear to the ambassador in Madrid, Jean Herbette, that the Republican government was the lawful government of Spain and a "friend" whose fight against the military rebels was "legitimate."[8]

The statement to Herbette suggested that consensus within the government was difficult to attain, or maintain, and the debate was not resolved by the cabinet decision of July 25. Public Health Minister Henri Sellier and his colleague Marius Moutet spoke at a Popular Front rally stating that a Nationalist victory in the civil war was sure to bring about world war and thus must be stopped by any and all means.[9] The vocal support of the Soviet Union for the Republican government in Madrid, which included early deliveries of oil and clothes, followed soon after by weapons and war materiel, raised tensions. The linkage of France to the Soviets in supporting the Republic was a common accusation made in places such as Berlin, where the Nazi government of Adolf Hitler considered the Spanish Republicans to be Marxist, as did Mussolini's Fascist regime in Italy.[10] Yet at the same time, reports from Spain indicated that in cities such as Burgos, the population had rallied around the military rebels, not the Republican government.[11]

In the press, newspapers associated with the Right, the Far Right (*L'Action Française*), and the more traditional (*Le Figaro*) vehemently opposed intervention, using the argument that aid to Spain, even to its legitimate government, represented an illegal act, as well as one that was not in French interests, which were to preserve European peace and maintain good relations with Italy and Germany.[12] From the opposite, anarchist, end of the spectrum, the newspaper associated with the Union anarchiste française, *Le Libertaire*, declared on July 31, 1936, that "the Spanish Revolution is ours" and in Marseilles, French, Spanish, and Italian anarchists formed a group in August 1936 to aid and promote the advent of revolution to Spain in the midst of civil war.[13] *L'Oeuvre* stated quite bluntly that defeat of the Spanish government would be a defeat for France.[14] Intervention was strongly favored by many parts of the Left.

It would be wrong, however, to assume that debates over intervention were always oppositional ones. France in 1936 was divided between a sense of solidarity with the Republican government among left-leaning activists and politicians, support for the Nationalist rebels on the right, and a belief, if half-hearted, that non-intervention was the policy to follow. For some, these were set positions aligned against each other, replicating the divisions of the civil war in Spain and raising the possibility of civil war or civil war-like tensions in France. Yet, for many it was not solidarity or non-intervention when it came to Spain, but aspects of both. This chapter seeks to outline the complex response within France to the outbreak of civil war in Spain, played out in politics but also in many other parts of society.

The Popular Front government, led by Léon Blum, had come to power in May 1936, as a coalition of Radicals and Socialists, supported by the Communist Party although the Communists took no positions in the cabinet. Blum became the first Socialist head of government in France. In Spain, a similar Popular Front government had been elected in February, again with Communist support but without Communist participation in government. For its first two months in office, domestic affairs consumed Blum's coalition as a series of strikes led to major policy initiatives on wages, benefits and social policies.[15] The Spanish Civil War was unexpected; indeed, on June 6, the French ambassador to Spain, Jean Herbette, reported that the Spanish Foreign Ministry did not expect war, although it acknowledged there were plotters within the military. It claimed that most soldiers desired to defend public order and the government, and Herbette agreed with this assessment.[16] Even on the day of the military uprising, on July 18, Blum met with Jimenez de Asua, a member of the Spanish parliament, who assured him all was well.[17]

Blum was especially concerned about the impact on national unity that the Spanish Civil War might have within France. His Popular Front government was a union of middle and working-class elements, and the outbreak of strikes and protests in June and July 1936 that greeted its ascendency to power, resulting in a series of major labor and other reforms, tested that coalition. While Blum himself was very much in favor of aid, not all members of his Socialist Party were, and the Radical Party, his coalition partner, was divided between pro-Republicans, such as Air Minister Pierre Cot, and those who were extremely hesitant, such as Foreign Minister Yvon Delbos, backed by people such as Léger in the Quai d'Orsay, as well as the French ambassador to Madrid, Herbette.[18] This helps explain the context of the July 25 cabinet meeting.

The Communist Party of France, a supporter of Blum's government while not a participant, was similarly divided, despite its clear sympathy for the Frente Popular government in Madrid. Many in the National Assembly, such as the Communist Florimond Bonte, raised the fear, on July 31, of a Fascist victory and demanded action.[19] Numerous Communists and others on the left, however, while eager to aid the Spanish Republicans, also wanted to preserve the French Popular Front; and many understood that fulfilling both desires would be a difficult if not impossible task. As Martin Hurcombe has pointed out, the French Popular Front was built on a paradox: to preserve the bourgeois liberal democratic system in the hope of building an alternative to traditional capitalist democracy.[20] Thus, the positions of the Left on aid to Spain were also fairly paradoxical and complex. The French Communist newspaper *L'Humanité* feared that intervention and a Republican victory might commit France to the defense of Spain in the longer term, which was not in the country's interest.[21] As David Wingeate Pike observed, the leftist press, for the most part, was "cautious and reserved" in the early days of the crisis.[22]

At a second cabinet meeting on intervention, on August 1, Blum was more active in his support, following news of Italian assistance to the Nationalists led by General Franco a few days earlier. However fear of a larger European war involving Italy and Germany led many Socialists and Radicals to abandon intervention, and the core group in favor of aiding the Republic shrunk.[23] Following the cabinet meeting, Blum began to authorize clandestine aid to Spain under a formula developed by Pierre Cot: sending planes to Spain without bomb-targeting equipment, thus appearing to conform with the French policy of selling commercial and not military aircraft to Spain; in reality, the conversion to military hardware could be easily done.[24] Seventeen aircraft were sent to Toulouse in preparation for movement to Barcelona while France publicly advocated an international non-intervention agreement and lobbied the British to consider aiding Spain as well. Orders given to local prefects indicated that the planes were not to leave Toulouse, although other, contradictory, orders were later issued by the Interior Ministry.[25] Some reports suggest five made it to Barcelona, although the truth is unclear.[26] Others indicate greater French assistance, with some 56 planes leaving Toulouse for Spain between August 9 and mid-October, 1936.[27] In any event, news of such deliveries hit the French press almost immediately, on August 6 in *L'Express du Midi*, forcing Cot to argue that they dated from orders made before the outbreak of civil war.[28] The tense atmosphere underlined the lack of clarity in government policy in the moment of crisis. The French ambassador in Berlin, André François-Poncet, reported that no one in the Nazi government doubted France was aiding the Republican government in Madrid.[29]

Concern that France might slide into a similar conflict was strong in the summer of 1936. The Popular Front victory in May and the resulting wave of strikes had stunned many political leaders and observers from the center and right-wing of the French political spectrum. On the right, press campaigns against Blum and his government intensified in newspapers such as that of Action Française.[30] Peter Jackson has shown how it was not just political movements that complicated the French response. Within the French military establishment, the election of the Popular Front government and the outbreak of strikes and popular protests raised fears of communist subversion in France, which led to the emergence of active anti-republican movements within the officer corps.[31] As a result the military leadership of the army was generally in favor of Franco's uprising and victory. The French military attaché in Madrid, Lieutenant-Colonel Henri Morel, predicted a victory for Franco as early as July 31, 1936, and grew even more certain of this once German and Italian military aid began to appear in Spain.[32] Similarly, Italian aid to the Nationalists in Spanish Morocco raised concerns that locals there, now armed, might rise up against their European rulers.[33] While these military and colonial issues were not at the forefront of Blum's concerns in the first week of August, they were important in that they were behind the hesitation of many decision makers and complicated the situation within the French government.

Between the meetings of the French cabinet on August 1 and 7, initiatives were taken to expand non-intervention to other countries and create some sort of international agreement, an appeal welcomed by France's strongest ally, Great Britain, as long as Germany and Italy also joined.[34] Meanwhile, on August 4, another request for arms came from the Republican government in Madrid.[35] Positive responses to meet on non-intervention were received from the Soviet Union, on August 5, and from Italy, on August 6.

The cabinet meeting of August 7 revealed deep divisions within the government, with Socialists such as Vincent Auriol, Marius Moutet, and others, alongside Radicals Pierre Cot and Jean Zay, strongly in favor of providing Republican Spain with military assistance.[36] Foreign Minister Delbos entered the meeting having just been taken to task by British Ambassador Sir George Clerk, who forcefully argued not only against military intervention but also against private sales of war materiel to Spain.[37] The British warning was much more direct than Foreign Secretary Anthony Eden's words to Blum in London, on July 24, to "be careful" when thinking about Spain. While it has long been established that domestic policy and the desire to keep the Popular Front unified was the primary factor in explaining the French decision to propose non-intervention,[38] foreign policy was not irrelevant in shaping the context of the debate.

At the meeting of August 7, about a dozen proponents of acting in favor of the Spanish Republic emerged among the 34 members of cabinet. Another dozen advocated prudence, led by Delbos, fresh from his meeting with France's ally Britain. Delbos forcefully defended non-intervention. Blum backed off from his August 1 position strongly favoring intervention. Non-intervention won the day. On August 9, France publicly declared a unilateral non-intervention agreement, which now also banned private sales to Spain and invited other nations to join an international pact. Great Britain signed a non-intervention agreement with France on August 15, the Soviet Union on August 23, and Germany and Italy on August 24, despite their continued aid to the Nationalist side. Eventually, the Non-intervention Agreement was joined by 27 nations. The Republican government in Spain protested this initiative, calling the closing of arms sales a "very effective intervention in the internal affairs of Spain, to the detriment of the legitimate regime."[39] Blum, however, did give volunteers going to fight in Spain the right to organize and enter Spain from France, his one concession to his support for the Republic.[40]

Blum stated simply that non-intervention was meant to prevent an arms race and an escalation of the Spanish civil conflict: "I have to fulfill a duty to the party and the nation."[41] While not enthusiastic, he was resigned; the right-wing press was content, and much of the press on the left was bitter. The political center welcomed France's diplomatic accomplishment. In other quarters, debates similar to those of the politicians continued along similar lines. Within the small Protestant community in France, strong support for the anticlericalism of the Spanish Republic was tempered by the belief that intervention would lead to a European war.[42] In this sense we can see how solidarity and a commitment to non-intervention were genuine. Non-intervention should not be seen only as an act led by Blum who had been backed into a difficult position, although it was that, too. On August 8, 1936, *L'Avenir du Bassin d'Arcachon*, a newspaper in the Gironde region, surveyed the history of French-Spanish military conflict and concluded that "we have paid dearly for our interventions in Spain," and "we hope our government takes account of these heavy lessons of history and not give in to the arguments of the Communists and their political coreligionists [who call for invention]."[43] *L'Echo de Bougie*, an official newspaper of the Union Republicaine, Democratique et Sociale in Algeria, which favored non-intervention, argued on September 27, 1936, that "this role of spectators, [which is] very new for us, has its advantages" since neither the Spanish Republicans nor the Nationalist rebels would be ideal allies for France.[44]

In French territory bordering Spain, along the Pyrénées, the impact of the civil war was immediate. Communication lines to Barcelona and the Basque country were lost from the start of the war, and the Socialist-dominated city of Toulouse became the center of communications and news from Spain, and the main point of contact for Spanish Republicans with France – not only the Republican government in Madrid but anarchist and other militia groups as well. In August 1936, many militia groups not only moved arms across the border but organized and mobilized their fighting units there.[45] By early September, movement was also noticed in the other direction, as the first refugees fled the Basque country for France. The leading newspaper in the region, the center-left *La Dépêche de Toulouse*, came to embrace support for non-intervention, seeing Blum's position as best representative of the majority of French Republicans.[46] In the Languedoc, the press was divided along political lines as in much of the country. In July 1936, the centrist, republican regional organ *Le Petit Méridional* reported the rise of Fascism in Spain, while the royalist *L'éclair* saw the civil war as a counter-revolutionary movement against anarchism.[47] These brief reviews of press coverage in July and August 1936 demonstrate that while the split between Left and Right in France was strong, the middle ground favoring non-intervention was consistent and well represented, not just in Paris but around the country.

As time went by, however, the Communist Party's demands for some form of action became increasingly more aggressive, although it did not rush to embrace military intervention as the answer. According to Martin Hurcombe, the sense of solidarity for a similarly constructed Popular Front coalition against Fascism motivated many French Communists, as well as the belief that Spain, perhaps, represented the next best chance for a Communist revolution and the formation of a Communist regime.[48] Enthusiasm for the establishment of popular militias and arming of women in Spain among French Communists in the summer of 1936 soon altered the position of the French Communist press, which now advocated for more direct intervention and a coordinated fight against Franco.[49] Eagerness for revolution faded and support for a regular war effort and the maintenance of social order and the Spanish Republic emerged. It is within this context that in September 1936 the Communist Party began to distribute pamphlets urging "planes for Spain," and to propose that intervention was possible without an offical French commitment to join the war and without the civil war in Spain developing into a broader European conflict.[50] The Communists contended that the choice was not just between neutrality and a continental-wide war. Intervention, according to this argument, was simply free trade with Spain, in support of an ally. Criticism of the Blum government for effectively closing down the border with Spain grew.

Some Socialists and Radicals were similarly motivated to counter the argument that intervention meant a French military commitment. By September 1, a new Franco-Spanish committee had been formed in Paris to advance such policy proposals, with the slogan "Frenchmen unite to end the blockade of Republican Spain!"[51] Some, however, maintained that unity of the Popular Front government was more important than what was happening in Spain, and Communist activism threatened this.[52] Meanwhile, anarchists, long critical of what they viewed as the hypocrisy of the Popular Front conception, similarly rallied to the idea of open trade instead of direct military intervention.[53] By October 1936, the Union anarchiste in France was crucial in the creation of the Comité pour l'Espagne libre, a union of anarchists and non-Communist others on the left, supported by the Spanish anarchist CNT-FAI and Marxist POUM party.[54] By autumn, then, the debate on intervention was very clearly between those on the leftist side of the spectrum in favor of selling military equipment to Republican Spain, and those on the right and center-left who, for different reasons, came to coalesce around non-intervention and the international agreement brokered by Blum and the French government. United in its position, the Right enjoyed the widening of divisions among Popular Front supporters.[55] Similar tendencies existed on the left in places like Britain, where much of the Labour Party also supported non-intervention, a fact French diplomats were quick to point out.[56]

In the midst of these developments, Léon Blum took to publicly defending non-intervention in a speech at Luna Park to supporters of Socialist movement. That same day, Irun, on the border of France, fell to Franco's Nationalist forces. As Jean Lacounture notes, Blum adopted a "confessional tone," declaring very clearly his support for the Spanish Republic and welcoming rallies such as those Spanish Republican leaders had recently held in France at the Véledrome d'Hiver.[57] He then transitioned to an argument about how intervention or the supply of arms to Spain would not, in fact, advance the Republican and Popular Front cause but only increase the likelihood of a full-scale European war. He emphasized to his audience that he was not the head of a Socialist government but of a coalition government that sought the best policy, which was non-intervention, in order to preserve the sovereignty of France and the current administration as well.[58] This speech was met with strong cheers from the crowd, if only for the moment.

It is important to note that beyond the Right's support for non-intervention was its more assertive support for the Nationalist cause and General Franco. Pierre Tattinger, leader of the Jeunesses Patriotes on the far right, sent a sword to Franco in an event covered by the press, and a committee formed in Perpignan to collect funds for the Nationalists, mainly through the distribution of pamphlets outlining atrocities against civilians committed by the Republicans in Spain.[59] On the border, newspapers on the right, such as *L'éclair de Montpellier*, reported on repeated incursions of the French border by Spanish Republican forces, and charged that Blum was leading a "belligerent neutrality." This prompted a call, answered by the French government, on September 19, 1936, to recommit to the August 8, 1936 decision to close the border to Spain.[60]

Within the Catholic Church, newspapers such as *La Croix des Pyrénées-Orientales* reported on attacks against churches and clergymen by Republicans in Spain, although such pro-Nationalist stories were not consistent in the Catholic press.[61] While the complex sentiments of solidarity and backing of non-intervention represented a majority of French politicians and public activists, support for Franco's Nationalists, the Catholic Church, and other elements opposed to the Spanish Republic was strong and certainly not silent.

In early October, French officials in Spain reported that Nazi agents were active throughout the zone occupied by Franco's Nationalist forces.[62] While there was little belief that Spain would become Fascist, the influence of Italian Fascism and Hitlerian Nazism was evident. Moreover, French military attachés concluded that Italian and German air support for Franco had been "decisive," rendering Franco's forces superior to those of the Republican government, which was beset by political in-fighting in its efforts to maintain a coalition and control political militias that had been authorized to support the regular army.[63] In this sense, non-intervention was a failure from the start and the ambassador in Madrid, Jean Herbette, concluded in October that a European war was no more distant than it had been at the start of the Spanish conflagration in July.[64] The Spanish government's first protest to the Non-intervention Committee concerning German, Italian, and Portuguese aid to Franco came on September 15, and was reiterated by the Soviet Union in a note on October 7.[65] While non-intervention seemed to rally many on the left and center-left, and thus must be understood as a popular policy, activism in support of supplying Republican Spain with military equipment and other war materiel did not fade, and even became more organized as fall progressed. This, combined with a growing realization that non-intervention was being blatantly ignored by Fascist Italy and Nazi Germanyrevived arguments and debates about France's non-intervention policy throughout the fall of 1936. The decision of the Soviet Union to withdraw from the Non-intervention Committee on October 28, 1936, only intensified the debate. French officials in Madrid, meanwhile, predicted the imminent collapse of the city, despite the "heroic" efforts of its inhabitants, who were organized in militias to supplement the Republican Army.[66]

In light of the situation on the ground, it is important to note that the French government did have concerns about the consequences for France of Republican loss of territory in the first months of the war. On October 31, 1936, the European Department circulated a memo considering the French response to a more or less autonomous Catalonia within the context of Francoist victories which, effectively, were closing off the region from the rest of Republican Spain. Fearing the potential of a unilateral declaration of independence by Catalonia, given the history of the Catalan movement over the previous 25 years, France had concerns about its own Catalan population in the Roussillon region, as well as about the partisans of Alsatian autonomy; in addition, it was anxious about the consequences for French relations with Belgium and Switzerland, allies with histories of their own autonomous movements. Not to mention, of course, the impact any French support or aid for an autonomous Catalonia would have on relations with the Republican government in Madrid.[67] These particular considerations reinforced France's general policy of prudence in Spain. Moreover, by the end of October, French diplomats could envision the ultimate victory of General Franco and the possibility that any Catalan government would be a Communist one.[68] All of these concerns meant the policy of non-intervention was the only option for France.

Advocates of non-intervention shared such views in the press, raising other factors, such as the more assertive Soviet position in favor of the Republic. *La Dépêche de Toulouse* argued that the Soviet move threatened the Franco-Soviet Pact of 1935, meant to secure peace in Europe. Right-wing supporters of non-intervention argued that the Soviet move was aggressive, meaning to provoke, not resolve, conflict.[69] In December, the newly formed Fascist party, the Parti Populaire Français (PPF) launched a campaign against Communist recruitment of volunteers to fight with the Republic in the International Brigades.[70] Meanwhile, the Spanish anarchist movements CNT-FAI, through their French language newspaper *L'Espagne antifasciste*, covered the battle of Madrid and the fighting of popular militia units, bringing this news to their members and other supporters in France.[71] These two press organs, and their stories that featured in fall 1936, demonstrated well how the political divisions over intervention in Spain unfolded in the various forms of media, most usually associated with existing political ideologies and parties.

The fierce battle for Madrid, from July through November 1936, captivated observers and was an important lens through which to see how the debate over what to do in Spain played out in France. Following the Soviet withdrawal from the Non-intervention Committee and the focus in Madrid on the use of popular political militias to augment the Republican army, *Action Française* concluded that the Spanish government was fully under the command of the Soviet Union and its techniques and practices.[72] Highlighting the hypocrisy of the non-intervention agreement and its violations by Germany and Italy, the bi-monthly journal *Feuilles Libres*, published in Lyon, demanded French and British action while Madrid was being fought over.[73] Meanwhile the

German and Italian governments moved to recognize Franco as a legitimate entity in Spain, leading Herbette to conclude that France must "accept the consequences of facts."[74]

This was the period during which the Comintern was creating the International Brigades of foreign volunteers to aid the Republic. Maurice Thorez of the French Communist Party visited Madrid and Moscow in September 1936, and played an important role in initiating the practical effort to move volunteers into Spain.[75] The first office and recruitment center of the International Brigades opened in Paris in October. Small groups of volunteers began crossing into Spain from Marseilles that same month. French volunteers were members of the 9th mixed brigade and the 11th mobile group, both formed in October 1936, and the French–Belgian André Marty group formed in November, as well as in mixed battalions formed at the end of December.[76]

Despite the changing situation, and the activism that the creation of the International Brigades represented, voices in favor of non-intervention remained strong. The newspaper founded by the late Radical leader Georges Clemenceau, *L'Homme libre*, argued that while it was clear the war in Spain was "growing less Spanish" due to foreign intervention, the Communist campaign was not popular in France since it risked a general war in Europe, which France did not want.[77] It was necessary to stay the course while responding to increased foreign activity.

Sensing continued and even growing dissatisfaction with his policies, Blum, together with Delbos and other European powers, sought to broker peace talks in fall 1936. In November 1936, Delbos, following Soviet proposals, put forward an agreement to end arms sales to the Republican government and pursue mediation, a development welcomed by much of the centrist press in France.[78] On December 5, 1936, France and Britain invited other European powers to jointly engage in efforts to bring about an armistice. On the whole, however, these initiatives were not greeted with much enthusiasm within France. The Left was more aggressively in favor of selling arms and supporting the Republic, while the Right grew increasingly confident of a Francoist victory. Additional proposals for peace talks came from Germany, but soon fell apart. The Non-intervention Committee did rally to ban foreign volunteers from going to Spain in December 1936, a position Blum now supported but one that once again ignited a polemic in the French press that paralleled the non-intervention debate of August and September.[79]

A final major debate on non-intervention took place in the Chamber of Deputies on December 4–5, 1936. Blum and Delbos spoke in defense of the government's position, emphasizing again the desire to limit the conflict to Spain and prevent a larger conflagration. By now, Blum, was also ready to ban the movement of foreign volunteers through France to join the fighting in Spain. Both Socialist and Radical members of the Popular Front supported this position in the Chamber. The Communist Party stand, outlined by leader Maurice Thorez, was that non-intervention was equivalent to intervention against the Republic. When the vote on non-intervention came on December 5, the Communists abstained. Members on the right argued that France needed to enforce non-intervention more clearly than it had, while some, such as Henri de Kérillis, voiced support for Franco and criticized Republican attacks on churches and priests in Spain. In January 1937, the Assembly voted in favor of continued non-intervention in December, and banned foreign volunteers from crossing through France en route to Spain.[80]

The December Chamber debate demonstrated that the different understandings of the war and its significance had not changed greatly since the outbreak of violence in July. Those on the left and center-left who were in favor of non-intervention feared, above all, that the conflict would spread to Europe, and thus non-intervention, despite their solidarity with Republican Spain, was the rational and only choice for France. Those on the right favored non-intervention for many reasons, including support for Franco, but many agreed with the conclusions reached by Blum. On the far left, the anarchists consistently favored intervention and revolution in Spain. Only the Communists had moved from non-intervention to intervention, mirroring the shift of the Soviet Union over the fall of 1936. The majority of France's political leaders and parties remained in the position of supporting non-intervention, despite empathy and solidarity with the Republican government in Madrid.

It is important to recognize that beyond the political debate, sympathy for the Spanish Republic was expressed in France in many ways. First, there were French volunteers who joined the fight in Spain. Even before the International Brigades had been organized by the Communist International in September 1936, French citizens crossed the border to join Spanish anarchist, Marxist and Communist militia groups, first in the Basque country and then, after the Nationalist capture of the city of Irun, in Catalonia.[81] Organized recruitment of French volunteers within France was led by the Communist Party, beginning in August 1936, and French Communist fighters joined the militias of the Catalan Communist Party in Barcelona, and were shipped from there to Madrid in the fall.[82] In factories and union clubs across France, as Sylvie Schweitzer has shown in the case of the Renault factory in the commune of Billancourt, speakers from the Communist Party, the trade union Confédération Générale de Travail (CGT), the Red Cross, and others spoke to the workers in August 1936, advocating aid and military intervention.[83] Following the withdrawal of the Soviet Union from the Non-intervention Committee, the Communist Party grew more aggressive in its clubs and unions over the fall, organizing short strikes at multiple factories around Paris, for example, to emphasize the plight of the Spanish Republic.[84] However, most of the activities aimed at direct assistance to Spain involved fundraising, allowing workers to express their sympathy without making a commitment to fight. By mid-December 1936, it was estimated that the Renault factory in Billancourt had raised 140,000 francs on its own for Spain.[85] Materiel of a civil, non-military nature, was also sent to Spain – such as an ambulance and two trucks from Billancourt in September 1936.[86]

As with left-leaning factory workers, many others in France also engaged in humanitarian and other activities to alleviate the plight of the Spanish people, showing the French people's ability to respond rather than focusing on the political debate over intervention. Communist groups like the *Mouvement contre la guerre et le fascisme* organized fundraising, and drives for basic supplies such as clothing and medical supplies.[87] Out of this a new organization, the *Comité international de coordination et d'information pour l'aide à l'Espagne républicaine* was formed to combat Blum's non-intervention policy but also to organize fundraising efforts across France. Similarly, the *Comité d'action socialiste pour l'Espagne* pushed Blum's Socialist Party on non-intervention while also engaging primarily in humanitarian fundraising and other efforts.[88]

Other endeavors reached across party lines and avoided the issue of non-intervention entirely. One of these emerged from the CGT and the *Ligue des droits de l'Homme*, the creation in September 1936 of the *Comité d'acceuil des enfants d'Espagne*. This organization, which raised funds and resettled refugee children from Spain in France, was supported in particular by female teachers across France.[89] In addition, junior sections of the French Red Cross held toy drives for Spanish children.[90] Laurence Brown states that the humanitarian efforts of organizations, both affiliated and unaffiliated with political parties, demonstrated the changing nature of the balance between political and humanitarian concerns.[91] As a result, the complexity of the political debate, balancing sympathy for the Spanish Republic with some recognition of the logic of non-intervention, was replicated outside of traditional political debate as well.

Throughout the summer and fall of 1936, France reacted to the outbreak of civil war in Spain with a great deal of self-reflection, debate, and a definite lack of any sort of consensus. The empathy many on the left felt with the Spanish Republicans, and/or with their leftist allies in Spanish political parties was clear. The strength of the Right and Center-Right in wanting to avoid any sort of commitment to the battle in Spain was equally apparent. Across the political spectrum, the fear of the potential of a civil war in France similar to that raging in Spain was present, but not as strong as the apprehension that events in Spain could lead to a wider European war. The result of all this was that both left- and right-leaning French parties, unions, and other groups came to embrace the non-intervention policy first proposed by the Popular Front government of Léon Blum. Never enthusiastic about this policy, Blum himself came to accept it as necessary for the unity of his coalition and for the mood of the country.

As the civil war moved into fall, and the advantage General Franco had established became clearer, despite his inability to take Madrid, the desire in France to embrace non-intervention as the only option increased. As the Soviet Union officially abandoned non-intervention, debate in France was revived, and the Communists in particular became more active in arguing for "planes for Spain," but nothing changed. Reluctantly, France's political arena came to accept the uneasy consensus that non-intervention was the only policy open to it.

Solidarity and empathy with the Spanish Republic was always present, and a stronger and more public expression of this was evident, compared with genuine but smaller-scale support for Franco's Nationalists. Yet those sympathetic to the Republic came to live with non-intervention. This identification was most visible in fundraising, clothing drives, and efforts to help Spanish refugee children. The desire to respond and be active in the face of the civil war was powerful, even in light of the inability to craft a political and foreign policy that would respond.

Thus, France met the zero hour of 1936 with solidarity, passion, and weakness. The realization that non-intervention was largely an ineffective policy was there from the start, leading to a lifetime of regret for someone like Blum. Yet it was the only policy that could be implemented. France expressed solidarity and acted only through the narrow window of non-intervention when faced with the conflict in Spain.

Notes

1 Robert Coulondre (French Ambssador to the Soviet Union) to Delbos, July 23, 1936, *Documents Diplomatiques Français, 1932–1939* (hereafter *DDF*), Série 2, vol. III (Paris: Imprimerie Nationale, 1966), 37; Herbette to Delbos, July 24, 1936, *DDF* Série 2, vol. III, 52.

2 For a description of the meeting, see Gilbert Grellet, *Un été impardonnable, 1936: La guerre d'Espagne et la scandale de la non-intervention* (Paris: Albin Michel, 2016), 25–29; Claude Thiebaut, "Leon Blum, Alexis Léger et la Decision de Non-intervention en Espagne" in *Les Français et la Guerre*

d'Espagne: Actes du Colloque de Perpignan, ed. Jean Sagnes and Sylvie Caucana, 3rd ed. (Perpignan: Presses Universitaires de Perpignan, 2008), who puts the meeting at a date somewhere between July 20 and 22, p. 26.

3 David Wingeate Pike, *France Divided: The French and the Civil War in Spain* (Brighton/Portland: Sussex Academic Press, 2011), 18.

4 François-Poncet, Berlin, to Delbos, July 25, 1936, *DDF*, Série 2, vol. III, 56.

5 Note de la Direction Politique, July 25, 1936, *DDF* Série 2, vol. III, 58.

6 Thiebaut, "Leon Blum, Alexis Léger et la Decision de Non-Intervention en Espagne," 24.

7 Salengro (interior minister) to Prefects of Spanish Border Region, July 28, 1936, *DDF* Série 2, vol. III, 69.

8 Delbos to Herbette, July 27, 1936, *DDF* Série 2, vol. III, 61.

9 François-Poncet to Delbos, July 28, 1936, *DDF*, Série 2, vol. III, 68.

10 François-Poncet to Delbos, July 30, 1936, *DDF*, Série 2, vol. III, 79; De Chambrun (ambassador to Rome) to Delbos, July 30, 1936, *DDF*, Série 2, vol. III, 86.

11 Morel to Daladier (defense minister), July 31, 1936, *DDF*, Série 2, vol. III, 96.

12 Pike, *France Divided*, 22–23.

13 David Berry, " Solidarité Internationale Antifasciste: Les Anarchistes Français et la Guerre Civile d'Espagne," in Sagnes and Caucanas, *Les Français et la Guerre d'Espagne*, 73, 79.

14 Pike, *France Divided*, 25.

15 Julian Jackson, *The Popular Front in France: Defending Democracy, 1934–38* (Cambridge: Cambridge University Press, 1990), 85–103.

16 Herbette to Delbos, June 6, 1936, *DDF*, Série 2, vol. II (Paris: Impirmierie Nationale, 1964), 437.

17 Jean Lacouture, *Léon Blum*, trans. George Holoch (New York: Holmes and Meier, 1982), 305.

18 Ibid., 320–1.

19 Jules Maurin, "La Chambre des Députés et la Guerre Civile Espangole," in Sagnes and Caucanas, *Les Français et la Guerre d'Espagne*, 62.

20 Martin Hurcombe, "Heroes of the Republic, Heroes of the Revolution: French Communist Reportage of the Spanish Civil War, 1936–38," *Journal of European Studies* 41, no. 1 (2010): 46.

21 Pike, *France Divided*, 24.

22 Ibid., 24.

23 Lacouture, *Léon Blum*, 323.

24 Michael Alpert, *A New International History of the Spanish Civil War* 2nd ed. (London: Palgrave Macmillan, 2004), 42.

25 Pike, *France Divided*, 35.

26 Alpert, *A New International History*, 45.

27 Pike, *France Divided*, 38.

28 Ibid., 34–5.

29 François-Poncet to Delbos, August 5, 1936, *DDF* Série 2, vol. III, 137.

30 Maurin, "La Chambre des Députés," 63.
31 Peter Jackson, "French Strategy and the Spanish Civil War," in *Spain in an International Context, 1936–1959*, ed. Christian Letiz and David J. Dunthorn (New York: Berghahn Books, 1999), 58.
32 Ibid., 62.
33 Delbos to Roger Cambon (French Chargé d'Affaires in London) August 2, 1936, *DDF* Série 2, vol. III, 99–100.
34 Cambon to Delbos, August 4, 1936, *DDF* Série 2, vol. III, 114.
35 Alvaro de Albornoz (Spanish ambassador to Paris) to Delbos, August 4, 1936, *DDF*, Série 2, vol. III, 119.
36 Grellet, *Un été impardonnable*, 140.
37 Lacouture, *Léon Blum*, 325–6.
38 See, for example, David Carlton, "Eden, Blum and the Origins of Non-Intervention," *Journal of Contemporary History* 6, no. 3 (1971): 40–55.
39 Albornoz to Delbos, August 10, 1936, *DDF* Série 2, vol. III, 174.
40 Pike, *France Divided*, 72.
41 Alpert, *A New International History*, 48.
42 Alain Boyer, "Le Protestantisme Français et la Guerre d'Espagne," in Sagnes and Caucanas, *Les Français et la Guerre d'Espagne*, 68.
43 *L'Avenir du Bassin d'Arcachon,* August 8, 1936, retrieved from Gallica, online service of the Bibliothèque nationale de France, on July 24, 2017, http://gallica.bnf.fr/ark:/12148/bpt6k54216531/f1.item.r=espagne%201936.zoom.
44 *L'Echo de Bougie*, September 27, 1936, http://gallica.bnf.fr/ark:/12148/bpt6k5578673k/f1.item.r=espagne%201936.zoom (accessed July 24, 2017).
45 Pike, *France Divided*, 46–7.
46 Ibid., 61.
47 Daniel Meyran, "La Presse Regionale Languedocienne et les Débuts de la Guerre d'Espagne," in Sagnes and Caucanas, *Les Français et la Guerre d'Espagne*, 108.
48 Hurcombe, "Heroes of the Republic," 47.
49 Ibid., 52.
50 Pike, *France Divided*, 59.
51 Ibid., 60.
52 Pike, *France Divided*, 61.
53 David Berry, "Fascism or Revolution! Anarchism and Antifascism in France, 1933–1939," *Contemporary European History* 8, no. 1 (1999): 60.
54 Ibid., 63–64.
55 Pike, 63.
56 Cambon to Delbos, August 21, 1936, *DDF*, Série 2, vol. III, 264.
57 Lacouture, *Léon Blum*, 336.
58 Ibid., 337–8.
59 Pike, *France Divided*, 65.
60 Jean-Louis Blanchon, "La Cerdagne Française face a l'Experiene Ananrchiste

fr Puigcerda (1936–1937)," in Sagnes and Caucanas, *Les Français et la Guerre d'Espagne*, 131–32.

61 Michel Cadé, "Le Clergé Roussillonnais face a la Guerre d'Espagne" in Sagnes et Caucanas, *Les Français et la Guerre d'Espagne*, 138.

62 Herbette to Delbos, October 5, 1936, *DDF*, Série 2, vol. III, 472.

63 Herbette to Delbos, October 6, 1936, *DDF*, Série 2, vol. III, 473.

64 Ibid., 474.

65 Note Soviétique au Comité de Non-Intervention, October 7, 1936, *DDF*, Série 2, vol. III, 479–81.

66 Morel to Daladier, October 14, 1936, *DDF*, Série 2, vol. III, 527.

67 "Note du Département au sujet des affaires catalanes," October 31, 1936, *DDF*, Série 2, vol. III, 663–65.

68 Ibid.

69 Pike, *France Divided*, 69–70.

70 Paul Schue, "The Prodigal Sons of Communism: Parti Populaire Français Narratives of Communist Recruitment for the Spanish Civil War and the Everyday Functioning of Party Ideology," *French Historical Studies* 24, no. 1 (2001)pp. 87–111.

71 See, for example, *LEspagne Antifasciste*, no. 22, November 21, 1936, http://gallica.bnf.fr/ark:/12148/bpt6k63560235.r=espagne%20novembre%201936?rk=21459;2 (accessed September 14, 2017).

72 "L'Espagne contre les Soviets", *L'Action Française*, November 4, 1936, http://gallica.bnf.fr/ark:/12148/bpt6k766507q/f2.item.r=espagne%20novembre%201936.zoom (accessed September 14, 2017).

73 *Feuilles Libres*, November 25, 1936, http://gallica.bnf.fr/ark:/12148/bpt6k61263835/f1.item.r=espagne%20novembre%201936.zoom (accessed September 14, 2017).

74 Herbette to Delbos, October 29, 1936, *DDF*, Série 2, vol. III, 652,

75 Fernando Schwartz, *La Internacionalización de la Guerra Civil Española* (Barcelona: Planeta, 1999 reprint, orig. 1972), 208.

76 Ibid., 218.

77 *L'Homme Libre*, November 26, 1936, http://gallica.bnf.fr/ark:/12148/bpt6k75996088/f2.item.r=espagne%20novembre%201936.zoom (accessed September 14, 2017).

78 Pike, *France Divided*, 89.

79 Ibid., 93.

80 Maurin, "La Chambre de Députés et la Guerre Civile Espagnole," 52.

81 R. Dan Richardson, "Foreign Fighters in Spanish Militias: The Spanish Civil War, 1936–1939," *Military Affairs* 40, no. 1 (1976): 9.

82 Ibid., 10.

83 Sylvie Schweitzer, "Les ouvriers des usines Renault de Billancourt et la guerre civile espagnole," *Le Mouvement social* 103 (1978): 112.

84 Ibid., 113.

85 Ibid., 114.

86 Ibid., 115.

87 Laurence Brown, "Pour Aidez Nos Frères d'Espagne: Huanitarian Aid, French Women and Popular Mobilization during the Front Populaire," *French Politics, Culture and Society* 25, 1 (2007): 32.

88 Ibid., 38.

89 Ibid., 40–41.

90 *Jeunesse: Organe de la section jeunesse de la Croix Rouge Française*, February 1937, http://gallica.bnf.fr/ark:/12148/bpt6k9689008k/f2.image.r=espagne%20novembre%201936?rk=386268;0 (accessed September 14, 2017).

91 Brown, "Pour Aidez Nos Frères d'Espagne," 43.

11

Chimerical Thoughts? Winston Churchill and Spain

EMILIO SÁENZ-FRANCÉS SAN BALDOMERO

> Naturally I was not in favour of the Communists. How could I be, when if I had been a Spaniard they would have murdered me and my family and friends?
>
> Winston Churchill, *The Second World War: The Gathering Storm* (Boston: Houghton Mifflin Company, 1948)

The Spanish Civil War had a polarizing effect on British politics. Labour leaned toward the Republicans while the Conservatives were much more divided. For the latter, Franco could mean – initially, at least – a return to political moderation, and even to a restored monarchy able to reinstate order – a significant feat indeed in an agitated Europe. Behind the many factors shaping the views of Conservative leaders on the conflict, fear of the expansion of Communism and a growing suspicion of Fascism combined with their sympathy toward the former monarchical regime in Spain. In the Foreign Office, calculated realism drove policymakers towards an analysis that suggested non-intervention in order to minimize risks in the peninsula. Little was known in 1936 about the upcoming regime, which would last for decades, only that it emerged as a strange mix between a nineteenth-century *pronunciamento* and a Fascist coup d'état. Moreover, the abdication crisis would shake British politics to the point where the only possible course of action on Spain was maintaining the status quo.

A good example of Conservative ambivalence toward the war was Julian Amery, son of Leo Amery,[1] who became an advocate of the Nationalist cause, as can be deduced from his personal documents, kept at the Churchill Archives Centre at the University of Cambridge.[2] His support, however, was probably more a result of fear of a Communist drift in Spain than any sympathy toward a Fascist victory. Amery's case is an accurate reflection of the Conservative party's ambiguity during the 1930s and later during World War II. It might be recalled that his brother John was executed after the war, accused of high treason for actively working for National Socialism, having been driven, too, by hostility toward Communism.

Franco's triumph, despite the fact that his regime would ultimately be maligned, was perceived as the lesser evil to a Communist victory. Yet, if on one side of the Conservative party's broad spectrum we find young Amery's growing sympathies for the Nationalist cause, relevant only since he was the son of one the party leaders, on the other, we find the Duchess of Atholl. An MP for Kinross and West Perth (Scotland), her active support for the Republican cause – a result of humanitarian rather than ideological motivations – aroused tensions with other party members, as Tom Buchanan points out.[3] Between two such extremes, we find a party entangled in its own appeasement policy and the decline of the cooperation policies designed after World War I, a process brilliantly described by Piers Brendon in his work *The Dark Valley*.[4] Moreover, the widespread anti-Communist sentiment in the party and a historic reluctance to intervene in Spanish politics reinforced the idea of not actively taking sides.

In the midst of all this was Winston Churchill, a noisy and influential figure, yet one with limited influence on party and government decisions. Indeed, in 1936 Churchill was among the most displaced figures within the Tories. This chapter looks at Churchill's position from the start of hostilities in Spain, in order to understand his specific posture regarding the war. This is important not only because of Churchill's critical leadership during World War II – which renders the evolution of his political thinking in the pre-war years relevant – but also because of what was a surprising attitude given his outspokenness on British foreign policy in the 1930s.[5] In the case of the Spanish conflict, Churchill appeared to be extremely complacent about his country's appeasement policy.

This chapter will first examine Churchill's earlier perceptions regarding Spain, and then analyze in detail the constraints and contradictions of his position on the eve of the civil war. The conclusions support the thesis that beyond his personal opinions regarding the conflict, in 1936 Churchill decided to join his party's fait accompli of non-intervention.

From the outset it should be noted that Churchill was driven by what is referred to in this chapter as "chimerical thought" when it came to Spain. He had strong sentiments about Spain and its history, which explains in part the bitter hostility he felt toward the Spanish Republic at the start of the conflict and a renewed, rampant anti-Communism, reminiscent of his post-World War I views.[6] Later, during the war, such feelings could also explain his utopic wish of reaching a peaceful agreement to end the conflict and thus prevent Spain from becoming an easy prey of Fascism and Nazism after a cruel and exhausting war.

Winston Churchill's political career has been studied extensively,[7] and continues to be so today. Indeed, his political positions are inseparable from the current political debate in the United Kingdom. However, his political motivations regarding the outbreak of the Spanish Civil War in 1936 have not yet been subject to much historical analysis,[8] a lacuna which it is hoped this chapter will fill, although mostly at a speculative level.

Churchill and Spain: A "Love Story"

Winston Churchill possessed a heartfelt empathy with Spain. His deep sense of history led him perhaps to idealize the shortcomings of the *Restauración*[9] and the worthiness of Spanish politicians who dominated that period, and in whom Churchill discerned similar aristocratic principles to which he himself felt so attached. To him, Spain remained the heir to a great European empire. It was "one of the oldest branches in the tree of the European nations,"[10] which had once rivalled and subsequently been defeated by England, and was thereafter demoted from the geopolitical frontlines. Like many other Englishmen of his class and ideological viewpoint, Churchill identified Spain and its people with an innate sense of honor, an appealing bravery, and a Quixotic spirit which had reached their zenith in the struggle, shared with Great Britain, to expel Napoleon from the Iberian Peninsula. For Churchill, Spain was an old European nation which, in his view of a fairer and more stable world, should occupy a prominent place within the continent's politics. However, it was also a country marked by certain peculiar, atavistic, and thus, dangerous and disquieting customs which had been imposed on the country by the miseries of the nineteenth century. All this led British politicians to a single conclusion: stay away from the Spanish hornet's nest.

Indeed, the founding father of his family, John Churchill, 1st Duke of Marlborough, had made his fortune and prestige in a war which, though essentially European, originated and took place in Spain: the War of Succession. Churchill greatly admired his ancestor, about whom he penned a massive biography, and this interest may have served to strengthen his sympathy for Spain.[11] Indeed, while the Spanish drama unfolded to its dramatic conclusion after the general election of 1936,

Churchill spent most of that summer at his countryside retreat, Chartwell, working on the fourth volume of his Marlborough magnum opus.[12]

With regard to his most personal experience of the country, in his youth Churchill fought alongside the Spanish troops against the Cuban rebels. It was baptism by fire, and as David Sarias[13] recounts, although he was critical of the Spanish administration of the island and the general conduct of the war, from the start he admired the Spanish soldiers' bravery and strength.

Winston Churchill was many things in his life, among which he saw himself as a member of the privileged class, his personal relations with Spain being based mainly on that principle. King Alfonso XIII was one of the Spaniards that most influenced Churchill's image of Spain at the beginning of the twentieth century.[14]

Churchill had met Alfonso XIII for the first time in 1914, shortly before World War I. They had got along famously, and their relationship was further strengthened by the king's subsequent visits to Great Britain.[15] As Roy Jenkins has stated, to some extent Churchill regarded European monarchs as his social equals, and therefore his relationships with sovereigns tended to be conducted on empathic terms; during World War II these were marked by a disposition on the part of the latter to accommodate Churchill's policies,[16] In the case of Alfonso XIII, the relationship appears to have been particularly natural and genuine, and Churchill's sorrow on the king's fall from power in 1931 was doubtlessly sincere.

On reading the chapter devoted to Alfonso XIII of Churchill's *Great Contemporaries*, the author's empathy for the already king is clearly evident. The text, written when Spain was already being wracked by a cruel civil war, offers a glimpse of the contempt and lack of confidence with which the future prime minister viewed the Republican regime of 1931.[17] It examines the reasons, besides the errors of the king and the weight of history itself, which may have accounted for the fall of the *Restauración* political system. In effect, Churchill explores the issue, and in his questioning, we hear echoes of the cries from a civil war which, five years after the fall of Alfonso XIII, was tearing Spain apart, and of the seemingly unstoppable rise of Nazi Germany in central Europe, two clarion calls to a world lurching towards disaster. His response could not evade this combined reality, and is extremely revealing: *the propaganda of Moscow.*[18] This conclusion reveals much about the frame of mind with which the British politician interpreted the Republic and the origins of the civil war.

Europe during Churchill's 'Wilderness Years'

The 1930s were for Churchill a period referred to as the "wilderness years."[19] In 1928, as Martin Gilbert indicates, he appeared to be at the apex of his career, on the brink of releasing his fourth budget as Chancellor of the Exchequer in Stanley Baldwin's government.[20] Yet the defeat of the Conservative Party a year later deprived Churchill not only of his political office but also propelled him towards political ostracism, since he had never been fully embraced by the Conservatives and was rejected by the Liberal Party which he had earlier abandoned. This situation would continue until 1935, when the Tories once again returned to power under Baldwin's leadership.[21] A year later, when the Spanish Civil War erupted, Churchill appeared to be a spent force, a shadow from the days of his adventurous policies in World War I. Fortunately, some believed, this past had been superseded by a more sensible epoch in which there was no place for mavericks of his type.

Yet, after 1929 the Europe that emerged from the Treaty of Versailles had begun to change with dizzying speed. The Spanish monarchy fell in 1931; in 1933 Adolf Hitler, riding the wave of fear about the advance of Communism unleashed by the tensions engendered by the economic crisis, came to power in Germany. During the following months, Hitler subverted the constitutional process to establish himself as dictator. His new Reich did little to conceal from the world its aim of reversing the effects of the Versailles Treaty. In 1935 Italy began its aggression against Abyssinia, and was met with a shameful answer from the democratic nations in the form of the Hoare-Laval Pact, which handed a virtual carte blanche to the Duce in that territory. In March 1936, Hitler militarized the Rhineland, effectively dealing a death blow to the Versailles Treaty and its Locarno corollary. The Kellogg-Briand Pact's explicit renunciation of the use of arms as an instrument of foreign policy, forged less than ten years previously, was revealed to be nothing more than a macabre and cruel grimace in the face of years of effort to avoid war. Winston Churchill's early denunciation of the dangers of the rise of Nazism, his call for British rearmament, his criticism of the soft belly of his country's foreign and imperial policy, from the Hoare-Laval Pact to India, and solitary support for Edward VIII's desire to marry Wallis Simpson during the so-called abdication crisis, which reached a peak by the end of 1936, were all controversial stands that helped to amplify his political sense of isolation and his image as an irresponsible warmonger.[22]

In July 1936, a revolt led by a section of the army against Spain's Popular Front government provoked a civil struggle which would devastate the nation for the following four years. The Spanish war became another pawn on the chessboard of European diplomacy, as the Communists, and German and Italian Fascists readied themselves – through their support of the contending parties – to fight a war by proxy, which though might prove to be a vital, would be suffused by the context of brutal politics then emerging in Europe. Spain, indeed, appeared to be another land of promise for a grandiose scheme, and for an open denunciation of what was to be the uncompromising British stand in relation to the conflict. It was not, however, the case.

Churchill, Spain, and 1936

Side-lined and half-forgotten, Winston Churchill, as seen, was criticized publicly by a new – or in some cases, not so new – generation of politicians due to his reactionary positions on how India should be governed, the rise of militarism in Germany, and his controversial stand regarding the abdication; in short, on almost all the questions then animating parliamentary discussion. Nor did Churchill neglect the Spanish war, a conflict that he viewed through a decidedly anti-Communist lens. For him, Communism was an old acquaintance, a supreme evil which had transformed itself into a permanent nemesis since the end of the Great War. Indeed, Churchill had already declared in his memoirs of those years that best strategy for the troops under Marshal Haig would have been to advance into Russia, thereby destroying the root source of the Communist menace.[23]

Undoubtedly, Churchill was a convinced anti-Communist. His accurate perception of the dangers of Leninism-Stalinism placed him, already in the years immediately following World War I, in a considerably more elevated position compared to that of most of his contemporaries. Yet, he was also a skilled and realistic politician, capable of distinguishing the priorities of the moment. Thus, mid-way through the 1930s, in an effort to broaden his political base and reacting to the rise of Fascist extremism, he initiated a cautious withdrawal from his most ferocious statements regarding leftist ideologies. As Roy Jenkins has stated, party colleagues jokingly began to refer to Churchill's "flourishing friendship with Mr Maisky [the Russian ambassador in London]."[24] Placing the blame on Communism for acting as the spark that had ignited the Spanish Civil War imperiled this political rapprochement.

Perhaps Churchill was already aware that, in order to defeat one evil, he would have to descend to hell and ally himself with another.[25] In that dark struggle, his education, trajectory, and political instincts pointed toward Nazism as a far graver threat than Communism to the survival of the British Empire. While Nazism was ready to pounce upon Europe and attempt to devour it, the peculiar and original characteristics of British society rendered Communism much less threatening in strictly national terms. However, this analysis was, in any event, really only applicable to Great Britain.

The future prime minister had never been a sympathizer of the Spanish Second Republic. He felt that it was a regime inspired by Moscow, which had established a conflict-ridden and non-inclusive democracy. In the final months of its existence, prior to the outbreak of the civil war, it had been marked by spiraling social conflicts and political radicalization which would eventually spark the war itself. For Churchill, these were the common ingredients of international Communist subversion in its purest form which, if not necessarily a threat to Great Britain, presented a grave danger to many European states. A few years earlier, when a coup d'état had engendered the Carmona regime in Portugal, Churchill had perceived the virtues of a stable and peaceful Portugal, ideological questions aside. In 1936 the situation in Europe had changed dramatically; yet in the final instance, the rebel forces seemed to represent, at least in the early stages, many of the principles that Churchill identified with "the good Spain." Socially, his Spanish friends and acquaintances were identified with the embryonic new regime, and almost all shared a ferocious hostility toward the Republic. Churchill, as he himself acknowledged, sympathized with the Nationalists in the early stages of the war, but moved to distance himself once Hitler and Mussolini began to be perceived as the sponsors of the new order in Spain.

At the start of the war, Great Britain and France adopted a policy of non-intervention, which in itself revealed the Republic's general lack of international prestige. For once, the British government, more focused on its own internal tensions, and Churchill himself, followed the same line of reasoning: it would be suicidal to interfere in a war in which even the slightest mistake might imperil essential imperial interests, such as Gibraltar or tacit control of the Straits. For most British politicians, non-intervention was a way of containing possible internationalization of the conflict and emanated from an intrinsic mistrust of the radical shift the Republic was taking. It was also a means of containing Communism and, to a lesser extent, Fascism and Nazism. What were the alternatives? Supporting the constituted government was not an option, but nor was fully supporting the rebels.

As Enrique Moradiellos points out,[26] the British government was both hoping for and expecting a short civil war that did not alter, at least substantially, the balance of power in the Iberian Peninsula. Yet, it also hoped for a war that could contain the revolutionary shift of a government that was on a truly radical path, described as the Kerenski phase by Churchill himself.[27] Britain believed that with its economic might it could tame a Spain that was becoming too close to Italy and Germany. Ultimately, it was merely a continuation of the appeasement policy that characterized Britain in the 1930s. In this sense, one of the Foreign Office's primary objectives in the short run was to prevent the Popular Front government in France from collaborating with the Republican government. By limiting the international scope of the conflict, the British were also hoping to contain the aid delivered to the Nationalists by Germany and Italy.

Surprisingly, the combative Winston Churchill appeared to welcome this approach during the first part of the civil war. In his internal debate of reasoning and political priorities, the Churchill of 1918 won, the Churchill whose biggest fear was the spread of Communism throughout Europe. As Tom Buchanan points out, Churchill refused to shake the hand of the new Republican ambassador in London, Francisco de Azcárate, mumbling "blood, blood" as he abandoned the meeting.[28] At this point it seems relevant to ask why a politician who was not in the first line of political action – but nonetheless still had a relevant say in Parliament – and whose primary cause by then was denouncing Fascist aggression, gave in when it came to the civil war, backing his own government instead of questioning it as he used to. In one of his first articles on the war (August 10, 1936), Churchill implicitly contemplated supporting the rebels, although he did note that it was not a desirable option, given the consequences this could have on Britain's relationship with France:

> French partisanship for the Spanish Communists, or British partisanship for the Spanish rebels, might injure profoundly the bonds which unite the British Empire and the French Republic. This Spanish welter is not the business of either of us.[29]

We can only speculate about what made Churchill behave as he did in relation to the Spanish conflict. On the one hand, Churchill was driven by that singular relationship he had with the country. On the other hand, his aristocratic idealization of Spain did not reach the point of blinding him to the threat the Nationalists posed; despite the strength of his anti-Communism. From the start of the war, both Italy and, in a more veiled manner, Germany showed their support for the Nationalist rebels. Churchill was well aware of this. Yet, his hostility toward Communism, together with his idealization of Spain prevailed, resulting in what has been called here "chimerical thought." Once again, as on many other occasions of his political career, the same hidden force within Churchill's personality disrupted rational thought, giving way to prolific imagination and sentimentality. It is this same force that explains his iconoclastic positioning a few months later during the abdication crisis.

For Winston Churchill, the Spanish Civil War not only a political tragedy but also a human one – a tragedy in which a major European nation was bleeding without reason, wounded by the Communist hordes. This explains his hopes for an early reconciliation of the Spaniards, bringing Spain back to serenity, and to the core of European politics. Indeed, Churchill dealt with the civil war with the same combination of "chimerical thought" and political calculation that defined his actions at many stages of his career, from Gallipoli to post-Hitler Europe. He acted this way because, at all such moments, and indeed in the case of the Spanish Civil War, he felt personally involved. Here, such engagement resulted in complete demonization of the Republic, beyond all rationality:

> Although it seems to be the practice of the Nationalist forces to shoot a proportion of their prisoners taken in arms, they cannot be accused of having fallen to the level of committing the atrocities which are the daily handiwork of the Communists, Anarchists, and the P.O.U.M., as the new and most extreme Trotskyist organisation is called. It would be a mistake alike in truth and wisdom for British public opinion to rate both sides at the same level.
>
> . . . the defence of the Alcazar by its unconquerable cadets will live forever in the history of Spain. If to a fibre so tense and a devotion so boundless the victors can add the quality of mercy, they may at the end of their journey make Spain a home for all its people.[30]

Be that as it may, it took Churchill only a few weeks to realize the inherent evil on the Nationalist side, especially in their conduct of the war and political alignment. Nevertheless, in all the articles Churchill published in 1936 and 1937, when it came to praising the running of the war or military achievements, he always sided with the Nationalists, in some cases to the point of flagrant exaggeration:

> There are large areas of Spain which returned whole blocks of Conservative members to the recent Cortes. Around Burgos and Valladolid, around Cadiz and Seville, dwell communities as solidly Conservative as our Home Counties. In these regions the army leaders find themselves upheld by a friendly population with a wealthy middle

> class and a daring martial youth. In the Carlist provinces there are other reserves of strength which provide, as long ago in La Vendée, the spectacle of a countryside passionately united in support of Church and Monarchy. Here are strong foundations and bases for the rebel armies. All history shows that armies without civil populations behind them are prone to collapse. No such weakness afflicts the Anti-Red movement.[31]

Beyond Churchill's reasoning, the inertia of British politics also played a decisive role in shaping his positioning in relation to Spain. From November 1936 onward, British politics was dominated by one of the most acute constitutional crises in its history, the so-called abdication crisis, after King Edward VIII declared his intention to marry the twice-divorced Wallis Simpson. The emergency consumed all Prime Minister Baldwin's attention and political skill. He even asked Anthony Eden, his foreign affairs secretary, not to disturb him with reports or memorandums on Spain, or on any other topic that would distract him from the crisis. Red boxes lay untouched for weeks. The same political crisis captured Churchill in another burst of chimera, this time resulting from his radical and romantic monarchism, which led him to support unconditionally the doomed monarch in a politically suicidal move.

Nevertheless, beyond the constitutional crisis, for Prime Minister Baldwin and Foreign Affairs Secretary Anthony Eden, and later for Neville Chamberlain and the appeasement-minded Lord Halifax, the war in Spain was an obscure and distant conflict in which Great Britain had nothing to win, and much to lose. By April 1937, there was also a reasonable prospect that international Communism might be defeated. In Churchill's mind, there was also the additional possibility that the victors in the war would not be unequivocally favorable to Rome and Berlin. The resulting regime might be authoritarian, but more akin to Carmona in Portugal than to Mussolini, and thus one with which it would be possible to negotiate.[32] Above all, it would put an end to Communist aggression in Spain, which Churchill always considered – above and beyond any other issue – to be the force ultimately responsible for the nation's blood-letting. For Churchill, the rise of Fascism in Spain was just an eventuality; Communism, on the other hand, had been the cause of the conflict. As the war progressed, Churchill's own perceptions on the military conduct of the war and the management of the home front continued to portray Nationalist war efforts in a positive light:

> Peace and order reign over the broad areas of Nationalist Spain, and industry and agriculture pursue their course. Trains run. Food and petrol can be freely purchased. All the decencies of civilised life appear upon

> the surface, but the slightest signs of disaffection are repressed with prompt and ruthless executions.[33]

Winston Churchill was an extremely cunning politician, which leads to the possibility that his positioning vis-à-vis the war could have been a way of keeping in tune with party and government. The breach between them was already deep. Widening it would have been politically unwise. The civil war was an opportunity for him to make his affinity to the government public, through several newspaper articles written at the time. The truth is that Churchill and the government essentially agreed on Spain, although probably not for the same reasons. And once all these views had been accepted, at governmental level it was extremely difficult to alter the initial non-intervention policy. After 1937, this was even more so, as the Nazi machinery began to expand, full steam ahead, in central Europe. The Aragon offensive of the Francoist forces coincided with the annexation of Austria to the Reich; just a few months later, while the Battle of the Ebro bloodily unfolded, Hitler imposed his will at Munich, and Czechoslovakia was reduced to an empty shell awaiting final destruction. Only a few weeks after the fall of Barcelona to Franco, Prague found itself in Hitler's hands.

Both of these conflicts, the European one anticipating a global explosion, and the Spanish one, which marked the fall of yet another country into the hands of a single ruler, were paradigms of this difficult moment in European history. In the balance of threats, Churchill – who was slowly regaining the attention of other MPs at Westminster, and had attacked, even if from a position of political isolation, the drama of the Munich "peace" – saw his "lesser-evil" view of the Spanish conflict increasingly strengthened. He hoped that Communism would not take root in Spain and that, in the process, the man who was on the way to becoming the absolute master of Alfonso XIII's former realm would be more reasonable than his counterparts in Rome and Berlin. This was still, as noted, his position in April 1937.[34]

Winston Churchill's stand on the Spanish Civil War was remarkably consistent. In October 1937, when it was clear that the near certain victory of the Nationalists would result in a Fascist-oriented regime, he still wrote in his articles about the possibility of a compromise, one of his mantras during most of the war. If this was ever possible is doubtful, but by late 1937 it was pure fantasy.

> In Spain also the war comes to an equipoise which should encourage Spaniards to come together for the rebuilding of their country. The Spanish Nationalists have proved their right to be respected. So have the

> stout-hearted defenders of Madrid. The frenzied ideologies of Nazi-Fascism on the one hand, and of Anarchy or Communism on the other, are fading. The problem becomes one in which brave soldiers who have fought each other hard, and are now organised in disciplined forces, may well find that they have much in common, including among other things their own tortured country. When human society is ruined in any country by villainous politicians and fanatics, it can only be rebuilt by its fighting men, who even on opposite sides develop a confraternity of their own. Let the Spanish soldiers come together on the basis of throwing out the foreign interlopers, and upon the slogan of "Spain for the Spaniards." This is a theme which is waxing and not waning.[35]

Churchill had made a similar proposal on April 14, 1937, during a debate in the House of Commons on the blockade of Bilbao. Even then Churchill made a bombastic proposal of joint intervention in Spain of the Great Powers in order to stop the war.[36]

At the close of the war in 1939, Franco seemed to give reason to expect the worst: Roman salutes filled the streets of Madrid, accompanied by the warlike anthems of an emboldened Falange. Yet there were also signs of hope: aesthetic matters aside, the regime retained its deeply Catholic and traditionalist attachments, and once victory was assured, it quickly provided guarantees of its peaceful intentions through the Foreign Secretary, the Count of Jordana.[37] A few months later, two men – Franco, but above all Churchill – would become major figures in another conflict, one far more horrific than that which had taken place in Spain.

Prior to Churchill's arrival at Number 10 Downing Street, and with more urgency still after the fall of France, it became an essential objective of British international activity to secure Spanish neutrality in the world-wide conflict. British concern was amply justified. More fascinated by Italian Fascism than by German Nazism, Spain imitated, one after another, the steps taken by Mussolini, who finally entered the war in June. Just as the Duce had done, the Caudillo modified his previous declaration of neutrality to one of "non-belligerence," which was interpreted in the corridors of power as signifying more likely belligerence.

Conclusion

When World War II was finally over, with the Allies victorious and a new world order emerging in which the globe would be divided between the Soviets and the Americans, Churchill elected to spend a few days resting in Hendaye, on the French-Spanish border, prompting the Franco regime press to speculate about a possible prime ministerial visit to San Sebastian; however, this yearning for international blessing led to nothing but loud frustration. A few weeks later, with the Potsdam Conference in full swing, Churchill's Conservative Party was unexpectedly defeated at the ballot box. At one fell swoop, Churchill therefore lost, at least temporarily, any capacity to directly influence Spanish politics. This was but one of the many prerogatives that the election result forced him to relinquish, and his acquiescence, while not entirely without bitterness, was characterized by a commendable dignity and aplomb that speak volumes of the entire British political system.

As stated at the outset, Churchill was genuinely fond of Spain. His understanding attitude, not to be confused with admiration or support toward Spanish policy during World War II, reflected that reality. During the conflict, and despite all its shortcomings, Spain had ultimately done what Great Britain had needed it to do.[38] Churchill was a realist, and his demands did not go any further than that. Nor did he fall into common traps, or feel the need to hold ideological vendettas in his dealings with Franco and the regime. To have favored any broader attempt at political maneuvering would have gone against his deeply-held sense of history.

When he viewed Spain, both during the suffering of the civil war and later, when Francoism reached its apex, more than anything else Churchill saw an unhappy people, imprisoned within the painful contradictions of the past. Yet this was a dilemma which he remained convinced had to be resolved by the Spaniards themselves.

In this, as in many other things, he stood over and above most of his contemporaries.

Acknowledgement

I would like to thank Dr. Julius Ruiz (The University of Edinburgh) and Dr. Enrique Moradiellos (Universidad de Extremadura) for their advice in preparing this chapter. Mr. Alberto Delclaux, and Dr Susan Jeffrey (Universidad Pontificia Comillas ICAI-ICADE) kindly helped with the English translation of the original manuscript.

Notes

1 Amery was a relevant member of the Conservative Party who played a significant political role during the twenties, serving in different key offices (Firt Lord of the Admiralty, Colonial Secretary . . .). In the thirties he opposed the policies of appeasement but without holding any significant political position. He served as Secretary of Statin for India during World War II. He disliked Churchill since their years together at Harrow School.

2 See Churchill Archives Centre GBR/0014/AMEJ.
3 Tom Buchanan, *Britain and the Spanish Civil War* (Cambridge: Cambridge University Press, 1997), 87–91.
Of course, most of the leaders of the Conservative Party favoured the Nationalist cause, including Samuel Hoare, David Margeson, and Maurice Hankey.
4 Piers Brendon, *The Dark Valley: A Panorama of the 1930s* (New York: Vintage, 2002).
5 See Neville Tompson, *The Anti-Appeasers: Conservative Opposition to Appeasement in the 1930s* (Basingtoke: Oxford University Press, 1971).
6 Winston Churchill, *The World Crisis,* vol. V (London: Blomsbury Academic, 2015). See also David Carlton, *Churchill and the Soviet Union* (Manchester: Manchester University Press, 2000).
7 See, among many other works, Roy Jenkins, *Churchill* (London: Pan Books, 2002); Martin Gilbert, *Churchill: A Life* (London: Pimlico, 2000); Geoffrey Best, *Churchill: A Study in Greatness* (London: Penguin, 2002). The relevance of Churchill to the current political debate in the UK is substantiated by the recent publication of a biography of the Conservative statesman by Boris Johnson, *The Churchill Factor: How One Man Made History* (London: Hodder, 2015). A recent issue of *Comillas Journal of International Relations* was devoted to Churchill's perceptions on Europe: Allan Packwood, coord., "Churchill and Europe," *Comillas Journal of International Relations* 7 (2017).
8 See Dorothy Boyd Rush, "Winston Churchill and the Spanish Civil War," *Social Science* 54, no. 2 (1979): 86–92. See also K. W. Watkins, *Britain Divided: The Effect of the Spanish Civil War on British Political Opinion* (London: Thomas Nelson and Sons, 1963), 84.
9 *La Restauracion* (The Restoration) was the name given to the political regime existing in Spain between 1874–1931, after the re-enthroning of the Borbon dinasty in the person of King Alfonso XII. While the regime was based during most of its existence on the rule of a parliamentary constitution and provided significant economic growth, it failed to address most of the country's most acute problems, including the final crisis of the Spanish Empire and the emergence of new political movements.
10 Winston Churchill, *Great Contemporaries* (Florida: Simon Publications, 2001), 156.
11 Idem, *Marlborough: His Life and Times* (Chicago: University of Chicago Press, 2003).
12 Martin Gilbert, *Churchill: The Wilderness Years* (London: Pimlico, 2004), 161.
13 David Sarias, *Caminando con el destino: Winston Churchill y España 1874–1965* (Madrid: Comunidad de Madrid-Churchill Archives Centre, 2011), 35–41.
14 Churchill, *Great Contemporaries,* 149–60.
15 Ibid., 152–53.
16 Jenkins, *Churchill,* 735.

17 Churchill, *Great Contemporaries,* 159–60.
18 Ibid., 157.
19 See Gilbert, *The Wilderness Years.*
20 Ibid., 9.
21 The achievements and failures of Baldwin as a premier are a matter of discussion among historians. See, for instance, Roy Jenkins, *Baldwin* (London: Collins, 1987) and Phillip Williamson *Stanley Baldwin: Conservative Leadership and National Values* (Cambridge: Cambridge University Press, 2007). It was precisely then, when visiting Majorca, he met for the first time Captain Alan Hillgarth, then British honorary vice-consul of the island. Hillgarth was to become a long-time friend and a conspicuous source of information for Churchill, both during the civil war and World War II. See Josep Massot i Muntaner, *El Cónsol Alan Hillgrath i les Isles Baleares. 1936–1939* (Monserrat: Publicacions de l'Abadia, 1995).
22 One of the most successful cartoonists of the time, David Low continuously mocked Churchill during the 1930s, presenting him as a dangerous warmonger. See Timothy Benson, *"Low and Churchill," History Today* 50, 2 (February 2000): 9–15.
23 See Antoine Capet, "The Creeds of the Devil: Churchill between the Two Totalitarianisms, 1917–1945," *International Churchill Society,* https://www.winstonchurchill.org/publications/finest-hour-extras/the-creeds-of-the-devil-churchill-between-the-two-totalitarianisms-1917-1945-1 (accessed June 15, 2017).
24 Jenkins, *Churchill,* 493.
25 This is a paraphrase of Churchill's comment to his private secretary Jock Colville on the evening of June 22, 1941, after the invasion of Russia by Nazi Germany: "If Hitler invaded Hell, I would at least make a favourable reference to the Devil in the House of Commons." See Winston Churchill, *The Second World War: The Grand Alliance* (London: Houghton Mifflin), 290.
26 Enrique Moradiellos, *Neutralidad benévola* (Oviedo: Pentalfa, 1990), 169–88. This is undoubtedly the best study of British positioning during the Spanish Civil War. Moradiellos also wrote the most relevant comparative study of both Hitler and Franco: *Franco frente a Churchill* (Barcelona: Peninsula, 2005). See also idem, *El reñidero de Europa: Las dimensiones internacionales de la Guerra Civil Española* (Barcelona: Peninsula, 2001); and Paul Preston, *La República asediada: Hostilidad internacional y conflictos internos durante la Guerra Civil* (Barcelona: Península, 1999).
27 Winston Churchill, *Step by Step 1936–1939* (New York: Rosetta Books, 2014), 50, https://play.google.com/books/reader?id=vsqWAwAAQBAJ&hl=es&printsec=frontcover&pg=GBS.PP1. This is a compilation of Churchill political articles published in the media in the period 1936–39. See also Moradiellos, "Neutralidad benévola," 70–75.
28 Julio Ponce Abarca, *Gibraltar and the Spanish Civil War: Local, National and International Perspectives* (London: Blomsbury, 2015), 69.
29 Churchill, *Step by Step,* 52.

30 Ibid., 68. Article originally published on October 2, 1936. See also Moradiellos, *El reñidero de Europa*, 106.

31 Churchill, *Step by Step*, 55–56. Article originally published on August 8, 1936.

32 Ibid., 123. Article originally published on April 2, 1937.

33 Ibid.

34 Ibid.

35 Ibid., 179. Article originally published on October 1, 1937.

36 The full debate in "Situation at Bilbao," Hansard 1803–2005, http://hansard.millbanksystems.com/commons/1937/apr/14/situation-at-bilbao#S5CV0322P0_19370414_HOC_454 (accessed August 6, 2017); see also Boyd Rush. "Winston Churchill," 91.

37 Emilio Sáenz-Francés, *Entre la antorcha. Franco en la Encrucijada de la II Guerra Mundial* (Madrid: Actas, 2010), 48–54.

12

The Impact of the Spanish Civil War on Imperial Japan, 1936–1940

HARUO TOHMATSU

The year 1936 was a great turning point for both Spain and Japan, two nations far apart from each other, one on the western edge, and the other, offshore the far eastern rim of the Eurasian continent.

On February 26 of that year a group of radical young officers of the Imperial Japanese Army (hereafter IJA) attempted a coup, together with 1,400 soldiers, killing several cabinet members and a high-ranking army official, and occupied the central area of Tokyo for four days (the so-called 2-26 Coup). The objective of the rebels was to overthrow the corrupt civil government, which they claimed was contaminated by decadent democracy and greedy capitalism, and to restore direct rule of the nation by the emperor.[1] Against the background of the coup was a factional struggle within the IJA between the so-called Control faction (*Tōseiha*) and the Imperial Way faction (*Kōdōha*). While the former was a group of technocrats pushing for the transformation of Japan into a state capable of pursuing a full-scale war, the latter was more fundamentalist, emphasizing the glory of the Japanese nation under the direct rule of the emperor. In the political sphere, the Control faction had a certain degree of affinity with the Soviet Union since it advocated a centralized planned economy and social mobilization. It had more interest in conquering north China in order to place the resources there under Japanese control. Therefore, a conflict with the USSR had to be avoided. In contrast the Imperial Way faction exhibited strong hostility to Communism and its priority was defeating the USSR, which it considered the major threat to Japanese interests in Manchuria.

The aforementioned coup by young officers from the Imperial Way faction, however, was aborted within four days. Ironically, the fatal blow to the rebels was dealt by Emperor Hirohito (1900–89) who was enraged when he heard of the killings of some of his trusted ministers. The rebel officers were executed, their supporters purged, and sympathizers of the Imperial Way faction in the IJA were sidelined.

Elimination of the Imperial faction meant the rise to predominance of the Control faction. After spring 1936, it began to gain influence not only within the IJA but also in Japanese decision-making circles. Its control of military affairs, politics, industry, and education in the country gradually transformed Japan, in the following few years, into a totalitarian regime under the collective leadership of the military. This great change was carried out without any domestic disturbance but with external wars, first, a major war against neighboring China beginning in 1937, and then a full-scale war against the United States and Great Britain from 1941. During this period all political parties were dissolved and unified into the Imperial Rule Assistance Association (*Taisei yokusankai*) in October 1940.

On the other side of the world, in the same year, a coup initiated by extremist officers of the Spanish army stationed in Morocco was a success. However, this victory eventually led the nation into four years of disastrous and bloody civil war. Unlike the Japanese rebels in February 1936, the Spanish counterparts led by Francisco Franco eventually gained control of the state. The prolonged civil war inevitably brought about a huge transformation in the social and political structure of the country. By 1940 Spain was an authoritarian regime headed by Franco. Leading a nation exhausted by the devastation of the civil war, Franco skillfully avoided joining World War II on the side of the Axis, in spite of a great amount of aid given by Nazi Germany and Fascist Italy during the Spanish Civil War (hereafter, SCW).

The SCW might seem less relevant to Japan in regard to its foreign policy and domestic politics in the late 1930s. However, it did have some impact and influence on Japan in certain fields and on particular issues. This chapter provides an overview of the complex relationship between the SCW and Japan.[2]

Japan in International Politics of the late 1930s

When the SCW broke out in July 1936 Japan was at a crossroads. Domestically, the Control faction was increasing its influence in politics while the infant parliamentary democracy was facing bankruptcy in the aftermath of the 2-26 Coup. Under pressure from the military, the new cabinet, headed by the former career diplomat Hirota Kōki (1878–1948), adopted a hardline stance toward China. However, this shift of policy did not ease the tensions with the USSR. Since the creation of the state of

Manchukuo in 1932, the IJA had been in charge of the security of the de facto Japanese protectorate in all but name. The Japanese seizure of Manchuria had greatly aroused Soviet anxiety and the Soviet army stationed in adjacent eastern Siberia was heavily reinforced. By 1935 Soviet ground forces in Siberia facing Manchukuo were three times larger than their Japanese counterpart, the Kwantung Army in Manchuria. Soviet superiority in air and tank forces was even greater. As a result, the IJA increased the size of the Kwantung Army and sought diplomatic and security cooperation with other anti-Soviet states. In terms of resources and arms production Japan was no match for the USSR.

Thus, IJA officials in Germany began to sound out the possibility of alliance, as the Nazi Party had been openly expressing an anti-Communist ideology. Although the Japanese government acknowledged the IJA initiative, it was more cautious in strengthening relations with Nazi Germany, for various reasons. First, as Germany was a former enemy in World War I, it had not dropped its potential claim to its pre-war interests in East Asia and the Pacific that had been taken over by Japan. Second, Germany was Japan's rival for the China market. Third, Germany was becoming a supplier of modern technology and weaponry to China. Until the dissolution of the first coalition of the Kuomintang (Chinese Nationalist Party; hereafter, KMT) and the Chinese Communist Party (hereafter CCP) in 1927, the USSR was the main provider of what China needed for modernization. Even the KMT military academy in Whampoa was established with Soviet aid and its instructors were under heavy Soviet influence. With the change in the KMT's policy toward Communism, China had to find a substitute for the USSR. Germany filled the gap neatly, especially in reforming the Chinese army. Many Wehrmacht advisers were sent to China. Replacing the Chinese army's weapons was an extremely attractive business opportunity for the German arms industry.[3] Even following the change of regime in Germany after January 1933, the new Nazi government pursued a similar China policy.[4] The Japanese Foreign Ministry therefore needed more clues to sound out Germany's designs and intentions regarding the near future of East Asia.

Complex strategic and political relations between China, USSR, Germany, and Japan characterized the international politics of East Asia in the late 1930s. The impact and influence of the SCW on Japan must be seen in this light.

The Spanish Civil War on the Eve of the Sino-Japanese War, 1936–37

Reports in the Japanese media

The SCW was initially covered quite widely in the Japanese media. Almost the only other occasion when Spain had become a topic of interest to the Japanese public to that date was the epidemic of Spanish flu after World War I. The outbreak of the civil war in the summer of 1936 attracted peoples' interest for two possible reasons. The military uprising led by radical Spanish army officers reminded the Japanese people of the attempted coup in Tokyo only a few months before. The strongly anti-Communist stance of the Spanish rebels made the Japanese people sympathetic to them, as the Japanese nation had been strongly indoctrinated with an anti-Marxist ideology since the end of the Meiji period.[5] As the limitations of this chapter preclude coverage of a wide range of media items and articles, it will introduce a typical case of media reportage by an eminent Japanese journalist, Sakai Yoneo (1900–78).

Sakai made in-depth observations of the SCW by reporting from the two confronting camps. His series of Spanish reports appeared chiefly in *Asahi Shimbun*, a major daily newspaper. They were later edited and published in the book *Bagabondo Tsūshin* (Correspondence from a vagabond), in 1939. The book sold several thousand copies and was welcomed by Japanese intellectuals who were keen on gathering the latest news of the SCW.

According to *Bagabondo Tsūshin*, Sakai visited Spain between June and September 1937, on two separate occasions. In early June 1937 he entered Nationalist territory from Portugal. Throughout July, Sakai toured the Nationalist frontline from south to north and carried out a face-to-face interview with Franco on the anniversary of the military uprising. During this meeting Franco emphasized the cause of saving Spain from the evils of Communism and asked for the support and sympathy of the Japanese people. Sakai noted that Franco had "a straight-forward, simple personality, quite different from that of Hitler or Mussolini."[6] After observing the battle of Brunete from the Nationalist side, Sakai left Spain for France where he gained permission from the Republican authorities to enter their territory. Between mid-August and mid-September Sakai visited Valencia, Madrid, and Barcelona, and interviewed Prime Minister Juan Negrin and other Republican leaders before returning to Paris.[7]

One of the most interesting accounts in Sakai's report regards the presence of Japanese volunteers in the two opposing armies. When Sakai was in Salamanca during his first visit to Spain, an American colleague told him the story of a Japanese volunteer in the foreign legion who had captured two Soviet-made tanks from the Republicans. Due to the fierce battle conditions at the time, Sakai was not able to make direct contact with the man in question. Later Sakai was invited by a Franco official to attend a ceremony decorating soldiers, including that Japanese volunteer. Sakai, however, declined the offer because his appearance in the Nationalist media might make it difficult for him to obtain permission from the Republican authorities to enter their territory.[8] The identity of the Japanese volunteer in the Nationalist army therefore remains undiscovered to this day.

During his second trip to Spain, this time on the Republican side, Sakai visited a field hospital in Castilejo. There, a wounded soldier of the International Brigades told him about a Japanese volunteer who had been killed in action in the battle of Brunete. Sakai was able to gather information about the volunteer and later it was discovered that the man in question was called Jack Shirai (1900?–37) by his comrades. Shirai was a Japanese Marxist worker who was born in Hokkaido and had spent his youth in New York. On hearing of the outbreak of the SCW, Shirai joined the volunteer force organized by the Communist Party of America. Shirai was in the 17th battalion of the 15th International Brigade when he was killed in action on July 11, 1937.[9] To date, Shirai is the most well-known Japanese associated with the SCW.

Sakai's reports were unique in the sense that he was among a very small number of people who were able to observe the two opposing camps at approximately the same time. His impartiality is well proved by his objective and detached depictions of zeal, passion, horror, and misery in civil war. Sakai not only interviewed eminent political figures, such as Franco and Negrin, but also officers and men in the field, foreign volunteers and observers, and ordinary citizens.

However, when Sakai's reports appeared in *Asahi Shimbum*, they were edited to give readers a quite different image of the civil war. While atrocities committed by the Republicans were exaggerated, Franco and the Nationalists were praised as defenders of the nation in the face of a Communist conspiracy. Sakai later vanished from the Japanese media due possibly to his "impartial attitude" in reporting the Sino-Japanese War.[10] Besides this self-imposed censorship by the press, intensification of the Sino-Japanese War took over media interest and the SCW gradually faded from the Japanese people's minds.

The Japanese government

On hearing of the outbreak of the SCW, the Hirota cabinet initially adopted a strict policy of neutrality. When the situation became serious, Hirota ordered the Japanese embassy in Madrid to evacuate, initially to San Sebastián, and later to Saint-Jean-de-Luz, in southwest France. Thereafter, the Japanese government gathered information on the civil war through its temporary embassy in Saint-Jean-de-Luz.

However, when it was discovered that foreign powers, such as Germany, Italy, and the USSR, were sending aid to the opposing camps, the Japanese government found in the SWC an ideal opportunity to gather intelligence regarding the respective intervening powers.

An important ongoing issue at the time was the possibility of concluding an anti-Comintern Pact with Germany. Although the negotiations were initiated by the IJA, the pact was on the official agenda of the Hirota cabinet. In this context, developments in the SCW turned out to be a precious information source of political intentions and military capabilities of Nazi Germany and the USSR.

Another potentially key issue was a plan to establish diplomatic relations with the Vatican. Since the visit of the young Emperor Hirohito (Crown Prince at the time) to the Holy See in 1921, this idea had been discussed intermittently. The failure to establish diplomatic ties was chiefly due to the strong anti-Christian ideology among influential circles in Japan. However, on hearing of the persecution of Catholics by the Republicans and Communists, the government realized the importance of Catholicism and the Catholic Church in international politics. Although it was not until 1942 that Japan and the Vatican officially exchanged delegations, during the SCW the Japanese government began to see Catholics and the Catholic Church in Japan as potential allies to counter Communism. The above issues will be returned to below.

The Imperial Japanese Army

The group most likely to be interested in developments in the SCW in Japanese decision-making circles was the IJA. As it was responsible for the security of Manchukuo, the IJA was keen on gathering intelligence regarding the political intentions and military capabilities of the USSR. Likewise, it had to prepare for possible retaliation by China in the future. It was evident that China under the KMT was rapidly modernizing its military capacity with German aid. A strategic nightmare for the IJA was a combined action of China and the USSR to take over Manchukuo. Since the battlefields of Spain were a testing ground for new weapons and tactics of Nazi Germany and the USSR, the IJA immediately sent an observer to the spot.

Captain (later Colonel) Nishiura Susumu (1901–70) was an elite IJA officer who occupied many pivotal administrative positions in the Ministry of the Army, including secretary to Prime Minister Tojo Hideki, who was also the army minister. He happened to be in France researching European military organizations when the SCW broke out. Under instructions from the Army Ministry and the General Staff, between November 8 and December 24, 1936, Nishiura made an undercover trip to the Nationalist-controlled area of Spain. He took a ship from Le Havre to Lisbon where he made contact with a secret agent of the Franco government. Having gained permission, Nishiura entered Salamanca on November 8. As the city was preoccupied with the arrival of German "volunteers," Nishiura's reception by the local Nationalist authorities was not particularly friendly. A Nationalist official flatly rejected Nishiura's request for assistance on the grounds that the Japanese government had not officially recognized the Franco government. Initially, Nishiura had to find his way without any official assistance. At this stage, he kept records of numbers of German "volunteers" in the town and correctly judged that most of them were pilots and crew members for air operations.[11]

However, when news of the conclusion of the Anti-Comintern Pact between Germany and Japan of November 25 was reported, official treatment of Nishiura improved dramatically. The local Nationalist authorities gave him permission to visit wherever he wished and provided various kinds of assistance, including a Spanish-French interpreter and an automobile. As a result, Nishiura made a thorough tour of the Nationalist front and gathered further intelligence.

On November 29, he witnessed the arrival of German regular troops in Salamanca. There he also experienced bombings by Soviet-made planes of the Republican air force.[12] Examining the body of a dead Communist "volunteer" in the field, Nishiura immediately identified him as a regular soldier of the Soviet army from Kiev military district. Nishiura also counted the types of shells and bullets abandoned by the Republican army in battlefields and discovered that they were products of 13 different states, including Mexico.[13]

As a military technocrat (Nishiura was an expert in artillery), what attracted him most were new types of weapons used by both camps, in particular tanks. While the German Type I tank used by the Nationalists was armed with only a pair of 7.92 mm machineguns, the Soviet-made T-26 tank and BA-10 armored vehicle, equipped with a 45 mm canon, were highly effective weapons used by the Republican army. The

Nationalist authorities on the frontlines gave Nishiura ample opportunities to examine the details of these captured Soviet-made weapons. Nishiura also gathered information from other foreign military missions. On one occasion the Italian mission was extremely helpful in sharing with Nishiura their experience of combat against the Soviet-made T-26 tank.[14]

One of the IJA's major concerns at that time was the inferiority of the Kwantung Army stationed in Manchukuo in regard to armor and artillery equipped by the Soviet army in eastern Siberia. While improvement and mass production of anti-tank weapons was planned, the IJA had to make do with makeshift means. Nishiura observed that in street-to-street fighting in towns, improvised petrol bombs utilizing a bottle (later called the Molotov cocktail) was fairly effective. However, as an artillery officer he recognized that the most effective anti-tank weapon, apart from the tank itself, was the high velocity anti-tank gun with a caliber of more than 37 mm (called in the IJA a "quick-firing gun").

Nishiura left Spain on Christmas Eve 1936 and returned to Tokyo via Paris. While in Paris, Nishiura wired Japanese General Staff on January 6, 1937, to explain the latest political and military developments in Spain. He had the impression that Germany was trying to make Spain its virtual colony.

On his return to Tokyo he submitted detailed reports to the Army Ministry and General Staff. In July 1937 he also lectured on recent developments in the SCW to a select audience in a study seminar organized by the Japan Association of Foreign Relations (*Nippon Gaikō Kyōkai*). Nishiura's report had considerable influence in forming an image of the SCW in Japanese decision-making circles, as members of the association included many present and former diplomats, as well as politicians and business leaders. On December 1, 1937, the Japanese government officially recognized the Nationalists as the sole legitimate government of Spain.

Japanese Catholics

One group in Japan that was heavily influenced by developments in the SCW was the Catholic Church. Despite a relatively small number of followers (approximately 300,000 out of a total population of 80 million in the 1930s), the Catholic Church had been increasing its influence in Japanese diplomatic considerations. Since the early 1920s a good number of urban Japanese intellectuals with a European background and training (academics, bankers, businessmen, diplomats, lawyers, and even some military officers) were followers of the Catholic faith or were sympathetic to the doctrine.[15] One of the most eminent Japanese Catholics was Rear Admiral Yamamoto Shin'jirō (1877–1942), who had the ear of Emperor Hirohito in diplomatic matters.[16] As it became more aware of the importance of the Catholic Church in Europe and Latin America, the Japanese government began to seek official diplomatic relations with the Vatican.

That said, with the increase of chauvinism in Japanese society following the Manchurian incident, the attitude of the government and general public toward Japanese Catholics was suspicious, if not hostile. Since the Meiji Restoration, the official stance of the government toward religion was freedom of faith within the limits of the Japanese *kokutai* (national foundation).

The ideology of *kokutai* was heavily based on State Shintoism (*Kokka Shintō*), an amalgam of traditional faith in Japanese gods and political nationalism. The emperor was revered for his divine origin: he was believed to be the direct descendant of Amaterasu, the goddess that created the Japanese nation. The idea of a Japan headed by the emperor was called *Kōkoku shisō*. As State Shintoism gained the status of a national religion by the mid-1930s, faiths of foreign origin were seen as potentially dangerous elements that might "contaminate" the *kokutai*.[17]

In the wake of extremist nationalism at home, Japanese Catholics found themselves in a difficult position. Worship of the Christian God was seen as a spiritual betrayal of Shintō gods. Christians, whether Catholic or Protestant, were accused of being *hikokumin* (un-patriotic, or traitors to the nation). In such circumstances, the SCW affected Japanese Catholics in a peculiar way.[18]

When news and comments on the SCW appeared in Japanese Catholic media, such as *Nippon Katorikku shimbun* (Japan Catholic press), *Katorikku gahō* (illustrated Catholic journal), and *Robi* (firelight), most supported the cause of the Nationalists, depicting Franco as a defender of the Christian faith against Communist atheism. Victims of the civil war on the side of Franco were praised as martyrs or Crusaders. As many foreign priests and nuns in Japan engaged in apostolic and education work had families and relatives in Spain, news of atrocities committed by the Republicans to Catholics in the civil war had strong credibility in the eyes of Japanese Catholics.

Meanwhile, *Divini redemptoris*, the papal encyclical issued by Pope Pius IX on March 19, 1937, strongly denounced Marxism as anti-Christian.[19] As a consequence of this official recognition, pro-Nationalist reports in the Catholic media gained wider currency among Japanese Catholics. It was symbolic that the Japanese Catholic press began to use the term "National" (not Nationalist) government for Franco's Burgos government from May, long before it was given official state recognition by the Japanese government on December 1, 1937. As long as they supported Franco, Japanese Catholics were not accused of being *hikokumin*. The triumph of Franco in the SCW served as a bulwark to protect Japanese Catholics from the fanatic *kokutai* ideology.

The Russian population in Manchukuo

The SWC had an impact on an unexpected group of people in an area not usually associated with Spain: the Russian population in Manchuria.

Since the Portsmouth Treaty of 1905 that put an end to the Russo-Japanese War (1904–5), the southern half of Manchuria had come under the Japanese sphere of influence. Although the northern half still remained under Russian sway, Russo-Japanese relations were relatively stable due to the conclusion of the Russo-Japanese Agreement of 1907, which confirmed the content of the Portsmouth Treaty. The agreement was revised in 1910, 1912, and finally in 1916, thus maintaining the status quo between the two countries in Manchuria.

The outbreak of the Russian Revolution in 1917 and the ensuing civil war greatly weakened the Russian presence in Manchuria for some time. However, stabilization of the USSR and its resurgence as a Great Power in the late 1920s shifted the balance of power in the region. In 1929, modernized Soviet forces crippled the Chinese military attempt to recover its railway interests in northern Manchuria (the Sino-Soviet War of 1929). The creation of Manchukuo in 1932 gave Japan the added burden of protecting the newly founded state from its Communist neighbor. As of 1934, IJA military doctrine was focused on an anti-Soviet strategy in northern Manchuria and eastern Siberia. In 1936 alone there were 152 small border disputes between Manchukuo and the USSR and the Soviet-sponsored Mongolian People's Republic.[20]

Under these circumstances, the Russian population in Manchukuo was a complex matter. Although Russians were a numerical minority (approximately 66,700 in 1940, only 0.16 percent of the population of Manchukuo), most of them lived in three major cities (Harbin, Mukden, and Dalian), forming the intellectual upper-middle and professional classes. On the one hand, Russians that fled the country to avoid Communist persecution were Japanese collaborators. Some of them worked for the Kwantung Army and the South Manchurian Railway Company, a semi-state company running the railway network and related business in Manchuria. The Kwantung Army secretly trained anti-Communist Russians for insurgency operations in the event of war with the USSR. On the other hand, Russians that had originally resided in northern Manchuria working mainly for the railway network under the USSR were potentially dangerous elements who were sympathetic to Communism.[21]

Thus, the impact of the SCW on the Russian population in Manchukuo was of great concern to the Japanese authorities. A detailed report dated August 25, 1936, sent to the Ministry of Foreign Affairs and other relevant government offices from Major General Tojo Hideki (1884–1948), vividly depicts the situation in Manchuria. Tojo at that time was chief of the Internal Security Department of the Kwantung Bureau. According to the report, entitled "Issues concerning Attitudes of Russians and Foreign Citizens in Manchuria towards the Spanish Revolution," the outbreak of the SCW revealed splits in the Russian community. Out of strong anti-Communist sentiment many Russians began a fund-raising campaign in favor of Franco's camp. Conversely, Soviet institutions maneuvered to organize support for the Popular Front.[22] Although the USSR did not give state recognition to Manchukuo, it established consular offices in major cities of Manchukuo for the practical reason of protecting Soviet interests there. There were even moves by both anti-and pro- USSR groups to organize a volunteer corps to send to Spain.[23] In charge of maintaining public order in Manchukuo, Tojo took extra care in gathering information regarding the moves of both rightist and leftist groups.[24]

However, by the time Manchukuo joined the Anti-Comintern Pact on January 16, 1939, followed by the Franco regime on March 27, the situation had greatly eased. After this date, Manchukuo and Spain became allies against international Communism.

The Spanish Civil War in the Context of the Sino-Japanese War, 1937–38

The Soviet involvement

Approximately a year after the outbreak of the SCW, a new war began in East Asia. A skirmish between local Japanese and Chinese garrisons in the suburbs of Beijing on July 7, 1937, and another clash between Japanese marine units and Chinese crack divisions on August 13, in Shanghai soon escalated into a full-scale war. Between August 1937 and March 1939, the two wars continued in parallel. Although their nature differed considerably, the SCW and the Sino-Japanese War had one thing in common: Soviet involvement.

From the Soviet point of view, the years 1937–39 were marked by a two-front involvement. Soon after the outbreak of the Sino-Japanese

War, in August 1937, China and the USSR concluded a non-aggression treaty.[25] The Soviet aim was to divert Japanese military strength away from Manchuria to China proper so that the Kwantung Army threat against eastern Siberia would be reduced. Stalin showed a good degree of realpolitik in aiding Nationalist China, that is, the KMT government, which was essentially anti-Communist.

Under this treaty, the USSR provided a considerable amount of military aid to China. As Chinese industry was not developed enough to produce modern weapons, apart from small arms, Soviet-made tanks, heavy artillery, and aircraft greatly improved China's military capability.[26] This was particularly apparent in air warfare. The Japanese air force suffered heavy losses in the bombing of Chongqing, the wartime capital of China, by Soviet-made interceptors.[27]

However, increased Soviet aid to China meant less military aid to the Spanish Republican government, which might have weakened the defense of Madrid.[28] In fact, the Soviet government made a decision to cease its aid to Madrid in the summer of 1938. Part of the rationale behind this decision was the rise of tensions in East Asia.

In July–August 1938 a military clash between the Japanese Korean Army and the Soviet Army occurred in Changkufeng, a location near Lake Khasan on the Soviet-Korea border. The two-week battle ended in stalemate, leaving a considerable number of casualties on both sides.[29] Around the same time, IJA troops in central China were about to launch a large-scale offensive on Wuhan, in the Yangtze Valley. The USSR therefore needed to strengthen its own forces in eastern Siberia, as well as support the crumbling Chinese forces in the defense of Wuhan. Above all, the possibility of a Republican victory in Spain was quickly diminishing.

The SCW and the Sino-Japanese War were thus interrelated through Soviet military aid. Naturally the IJA's interest in developments in the SCW, after the outbreak of the Sino-Japanese War, shifted specifically toward observing the amount of Soviet military aid sent to Madrid.

Official approach of the IJA to the Nationalist Government

Following state recognition of the Nationalist regime on December 1, 1937, a new IJA officer was sent to Spain. In January 1938, Lieutenant Colonel (later Major General) Moriya Seiji (1896–1943) was appointed military attaché to Salamanca. Half a year later, in June 1938, Major Sato Hiro'o joined Moriya. Sato had been an intelligence officer based in Warsaw for some years. Poland and Japan had established diplomatic relations in 1919. Since then the IJA and the Polish military had maintained intelligence cooperation against the USSR. Sato was chosen for his expertise in anti-Communist intelligence and counter-intelligence activities. Both Moriya and Sato were welcomed by the Nationalist government.

While Sato worked mostly undercover, Moriya maneuvered openly to strengthen cooperation with the new Spanish government. One such action was Moriya's support for promoting the handover of Imperial Japanese Navy (hereafter IJN) destroyers to the Nationalist government. The request for Japanese aid in naval matters began as early as January 1938 when Yamamoto Shin'jirō, the "admiral monk," visited Burgos as a member of a Japanese goodwill mission. Yamamoto had meetings with Nationalist navy leaders, including Admiral Juan Cervera. However, the direct cause for the request for destroyers was an acute need to replace the loss of a navy vessel. On March 6, 1938, the Nationalist navy cruiser *Baleares* was torpedoed and lost in the battle of Cabo de Palos. Since an intense struggle for trade routes in the Mediterranean was currently under way, the Nationalist navy desperately required substitutes for the lost cruiser. At one stage, the transfer of two IJN destroyers to the Nationalist navy was considered.

However, due chiefly to the reluctance of the Japanese government to commit itself to handing over naval vessels to a state still in the midst of a civil war, but also to the difficulties of providing technical assistance to the Nationalist navy, the plan did not materialize.

In the spring of 1938, Moriya took part in the military planning of the Nationalist force in the battlefield. The documents that remain suggest that in May 1938 Moriya accompanied Nationalist forces operating in Alcañiz and Zaragoza.[30] This enabled him to closely observe tactics and weapons adopted by the Republican forces. Moriya even managed to obtain captured tanks and field guns for detailed examination in Japan. Documents from October 1938 suggest that a considerable amount of captured Soviet weapons and equipment, such as armored tank plate, fighter plane engines, field- and machineguns, and range finders were sent secretly to Japan.[31]

Moriya remained in Spain until June 1941, organizing the intelligence network in Spain and related countries.

Madrid and Wuhan

The year 1938 marks the battle for two cities, Madrid and Wuhan. In Spain, the confrontation was part of a civil war between two political camps; in China, it was part of a war between two states, China and Japan. However, as China fought Japan through a coalition of the KMT and the

CCP, the war was seen by some foreigners as heroic resistance by the Asian version of the Popular Front against Japanese imperialism. In *Bagabondo Tsūshin*, Sakai points out that many volunteers from the International Brigade he had met in Spain were keen on going to China to join the war against Japan.[32]

In that sense, the year 1938 was a moment when the two wars became most closely interrelated ideologically. From June 11 to October 7, Japanese and Chinese forces fought a massive battle for control of the river and railway center of Wuhan, in Hubei Province, central China. Although the official capital had been transferred to Chongqing, Sichuan Province, in the previous year, Wuhan as the second largest urban area in the country was the symbol of national resistance of the Chinese people against Japanese aggression.[33] In this context Wuhan was often compared to Madrid in Chinese propaganda.

Madrid, the capital of the Republic and center of the Popular Front, stood undefeated from the first day of the SCW until March 29, 1939, three days before the end, repelling every attack mounted by the Nationalists. For many observers, the decisive factor in the successful defense of Madrid was the existence of politically aware workers' militias. This new group of people belonged to the social class which Karl Marx named the proletariat. Madrid therefore was idealized by liberals and Communists throughout the world and it was this image that China tried to adopt for Wuhan.

The reality was quite different, however. The Chinese force in charge of defending Wuhan at the time was composed chiefly of troops under the central government and forces of various former warlord armies. The participation of Communist militias was minimal, if not nominal. The main body of the CCP force was in the far north, in Yan'an, and had nothing to do with the battle of Wuhan. The political configuration of China at that time consisted of a coalition of the KMT under Chiang Kai-shek and the CCP of Mao Zedong. As Chiang's source of power was control of the military, he was much closer to Franco in character. Putting this picture into the Spanish context, it was as if Franco and the Communists were collaborating to fight a foreign power.

On October 26, 1938, the city of Wuhan eventually fell to the Japanese without substantial resistance by its Chinese inhabitants. Five months later Madrid also fell in spite of the stiff resistance of its highly motivated working-class citizens.

The Aftermath: Two Authoritarian Regimes, 1939–40

On March 27, 1939, the day Madrid fell to the Nationalist army, the Franco government joined the Anti-Comintern Pact.[34] On April 1, the end of the civil war was officially announced by the triumphant Nationalists. In contrast, the prolonged Sino-Japanese War was well into its third year and Japan was suffering from a stalemate. To make matters worse, termination of the SCW meant increased Soviet aid to China and the expansion of the Soviet army in eastern Siberia.

In fact, the Soviet threat on the Mongolian-Manchukuo borders culminated in the Nomonhan (or Khalhin-Gol) incident of May-September 1939 – a full-scale war between the Soviet Far Eastern Army and the Kwantung Army in all but name. As a result of the destruction of the 23rd division of the IJA on the ground the incident ended in Soviet victory. However, the Soviet army and air force suffered heavy losses due to Japanese anti-tank tactics and interceptors.[35] This was chiefly thanks to Japanese examination of captured Soviet-made weapons in the SCW.

The civil war ended in Franco's victory but the Nationalist government faced the heavy task of reconstructing Spain's decimated infrastructure. An interesting observation on this period can be seen in a report made by a Japanese diplomat. In November 1939, a mid-rank Japanese embassy official in Rome named Inomata made a two-week, unofficial tour of Spain, at the invitation of various Spanish Nationalist organizations.[36]

Inomata and his assistant left Genoa on October 31 and, between November 2 and 18, visited Barcelona, Madrid, Toledo, Seville, Spanish Morocco, and the island of Mallorca, before returning to Rome. Wherever they went they were welcomed enthusiastically by the authorities, both national and local. The report therefore chiefly represents the perceptions of people from the Nationalist camp. That said, it also includes interesting information regarding post-civil war Spain.

Inomata's main interest was anti-Communist measures adopted by the Nationalist government. The police system, investigation methodology, thought control schemes, and education plans were examined in detail. He also looked at welfare policy promoted under the Nationalist government, which Inomata identified correctly as an effective means to counter Communism.[37] Referring to the huge human and material losses of the country as a result of the civil war, the report explains that Spain's top priority was economic rehabilitation. And as Inomata points out, Franco was realistic and cautious enough to keep Spain out of World War II. Despite repeated pressure from Hitler, Franco adamantly rejected entering war on the Axis side and sent only a nominal volunteer force to the Eastern Front.

While Spain was struggling to reconstruct itself in the aftermath of the war, Japan was entering a new phase. All political parties were dissolved and a single party, the Imperial Rule Assistance Association, was established under Prime Minister Konoye Fumimaro (1891–1945). This move was obviously aimed at transforming Japan into a single-party, totalitarian state modeled after Fascist Italy, Nazi Germany, and perhaps the USSR under Stalin. However, in substance the Imperial Rule Assistance Association ended up as a loose collaboration of assorted conservative and nationalistic interest groups. In some ways it resembled the Falange Party in Franco's Spain. To make matters worse, the Imperial Rule Assistance Association lacked strong leadership such as that of Franco. As Japanese constitutional law (*Dainipponteikoku kempō*) at the time defined the emperor as the supreme, sole ruler of state, it prevented the formation of a centralized leadership similar to those in other totalitarian states. When Tojo was appointed prime minister in October 1941, and concurrently he assumed the post of president of the Imperial Rule Assistance Association, he was hampered by the defused decision-making structure of the organization. In December 1941, Japan entered the Asia-Pacific War under a political regime similar to that of Spain, but without a powerful leadership. Tojo was not Franco.

The SCW was not an issue central to Japanese diplomacy in the latter half of the 1930s. However, it functioned as a link that connected various issues in Japan in diverse and sometimes unexpected ways.

Notes

1 On the 2-26 Coup, see Tsutsui Kiyotada, *Fifteen Lectures on Showa Japan* (Tokyo: JPIC, 2016), 121–40.

2 For a general background to this period, see Haruo Tohmatsu and H.P. Willmott, *A Gathering Darkness: The Coming of War to the Far East and the Pacific 1921–1942* (Lanham: SR Books, 2004), Ch. 2.

3 For German military advisors and aid sent to China, see Zhan Baija, "China's Quest for Foreign Military Aid," in *The Battle for China*, ed. Mark Peattie, Edward Drea, and Hans Van de Ven (Palo Alto: Stanford University Press, 2012), 283–88.

4 For Nazi Germany's China policy, see John P. Fox, *Germany and the Far Eastern Crisis 1931–1938* (Oxford: Clarendon Press, 1982), especially Ch. V.

5 In 1910–11 political activists allegedly planning to assassinate Emperor Meiji were arrested. As many of them were Socialists and anarchists, the left-wing movement was heavily suppressed by the government (*Taigyaku jiken*). In 1925, when Japan established diplomatic relations with the USSR, the Peace

Preservation Law (*Chian ijihō*) was introduced to prevent the expansion of Marxism in Japan.

6 Sakai Yoneo, *Dōran no supein hōkoku: Bagabondo Tsūshin* [Reports from tumultuous Spain: Correspondence from a vagabond] (Tokyo: Sairyusha, 1980), 74–78.

7 Ibid., 157.

8 Ibid., 85, 195–96.

9 Ibid., 158–59, 165–66.

10 Sakai spent most of his remaining life in the United States. See Sakai, *Bagabondo Tsūshin*, 204–13.

11 *Supein naisen wo miru* [Observing the Spanish Civil War], Lecture by Artillery Captain Nishiura Susumu, edited by Nippon Gaikō Kyōkai (July 1937), Japan Center for Asian Historical Record, National Archives of Japan (hereafter, JACAR), Reel No. A-0360, p. 102. JACA Ref. no. B02030915800.

12 Ibid., 136–37.

13 Nishiura Susumu, *Shōwa Rikugun Hiroku* [Secret testimonies of the IJA in the Shōwa period] (Tokyo: Nippon Keizai Shimbun Press, 2014), 135.

14 Ibid., 135.

15 For Catholicism and the Catholic Church in modern Japan, see Kevin Doak, ed, *Xavier's Legacies: Catholicism in Modern Japanese Culture* (Vancouver: University of British Columbia Press, 2012).

16 Yamamoto served Hirohito as personal tutor when he was crown prince. Young Hirohito's visit to the Vatican in 1921 was arranged, against considerable opposition at home, by Yamamoto. Stern and serious, he was nicknamed "a monk in naval uniform." At the outbreak of the Asia-Pacific War, Emperor Hirohito saw the Vatican as one of the mediators among the Allies for a negotiated peace. The establishment of diplomatic relations between the Holy See and Japan in 1942 was made possible due to Hirohito's strong appeals.

17 After 1935 *Kokutai meichō undō* (action to clarify the national foundation of the state) was enthusiastically promoted by the Ministry of Education and right-wing activists, who rejected modern concepts of constitutional monarchy and parliamentary democracy. Strong anti-Western thought that emphasized traditional values based on State Shintoism accompanied this movement.

18 The following account chiefly depends on Watanabe Chiaki, "Nippon no katorikku shuppanbutsu nimiru supein naisen hōdō" [Reports on the Spanish Civil War that appeared in Japanese Catholic publications, 1936–1939], *Aoyama Kokusai Seikei Ronshū* (Journal of International Politics and Economy, Aoyama Gakuin University, Tokyo), no. 63 (May 2004): 221–39.

19 The text of *Divini redemptoris* can be seen in http://w2.vatican.va/content/pius-xi/encyclicas/documents/hf_p-xi_enc_1937031.

20 For border disputes, see Alvin D. Coox, *Nomonhan: Japan against Russia*, 1939 (Palo Alto: Stanford University Press, 1990), 156–57.

21 For Russian elements in Manchuria, see Yoshihisa Tak Matsusaka, *The*

Making of Japanese Manchuria, 1904–1932 (Cambridge, Mass: Harvard University Press, 2003).

22 "Supein nairan ni taisuru hakkei rojin wo hajimeto suru zaimanshū shogaikokujin no han' nō ni tsuite" [The Attitude of Russians and Foreigners Residing in Manchuria toward the Spanish Civil War], Report no. 3236, (dated August 25, 1936), sent by Tojo Hideki to Deputy Foreign Minister Horiuchi Kensuke, doc. no. 121, vol. 5, Part II, Showa Period, Nippon Gaiko Bunsho [Records of Japanese Diplomatic History] (Tokyo: Ministry of Foreign Affairs, 2007), 247–51.

23 Ibid. 250.

24 In 1936 Tojo was concurrently head of the military police of the Kwantung Army. He was promoted to lieutenant general in 1937 due to his achievements in persecuting Communist elements and suppressing radical supporters of the 2-26 Coup in Manchukuo. Ascending the leadership ladder, Tojo was appointed prime minister in October 1941.

25 For the Sino-USSR Non-aggression Treaty and its implications for the Sino-Japanese War, see James C. Hsuing & Steven I. Levine, *China's Bitter Victory* (New York: Sharpe, 1992), 109.

26 The amount of aid to China from the USSR between August 1937 and June 1941 is estimated as follows: 800 aircraft, 50 tanks, 960 field artillery piece, 1,200 trucks, 100,000 rifles, totaling the equivalent of 450 million US dollars between 1937 and 1940. In addition, approximately 1,000 advisers and volunteers (chiefly pilots) were sent. See Zhan, "China's Quest for Foreign Military Aid," 288–93.

27 The Japanese bombardment of Chongqing was one of the early cases of strategic bombing aimed at destroying the morale of enemy civilians.

28 Soviet aid to the Republicans between October 1936 and August 1938 is estimated as follows.1050 aircraft, 700 tanks and armored vehicles, 1,200 field artillery pieces, 4,000 trucks, and 28 cargo ships. Approximately 80 military advisors and instructors, 70 language interpreters, 100 engineers, 30 gunners, 100 tank crew, and 140 pilots were sent as "volunteers."

29 For the Battle of Lake Khasan, see Coox, *Nomonhan*, 124. Casualties were approximately 1,400 (Japan) and 2,400 (the USSR) killed and wounded, respectively.

30 Moriya's participation in the Nationalist government's military campaign is documented in telegram no. 22 sent to the General Staff, May, 25, 1938, JACAR Ref. no. C01004553700.

31 Report sent by Moriya to Vice Army Minister Tojo, "Supeinkoku kokumingun rokaku ni kakawaru sorensei heiki sōfu no ken" [Transportation of Soviet-made weapons captured by the Spanish Nationalist Army], October, 5, 1938, JACAR Ref no. C01004553700.

32 Sakai, *Bagabondo Tsūshin*, 158.

33 For the battle of Wuhan and its political implications, see Stephan R. Mackinnon, *Wuhan, 1938: War, Refugees, and the Making of Modern China* (Berkeley, CA: University of California Press, 2008).

34 For Spain and the Anti-Comintern Pact, see Shiozaki Hiroaki, "Furanko seiken no nichidokui bōkyōkyōtei sanka nitsuite" [On the participation of the Franco government in the Japan–German–Italy Anti Comintern Pact] in *Supein naisen no kenkyū* [A study of the Spanish Civil War], ed. Saitō Takashi (Tokyo: Chūō krōnsha, 1979), 258–74.

35 It is evident that the dispute was settled in favor of the USSR. However, after the end of the Cold War documents in Russian archives revealed that Soviet casualties were much higher than those of Japan. It is estimated that 25,000 Soviet soldiers were killed or wounded versus 19,000 Japanese. The former also lost 400 tanks and armored vehicles and 360 aircraft, versus 30 and 160, respectively.

36 "Supeinkoku shisatsu hōkokusho, Inomata jimukan, zai itaria" [Report on visit to Spain by officer Inomata, Embassy of Japan in Italy], April 1940, submitted to Ambassador Amou Eiji, the Japanese ambassador to Italy, Reel No. A-0670, 1–3, JACAR Ref. no. B02031637400.

37 Ibid., 38–39.

13

Argentina's Diplomatic and Naval Asylum Policy in the Spanish Civil War

LEONARDO SENKMAN

The aim of this chapter is to assess the practice of diplomatic and maritime asylum granted by Argentina during the first two years of the Spanish Civil War, as well as to re-examine those who benefited from this humanitarian activity.

It is estimated that the diplomatic policy of asylum carried out by several Latin American and European countries protected a total of 11,1130 asylees during the Spanish Civil War, with 6,196 of them benefiting from asylum in Latin American embassies. Argentina ranked second, after Chile, among Latin American countries in carrying out and defending the Latin American legal tradition of the right of asylum from a principled and doctrinaire perspective.[1] The largest number of protected people – no fewer than 1,200 – found refuge in the Chilean embassy, while the estimated number in Argentina did not exceed 450 asylees in all.[2]

The asylum policy was criticized by the Ministry of Foreign Affairs of the Spanish Republic, especially once Alvarez del Vayo took office, with the claim that it benefited rebels from the Nationalist camp. In response, Argentina invoked the humanitarian principles of Latin America's tradition of the right to asylum, and its absolute non-interference in the internal politics of Spain, in accordance with the position of the Anglo-French Non-intervention Committee.[3]

Protection of the 450 asylees was considered a priority among the duties of the Argentine ambassador, Daniel García Mansilla. From the summer of 1936, he had been relocated, along with other ambassadors, to Zaráuz, on the coast of the Guipúzcoa province in the Basque Country, after the government of President Azaña moved his offices to the

Ministerio de Jornada in San Sebastian. The asylees in the Argentine embassy in Madrid were managed by the chargé d'affaires, Edgardo Pérez Quesada.

Most of the Argentine and Chilean asylees were sympathetic to the rebel camp. Their number increased even more, with a contingent of 257 asylum-seekers in the Uruguayan embassy, when Argentina took over the affairs of this neighboring country, after it severed diplomatic relations with Spain in September 1936, in retaliation for the execution of two Uruguayan citizens.[4]

From the end of July 1936, Alvarez del Vayo's mistrust, and the violence of militiamen against, the asylees – who were characterized as "enemies, *señoritos*, and reactionaries" – worried Ambassador García Mansilla and other Argentine diplomatic officials. The ideological orientation of the asylees left no doubt in the minds of the Republican authorities. In her pioneering study on asylum carried out in the Argentine embassy in Madrid and the residence in Zaráuz, Beatriz Figallo documented the first entry of D. Pedro M. Anzoátegui in Madrid Embassy , a Carlist neighbor of the ambassador, followed later "by industrialists from the zone, politicians of the Right, and members of the nobility."[5]

In a report from early 1939, Ambassador García Mansilla recalled the first two anti-Republican figures to whom he granted asylum in the Zaráuz residence: "Honorio Maura, a deputy of the Right whose election was fraudulently annulled by the Left, as well as Pelayo Olazabal, Marqués de Cantillana, a known Carlist."[6] On July 25, the ambassador also granted asylum to "two known Falangist young people from Zaragoza, companions of José Antonio Primo de Rivera." On July 28, Pedro Caro, Marqués de Sobroso, a well-known figure who had taken part in the repression of Asturias, requested protection within the Argentine embassy. The list of these first asylees ends with a factory owner hated by his anarchist workers.[7]

In the days that followed, three aristocratic women received asylum at the residence of the Argentine ambassador: Teresa Osores de Valdés (daughter of the Marquis of Aranda), and her daughters, María Falco, Marquess of Romanal, and Rosario Gurtubay, Duchess of Hijar (mother-in-law of the Duke of Alba). In the diplomatic headquarters of Madrid, other members of the nobility and Falangists were also protected, including Carmen Angoloti, Duchess of Victoria and former president of the Spanish Red Cross, as well as Jacinto Miquelare, a well-known Falangist journalist and Basque intellectual.[8] In addition, asylum was granted to the Falangist military chaplain Adolfo Suarez, and to the wife and daughters of the Falangist commander, Tuevo, one of the defenders of the Alcázar of Toledo.[9] The most complete list of asylees in the Argentine embassy was registered by another Falangist, Francisco Cásares.[10]

On August 1, 1936, militiamen of the Popular Front of Zaráuz attacked the residence of García Mansilla with incendiary bombs, demanding that the ambassador hand over the asylees, but he refused. Two days later, an even more serious incident occurred, with militias threatening to take the residence by storm. The civil governor of Guipúzcoa took measures to halt the violence. An example of García Mansilla's determination to enforce the right of asylum was his resistance to the physical threats of the Junta Popular Front in Zaráuz, and their chants demanding that he hand over Carlist Arocena and the Falangist Anzoátegui brothers, with threats of retaliation against their families.[11]

Some of the refugees in the diplomatic Zaráuz residence, such as García Mansilla's wife, were evacuated to French territory in British battleships. Both the Argentine and Swedish ambassadors traveled by car to Irun, but on the way they were bombarded from the air and fired at from the ground. They finally managed to cross the border and settle in San Juan de Luz, France, where dozens of diplomats from various countries were located.[12]

The Argentine Humanitarian Exchange Initiative, August 1936–February 1937

In this atmosphere of violence and insecurity, Ambassador García Mansilla himself embarked upon an ambitious diplomatic initiative in August 1936, aimed at "humanizing the civil war as much as possible." He presented a proposal to the Latin American ambassadors, who were summoned to Ciboure, San Juan de Luz,[13] and then submitted it to the government of Burgos and the Basque government. The García Mansilla initiative was inspired and supported by the humanitarian action of both the International Red Cross and the British ambassador to rescue non-belligerents, the elderly, women and children from both sides. It also provided for helping to preserve works of art and religious and cultural items vandalized in churches and museums.[14]

However, the initiative was not successful. In a January 1939 memorandum to Foreign Minister Carlos Saavedra Lamas, Ambassador García Mansilla did not hesitate to blame the Republican government in Madrid for its alleged action "to divert and hypocritically reject the reasons for the initiative," while stating that, by contrast, it "was accepted without exception, with goodwill and gratitude, by the Nationalist camp."

To further clarify his anti-Republican orientation, the Argentine diplomat also reflected in the memorandum that, "it is astonishing that these men, led astray by hatred, have succeeded in being called Republicans and Loyalists due to the discontent (OK) that is the victim of today's civilization, while those denominated Rebels are men shedding their own blood and that of their children fighting in defense of it."[15]

Chilean ambassador Aurelio Nuñez Morgado joined the humanitarian initiative by offering to intercede and manage the exchange of Euskadi nationals of military age who had fallen prisoner in Laredo and Santoña. However, the mediation of the Chilean diplomat was less ambitious than that of the Argentine ambassador. Nuñez Morgado obtained the authorization of the Euzkadi (Basque) government to exchange 1,080 people. But according to Chilean diplomatic documentation, the exchange was hampered by the intransigence of the Nationalist faction, as the Francoists gained positions in Republican territory and the fall of the Basque Country approached.[16]

Conversely, when the Argentine ambassador interceded with the Burgos and Bilbao authorities in January 1937 with his important initiative – in cooperation with Britain and the Red Cross – to achieve the simultaneous exchange of 4,000 prisoners, he blamed its failure on the president of the Euzkadi government. The initiative proposed the evacuation of 2,000 prisoners on each side, whether or not they had been prosecuted, in accordance with the spirit of the August 1936 agreement, to "humanize" the consequences of the bloody civil war.

However, on February 7, 1937, Lehendakari Jose Antonio Aguirre, president of the Basque Country government, informed Ambassador García Mansilla that he was refusing to carry out the exchange unless the bombing of the Franco air force ceased immediately. In addition, he demanded the end of the expulsions and violence against civilians in the Loyalist militias and their families – aggression that Aguirre considered to be "an obvious violation of the humanitarian agreement signed in Geneva with the International Red Cross Committee."[17].

Although the Argentine ambassador acknowledged that he had succeeded in obtaining President Aguirre's release of some prisoners and pardoning convicts on the rebel side in the Republican autonomous zone of the Basque Country, García Mansilla criticized the Aguirre Euskadi goverment "intransigence and delays," which supposedly would frustrate the exchange of prisoners. However, the Argentine ambassador refrained from mentioning another cause of Aguirre's delays: the bombings of the Francoist air force:

> The slow and difficult negotiations that I have been carrying out jointly with my colleague, the ambassador of England, have been constantly delayed by new demands of the Bilbao government. Unfortunately, the military operations have been paralyzed for the moment . . . [18]

In his last communication to the president of the Basque state – a telegram sent jointly with the British ambassador on April 7, 1937 – García Mansilla wrote that he trusted that the president "would take all necessary measures to prevent prisoners innocently suffering from the failure of the negotiations"; both diplomats refrained from requesting such measures from the Francoist camp.[19] García Mansilla warned against a possible "extermination of two thousand Nationalist prisoners" in the jails of the Basque country. However, three months previously, he had abstained from informing Saavedra Lamas that even the Basque government had approved the exchange agreement, and presented a list of 2,000 prisoners in Bilbao who could be included in such a deal. The mediator of the International Red Cross, Dr. Marcel Junod, had already denounced the Nationalist authorities in Salamanca for refusing to give him the official lists for exchange. Instead, on December 27, 1936, 11 bomber planes and 7 fighter jets of the Francoist air force attacked the civilian population in Santander. Revenge was not long in coming, and numerous Nationalist prisoners on prison ships in the port of the city were killed by militiamen.

Nor did the Argentine ambassador inform to Argentine Foreign Minister that despite a second pledge by the Franco authorities to Red Cross mediator Junod, to supply all documents and lists of detainees on January 5, 1937, for carrying out the exchange, the Francoist authorities recanted the exchange agreement that same day, claiming that this would be a privilege for the Basque people only. On the other hand, the Francoists did not oppose a general exchange of prisoners in all Spanish territory, on condition that it would be negotiated with the Republican government.[20]

In any event, after indiscriminate executions of Nationalists in four Bilbao jails on January 4, 1937, in retaliation for the resumption of bombings on Bilbao by the Francoist air force, any humanitarian possibility of exchange was abandoned, even when President Aguirre tried to propose a new negotiation scheme one month later.[21]

Ambassador García Mansilla was fully aware that the delay of the Basque government in implementing the exchange of prisoners stemmed from Aguirre's deep suspicion that once the liberation of prisoners from Bilbao jails was completed, Franco would bomb the capital of Euskadi. Indeed, García Mansilia and the British ambassador received a note from

President Aguirre stating that the Basque government would deliver the hostages if Franco formally promised not to bomb Bilbao.

The ambassador transmitted this message to the Generalissimo. But Franco's response was that his armies had never bombed targets other than strategic military fronts, and he could not commit himself to what could be a reason [for his people] to reproach him for infidelity. Franco also replied to García Mansilla that "military and humanitarian [considerations] cannot be mixed."[22]

Documentation in the archives of the Argentine Ministry of Foreign Affairs reveals evidence of the high esteem those closest to Franco held for Ambassador García Mansilla who, they considered, showed diligence and effectiveness in interceding with the Basque Republican government in favor of important figures among Nationalist prisoners in Coruña, Bilbao, and territories under the Loyalist government. This is illustrated in a letter written by Nicolás Franco, brother and one of the main collaborators of Francisco Franco. Writing to García Mansilla from the General Secretariat in Salamanca on February 14, 1937, he expresses "great appreciation and gratitude for your work [that is] filled with sympathy and affection toward the Spaniards," during the prisoner exchange process.[23]

Franco's brother had already thanked the Argentine ambassador for his mediation on October 13, 1936, when García Mansilla was asked by the Bilbao government to accept a joint proposal of the British and the International Red Cross to liberate 130 women of the Nationalist faction who were detained in Larrinaga Prison. They would leave aboard two destroyers of the Royal British Navy, bound for San Juan de Luz, in exchange for the freedom of equal numbers of Basque Republican women prisoners. In addition to this successful exchange, the Argentine ambassador secured the liberation of the monarchist Ramón Colón y Carvajal, who was transferred to his residence in San Juan de Luz.[24] An indeterminate number of nuns and clerics also received asylum in that residence. They included the mother superior of Valdecilla; a group of Salesian nuns from Madrid; another group of nuns from the Don Bosco Institution, Barcelona; Ursulines from Chabañes de Benedo, Valencia; and various Jesuits from the Pontifical University of Comillas, Santander.[25]

Reciprocally, the Nationalists acceded to some intercessions of the Argentine ambassador in favor of Republicans sentenced to capital punishment. One example was his success in preventing the execution of a young Republican sentenced to death, as requested of him by Manuel Irujo, a Euskadi minister without portfolio, the brother of the convicted man.[26]

Argentine Naval Asylum: Evacuation of Argentine Citizens in Danger, or Operational Humanitarian Aid to the Nationalists?

The naval asylum operation ordered by President Agustín P. Justo, widely publicized as Argentina's humanitarian effort to save lives in danger, was carried out between 1936 and 1938, using two vessels of the Argentine Navy, the *25 de Mayo* and the *Tucumán.* But it is necessary to further re-examine the humanitarian motivation of this powerful and effective Argentine mission.The *25 de Mayo* sailed on August 8, 1936, under the command of Captain Miguel A. Ferreyra, under the mutual instruction of Argentine Foreign Minister Dr. Carlos Saavedra Lamas and Naval Chief of Staff Rear Admiral León L. Scasso. Its specific mission was to ensure respect for the rights of Argentine citizens and the diplomatic corps, and to implement the asylum policy. The immediate purpose of its arrival was to transport García Mansilla, the entire embassy staff and the asylees to the town of Zaráuz, near the port of Guetaria. The commander of the ship was placed under the immediate authority of García Mansilla.

However, on August 17, 1936, Ferreyra was informed of a change of course toward the port of Alicante, since García Mansilla and the asylees in Zaráuz had already been evacuated on August 14, with the help of the French ambassador. On August 22, when the Argentine warship arrived in Alicante, a port controlled by the Republican government, other naval missions of Germany, France, Britain, Italy, and Portugal were already docked there. The Argentine warship anchored away from the docks, as the captain wanted to avoid exposure to the bombing of the Nationalists; in addition, he wanted to prevent those who sought to escape from swimming away and circumventing government authorities. Regarding the latter, the commander and crew had committed to giving asylum to those who were in danger but had no criminal record.[27]

Although President Justo's government publicized the humanitarian mission without any ideological orientation, a careful examination of the evacuees shows that most of those rescued were Spanish nationals returning to Franco's Spain. The *25 de Mayo* made five trips between August 27 and December 8, 1936, evacuating 451 refugees from Alicante, Valencia, and Barcelona via the ports of Marseille, Genoa, and Lisbon. According to a report by the consul general in Barcelona, in early December 1936, only 201 Argentinean citizens were repatriated, and 383 awaited evacuation.[28] At the end of 1936, the Chilean embassy made arrangements on behalf of the family of Manuel Azaña, Indalecio Prieto, the family of Deputy Sánchez Román, and other leftist politicians, including the daughters of Largo Caballero, to travel on the *25 de Mayo* from Alicante to Marseilles.[29]

On December 5, the torpedo boat *Tucumán* arrived to replace the *25 de Mayo*. On November 11, Perez Quesada had asked the naval minister, Rear Admiral Eleazar Videla, and Foreign Minister Dr. Carlos Saavedra Lamas that the ship remain in Mediterranean waters, due to "the seriousness of the increasingly alarming situation, as well as the necessity [of] protecting and transporting 300 Argentines."[30] The situation in Barcelona had become very difficult. Support was needed by the staff of the Barcelona consulate to facilitate the departure of Argentine citizens and to close the consular office. In addition, for the entire month prior to that time, the Republican government had placed obstacles before the rescue mission in Madrid, restricting the right of asylum by allowing only the evacuation of Argentines and denying guarantees for the Madrid-Alicante route.Eventually ,between November and December 1936, the consulate was dismantled in Barcelona and its personnel evacuated, and between March 7 and 10, 1937, the Madrid embassy was shut down.[31]

Most of the evacuees on the second ship, the *Tucumán* torpedo boat, were not Argentines but Spaniards. Between November 5, 1936 and June 4, 1937, the ship operated between the Mediterranean ports of Alicante, Almería, and Valencia, and carried out ten rescue journeys, transporting 1,489 asylees to the ports of Marseilles, Lisbon, and Gibraltar. According to Figallo, 69 percent of those transported were Spaniards.[32] The first contingent of evacuees on the *Tucumán*, composed of 11 Argentines and 126 Spaniards, arrived on November 29, 1936. The Argentine vice consul in Alicante, Lorenzo Barrera, signed the authorization for the embarkation of the trip on January 23, 1937, overcoming the opposition of the anarchists of the FAI trade union federation, which had identified "enemies" among its passengers.[33]

Indeed, there were several Falangists whose destination was a French port from which they would later return to territory controlled by the Nationalists. One of them was the journalist Jacinto Miquelarena, for whom Perez Quesada, the chargé d'affaires, obtained safe conduct from the Delegated Board of Defense of Madrid on January 19, 1937, enabling his transit to Alicante. Miquelarena was included in a group of women, children, and men aged over 45.

In his memoir, Miquelarena relates that important personalities such as Julio Wais, former minister of economy and finance during the dictatorship of General Primo de Rivera, were also evacuated.[34] Once they arrived in Marseilles, pro-Franco asylees returned to Spain, via a route that took them by train from Marseilles to Hendoya, while others did so via St. Jean de Luz, Bayonne, or Biarritz.[35]

In a recent study on the asylum and evacuation of Jacinto Miquelarena from the Argentine embassy to Marseilles, Rafael Castaño

Dominguez presumes that he would have chosen to return to Spain via Hendoya.[36]

Miquelarena recalls his evacuation experience on the *Tucumán* in his chronicle titled *In That Argentine Warship*, published by the Falangist magazine *Vértice* (no. 18). He also describes some refugees from the Argentine embassy who traveled with him from Alicante to Marseilles, from where they returned to the Nationalist zone in Spain. Settling in Salamanca in February 1937 – with sporadic trips to other places, such as Bilbao, after the conquest of this city by Franco's army – Miquelarena continued his journalistic work for the newly founded Spanish National Radio, headed by Antonio Tovar.[37]

The *Tucumán* not only helped supply food to the Republican authorities, but also boosted the confidence of Argentine diplomats regarding the evacuation of asylees in the embassy and diplomatic offices in Madrid, Alicante, and Valencia, as well as in the Chilean embassy. The *Tucumán* was one of the points used by the Argentine Foreign Ministry in its negotiations with the Spanish Republican government in managing the safe conduct and guaranteeing the security of each subsequent evacuation. In its voyage of December 21, 1936, the *Tucumán* was used for the transfer of Spanish Republican officials. However, the Republican authorities did not accept the evacuation of young Spaniards of military age, and distrusted the refugee Nationalists.

The departure of asylees from the Madrid embassy was risky. The Republican government allowed the first evacuation in November 1936. The second, on January 5, 1937, consisted of a convoy of women, children, and men of non-military age. The evacuations that followed – on January 23, February 14, and February 28, 1937 – involved the quiet transfer of small groups from Madrid to Alicante.[38]

Evacuation operations necessitated the mediation of the Argentine delegation, in collaboration with the captain of the *Tucumán*, for the departure of asylees from the Chilean embassy in Madrid in March and April 1937,[39] as well as that of Uruguayans and some consular agents of European and Latin American countries.

The captain of the ship sought to respect the government's procedures for evacuation, with a view to gaining the confidence of the Republican custom authorities. However, the list of evacuees were handed over to the port authority (the authority in Alicante was headed by two anarcho-syndicalist workers' group) only at the time of departure, as the captain wanted to avoid investigations regarding names, documents, ideological orientation, and nationality of the passengers. Nevertheless, the majority of the evacuaees were affiliated with the Nationalist camp. The total number of Argentine citizens repatriated on the *25 de Mayo* and the

Tucumán by June 1937 was less than the total number of Spanish evacuees and those of other nationalities. The *25 de Mayo* rescued 251 people on three trips. The *Tucumán* made 12 trips between the Mediterranean ports of Alicante, Almería, and Valencia from November 5, 1936 to June 1937, taking 1,489 asylees to the ports of Marseilles, Lisbon, and Gibraltar.

From the beginning of the civil war until May 1937, a total of 1,940 people were evacuated, of whom 553 were Argentines, 651 Spaniards and the rest of different nationalities – among them from the bordering countries of Bolivia, Chile, and Paraguay. Some evacuees remained in France, while the number that traveled to Argentina is unknown. The lists published by the Argentine navy contain all of the travel tickets from the port of Alicante, but indicate neither nationality nor citizenship, nor those whose destination was Buenos Aires. Numerous names are assumed to be false identities.[40] Others returned to Spanish territory from Genoa, Malaga, Almeria, and Gibraltar.

In addition, the Argentine torpedo boat evacuated Bolivian asylees in Paris and asylees in the Chilean embassy in Madrid, some 360 refugees in all. Prior to the evacuation of the Chilean embassy, the *Tucumán* took care of supplying food to those asylees. The government of Chile had made numerous efforts for the *Tucumán* to assist its compatriots in Spain. On April 11, 1937, the *Tucumán* evacuated 96 asylees from the Chilean embassy in Valencia and on April 24, another 153 embarked, including the ambassador, Aurelio Nuñez Morgado.[41]

Besides carrying boatloads of authorized passengers, as mentioned previously, the captain of the *Tucumán*, Captain Mario Casari ,also hosted fugitives from the Nationalist camp, all of them admitted clandestinely. Casari himself acknowledged that the practice of asylum law was being carried out far more broadly than usual, because the norms pertaining to the system of admitting asylum seekers were being loosely interpreted. Hundreds of letters and personal and official communications with appeals for asylum reached the hands of Casari and his officers. These requests came from Argentina, Uruguay, Portugal, England, France, and Nationalist Spain.

Captain Casari did not conceal his ideological criticism of the Republicans, which he expressed explicitly in a report from Marseille to Admiral Eleazar Videla, on January 7, 1937:

> The struggle in Spain is the struggle between two tendencies within the European nations: the Fascists and the Marxists. The first are characterized by active participation, with help in men and money coming from Germany, Italy, and Portugal; the other side have received support first

> from the Russians, followed by France. In analyzing the causes of the current state, it can be said that the guilt for the fate of Spain has long lain with the leaders, due to the government's lack of concern for public education, public health, and the mass welfare of the people . . . The Republicans, who were impotent to carry out the new Constitution of the Republic – which I consider to be moderate – had to appeal for the help of Socialist, Communist, Marxist and anarchist organizations, all of them affiliated to the Third International and obedient to the orders of Moscow in opposing the conservative parties.

The clandestine transports increased as many young people escaped from the mandatory military draft decreed by the Republic. From the memoirs of a sailor on the *Tucumán*, we know that the captain and a select group of his crew sometimes carried out secret rescue missions on land for those who were to be boarded without official authorization .In general, the names of all refugees were unknown to the crew.[42]

As early as December 1936, the Argentine consul in Marseilles was alarmed by veiled criticism from the Argentine ambassador in Paris, Tomás Le Breton, regarding the preponderance of Spaniards among those evacuated by the *Tucumán*. In his reply, García Mansilla emphasized that "it would not be justified for the Argentine Republic to deny Spanish citizens protection provided freely by the English and the French." On the contrary, García Mansilla attributed the protest of the consul in Marseilles to the behavior of "subversive elements, both Spaniards and Argentines," whom the Argentine ambassador aimed to differentiate from the Spanish evacuees of the Nationalist camp.

Various schemes were devised to save lives by circumventing customs controls: the consulate disguised future asylees in Argentine sailors' uniforms, simulated visits of women and children to the ship, and often registered passengers under false names. An example is the clandestine embarkation of 112 people, carried out between March 7 and 13, 1937. The port agents of Alicante turned a blind eye as the commanders and crews had gained their trust by furnishing them with scarce supplies, especially meat.[43]

Among well-known clandestine fugitives from the Nationalist camp who were transported by the *Tucumán* to Marseilles was Franco's future chancellor, his *brother- in- law* Ramón Serrano Suñer. Serrano Suñer managed to save his own life in the Modelo Prison of Madrid, when a mob of militiamen carried out an assault there in August 1936. Months later, Manuel de Irujo, a minister without portfolio, would authorize his transfer to a private clinic. On January 20, 1937, Serrano Suñer managed to escape, dressed as a woman. He took refuge in the diplomatic legation of the Netherlands, from where, with a forged safe-conduct pass of the Republican military, he left for Alicante. Serrano Suñer moved to the Argentine consulate in Alicante until he was evacuated to Marseilles on the *Tucumán*. Understandably, the name Serrano Suñer does not appear on the list of passengers embarking on January 22, 1937, as his documents were false.[44]

Another celebrated Falangist protected by the Argentine embassy was Pilar Primo de Rivera, sister of José Antonio and daughter of the dictator general. Two years previously, she had founded the Women's National Falange Section, and afterwards had secured refuge from the Argentine ambassador in the Republican zone. Thanks to a false passport provided by the German ambassador, Pilar Primo de Rivera managed to escape from Alicante on the German warship *Admiral Graaf Spee*. The Argentine consul did not receive authorization to evacuate her on the *Tucumán*, presumably because the Republican government demanded that an exchange of the Primo de Rivera family be negotiated with the central government.[45]

Less well-known than Serrano Suñer and Pilar Primo de Rivera were several writers and journalists of the Nationalist camp who traveled on the *Tucumán*. An example is the *madrileño* playwright Joaquín Calvo Sotelo, who first took refuge in the embassy of Turkey, and later in the Chilean embassy, before being evacuated on the *Tucumán*. Calvo Sotelo returned from Marseilles to the Francoist zone, and from 1939 until 1942 served as general secretary of the Official Book Chamber of Madrid, which, thanks to his efforts, was later renamed the National Institute of the Spanish Book.[46] Another evacuee on the *Tucumán* was the Francoist journalist Francisco Cáceres, who spent seven months in the Argentine embassy in Madrid. He left on the *Tucumán* in February 1937, but immediately returned from Marseilles to Spanish territory controlled by the Nationalists.

The case of this journalist is significant, because he was commissioned by the Francoist authorities to travel to Argentina in May 1937 to propagandize in favor of the Nationalist cause. In his book, *Argentina–Spain 1936–1937*, published in Buenos Aires,[47] Caceres not only praises Edgardo Pérez Quesada for his help in escaping from the "Red Republicans," but also thanks the Argentine government for "the benefits received by those who were lucky enough to be given asylum by the embassy."

Another F. Cáceres propaganda book, *Spain and Its Revolution*, was published in Buenos Aires in the same year, 1937, by the Office of Press and Propaganda of the Representation of the National Government of Spain.[48]

Along with these notorious Francoists, some well-known Republicans were accepted as exiles aboard the *Tucumán*. Such was the case of politician Federico Fernández Castillejo, who ran for the Cortes three times during the Second Republic, in 1931, 1933, and 1936. In 1933 and 1936, he was included in the Progressive Republican Party's list for Córdoba, alongside the President of the Republic, Niceto Alcalá Zamora. He boarded the *Tucumán* in Alicante on February 13, 1937. During his Argentine exile, he published – together with Clara Campoamor, another former Republican deputy in exile and renowned feminist – a book detailing his evacuation, including the escape of his family and that of many passengers on both the *25 de Mayo* and the *Tucumán*.

At the outbreak of the civil war, Clara Campoamor escaped, first in Paris, where, in 1937, she published *The Spanish Revolution Seen by a Republican*, which criticized the behavior of Spaniard Republicans. Immediately afterward, she departed for Buenos Aires, where she resided for a decade.[49]

Conclusions

Argentina's foreign policy adhered to the Anglo-British position of non-intervention in the civil war, and despite the sympathies of Argentine diplomats toward the insurgents of the Nationalist camp, the Argentine position did not result in confrontation with the Republic, as happened with Chile in the General Assembly of the League of Nations.[50]

This non-confrontational approach allowed Foreign Minister Saavedra Lamas to demand unrestricted respect for his country's diplomatic and maritime asylum policy. Exercised by García Mansilla and Pérez Quesada, this policy benefited a smaller number of Argentinean citizen returnees than Spanish pro-Franco Nationalists, asylees, and other evacuees, the majority of whom soon returned to Spanish territory under Franco's rule.

The Nationalist camp authorities valued the asylum and intercession efforts of Argentine diplomats, along with the two navy warships that allowed important figures on the Franco side, as well as monarchists and Carlist anti-Republicans, to be aided and evacuated between July 1936 and late 1937.

The decision of President Justo in June 1937 to put an end to the evacuation carried out by the *Tucumán* coincided with the advance of the Nationalist forces, abruptly aborting the humanitarian effort of evacuating many persecuted and imprisoned anti-Franco Argentine citizens at the end of the civil war.

During the course of the civil war, and even a few years after it ended, there were delays in the repatriation of numerous prisoners of Argentine nationality who were detained in concentration camps under the Franco regime, in spite of Argentina's recognition of his government in February 1939. As late as February 1942, the Argentine ambassador in Madrid appealed to the Minister of Foreign Relations and Culture in Buenos Aires, for expedited action in the liberation and repatriation of 1,527 Argentines held in concentration camps, jails, or battalions of forced laborers. In his request, the ambassador reiterated "the identical humanitarian and patriotic sense" with which the ships *25 de Mayo* and *Tucumán* had been sent during the civil war, "to save from revolutionary danger the numerous Spaniards who took refuge in the diplomatic representation in Madrid."[51].

This late and morose repatriation of Argentine nationals who suffered under Francoist repression has remained an unresearched chapter in post-civil war relations between Argentina and Francoist Spain, in sharp contrast to the expedited action of the Argentinian diplomatic and humanitarian initiative in mid-1936.

Notes

1 Antonio Manuel Moral Roncal, "El asilo diplomático: un condicionante de las relaciones internacionales de la República durante la Guerra Civil, Congreso Internacional," *La Guerra Civil* (2006): 3, https://www.researchgate.net/publication/28210028; idem, "An Analysis of Foreign Diplomatic Aid to the Catholic Clergy during the Spanish Civil War (1936–1939)," *Religions* 4, 1 (2013): 96–115, 99.

2 Javier Rubio, *Asilos y canjes durante la guerra civil española: Aspectos humanitarios de una contienda fratricida* (Barcelona: Planeta, 1979), 45; Crisitián Garay, *Relaciones Tempestuosas: Chile y España 1936–1940,* Instituto de Estudios Avanzados (Santiago: Unversidad de Santiago de Chile, 2000), 22.

3 Ministry of Foreign Relations and Culture, Republic of Argentina, *Memoria presentada al Honorable Congreso Nacional correspondiente al período 1937–1938,* vol, I, part 1, *Relaciones Exteriores,* section C: *Política internacional,* ch. 1 (Buenos Aires: Peuser, 1938), 37–38.

4 Cesar Vidal, *Las checas de Madrid: Las cárceles republicanas al descubierto* (Barcelona: Carrogio, 2003), 83. In December 1937, Uruguay recognized the government of Burgos de facto, and in February 1939, de jure. Carlos Zubillaga, *Una historia silenciada: Presencia y acción del falangismo en Uruguay (1936–1955)* (Montevideo: Cruz del Sur y Linardi & Risso, 2015), 57.

5 Beatriz Figallo, *La Argentina ante la Guerra Civil Española: El Asilo Diplomático y el Asilo Naval, Rosario,* Instituto de Historia (Buenos Aires: Pontificia Universidad Católica Argentina, 1996), 178.

6 Only the Argentine wife of Maura and her three children succeeded in getting asylum in the embassy. Carlos María Gelly y Obes (hereafter, Carlos María Gelly y Obes), *Embajador Daniel García Mansilla*, Anexo 1, Consejo Argentino de Relaciones Internacionales, Los Diplomáticos, no. 22 (Buenos Aires, 2004) 29–30. Gelly y Obes wrote a biographical book on ambassador Daniel García Mansilla, comprised in it Anexos of archival documentation from the Argentine Ministery of Foreign Relations, related to García Mansilla diplomatic performance,

7 Ibid., 30.

8 Jacinto Miquelarena participated in the literary *cenacle* of Falange Española with José Antonio Primo de Rivera. After his release he wrote two books relating his experiences during the first two years of the civil war and his asylum in the Argentine embassy. Both books were written under the pseudonym, El Fugitivo, *Cómo fui ejecutado en Madrid* (Madrid: Avila Sigiriano Díaz, 1937), and *El otro mundo* (Burgos: Imprenta Aldecia, 1938); Rafael Castaño Domínguez, "Asilado en Madrid: La vida de Jacinto Miquelarena en la embajada argentina durante la Guerra Civil Española," (MA diss., University of Seville, 2016).

9 Francisco Cáceres, *Argentina-España 1936–37: Apuntes y recuerdos de un asilado en la Embajada Argentina en Madrid* (Buenos Aires: Poblet, 1937), 76.

10 Ibid.,126–34.

11 Carlos María Gelly y Obes, 31–32; also, Archivo Ministerio Relaciones Exeriores y Culto de la República Argentina (hereafter AMREC), España, Divisi6n Política, Exp. 1/1936, Anexo 1, legajo 69.

12 Carlos María Gelly y Obes, 21–22.

13 Juan Archibaldo Lanús, *Aquel Apogeo: Política internacional argentina 1910–1939* (Buenos Aires: Editorial Emece, 2001), 540.

14 AMREC, Embajada en Madrid, 0130, Box 23, Exp.19, "Iniciativa del Embajador argentino con el fin de humanizar en todo lo posible la guerra civil," Ciboure, August 29, 1936 , fol. 1–14.

15 Carlos María Gelly y Obes, Memorandum presentado al Ministerio de Relaciones Exteriores por el Embajador Daniel García Mansilla, Buenos Aires, April 1939, 40–41.

16 Elena Romero Perez, "Vida y muerte en la Embajada: Un estudio de la vida cotidiana en las legaciones a cargo de Chile durante la guerra civil española (Julio 1936–Abril 1939)," paper presented at the First Meeting of Young Researchers on Contemporary History, Zaragoza, September 26–28, 2007, https://www.academia.edu/14183042/Vida_y_muerte_en_la_Embajada._Un_estudio_de_la_vida_cotidiana_en_las_legaciones_a_cargo_de_Chile_durante_la_Guerra(accessed July 17, 2017). Also, the Chilean ambassador Morla Lynch recorded the delays of the Nationalists in his memoirs: "I have been striving to obtain the rapid evacuation of 100 sick patients housed in the embassy. The first impression that is always received at the beginning of these efforts is favorable, but then (. . . .) what one finds facilities on the

Republican side for evacuation fails because of the intransigencies with which one stumbles on the Nationalist side," Carlos Morla Lynch, "*Informes Diplomáticos sobre la Guerra Civil Española,*" RIL ediciones, ADICA,(Santiago de Chile, 2003), 84.

17 AMREC, Embajada en Madrid, AH01, 23, 1936–1938, Mensaje del Presidente de Euskadi a Embajada Argentina a través del Consulado Español en Bayona, Bilbao, February 24,1937.

18 Idem, from Ambassador García Mansilla to Minister Carlos Saavedra Lamas, Ciboure, March 2, 1937.

19 Idem, AHOI 23, 1936–1938, from Argentine Ambassador García Mansilla to Minister Carlos Savedra Lamas, Ciboure, April 9, 1937.

20 José Manuel Ascona Pastor y Julen Lezamiz Lugarezaresti, "Los asaltos a las cárceles de Bilbao el día 4 de enero 1937," *Investigaciones Históricas* (Universidad de Valladolid) 32 (2012): 223–24.

21 Rubio, Asilos y canjes durante la guerra civil Española, ch. 8; Carlos María Gelly y Obes, Anexo 18 B, 79, From Juan de Jauregui, Diputado por Vizcaya to Ambassador García Mansilla, San Juan de Luz, February 23, 1937.

22 Carlos María Gelly y Obes, Anexo, "Memorandum presentado al Ministerio de Relaciones Exteriores," 45.

23 AMREC, Embajada en Madrid, AH/0136/10,C23,1937. From the Secretary General in Salamanca to Ambassador García Mansilla, February 13, 1937. On several occasions authorities on the Francoist side asked the Argentine ambassador to intercede to help Franco's distressed relatives in Madrid. See letter from Director Diplomatic Cabinet of Franco to García Mansilla, Cáceres, September 24, 1936, AMREC, Embajada en Madrid, AH/0130, 1936–38.

24 For the list of 130 women of Basque ancestry resident in the region (Alava, Guipúzcoa, Vizcaya, and Navarra) who embarked on October 12, 1936, for San Juan de Luz in two ships of the British navy, see, Carlos María Gelly y Obes, Annex 9 , 73–74; 38 women on the list decided to remain in Basque lands and not to embark. On the liberation of Ramón Colón and Carvajal, nephew of the Duke of Veragua, by the Argentine ambassador, see La Nación, October 12, 1936, and the telegram sent to President Justo from Ciboure, on October 11, 1936, Carlos Maria Gelly y Obes, Annex no.13, 49.

25 Moral Roncal, "An Analysis of Foreign Diplomatic Aid," 104.

26 AMREC, Embajada en Madrid, Box 0129, 1936–38, exp 1, Letter from García Mansilla to Saavedra Lamas and request from Argentine Consul in Barcelona, February 8, 1937.

27 Beatriz Figallo, "Participación de la Armada Argentina durante la guerra civil Española," *Revista de Publicaciones Navales*, no. 647, tomo CXIX, año LXXXIX (Buenos Aires, 1988): 434.

28 AMREC, Embajada en Madrid, Box 0129, 1936–1937, Exp/6, from the Argentine Consul in Barcelona to Argentine Embassy, Madrid, December 4, 1936.

29 Lynch, Informes Diplomáticos sobre la Guerra Civil Española, 129; Figallo, "Participación de la Armada," 443.

30 Ricardo Irurzún, Crucero 25 de Mayo: Proa al Mediterráneo (Buenos Aires: Ediciones Theoria, 1994), ítem 104.

31 Fabiola Serralunga, "Primera misión naval humanitaria argentina (1936–1937)," Estudios Históricos Navales – Armada Argentina, Revista del Mar (Buenos Aires), no. 166 (2011): 5. (accessed June 4, 2017).

32 Beatriz Figallo, *Diplomáticos y marinos argentinos en la crisis española. Los asilos de la guerra civil* (Buenos Aires, Editorial-Librería Histórica, 2007), 71–72.

33 Rubio, *Asilos y canjes durante la guerra civil española*, 244; Tomás Merino, "El Asilo Diplomático y Naval Argentino durante la Guerra Civil Española: Los marinos argentinos del torpedero Tucumán y del crucero 25 de Mayo en 1936/1937," *Boletín del Centro Naval*, no. 844 (September–December 2016): 286–87.

34 Jacinto Miquelarena, *El otro mundo* (Burgos: Imprenta Aldecia,1938), 191.

35 Rubio, *Asilos y canjes durante la guerra civil española*, 309; Moral Roncal, "El asilo diplomático argentino durante la Guerra Civil Studia Historica". *Historia Contemporánea*, vol. 19–20, Universidad de Salamanca (2001–2002), 285–86. A Spaniard who embarked on the Tucumán on February 13, 1937, for Marseilles, recalls his return to Spain via what he calls "the {escape route from Marseilles," where he arrived on February 15. The next day he reached San Juan de Luz, from where he took a ride to San Sebastian and on the 19th he arrived in Burgos, and from there he traveled to Seville. "Carta de un Refugiado en el Tucumán," Historia y Arqueología Marítima, "El rescate de refugiados políticos por parte de buques de la Armada Argentina en la Guerra Civil Española" (2005). http://www.histarmar.com.ar/InfHistorica/ARA-GCivilEsp.htm (accessed May 7, 2017).

36 Dominguez, "Asilado en Madrid," 8.

37 José María Martínez Cachero, "Miquelarena, un escritor en la Guerra Civil," *Razón Española* 29 (1988): 281–300.

38 Merino, "El Asilo Diplomático y Naval Argentino," 287; Moral Roncal, "El asilo diplomático argentino," 286.

39 By March 1938, Chile's embassy in Madrid was housing 730 asylees, including those from the embassies of Guatemala and El Salvador, countries that had broken off diplomatic relations with Spain, and Chile agreed to represent their interests. Of the total number of asylees, 135 belonged to the Spanish armed forces, 94 of them on active duty. To these were added 509 civilians of military age and 103 over 45 years, in addition to women and children. On that day the Chilean embassy managed to evacuate 1,200 people to Valparaiso, of whom only 55 were of military age. Romero Perez, "Vida y muerte en la Embajada," 7.

40 http://www.histarmar.com.ar/InfHistorica/ARA-GCivilEsp.htm (accessed July 12 2017).

41 Merino, "El Asilo Diplomático y Naval Argentino," 288.

42 Figallo, "Participación de la Armada Argentina," 446.

43 "La misión naval Argentina durante la guerra civil española," Historia militar argentina, August 6, 1914, (accessed May 3, 2017).

44 http://www.histarmar.com.ar/InfHistorica/ARAGCivEsp/ListTucuman.htm (accessed May 4, 2017).

45 AMREC, Embajada en Madrid, AH Box 0129, Exp. 1, Encrypted telegram from Consul in Alicante, January 4, 1937 to Ambassador in Ciboure, for consultation exchange possibilities of Maria Primo Rivera and her niece Carmen; also, AH Box 0130, Letter from García Mansilla to Saavera Lamas, asking for instructions on evacuation of refugees, Ciboure, September 16, 1936; Adrián C. Escobar, *Diálogo íntimo con España. Memorias de un embajador durante la tempestad europea* (Buenos Aires: Club de Lectores, 1950), 316–18; 320.

46 José María Martínez Cachero, "Literatura y cautiverio: el caso de las embajadas madrileñas durante la guerra civil," http://www.cervantesvirtual.com/servlet/SirveObras/12471630933481506321657/p0000001.htm.

47 Cáceres, *Argentina-España 1936–1937.*

48 Idem, *España y su Revolución* (Buenos Aires: Oficina de Prensa y Propaganda de la Representación del Gobierno Nacional de España, 1937).

49 Clara Campoamor and Fernández Castillejo, *Heroísmo criollo: la Marina Argentina en el drama español* (Buenos Aires, 1939; reprinted in 1983, by the Institute of Naval Publications of Buenos Aires). Includes emotional and grateful chronicles of the rescue actions of Argentine sailors on the warships 25 de Mayo and Tucumán.

50 The Chilean representative frustrated the re-election of Spain as a semi-permanent member of the Council of the League of Nations at the XVIII General Assembly held on September 13, 1937. David Jorge Penado, "México y Chile ante la guerra civil española: Dos polos opuestos de actuación latinoamericana en la Sociedad de Naciones," in Heriberto Cairo Carou, et al., *XV Encuentro de Latinoamericanistas Españoles* (Madrid, Trama/CEEIB, 2013),1449–60.

51 AMREC, Embajada en Madrid, Box 0142, confidential letter from Embajada Madrid, February 26, 1941 to Minister of Foreign Relations and Cult Guillermo Rothe.

14

A Spanish Destiny: Renzo Giua and Giustizia e Libertà *In Memoriam*

MANUELA CONSONNI

Prologue

In her compelling book on the Spanish Civil War, Paola Lo Cascio writes that the social, cultural, economic, diplomatic, political, and ideological conflicts that marked the entire history of the twentieth century found their physical representation in this most violent confrontation that unfolded between 1936 and 1939 to the south of the Pyrenees.[1]

This war aroused the interest not only of historians, but also of writers, filmmakers, and journalists, provoking heated public debates around the world. On the one hand, it was the result of internal dynamics specific to the frail, young Spanish Democratic Republic, whose government was unable to halt the troops led by the generals in revolt. On the other, the Spanish Civil War was a decisive, crucial, and specific event tied to the history of Europe in the twentieth century. In the words of Massimo Mila, it became the "dress rehearsal" of World War II, the arena of a deadly struggle in which the fate of the ideals and values of democracy were at stake. Spain was only the initial phase in a period encompassing the most violent years in modern world history, marked by bloody fratricidal confrontations, mass violence, and the extermination of the Jews.[2]

The "Red Revolution," the expression used by the Italian weekly *Domenica del Corriere* in July 1936, has acquired the value of a historiographic topos of the same quality and hermeneutic strength as that of the Russian Revolution and the American Civil War. Western European democracies – anti-Communist, anti-revolutionary, and fearful of possible Soviet influence – sacrificed the Spanish Popular Front. Not intervening in favor of the young democracy on July 19, 1936, the day of the *alzamiento militar*, led by José Sanjurjo, meant surrendering to Fascism. The fighters of the International Brigades arrived to compensate for this tragic absence. They risked their lives, fighting on Spanish soil alongside the Republican government, for the freedom and national independence of Spain, and for the liberty of Europe. Their struggle transformed the Spanish experience into a litmus test of European anti-Fascism and of Italian Fascism in particular. Many Italian fighters left for Spain a few days after the rebellion of the generals. They were of various political orientations: anarchists, liberals, Communists, and republicans. Among them, the Giustizia e Libertà (Justice and Freedom) group stood out. It was a politically eclectic anti-Fascist formation, headed by Carlo Rosselli, its founder and recognized leader, and one of the major figures of Italian anti-Fascism in exile.[3] Renzo Giua, a young man from a Turin-based Italian anti-Fascist family, was very active in the movement.

This study reconstructs Giua's paradigmatic story. It is intertwined with the story of the Italian clandestine resistance in Turin, in Paris, and lastly in the Italian anti-Fascist struggle in Spain, where he fought with great courage. Italian participation in the Spanish war was the first true form of political and military praxis against Fascism; it laid the foundations for what would later become the partisan struggle in Italy against the regime of Mussolini between 1943 and 1945. Giua could not fight against Fascism for Italy's freedom because he fell earlier in Spain, with guns blazing, in the battle of Extremadura in February 1938.

The structure of this essay is inspired by Hans Magnus Enzensberger's magnificent biography of Buenaventura Durruti, the Spanish anarchist hero who remains one of the most beloved legendary figures of the Spanish Civil War. The choice was determined by Giua's life, which was filled with passion, as well as a sense of justice and existential necessity that impelled him to join the struggle for Spanish liberty; in spite of the differences in age, class, and upbringing, his story resembles that of the Spanish anarchist. This chapter is therefore a narrative that interweaves the personal story of Renzo Giua, related partially through testimonies of his human qualities and political militancy, with the *stimmung*, the ambiance of those years, with its range of concrete historical situations without which Giua's life and death would be unimaginable.[4] Giua is defined "through the struggle that he led . . . a fight that, at the same time, shapes whatever he did, expressed, and undertook." A portrait emerges of a young man whose human path, as Mila wrote, seemed at first sight, crossed and obstructed "by a blind and unjust fate"; then it seems to be guided by a deep harmony. Renzo Giua's life was marked by

> a thick plot containing internal symmetries, as if it was governed by a far-sighted mind to whom the unknown is known, a life where . . . everything is kept together, and that is determined not by the foolish violence of external events, but by personal, moral, and physical qualities, of which . . . it presents itself as the most complete and natural expression.[5]

Giua's deeds are recounted here partly through the memories of those who knew him very well or very little. All were extremely impressed by the pride and passion of this young anti-Fascist exile, who touched the heart of Carlo Roselli and many others of his comrades. His brief, intense life, and prematurely early death, meant he left behind no scholarly works or expansive autobiographical writings. Only traces, letters – especially to his mother and friends – memoirs, and testimonies tell the story of his life and death as reflected in action.[6]

First Gloss

Giustizia e Libertà

After escaping from the island of Lipari, where he had been sentenced to five years' exile, Carlo Rosselli reached Paris via Marseille in July 1929, with Emilio Lussu and Francesco Fausto Nitti. There, on August 1 of that same year, he and his comrades founded the Giustizia e Libertà (henceforth, GL) movement. The group was intended to be structured like a party rather than an insurrectional, revolutionary, ideologically non-Marxist movement, but with an affinity to anarchist thought. Anarchists traditionally hostile to collaboration with other political forces thus welcomed its birth with interest. Luigi Fabbri, the second most prominent figure after Errico Malatesta in the Italian anarchist movement,[7] defined the emergence of GL as a "revolutionary fact," claiming it could be a primary factor in an Italian revolution.[8] The political goal of GL – which was a self-defined unitary action movement for workers' autonomy, a Socialist republic, and a new humanism – was to unite all non-Communist groups that sought to fight against the Fascist regime.[9] The movement was headed by a central committee based in the French capital; in Italy, some action groups existed, mostly in the major cities of the north, with the center in Milan, which maintained close contact with the Parisian group. Carlo Rosselli aimed at a synthesis between a pluralistic and republican democracy: a Socialist party along the lines of the British Labour Party. The main points of his program included: the revolution; the republic; a social constitution in which, alongside the socialization of certain sectors, small and middle-sized property could remain; and guaranteed local autonomy. Turin's core of GL, composed of Aldo Garosci, Carlo Levi, Michele Giua, and Mario Andreis was particularly interested in political action with the local working class; on the other, the Milanese core, represented by Alberto Tarchiani and Riccardo Bauer, focused on the positions of the liberal matrix, as did the Florentine Ernesto Rossi. Along with Nello Traquandi and Piero Calamandrei, Rossi had participated in the Gaetano Salvemini campaign *Non Mollare!* (Don't give up!); in Puglia, the followers of Tommaso Fiore, supporters also of Salvemini's southern battle, were initially influenced by Benedetto Croce, but subsequently they adhered to the critical liberal-social critique advocated by Guido Calogero. They shared the same idea of pursuing an immediate anti-Fascist action abroad and, in Italy, of overcoming the hesitations of the traditional currents of Socialism and republicanism that had been ineffective against Fascism.[10] Indeed, at the beginning of the 1930s, GL had conducted an intense, widespread anti-Fascist propaganda campaign, to which the Mussolini regime reacted violently. On October 30, 1930, 24 people – members and leaders – were arrested in Italy, including Rossi, Bauer, and Umberto Ceva, who committed suicide in jail. Following the arrests, the organization postponed the idea of an armed insurrection, dedicating itself to a long-term political program. In 1931, GL in Paris signed an agreement with the anti-Fascist group Concentrazione d'azione antifascista, formed by members in exile of the Socialist and republican parties, the Lega italiana dei diritti dell'uomo (Italian Human Rights League) and the Communist workers' organization CGIL. GL, which renounced its political autonomy abroad only for a short while, attained recognition as a legitimate representative of the anti-Fascist alliance in Italy. With the dissolution of the latter in 1934, GL regained its status of an autonomous political movement whose program focused on the quest for a democratic revolution that found its synthesis in *Quanderni di Giustizia e Libertà*.[11]

Renzo Giua

Renzo (Lorenzo) Giua was born in Milan to a Turin-Sardinian family, on March 13, 1914, the first son of Michele Giua, an illustrious chemist, and Clara Lollini, also a scientist.[12] His parents were prominent figures in Italian Socialist and anti-Fascist circles. Until the age of six, Renzo Giua lived in Sassari, where his father held the chemistry chair at the university. The family moved to Turin when Michele Giua, his father, started to teach at the Polytechnic Institute of Turin in 1925, subsequently becoming one of the most important figures of GL in the city. Renzo Giua studied at the Liceo Massimo d'Azeglio, the famous forge of Italian anti-

Fascism, where he was a pupil of Augusto Monti, the distinguished anti-Fascist, and became active in GL. In September 1931, when he was still an adolescent, he founded the newspaper *Voci d'Officina*, with other GL friends, among them, Aldo Garosci, Vittorio Foa, Franco Venturi, Paolo Sabbione, Barbara Allason, Giandomenico Cosmo, and the anarchist Michele Guasco.[13] The publication, a simple leaflet of which only three issues were published, reflected a strong working-class orientation inspired by Gobetian-Gramscian thought. It aimed to establish a relationship with the workers, and sought the support of other anti-Fascist political forces. Giua was arrested in January 1932, together with Remo Garosci, Luigi Scala, and Cosmo, and referred to the Special Tribunal. He was first put in a correctional home because he was still under-age, but was transferred to the Regina Coeli prison in Rome when he reached the age of eighteen. Tried by the Special Tribunal, he was then released for lack of evidence. At the university, Giua chose to study Spanish Medieval literature, writing a thesis on Juan Ruiz, the Spanish poet, better known as Archbishop de Hita. His friends, who were absorbed in the discovery of America and the American novel, translated by Cesare Pavese, reacted with surprise to his decision. It seemed to them an incomprehensible choice, one that boded something for the future. It was as if Spain was attracting him, as an inner vocation, his destiny.[14] Thus Mila wrote in his memoir:

> For us . . . Spain was then a country on the edge of civil life, a remnant of a medieval age preserved and forgotten by a mistake of history, totally incapable of arousing intellectual interest . . . Spain . . . remained outside of our spiritual interests, and we were amazed by Renzo's surety in taking up the subject.[15]

Giua's interest in Spain was not only intellectual but also political. He was the one who introduced his comrades to the figure of Largo Caballero, adopting his political position, and admiring his work as an organizer and head of the Spanish workers. The decisive event that accelerated and changed the course of Giua's life, directing him to his Spanish destiny, was the episode of Ponte Tresa on March 11, 1934.[16] This event led to the arrests of 14 people, among them Leone Ginzburg, Carlo Levi, and his brother Riccardo, Gino and Giuseppe Levi (brother and father of Mario and Natalia Ginzburg), and Allason, whose political salon Renzo used to attend.[17] OVRA's (Italian secret police service) operation thus undermined the organization. As a precaution, Renzo's parents decided to send him away to the mountains, in the Balme area, which he knew very well. Had the situation gotten out of control, Giua could have crossed the border. Without waiting, the young anti-Fascist made his way from Balme, in the direction of the neighboring Viù Valley, to Malciaussia. Alone he skied at 3,000 meters across Auteret Mountain, weathering stormy weather and spending two nights in the cold, until finally he reached France.[18] In Paris, he found his old Turin friends, Aldo Garosci, Mario Levi, and Franco Venturi, who were joined by another anti-Fascist in exile, Nicola Chiaromonte. Those young militants, with their intellectual involvement, their political passion, and their encompassing anti-Fascism, encapsulated Rosselli's hopes and desires to such an extent that he established with them a tight, complex political and cultural dialogue.

Ursula Hirschmann;[19] Renzo Giua, a Memoir

. . . I met Renzo Giua, in the spring of 1935 in Paris. My memory of him goes hand-in-hand with that of his infectious laugh. He was a handsome boy with steel gray eyes, short eyebrows, and shiny teeth. He laughed at everything: my questions, my pronunciation, my shyness. He laughed without thinking, for fun, and after a while, I was laughing too, without any shyness. In a disarming way, we questioned each other, of course, on the reasons for our anti-Fascism, to which group we felt we belonged, and much more on our ideas and projects for the future. During the lessons, Renzo told me about Turin, his city, about Giustizia e Libertà, about the life of the Italian anti-Fascists in exile in Paris, bursting every now and then into one of his laughs, making fun of the most serious things. Then it was my turn . . . My Marxist beliefs were becoming shaky at that time . . . I told Renzo of our ideological divisions, of our renewal efforts, without mentioning any name because this was contrary to the practice of our clandestine life. Renzo then asked me, on the spot, whether I really believed in all that illegal farce that the anti-Fascist Germans used to recite in Paris, because probably few of them would ever return to Germany . . . That mixture of personal and political discourse did not exist in our German circles, which had been quite ascetic . . . I then inquired about Italian anti-Fascist organizations. He answered, telling me everything he knew. I reproached him, accusing him of behaving in an irresponsible way: after all, he did not know me, I could be a spy, a collaborator or at least a big mouth who endangers the life of the people she knows. He looked surprised, cheerful. He wondered whether I took him for a fool, unable to distinguish between a spy and a friend, a gossiper and a serious person. He did not say the word comrade. *I noticed that he did not willingly use the jargon of Marxist anti-Fascism that I did. Renzo's personality attracted me, and we became very close just because he was so different from the people I knew . . . He told*

me, one day, the story of a high school teacher in Italy who, during a Fascist ceremony, had stood up after the principal speech and publicly criticized the Italo-Abyssinian war, condemning the Fascist regime. As a consequence, the teacher was fired and sent to prison. "Well done," I said, "so you have one less anti-Fascist; he has done his best to follow his conscience . . . but if he had acted according to the rules of clandestine work, he could have continued to be useful to the movement." Renzo laughed. "Being useful to the movement," he mocked me. "How important your language is! The one who stands up and speaks the truth is more important than all your wise network of clandestine people who do not open their mouths but murmur the news in each other's ears. In the long run, remaining silent, they will become good Nazis, too." I protested. This Italian, inconsistent and anarchist, was different from us, could not understand . . . Renzo lost patience: "The soul of your working class! It seems to me that the time has come to lose some confidence . . . Twelve million Socialist and organized Communists, the most powerful labor movement in Europe . . . and then Hitler rose to power, and everyone is standing still, nobody moves! Is this your discipline? What's wrong?" Here was my most painful point . . . The great, generous German working class, which for years, conscious of its own responsibility, had tolerated the provocation of the Fascist squads, now bowed its head like a poor Christ on the cross . . . And if Renzo was right? If adapting to the Nazi environment, the first rule of "domestic action" in Germany, became a pretext to no longer do anything to damage the Gleichschaltung?[20] *Perhaps our clandestine method was good for times of brief reactionary oppression that could be violent, but it was not meant to conquer souls. In the face of Nazism, with its total aggression, perhaps it was necessary to return to individual political romanticism, to the courage of the individual, perhaps it was necessary, occasionally, to provide the example of a person who says no, as von Ossietzky, Mühsam, and a few others had done. Indeed, political opponents in Germany did not end up in the prisons but were tortured and killed in concentration camps, but they offered a shining example to many others . . .*

Renzo's questions thus led me to those thoughts, perhaps without his noticing it, because nothing was stranger to him than to persuade somebody . . . It was his way of being that was so persuasive . . . When Renzo died in Spain, I was already in Italy. I do not know the details of his death and even when, many years later, I could have asked about them, I never did. But in his death, the traits of his personality are fused for me into a picture of great beauty. Each one of us became anti-Fascist for different reasons, but almost every one of us shared the awareness of what we left behind us, sometimes feeling the weight of the decision and the austere moral commitment that ordered us to continue along our chosen path. Renzo, on the other hand, was anti-Fascist not because of reasoning or the need for moral purity. He was anti-Fascist for the sake of life, because he could not do otherwise, for a kind of noble game. Everything in him was impromptu: his life, his action, his death. He fought in Spain against the Falangists and the Fascists with the cheerfulness of an Ariosto hero; and, certainly, he continued to mock irreverently the famous anti-Fascists who remained in Paris, as before . . . those solemn anti-Fascists who wrote lively letters to their wives from prison, praying for them, for posterity. Then he rose to the sky, riding a flashy rose-colored cloud, laughing forever, with his heart broken by a Falangist bomb.

Second Gloss

Clashes within GL and the Way to Spain

The divergence of views, which had already emerged in the last months of 1931 between Rosselli and the Turin group of GL about the kind of state that should be formed after the fall of Fascism, caused a profound split among the young anti-Fascists in exile. One side favored the parliamentary democracy of Rosselli, Giua, and the *novatori* (innovators; Levi, Chiaromonte, Venturi, and Andrea Caffi). The other advocated a democracy based on Gramscian-type councils, founded on powers legally recognized and represented by workers and peasants.[21] The disagreement led to a devastating schism, in 1934, of the anti-Fascist alliance. Rosselli wanted GL to become a Socialist party organized on completely new grounds than those of the Socialist movement of the pre-Fascist state, a force able to direct its choices in a more revolutionary direction. Giua and the other novatori criticized both the transformation of GL into a party and the maintenance of the organizational status of the movement, which, without a vital relationship with the masses, remained oriented toward parties of the historical Left. Ultimately, these young anti-Fascists distrusted Rosselli's political vision, which, in their view, inhibited the growth of new values and new ideas within an active but concrete political program.[22]

Although Rosselli had attempted to prevent the rupture in a meeting with the young dissidents in mid-December 1935, at the end of the same year, the novatori decisively broke with Carlo Rosselli and GL. It was an extreme confrontation, with Rosselli accusing the dissidents of political infantilism and abusive intellectualism, to which Giua and Levi replied:

> And yet, one last observation. You say (implicitly): if we separate what will you be able to do? Probably nothing. If this is the eviction [order]

> given by the "owner," we have nothing to say. It is likely that without means we "shall continue on our destined road"; we will not be able to compete with GL. The fact that we are unable to do anything does not mean, however, that our opinions are worthless. If we were to measure people (or political groups) by the amount of things they undertake, and not by what they are, the comparison between, let's say, Fascism and GL, would not be exactly in favor of the latter.[23]

In May 1935, the news of his father's arrest reached Renzo Giua. His deep affection and anxiety for the fate of his father, who had followed and sustained Renzo's anti-Fascist activities, did not break him but reinforced his strong and decisive commitment to fight the Fascist regime. He had burned his bridges with the past; he was now ready, at peace with himself, to embark on a journey that had become the main path of his destiny. He spent some time in Switzerland, in the Canton of Ticino, where he contacted other Italian anti-Fascists, and returned to France just when his presence had been reported by the Italian police to the Swiss authorities. Relentlessly, Renzo Giua continued his clandestine work: Paris, Chambéry, Lyon, Nice, Marseille, in the organization of political groups, collecting donations, and sending anti-Fascist material to Italy. The decision to move to France, the refusal to return to Italy, and his intense political activity made the French experience just a step on the road to the Pyrenees, the plot around which his life was gradually unfolding.

Third Gloss

Today in Spain, Tomorrow in Italy

The profound conflict with the young innovators restored vitality to Rosselli's thought. While again reaffirming his desire to pursue some form of unity among the various anti-Fascist political groups, it confirmed the need for a less bland and bureaucratic political approach, which would incorporate more culture and humanity in the movement's streams, especially in exile. At the outbreak of the civil war, GL immediately mobilized funds, weapons, and people in support of the Spanish republic. The possibility of GL's direct participation in the war was discussed in Paris during a meeting held on July 22, 1936. At that time, in addition to Renzo Giua, some of the most important figures of the Italian anti-Fascist emigration were in Spain, among them the Communists Nino Nanetti and Vittorio Vidali (Carlos Contreras), who arrived in Catalonia after the rebellion of the generals, and the anarchist Camillo Berneri, who had been in Barcelona since 1934.[24]

Rosselli saw the Spanish Civil War as offering an opportunity for political and military concretization of the dialogue developed in the early 1930s among the various political components of the anti-Fascist movement in exile – that is, moving in the direction indicated by the young novatori, thereby transforming Giustizia e Libertà into the leading force of Italian anti-Fascism. Rosselli thus declared: "The Spanish Revolution is our revolution."[25] Rosselli perceived that the importance of the conflict went beyond the borders of Spain because the Spanish defeat would be a further step toward the fascistization of Europe. Rosselli insisted on the need for anti-Fascist unity among Italian volunteers by sending an appeal, which remained unanswered, to Communists and Socialists a few days before his departure for Barcelona. Immediately upon his arrival, on August 10, 1936, he founded, with Berberi, the Italian section of the Ascaso Column.[26] Rosselli's speech, broadcast over the radio from Barcelona on November 13, 1936, reiterated his urgent plea:

> Comrades, brothers, Italians, listen. An Italian volunteer speaks to you . . . to bring you the greetings of the thousands of exiled Italian anti-Fascists who are fighting in the ranks of the revolutionary army. An Italian column has been battling for three months on the Aragon front. Eleven dead, twenty wounded, according to the estimate by the Spanish comrades: here is the testimony of their sacrifice . . . There are Italian volunteers in all units; men who have lost their freedom in their own land are beginning by regaining it in Spain, with a rifle in hand . . . The ongoing experience in Spain is of extraordinary interest to everyone . . . [It is] not just a party that, by pretending to be infallible, delays the revolution for a concrete and realistic program: anarchists, Communists, Socialists, and republicans here are collaborating in public affairs, at the front, in social life. What a lesson for us Italians![27]

As Aldo Garosci recalls, the Italian section of the Ascaso Column was made up of men "with beards of all sizes and shapes, dressed in the strangest rags, with red-black, red, and multi-colored flags," seized by a desire and a passion, by the will to learn, "a great will of revolutionary discipline."[28] The Italian section fought valiantly on the Aragon front, alongside the Catalan anarcho-syndicalist militias on August 28, 1936, in the Battle of Mount Pelato, where it repelled the Falangist attack, suffering many losses including Mario Angeloni, while Rosselli himself was wounded.[29] Following the Battle of Almudévar (November 20, 1936), a political-ideological crisis developed within the group, which culminated on December 16, when the anarchist representatives of the column formed a majority against Rosselli. Sick with phlebitis, Rosselli returned to France in January 1937. On June 9, that same year, he was murdered, along with his brother Nello, in Bagnoles-de-l'Orne by the "sicari" of the Fascist group Cagoule, on the orders of Benito Mussolini himself.[30]

In Spain, His Death

At the outbreak of the Spanish Civil War, on July 18, 1936, Renzo Giua was 22-years-old. After Paris, he had settled in Annemasse, in Haute Savoie, not far from Geneva. In Saint Cergues or in Geneva, he met the Italian anarchist Antonino Nino Napolitano, to whom he confided: "You know that Malatesta intrigues me. What a great ideal he cherishes, you can argue, as he does, keeping his feet on the ground, standing close to reality, it's amazing."[31] Helped by the Foyer des réfugés politiques antifascistes, Giua left for Spain, with the Italian anarchist Francesco Barbieri, and other Italian anti-Fascist militants.[32] When he arrived in Barcelona shortly thereafter, he enrolled in the international group of the Durruti Column.

In September 1936, he was injured in the battle of Barbastro, in the province of Huesca, and sent to France to recover. Giua returned to Spain in November 1936, and then to Geneva, on leave, from January to February or March 1937. After the Battle of Guadalajara, Giua travelled to Albacete in Castile to attend an officers' course at the military headquarters of the International Brigades, receiving the rank of lieutenant. In May 1937, after arriving in Barcelona with Antoine Gimenez, Giua was integrated into the Battalòn Italo-Espanol of the Twelfth International Brigade, commanded by Randolfo Pacciardi, with the rank of captain, demonstrating once more his military talents and courage. He was injured again on July 16, and spent a period of convalescence in Sitges, near Barcelona, where he met his old comrade and friend Aldo Garosci. He then set off for the front, where he was wounded for the third time, in Zaragoza. During the offensive on the Estramadura front, on the night of February 16–17, 1938, in the Sierra Quemada area, at Zalamea de la Serena, Badajoz, Giua, against all odds, took command of the battalion, after three of his commanders fell one after the other during the battle. Renzo Giua was killed by a bullet in the abdomen. He was buried in a common pit in Zalamea della Serena. His cenotaph is at the cemetery in Turin next to his brother Franco's tomb.[33]

Spanish Destiny: Letters and Remembrance

Letter from Renzo Giua to his mother, Clara Giua Lollini:[34]

BARCELONA, August 20

Dearest Mamma,
I am alive, and if I am so late in answering, do you really believe that it is this revolution that prevents foreign postal services from working as one would expect in a civilized nation? In the end, I would say that, at least with some reservations, this civilization suits me perfectly. I am in good physical and moral health; to tell you one story, I am growing a beard, which, according to all opinions, suits me well. I'm not telling you other stories because they are not worth much.

I guess you'll ask me: what are you doing there? Strange question: There is a story that a husband came home slightly drunk, opened the closet to hang up his jacket, and found his wife's lover, as God created him, under his wife's anguished gaze. Dumbstruck, he immediately asked: "What are you doing here?" The man readily replied: "I am waiting for the tram." . . . Actually what I'm really doing here, leaving aside jokes and metaphors, is resting in a social environment where I can relax: you know I've always liked to relax on the first sofa I saw . . . This has not been possible for some time, and here I have found a very comfortable one.

The second question, I imagine. And your exams? The answer is simple. When I can go and take them, I'll do so. For now, I am studying the Spanish language, which will serve me for the long-planned study on the Archbishop de Hita, which I hope to write, if they will not shoot me in these dramatic moments. What I'm most sorry about, dear Mamma, is not having your news and not being able to . . . give you any for some time yet. I'll try to do so in every way, and as soon as I have the chance, I'll give you an address. You would be wrong to worry; you should keep calm, as I could not feel better than I do here. And this, in my opinion, is the essence. Perhaps your maternal selfishness would prefer me to have an address among the tall Helvetians than to be without one under the hospitable sombrero? I'm sure I will continue to give you my news, because I keep thinking about you and Papa. Kiss the children for me and yourself, the usual affectionate embrace. Tuo Renzo.

Letter from Renzo Giua to his mother, Clara Giua Lollini:[35]

Dearest Mamma,
Two words: do you know I've written you every week? Do you know there are accidents which determine whether or not a letter arrives? They tell me you caused havoc in Geneva, with telegrams, etc. Blessed Mamma, but if I do something, how can I do something else. Consider that I am as if paralyzed toward you, so how can a letter matter so much? It's obvious that if something had happened to me, you would have known it right away; I have never been so happy, never as strong as now. What do you want me to do next? Be patient, and believe and be assured that my first thought, if only because it is my first duty, is of you. It would be stupid if this thought of you would eliminate my freedom of action; indeed, it is necessary for me to do that. When, after the various storms, when the sky will be calm, the hens will return to the yard, then will be the time of our reunion. If by accident, the storms will continue, after all, cutting off the water supply, what will be will be, as men depend on events and not the other way round. So listen to me: I kiss you, and I kiss Lisetta and Franco, tuo Renzo.
P.S. I do not have any doubt as to how you and Papà feel, so I know it would be a futile question to ask.

Letter from Renzo Giua to his mother, Clara Giua Lollini:[36]

Dearest Mamma,
I'm sending you kisses, with filial affection, after so long. Tell me truly, are you really worried about me? That is what they say to me, and frankly, I become embarrassed, because I cannot see how to remedy these epistolary deficiencies, on the one hand, and the reasons for your anxiety, on the other. I will tell you: I cannot do otherwise. It seems to me that this solves the question of your worries. So be a sport, be a philosopher: say OK and let's hope that I will be fine. And think that this world, as bad as it is, is a vast rigolade[comedy] that is always worth seeing, and does not leave anything out. With the usual phrases, I embrace the fairy Lisetta, the . . . rogue Franco, and you of course. Tuo Renzo
P.S. I know you published a book with the Laterza publishing house. I do not know whether I shall ever be able to publish one! R.

Letter from Renzo Giua to Emilio Lussu, autumn–winter 1937:[37]

I forge ahead, from one wound to another, from one battle to another, driven by the healthy instinct of not wasting even one hour of this war. I do not know whether you occasionally receive news of my father. I feel a great need of him: the most beautiful aspect of this militia is the sense of fulfilling a duty as his son. And the most meaningful one is to give a son back to his father. Even if they "make holes in me," the account will be closed with a profit. Renzo

Magrini (Aldo Garosci), in memoriam:[38]

Renzo Giua belonged to the race of the De Rosa, the Vezzoli, the Scala. Despite the differences in their temperaments – taciturn or intemperate, gay and cordial, or introvert —one characteristic is prominent in all of these heroes: the strength and frankness of their nature, the total faith in the value of their actions . . . In Giua, this heroic characteristic was, in my opinion, the most salient one, through the contrasts and surprises that the self-confidence of such a temperament could not but ignite at every major turning point in his life. I remember what Scala told me about Giua . . . maybe a year before his first arrest, in Turin. There were, I was told, two high school students who greedily read our press, who had found a way to contact us, and who planned large-scale acts against the regime. One was Giua . . . A few months later . . . Giua was arrested and then convicted by the Tribunale Speciale, with Scala . . . he was part of the Turin political group that was formed at that time, and after 1930 was brutally crushed by prison and death . . . As a story of ideas, it is a major part of the life and formation of Giustizia e Libertà; as a story of action, it would be better to leave it as it is . . . Renzo Giua was the embodiment of such action with his fierce and fiery spirit . . . He had . . . the ability to command, a strong sense of order, and a capacity to make rapid decisions. On the morning of his friends' arrest, before leaving for the mountains, he quickly destroyed all the propaganda material . . . and then left. Three days later, he was in Paris. When we met him, his face was scarred by the dreadful frost, after two nights on an ice floe, in the winter. But the flame of action was shining in his eyes . . . I saw him in Barcelona. I had already heard in September, a year earlier, from the comrades of the Durruti international group in the hospital of his calm heroism. He had spent his recovery in Sitges, and the next day he had to leave for Madrid. In the morning, we discussed politics; as always, he was hard, tough, merciless. In the evening, I spent an hour with him; he was a delightful friend, not a moment of posing, and full of humanity and fraternity in what he said. He spoke with affection about Rosselli and Lussu: he talked about his experience at the Aragon front, and I do not wish to repeat what he said in this context . . . "And now," he concluded, "if I wish I could go back to Sitges; I could stay as much as I want in Barcelona. Instead," he said in a lower voice, "tomorrow morning I will travel to Madrid." I did not get to see him again, as he left at night, faithful to the model he had set for himself, struggling to the end, and he died. He did not leave the thesis on Archbishop de Hita, or the political writings he had, at certain times of his life, thought to write; he did not leave any political and military feats which, as a born man of action, he would have accomplished. He left us a bunch of memories, some scattered writings, and some letters.

He leaves us, however, an example of action, of a new Italian temperament, which, even for the most disheartened, can open their eyes to great things that can be expected from young, adolescent Italians. He leaves us the duty to act, and he makes us understand that we must persevere until the end. He leaves to his friends this almost physical memory of indomitable boldness, of will, of courage. It may seem a bit sentimental, one of those things that are said when instead you can do something . . . but each one of us, I am sure, says to himself: "Happy are you, Giua; happy are you, you who have known how to suffer and to endure until your death – "dragging yourself from hospital to a battle," always faithful to yourself, always equal to the task you had to fulfill! May fate grant that we, too, at the supreme moment, will not deny what is most valid in human nature!

Emilio Lussu: The fighter in Spain:[39]

Renzo Giua was one of the first to rush to Spain in July 1936. He had been preparing to spend years studying at the University of Geneva but, instead, he put his books aside to take up the rifle. The Italian columns in Spain had not yet been formed, even in Catalonia, and he did not have time to find a place to fight at the Aragon front . . . Renzo Giua was part of a vanguard column composed at first of 150 volunteers and commanded by a Frenchman whose name I forget, but whom he always remembered with great admiration and deep affection. The column was decimated in continuous attacks and reduced to thirty men. Even his commander, who seemed invulnerable, fell, fighting alongside Giua . . . Very few survivors, Giua, among them, went to the Durruti column and continued the struggle. He did not waste time in Spain except for recu-

perating in the hospital from the injuries he suffered. Obliged to it, he attended the young officers' course; he was at Albacete's headquarters, in the organization of the International Brigades under the command of Platone,[40] *whom he held in great esteem . . . He joined the Garibaldi Brigade, shortly after Guadalajara, took part in all the battles, and remained there until his death . . . He was still a boy when, to escape his second arrest, he crossed the Alps and sought refuge in France. The Spanish war matured him, transforming him into a man. He thought he would stay in Spain until the end of the war. He had become a soldier and did not want to be anything but a soldier. He was studying military problems generated by the war, and nothing but the war attracted his attention.*

"Now," he said, "politics is war." Even after having matured as a commander of volunteers . . . he still retained his gullible, sporting character, together with a vision of life in which irony seemed to drive his skepticism, denying all of life's absolute values. Yet he was an idealist. "Bourgeois Liberal – I used to call him, jokingly – the Croce of the FAI."[41] *And he would laugh loudly . . . "You will always take care of him," his father once said to me, "because he is a messy boy . . . "* Messy! *. . . And I laughed at him, asserting that the student had nothing to learn from the pedagogues. Now the fight is tough. His father is in jail, and he has sacrificed everything for the sake of his moral conscience: the university, his favorite studies, a comfortable life, his family . . . And now his son. The first born, his first hope, has fallen, to rise no longer. This is the heavy duty of our struggle. The fathers fall and their children fall. Two generations are sacrificed. But, in sacrifice, and only in sacrifice, the right to build tomorrow's Italy is affirmed.*

Letter from Renzo Giua to his mother, Clara Giua Lollini:[42]

Dearest Mamma,
Enduring the distance feeds my love and my nostalgia. Well, is not Turin's Sacchi Street one of the best places where your son could live the quietest of lives? There is no doubt [about that]. And in the meantime, I am entrusting to this postcard the assurance of my well-being; to you for Franco and for dear Lisetta, to whom I wish the most beautiful snowy holidays, to you my most loving and delicate feelings, including Papá, the object of my dearest thoughts. Renzo.

Epilogue

If at the beginning of 1936 anti-Fascism in Western countries had its strongholds in Spain and France, three years later, despite the defeat of the Spanish Republic, anti-Fascism became a powerful force capable of mobilizing Western public opinion. Even though the struggle of international volunteers in Spain did not save the Spanish Republic, in this drawn-out, difficult war, the partisan leadership that fought Fascism in Europe took shape. In Italy, the civil war in Spain represented, symbolically, the beginning of the fall of Fascism: from Guadalajara to the Italian uprising of April 25, 1945. Rosselli's motto "Today in Spain, tomorrow in Italy" summarizes better than any other the meaning of Giua's sacrifice, and Italian participation in the heroic war for Europe's freedom from the Fascist yoke.

Notes

1 Paola Lo Cascio, *La guerra civile spagnola: Una storia del Novecento* (Roma: Carocci, 2014).

2 Cf. Massimo Mila, "Destino spagnolo (Ricordo di Renzo Giua)," *La Rassegna d'Italia* 6–10 (June–October 1947): 12; Gabriele Ranzato, *La grande paura del 1936: Come la Spagna precipito nella guerra civile* (Bari: Laterza, 2011); Hannah Arendt, "The Decline of the Nation-State and the End of the Rights of Man," *The Origins of Totalitarianism* (London: Andre Deutsch, 1973) [1951], 278. See also Arno Maier, "The Economics: The Endurance of Land, Agriculture, Manufacture," *The Persistence of the Old Regime: Europe to the Great War* (New York, NY: Pantheon Books, 1981), 17–79; Dan Diner, *Cataclysms: A History of the Twentieth Century from Europe's Edge*, George L. Mosse Series in Modern European Cultural and Intellectual History (Madison: University of Wisconsin Press, 2008).

3 Carlo Rosselli (Rome 189? -Bagnoles de l'Orne, France, 1937) was born to a Jewish family of republican and Risorgimental traditions, both maternal and paternal (grandmother Hariett, Enrichetta Nathan was the daughter of Sarah Nathan Levi). An interventionist, he participated in World War I and founded the Circolo della Cultura in Florence, in which Gaetano Salvemini, Ernesto Rossi, and Piero Calamandrei took part. Upholding strong anti-Fascist positions, Rosselli drew close to the Socialist Party, and collaborated with the journal *Critica sociale.* After meeting Piero Gobetti, he began his collaboration with *Liberal Revolution,* developing a non-Marxist and non-class oriented Socialism, and joining the reformist current. He was arrested in 1927 and sentenced to five years forced exile in Lipari, from where he escaped on July 27, 1929. In Paris, he founded the GL movement, which also had group affiliations in Italy. In May 1934, he began publication of the weekly *Giustizia e Libertà,* alongside the *Quaderni,* published from 1932.

Stanislao G. Pugliese, *Carlo Rosselli: Socialist Heretic and Antifascist Exile* (Cambridge, MA: Harvard University Press 1999).

4 Cf. Hans Magnus Enzensberger, *La Breve estate dell'anarchia: Vita e morte di Buenaventura Durruti* (Milan: Feltrinelli, 1973[1972]), 12.

5 Massimo Mila (1910–1988) was an Italian musicologist and an anti-Fascist linked to GL; he was convicted by the Special Tribunal to seven years imprisonment. Mila, "Destino spagnolo," 3.

6 The Renzo Giua file in the State Archives of Rome contains about 60 unpublished letters written to his mother, Clara Lollini Giua, and by her to Renzo. I could utilize only a few of them. The oleographic copies have been destroyed, but copies typed by the Fascist censorship authorities are available.

7 Luigi Fabbri was born in Fabriano, in the province of Ancona, on December 22, 1877, to Curzio and Angela Sbriccioli. In 1908, two collections of his political-ideological writings, *Sindacalismo y anarchismo and Marxismus* and *Anarchismus*, focusing on the confrontation between anarchist doctrine, Marxist Socialism, and revolutionary syndicalism were published in Spain and Germany.

8 Cf. Enrico Acciai, "Memorie difficili: Antifascismo italiano, volontariato internazionale e guerra civile spagnola," *Diacronie* 7, no. 3 (2011): 2–4; Santi Fedele, *Storia della Concentrazione Antifascista, 1927–1934* (Milano: Feltrinelli, 1976), 74–75, quoted in Acciai, "Memorie difficili," 3.

9 Thus, in 1934, the first issue of the periodical *Giustizia e Libertà* came out: "Deriving from various political currents, we are now putting aside party membership and organizing united action. A revolutionary movement, not a party, Giustizia e Libertà is the name and symbol. Republicans, Socialists, and democrats, we fight for freedom, for the republic, for social justice. We are no longer three different streams but an inseparable trinity." *Giustizia e Libertà*, May 18, 1934, 1.

10 Simona Colarizi, *Classe operaia e ceti medi: Rosselli, Nenni, Morandi: il dibattito sulle alleanze negli anni trenta* (Venice: Marsilio, 1976); Marco Gervasoni, ed., *Giustizia e Libertà e il socialismo liberale*, preface by Valdo Spini (Milan: M&B, 1999).

11 *Quaderni di Giustizia e Libertà. 1932–1935* (Torino: Bottega d'Erasmo, 1975 [1959]); Mario Giovana, *Giustizia e Libertà in Italia: Storia di una cospirazione antifascista, 1929–1937* (Turin: Bollati Boringhieri, 2005).

12 Michele Giua (1889–1966) was born in Sassari, Sardinia. In 1926, in the climate of academic fascistization, his university career was blocked because of his political positions, and he began to teach courses at the Scuola di applicazione di artiglieria e genio of Turin. In 1933, he renounced teaching entirely in order not to be forced to swear allegiance to the regime, and he opened a private research lab. In 1935, betrayed by the writer Pitigrilli – Dino Segre – a spy of OVRA (the Fascist secret police), Giua was arrested along with Vittorio Foa, and other anti-Fascists. Brought before a Fascist special tribunal, he was sentenced to 15 years in prison and released in August 1943,

after serving eight years. In September that same year, he went into hiding in Torre Pellice to escape the Germans. After liberation, Giua became the president of the Turin Provincial Epuration Commission for the political cleansing of the Italian state apparatus. He was a deputy in the Constituent Assembly and a senator of the republic. He retired from active politics, devoting his last years to chemistry studies. In 1945, Giua published *Ricordi di un detenuto politico 1935–1943,* with the Chiantore publishing house. Clara Lollini (1888–1987) was an Italian chemist. In 1912, she graduated with a degree in chemistry, and in the following year, she married Michele Giua, professor of chemistry, writing several books with him. In the 1930s, after her husband's arrest, Clara, mother of three, Renzo, Franco, and Lisa, continued her work as a translator from German to support the family. Renzo's sister, Lisa Giua (1923–2005), Lisetta – as she was called, and as Natalia Ginzburg remembers her in *Lessico Famigliare* – was a member of Turin's anti-Fascist conspiracy, where she met and married another leading protagonist of Italian anti-Fascism, also a member of the GL group, and one of the founding fathers of the Italian Republic: Vittorio Foa (1910–2008). After the war, Lisa Giua Foa was a member of the Italian Communist Party, a close collaborator of Palmiro Togliatti, and one of the inspiring figures of the Lotta Continua group.

13 Barbara Allason, *Memorie di un antifascista* (Roma-Firenze-Milano,1947), 106, 109; Giovana, *Giustizia e Libertà in Italia,* 274–303. Cf. Vittorio Foa, "La Torino degli anni '30," *Nuova Antologia* no. 2183 (July-September 1992): 71–82 (interviewed by G. Zanfarino). FOA

14 Cf. Mila, *Destino spagnolo,* 13.

15 Ibid., 12.

16 At Ponte Tresa, on the border with Switzerland, the police stopped Sion Segre and Mario Levi, who were on their way back from Lugano, where they had gone on behalf of GL. In their car, the police found anti-Fascist material, a copy of the weekly of the anti-Fascist alliance *La libertà,* and copies of leaflets that incited against the March 25 elections. On the way to the police station, Levi threw himself into the River Tresa and swam to the other side of Lake Lugano. Segre was stopped and transferred to police headquarters in Varese, where he was beaten up and tortured.

17 Carlo Mussa Ivaldi, Giovanni Guaita, Giuliana Segre, Marco Segre, Attilio Segre, Cesare Colombo, Leo Levi, and Camillo Pasquali were arrested. Not everyone was a GL militant and not everyone had the same fate in court. After Ginzburg's return in 1932 from Paris, where he met Rosselli, a clandestine network formed, characterized by an interesting social milieu consisting of people who were tied to each other by family relations, friendship, and intellectual and cultural affinities. This included the Massimo d'Azzeglio High School; the salon of Barbara Allason, which hosted evenings of cultural discussions and conspiracy; the circle of intellectuals out of which the publishing house Einaudi was established; and Olivetti of Ivrea. Many of the Turin arrestees of 1934 were of Jewish origin.

18 Cf. Mila, *Destino spagnolo*, 13.

19 *Tempo Presente*, no. 3–4 (March–April 1963). Ursula Hirschman (1913–91) was born in Berlin and raised in a middle-class Jewish family. As a young student of economics, she took part in a range of events organized by both the Socialist and German Social Democratic Party. She became involved with Communist resistance groups and was later forced to escape to France with her brother, Albert O. Hirschman, later a candidate for the Nobel Prize, who fought in Spain in the International Brigades during the civil war. In France, she met Renzo Giua, her brother's Italian teacher.

20 *Gleichschaltung* – way in which Nazi Germany succeeded in imposing totalitarian control and coordination over all aspects of society.

21 Renzo Giua, "Polemica sullo Stato," *Quaderni di Giustizia e libertà*, October 5, 1934, number22.

22 Cf. Paolo Bagnoli, "Di un dissidio in Giustizia e libertà. Lettere inedite di Mario Levi, R.G Mario Levi (1905–73), Italian anti-Fascist son of Giuseppe Levi and Lidia Tanzi, brother of Natalia Ginzburg, was born in Florence. In Turin, where the family moved in 1919, he attended the D'Azeglio High School and had his first contacts with the anti-Fascist GL. At the time of the German occupation, he moved to the Toulouse region, where in March 1942, he was arrested by the Vichy police and interned for a period in the Vernet camp. Later, he took part in the Resistance, joining the Front National de l'indépendance de la France, inspired by the PCC. In the postwar period, he stayed in France, taking French citizenship, and worked for French radio and UNESCO. , N. Chiaromonte, C. Rosselli, A. Garosci (1934–35)," in *Mezzosecolo, Annali 1978–1979*, no. 3, 5–54, 8.

23 Typed letter in, "Lettere di un dissidio in Giustizia e Libertà," *Una città. Rivista, Mezzo secolo* (1978), signed by Mario Levi (Selva) and Renzo Giua (Bittis), Paris, May 14, 1935. Mario Levi (1905–73), Italian anti-Fascist son of Giuseppe Levi and Lidia Tanzi, brother of Natalia Ginzburg, was born in Florence. In Turin, where the family moved in 1919, he attended the D'Azeglio High School and had his first contacts with the anti-Fascist GL. At the time of the German occupation, he moved to the Toulouse region, where in March 1942, he was arrested by the Vichy police and interned for a period in the Vernet camp. Later, he took part in the Resistance, joining the Front National de l'indépendance de la France, inspired by the PCC. In the postwar period, he stayed in France, taking French citizenship, and worked for French radio and UNESCO.

24 Berneri was killed in May 1937, together with Francesco Barbieri, shortly after their arrest by the PSUC (Partit Socialista Unificat de Catalunya) Stalinist Communists during the unremitting battle of the Spanish anti-Fascist front in May, which took place in Barcelona between Communists and anarchists. See Giulia Canali, *L'antifascismo italiano e la guerra civile spagnola* (San Cesario di Lecce: Manni, 2004), 11. Cf. ibid., 12ff; also Giulia Medas, *¿Quiénes Fueron Los Voluntarios? Identità, motivazioni, linguaggi e*

vissuto quotidiano dei volontari italiani nella guerra civile spagnola, (PhD diss., Università degli Studi di Cagliari/Universitat de València, 2014), 63.

25 Medas, *¿Quiénes Fueron Los Voluntarios?* 64–66; Carlo Rosselli, *Oggi in Spagna, domani in Italia* (Turin: Einaudi, 1967), 19. The book came out, with a preface by Gaetano Salvemini, in issues of *Justice and Freedom* in Paris in 1938; the second edition, 1967, was published by Einaudi, with an introduction by Aldo Garosci .

26 Cf. Canali, *L'antifascismo italiano,* 11–13ff; Acciai, "Memorie difficili," 5. On the Ascaso column, see Enrico Acciai, "Berneri e Rosselli in Spagna, l'esperienza della 'Sezione Italiana della Colonna Ascaso'," *Spagna Contemporanea* 38 (2010), and "Una scelta di vita. Il primo volontariato italiano nella guerra civile spagnola," *Storia e problemi contemporanei* 55 (2010). The column was organized by Rosselli himself, with Mario Angeloni, Umberto Calosso, and the anarchist Camillo Berneri; the Italian contribution was extensive and effective and was dissolved in April 1937.

27 Carlo Rosselli, *Oggi in Spagna,* radio broadcast, Barcelona, November 13, 1936; Canali, *L'antifascismo italiano,* p. 5.

28 Aldo Garosci, "Francesco De Rosa, Renzo Giua e Carlo Rosselli in Spagna," *Trent'anni di storia italiana 1915–1945: Lezioni con testimonianze,* a cura di Franco Antonicelli (Torino: Einaudi, 1961), 247–53, 250.

29 Cf. Enrico Acciai, "Memorie difficili," 4. According to the account of Umberto Calosso, a member of GL who was present that day on the front, it was the "first instance of partisan Italian weapons in the European war."

30 After the assassination of Rosselli, the movement's leadership was assumed by Emilio Lussu, who gave GL a strong Socialist imprint. This caused disagreement and numerous elements left GL, including Alberto Tarchiani. With the entry of German troops into France in 1940, almost all GL leaders fled elsewhere. Alberto Tarchiani joined Salvemini in New York and assumed the secretariat of the Mazzini Society. Paolo Vittorell left for Cairo, founding GL Egypt, which carried out intense propaganda activity, especially among Italian prisoners of British soldiers. In October 1941, Silvio Trentin and Francesco Fausto Nitti signed a unification agreement with Communists and Socialists in France, still on behalf of GL, even though the movement had ceased to exist. In 1942, the various components of the group joined the Partito d'Azione (Party of Action), which called their own partisan brigades Giustizia e Libertà. Cf. Marta Bonsanti, ed., "Archivi di 'Giustizia e Libertà', Revisione e Integrazione, 2013," Istituto Storico della Resistenza in Toscana.

31 Nino Napolitano, *Adunata dei refrattari,* April 9, 1938.

32 Francesco Barbieri was born in Briatico (then a province of Catanzaro) on December 14, 1895, to Giovanni and Domenica Arena. Cf. *Epistolario inedito* a cura di Aurelio Chessa, Pier Carlo Masini, Paola Feri e Luigi di Lembo, Pistoia, Ed. Arch. Fam. Berneri, 1980 e 1984.

33 Discrepancies exist with regard to Giua's death. Andreu Castells, *Las Brigadas Internacionales de la Guerra de España* (Esplugues de Llobregat:

Ariel, 1974); Álvaro López, ed., *Antifascisti italiani caduti nella guerra di Spagna 1936–1939: combattenti antifascisti di Spagna caduti nella lotta di liberazione in Italia* (Rome: AICVAS, 1982) (Quaderno. Associazione Italiana Combattenti Volontari Antifascisti). Castells reports his date of death as March 17, 1938, at a site in Ciudad Real, Castile-La Mancha.

34 Buaraloz-Zaragoza postal stamp, August 20, 1936, ACS, Pol. Pol. (Political Police), envelope no. 606, fasc. n. 41, folders nn. 22, 23 (Giuseppe Renzo di Michele). Handwritten letter to Clara Giua Lollini, Via Sacchi 42, Turin. Copy conforming to the original, containing transcript errors.

35 Ostende postal, October 1, 1936, written by Giua on September 25, 1936, ACS, Pol. Pol., envelope n. 606, fasc. n. 41, folders nn. 22, 23 (Giuseppe Renzo di Michele). Handwritten letter sent to Clara Giua Lollini, Via Sacchi 42, Turin. Copy conforming to the original, containing transcript errors.

36 Handwritten letter, October 15, 1937, ACS, Pol. Pol., envelope n. 606, fasc. n. 41, folders nn. 22, 23 (Giuseppe Renzo di Michele). Handwritten letter sent to Clara Giua Lollini, Via Sacchi 42, Turin.

37 Cited in Mila, *Destino spagnolo* (Ricordo di Renzo Giua), p. 25.

38 "Un eroe della nuova generazione: Renzo Giua," *Giustizia e Libertà*, March 18, 1938.

39 Loc. cit.

40 Felice Platone (1899–1955), a journalist and Communist leader, was in Spain in 1936 as chief commander of the International Brigades.

41 Benedetto Croce, the Italian philosopher; FAI (Federazione Anarchica Italiana).

42 Postcard sent from Annemasse, near Geneva, by a comrade on March 30, 1938, that reached the family a month and half after his death. ACS, Pol. Pol., envelope 606, 41, cartelle nn. 22, 23 (Giua Renzo di Michele).

The Editors and Contributors

Pedro Aires Oliveira holds a PhD in Political and Institutional History and is an Assistant Professor at the History Department of FCSH-NOVA, as well as a researcher of the Institute of Contemporary History in Lisbon. His main research topics are the history of Portuguese foreign relations, colonialism and decolonization. He has published several articles in academic journals (*Portuguese Studies, Cold War History, International History Review, European Contemporary History*), as well as the books *Os Despojos da Aliança. A Grã-Bretanha e a Questão Colonial Portuguesa 1945–75* (2007), *História da Expansão e do Império Português* (with J. P. Costa and J. D. Rodrigues, 2014), and *O Adeus ao Império. 40 anos de Descolonização Portuguesa* (co-edited with F. Rosas and M. Machaqueiro, 2015).

Luciano Casali is a member of the Grup de Ricerca sobre l'Epoca Franquista at the Universitat Autònoma de Barcelona. He taught Contemporary History and History of Spain at the Università di Bologna and was visiting professor at the Universitat de Valencia. He has published extensively on the topics of labor movements, European fascisms, and antifascism in Italy, France, Spain, and Portugal.

Alexandra Cheveleva Dergacheva has completed her Ph.D. dissertation in Artistic, Literary and Cultural Studies at the Autonomous University of Madrid. Her main research interests focus on the avant-garde movement in poetry in the interwar period, and on the mutual reception and translation of Russian and Spanish avant-gardes authors, a topic on which she has published various articles. She is also the author of a fiction book, *Cantiga about Maria Blanca*, winner of the first prize of Strelbitsky Novel Writers Competition in 2016.

Manuela Consonni holds the Pela and Adam Starkopf Chair in Holocaust Studies, Department of Jewish History, at the Hebrew University of Jerusalem. She heads the Italian Studies Program at the Department of Romance and Latin American Studies and is currently the Director of the Vidal Sassoon International Center for the Study of

Antisemitism. Consonni is the author of *Resistance or Holocaust:* The *Memory of the Deportation and Extermination in Italy, 1945–1985,* (Magnes University Press 2010, in Hebrew), and *L'eclisse dell'antifascismo. Resistenza, questione ebraica e cultura politica in Italia dal 1943 al 1989* (Laterza Publisher 2015), awarded the 2016 Polonsky Prize.

Daniel Kowalsky is lecturer in European Studies at Queen's University, Belfast. He is the author of numerous books and articles on the civil war in Spain, including *La Unión Soviética y la guerra civil española* (Barcelona, Editorial Crítica, 2003), *Stalin and the Spanish Civil War* (New York: Columbia University Press, 2004) and *History in Dispute: The Spanish Civil War* (Detroit: St. James Press, 2005).

David A. Messenger is Professor of History and Chair of the Department of History at the University of South Alabama in Mobile, AL. He is the author of *Hunting Nazis in Franco's Spain* (Louisiana State University Press, 2014) and *L'Espagne Republicane: French Policy and Spanish Republicanism in Liberated France* (Sussex Academic Press, 2008) as well as co-editor, with Katrin Paehler, of *A Nazi Past: Recasting German Identity in Postwar Europe* (University of Kentucky Press, 2015). He has published numerous articles in peer-reviewed journals on Franco Spain's relations with France during and after the Second World War, on Allied and Nazi intelligence in Spain during the Second World War, and on contemporary memory of the Spanish Civil War in Catalonia.

Xosé M. Núñez Seixas is Full Professor of Modern History at the University of Santiago de Compostela; between 2012 and 2017 he was also professor at the Ludwig-Maximilians University of Munich. He has published widely on the comparative history of nationalist movements and national and regional identities, as well as on overseas migration from Spain and Galicia to Latin America, and the cultural history of war in the twentieth century. Among his latest books are *Camarada invierno. Experiencia y memoria de la División Azul, 1941–1945* (Barcelona 2016); with J. Moreno (ed.), *Metaphors of Spain. Representations of Spanish National Identity in the Twentieth Century* (Oxford/New York 2017); and with L. Gálvez and J. Muñoz Soro, *España en democracia, 1975–2011* (Barcelona/Madrid 2017).

Inbal Ofer is Associate Professor of Modern European History at the Department of History, Philosophy and Judaic Studies. She specializes in the social, gender and urban history of 20th century Spain. Amongst her publications are: *Señoritas in Blue: The Making of a Female Political Elite* *in Franco's Spain. The National Leadership of the Sección Femenina de la Falange* (Sussex Academic Press, 2009); *Claiming the City/Contesting the State: Squatting, Community Formation and Democratization in Spain* (Routledge, 2017); *Taking Citizenship Personally: Social Movements and Spain's Transition to Democracy*, co-authored by T. Groves, N. Townson, I. Ofer, A. Herrera (Palgrave, 2017).

Raanan Rein is the Elias Sourasky Professor of Latin American and Spanish History and Vice President of Tel Aviv University. He is also the Head of the S. Daniel Abraham Center for International and Regional Studies. Rein is the author and editor of more than thirty books and well over a hundred articles in academic journals and book chapters, in several languages. He is a member of Argentina's National Academy of History. The Spanish king awarded him the title of Commander in the Order of the Civil Merit for his contribution to Spanish historiography and Spanish-Israeli relations. In 2016 he won the Reimar Lust Award (co-sponsored by the Alexander von Humboldt Foundation and the Fritz Thyssen Foundation).

Emilio Sáenz-Francés is senior lecturer in History and International Relations at the Universidad Pontificia Comillas ICAI-ICADE, in Madrid. In 2008 he completed his PhD at the Universidad de Deusto, focusing on the study of Spanish Foreign Policy during the central years of World War II. His dissertation received the Spanish Royal Academy of Doctors Award for the best humanities doctoral thesis of the year. He was granted with a one-year scholarship to continue his research at the Centre for the Study of the Two World Wars at the University of Edinburgh. In 2014 he was appointed Archives By-Fellow at the Churchill Archives Centre of Churchill College (Cambridge University). He is Editor of *Comillas Journal of International Relations.*

Silvina Schammah Gesser specializes in the cultural history of Spain with an emphasis on the first half of the 20th century. Her new interests focus on the economy of memory, ethnicity and representation in post-dictatorial societies. Her books include *Madrid's Forgotten Avant-Garde. Between Essentialism and Modernity,* (Sussex Academic Press, 2015) and *El Otro en la España Contemporánea* (Fundación Tres Culturas, 2011), co-edited with Raanan Rein. Her publications have appeared in *Gender and Society, Racial and Ethnic Studies, Journal of War and Culture, Revista de Historia Contemporánea* and *Casa de Velázquez,* among others. Since 2010 she lectures at the Department of Romance and Latin American Studies and is a fellow researcher at the Harry S. Truman

Institute for the Advancement of Peace at the Hebrew University, Jerusalem.

Michael Seidman is professor of history at the University of North Carolina Wilmington, having studied at the University of Amsterdam, University of California Berkeley, and Swarthmore College. His first book, *Workers against Work: Labor in Barcelona and Paris during the Popular Fronts, 1936–38* (1991), has been translated into six languages. Other publications include *Republic of Egos: A Social History of the Spanish Civil War* (2002); *The Imaginary Revolution: Parisian Students and Workers in 1968* (2004); and *The Victorious Counterrevolution: The Nationalist Effort in the Spanish Civil War* (2011). His most recent book is *Transatlantic Antifascisms from the Spanish Civil War to the end of World War II* (Cambridge University Press, 2017).

Leonardo Senkman holds a Ph.D in History (Universidad de Buenos Aires) and is Research Fellow at the Harry Truman Institute for the Advancement of Peace, The Hebrew University of Jerusalem. He recently co-authored with L Roniger, M.Sznajder, and S.Sosnowski *Exile, Diaspora, and Return. Changing Cultural Landscapes in Argentina, Chile, Paraguay, and Uruguay* (Oxford University Press, 2018).

Joan Maria Thomàs is ICREA Academy Researcher and professor at the University Rovira-Virgili. He is the author of eleven books on the Francoist Regime, the Spanish Fascism, the Single-party FET y de las JONS, and on US-Spanish relations during the Second World War. He has been visiting researcher or lecturer in universities of the United States, China, Japan, Australia, New Zealand, Israel and Great Britain. He has been awarded with The City of Barcelona History Award, the "Serra d'Or" Critics Award and the Narcís Monturiol Medal for Scientifical and Technical Merit.

Haruo Tohmatsu is professor of diplomatic and war history at the National Defense Academy of Japan. He initially read modern European history at the University of Tsukuba and later obtained an M.A. in politics from Waseda University. He holds a Ph.D. in international relations from the University of Oxford. His research interests include international administration of territories focusing on the League of Nations mandate/United Nations trusteeship systems, history of Anglo-Japanese relations, the Russo-Japanese War, the Manchurian Incident, Japan's Micronesian mandates, the Sino-Japanese War of 1937–1945, United Nations peace-keeping operations, and disputes between nations over different interpretation of history.

Index

25 de Mayo, warship, 257–60, 263–4
Abraham Lincoln Brigade, 23–4
Abyssinian crisis, 116, 119
Acción Española, 78
Action Française, 199, 201, 207
Addis Ababa, 133
Aegean Sea, 139
Africa, 7, 23, 71, 82, 126, 128, 133–6, 138–9, 142
Agrupación de Mujeres Antifascistas; AMA, 93, 100–1, 110
Albania, 124, 138
Alberti, Rafael, 7, 22, 174–85, 187–90
Alcázar of Toledo, 121, 253
Alfonso XIII, King of Spain, 35, 61, 66, 114, 153, 219, 226
Alianza de Intelectuales Antifascistas, 22
Allason, Barbara, 273
Alsace/Alsatian, 44, 207
Álvarez del Vayo, Julio, 183, 251–2
Amaterasu, Japanese goddess, 240
Amery, John, 217
Amery, Julian, 216–7
Amery, Leo, 216
Anarchist/ anarchism, 6, 17–21, 25, 27–8, 44, 48, 65, 67, 96, 101, 103, 107, 110, 118, 153, 159, 160, 166, 184, 199, 203–5, 207, 209, 224, 252, 258–9, 261, 270–1, 273, 275, 277–9
Andreis, Mario, 272
Anglo-Portuguese Alliance, 115, 117, 119, 123
Anti-Comintern Pact, 126, 237–8, 242, 246
Antonov-Ovseenko, Vladimir, 159–60
Aquist, Robert, 49
Argentine humanitarian exchange initiative, 253–4, 264
Asahi Shimbun, Japanese daily newspaper, 235–6
Ascaso Column, 278
Asociación de Amigos de la Unión Soviética, 154, 176
Asociación de Escritores y Artistas Revolucionarios, 176
Auriol, Vincent, 202
Auslandsorganisation of NSDAP, 79
Auxilio Azul, 99, 106
Auxilio Social, 81, 98
Azaña, Manuel, 15, 22, 25, 115–16, 118, 120, 158–9, 251, 257

BA-10, Soviet armored vehicle, 238
Badoglio, Pietro, 133
Bagabondo Tsūshin, 235, 245
Balbo, Italo, 138
Baldwin, Stanley, 26, 220, 225
Baleares, Nationalist navy cruiser, 124, 244
Bank of Portugal, 120
Barbieri, Francesco Ciccio, 279
Barcelona, 5, 15–17, 19, 24, 28, 34–49, 56, 75, 94, 97, 102, 108, 146, 159, 166, 176, 201, 203, 209, 226, 235, 246, 256–8, 277–80, 282–3
Barzini, Luigi, 143
Basque (Euskadi) government, 253–6
Bauer, Riccardo, 272
Bellón, Ildefonso, 59
Ben Hach Abd el Krim Ganmia, Sidi Ahmed, 60
Benda, Julian, 175
Beneyto, Juan, 77
Berlin, 5, 9, 35–8, 40–1, 43, 50, 70–1, 77–82, 125, 157, 198–9, 201, 225–6
Berlin 1936 Olympics, 5, 35–6, 38, 40–1, 50
Bermúdez Cañete, Antonio, 78
Bernays, Edward, 133
Berneri, Camillo, 277
Bernhardt, Johannes, 70, 79
Billancourt, 209–10

Blum, Léon, 8, 25–7, 36, 38, 198, 200–5, 208–11
Boaventura, Armando, 125
Bocchini, Arturo, 146
Bohle, Friedhelm, 79
Bologna, 134
Bonacorsi, Arconovaldo, 139
Bonfanti, Luigi, 145
Bonte, Florimond, 200
Borbón-Austria Este, Alfonso Carlos, 66
Borbón-Battenberg, Juan de, 61
Borbón-Parma, Javier, 66
Boris III, 138
Botelho Moniz, Jorge, 121–2
Bottai, Giuseppe, 143, 146
Bowers, Claude, 158
Brendon, Piers, 217
Bricchetto, Enrica, 137
British Trade Union Congress, 38
Broz, Josip, 24, 164
Buchanan, Tom, 217, 223
Bulgaria, 138
Bund deutscher Mädel, 81

Cabanellas, general José, 57, 60
Cabo de Palos, battle of, 244
Caffi, Andrea, 276
Caixa Geral dos Depósitos, 121
Calamandrei, Piero, 272
Calogero, Guido, 272
Calvo Sotelo, José, 15
Campidoglio, 134
Canaris, admiral Wilhelm, 71
Cantalupo, Roberto, 69–71
Carlism, 68
Carmi, Israel, 41, 43 ,45–8
Carmona, 222, 225
Carpi, 144
Carrero Blanco, Luis, 63
Casali, Luciano, 7, 133, 291
Casals, Pablo, 44
Casares Quiroga, Santiago, 1, 15
Castillo, Peña, 121
Catalan Communist Party, 209
Catalonia, 20, 34–7, 39, 41–2, 44, 144, 159–60, 206–7, 209, 277, 283, 292
Catholic Church, 78, 81, 142, 206, 237, 238–40
CEDA (Confederación Española de Derechas Autónomas), 64, 79, 116
Cervera, Juan, 244
Ceva, Umberto, 272
CGIL, Confederazione Generale, 272
Italiana del Lavoro, 71
Chamber of Deputies, 164, 208–9
Chamberlain, Neville, 124, 225
Changkufeng incident (1938), 243
Chiaromonte, Nicola, 274, 276
Chicherin, Georgy, 152
Chinese Communist Party (CCP), 234, 245
Chongqing, 243, 245, 249
Churchill (1st Duke of Marlborough), John, 218
Churchill, Winston, 8, 28, 216–28, 293
Ciano, Galeazzo, 136, 138, 143
Clemenceau, Georges, 208
Clerk, Sir George, 202
Codovilla, Victorio, 19
Colorno, 145
Comintern, 7, 14, 18–19, 24, 35, 37, 126, 153–5, 162, 167, 176–7, 181, 184, 208, 237–8, 242, 246
Comintern Executive Committee (ECCI), 154–5, 164–5
Comité d'Acceuil des Enfants de l'Espagne, 210
Comité d'Action Socialiste pour l'Espagne, 292
Comité International de Coordination d'Information pour l'Aide à l'Espagne Républicaine, 210
Communist party of America, 236
Communist Party of France, 164, 200, 208
Communist Party of Great Britain, 27
Companhia de União Fabril, 131
Companys, Lluís, 37, 39, 159–60
Comunión Tradicionalista, 64–8, 97
Concentrazione d'Azione Antifascista, 272
Conde, Francisco J., 82
Condor Legion, 2–3, 23, 79
Confederación Nacional del Trabajo (CNT), 17, 19, 153, 205, 207
Confédération Générale de Travail (CGT), 209–10
Corfu, 138
Corpo Truppe Volontarie (CTV), 143
Corsica, 138–9
Cosmo, Giandomenico, 273
Cot, Pierre, 198, 200–2

Coverdale, John, 138
Croce, Benedetto, 272

D'Alessandro, Leonardo Pompeo, 141–2, 145
da Cunha, Vasco, 125
da Matta, José Caeiro, 124
da Silva, Alfredo, 121
Dainipponteikoku kemp (Constitutional Law of the Japanese Empire), 247
Danzi, Guglielmo, 69–70
Dávila, general Fidel, 57, 61, 67
de Asúa, Jiménez, 176
de Azcárate, Francisco, 223
De Felice, Renzo, 136, 138
de Fragoso Carmona, António Óscar, 222, 225
de Kérillis, Henri, 26, 209
de Oliveira Salazar, António, 7, 114–28
de Sagarra, Josep Maria, 38
de Sampayo, Luiz Teixeira, 117–19
Del Boca, Angelo, 117–19
Delbos, Yvon, 198, 200, 202, 208
Deutsch-spanische Gesellschaft, 82
Di Jorio, Irene, 140
Dimitrov, Georgi, 18, 180–1, 184–5
Diplomatic asylum policy, 8, 251–2, 257, 260, 262
Divini redemptoris, Papal encyclical, 240
Duke of Alba, 123, 252
Durruti Column, 48, 279, 283
Durruti, Buenaventura, 270

Echevarrieta, Horacio, 116
Eden, Anthony, 119, 202, 225
Ehrenburg, Ilya, 159, 179, 184, 190
Eisler, Hans, 38
El Debate, 78
El Mono Azul, 22, 180
Elkon, Chaim, 34, 49–50
Ensner-Thalmann, Clara, 48
Enzensberger, Hans Magnus, 270
Esquerra Republicana Catalunya, 37
Esquivias, 164
Ethiopia, 16, 133, 135–7
Europe, 4, 9, 13–14, 16, 18, 24–5, 27–9, 34, 36, 38–40, 47, 49–50, 75, 78, 80–3, 85–6, 116–17, 126–8, 133–5, 138–9, 143, 152, 155–6, 161–2, 167, 174, 189, 199, 201–5, 207–9, 211, 216, 218–24, 226, 238, 240, 251, 259–60, 269–70, 275, 278, 285, 291–2, 294

Fabbri, Luigi, 271
Fal Conde, Manuel, 66–7, 69, 86, 97
Falange Española, 1–2, 6, 64–8, 70, 78–81, 83, 85, 93, 97–9, 115, 122, 125, 139, 227, 247, 262, 293
Falange Española de las JONS, 64–5, 68–70, 76, 78–9, 81
Falange Española Tradicionalista y de las JONS, 68, 70, 97
Falangism, 6
Farinacci, Roberto, 69–70
Fascism, 6, 8, 14, 16, 18, 23–6, 28, 35, 40–1, 62, 75, 78, 81, 84, 96, 101, 133–4, 138–9, 141–2, 145–7, 155–6, 179, 184, 204, 206, 216, 218, 222, 225, 227, 270, 272–4, 276–8, 285, 294
Faupel, general Wilhelm, 80–1
Federación Anarquista Ibérica (FAI), 65, 153, 159, 205, 207, 258, 284
Fédération Sportive et Gymnique de Travail, 38
Fernández Arias, Adelardo, 77
Ferro, António, 117
Feuchtwanger, Lion, 174, 182, 185, 188–9
Feuilles libres, 207
Fiore, Tommaso, 272
First Congress of Soviet Writers, 177–8
First Portuguese Republic, 114
Foa, Vittorio, 273
France, 5, 8, 13–14, 16, 23, 25–7, 38–9, 48–9, 66, 70–1, 79, 83–4, 122, 126, 128, 139–40, 153, 155–6, 175–6, 188, 198–211, 222–3, 227, 235, 237–8, 253, 257, 260–1, 274, 277, 279, 284–5, 291–2
Franco-Soviet Pact, 207
Franco, Francisco, 1–4, 6, 8–9, 15, 19, 23, 27, 34, 45–6, 49, 56, 59–64, 66–71, 80–4, 94, 96, 100, 111, 117, 120–6, 138, 140–3, 156, 163, 167, 201–2, 204–9, 211, 216–17, 226–8, 233, 235–6, 238, 240–2, 245–7, 254, 255–9, 261, 263–4, 273–4, 279, 281, 284, 292–3
Franco, Nicolás, 62–3, 69, 256, 279
François-Poncet, André, 201
French Popular Front, 14, 25–6, 200

French Revolution, 13, 16, 18, 27
Frente de Juventudes, 81
Frente Único Antifascista, 176
Friends of the Soviet Union (Amigos de la Unión Soviética, or AUS), 154, 165, 175
Fusignano, 145

Gabinskiy, Nikolai, 179
Gaeta, 146
Gambara, Gastone, 146
García Lorca, Federico, 178
García Mansilla, Daniel, 251–7, 261–263
García Oliver, Juan, 27
Garcia Queipo de Llano, Genoveva, 60–1
Garosci, Aldo, 272–4, 278–9, 282
Gaulle, Charles de, 28
Gay, Vicente, 77
General Motors, 24
Generalitat, 16, 17, 37
Gentile, Emilio, 136
Germany, 1, 5–6, 9, 14, 19, 26, 35–6, 38, 40–1, 44, 47, 49, 61, 70–1, 75–84, 86, 120, 123–8, 138–9, 141, 155–6, 176, 186, 199, 201–3, 206–8, 219–21, 223, 233–4, 237–9, 247, 257, 260, 274–5
Gide, André, 174–5, 178, 182–3, 185–9
Gil Yuste, general Germán, 57
Giménez Caballero, Ernesto, 62, 69, 7
Ginzburg, Leone, 273
Ginzburg, Natalia, 273
Giovanna di Savoia, 138
Giral, José, 15, 27, 198
Giua, Clara Lollini, 280, 284
Giua, Franco, 281, 284
Giua, Michele, 272
Giua, Renzo, 7, 269–74, 276–7, 279–285
Giustizia e Libertà, 269–72, 274, 278, 282
Glowinsky, Haim, 34–7
Gómez-Jordana (Count of Jordana), Francisco, 126, 227
González Ruano, César, 77
Gorev, Vladimir, 163
Göring, Hermann, 80
Gorki, Maxim, 178
Gottwald, Klement, 24
Great Britain, 5, 26–7, 81, 83, 123, 139, 202–3, 218–19, 222, 225, 228, 233, 294
Griner, Massimiliano, 141
Guadalajara, 143–4, 163, 279, 284–5
Guardia di Finanza, 145
Guasco, Michele, 273

Haig, Douglas, 221
Hakoah Vienna, 34, 42–3
Hapoel sports federation, 5, 35, 4–44, 49
Hartmann, Nicolai, 75
Hedilla, Manuel, 66, 70, 81
Heiberg, Morten, 139
Heidegger, Martin, 75
Heidelberg, 75
Herbette, Jean, 26, 199–200, 206, 208
Hess, Rudolf, 70
Himmler, Heinrich, 81
Hirohito (Japanese emperor), 232, 237, 240
Hirota, Kōki, 233, 237
Hirschmann, Ursula, 274
Histadrut, 40
Hitler, Adolf, 2, 22–3, 27, 38, 40, 47, 70, 75–86, 119, 127, 138, 140, 186, 199, 206, 220, 222, 224, 226, 235, 246, 275
Hoare, Samuel, 220
Hodgson, Robert, 124
Hull, Cordell, 24

Ibarruri, Dolores, 181
Imperial Japanese Army (IJA), 232–4, 237–9, 241, 243, 246
Inomata, 246
Instituto de Estudios Políticos, 82
Integral Catholicism, 118
International Brigades, 7, 16, 35, 48–9, 100, 143, 162, 164–5, 167, 185, 207–9, 236, 270, 279, 284
International Olympic Committee, 35, 38, 40
Italian Anarchic Federation (FAI), 153, 159, 258, 284
Italian Communist Party (PCI), 164
Italy, 5–7, 9, 19, 26, 61, 71, 76, 123–4, 127–8, 133–44, 146–7, 156, 199, 201–3, 206–7, 220, 223, 233, 237, 247, 257, 260, 270–2, 275, 277, 284–5, 219–20
Izvestia, 179, 181–2, 190

Jacoby, Imre, 34–5, 49–50
Jenkins, Roy, 219, 221
Jeunesses Patriotes, 205
Juliá, Santos, 94

Juntas Castellanas de Acción Hispánica, 76
Juntas de Ofensiva Nacional, 76
Sindicalista (JONS), 64, 65, 68–70, 76, 78–9, 81, 97, 294

Karmen, Roman, 157
Katorikku gahō (illustrated Catholic journal), 240
Kellogg, Frank B., 220
Kélyin, Fyodor, 178–80, 183, 185, 187, 190
Kerensky, Alexander, 15
Kérillis, Henri de, 26, 209
Kharitonova, Natalia, 182
Kindelán, general Alfredo, 58, 61
King Edward VIII, 220, 225
Kōdōha (Imperial Way Faction), group of officers in IJA, 232–3
Kokka Shintō (state Shintoism), 240
Kōkoku shisō, 240
Kokutai (national foundation), 240–1
Koltsov, Mikhail, 157, 166, 178–9, 184, 188, 189
Konoye, Fumimaro, 247
Kuomintang (Chinese Nationalist Party, KMT), 234
Kuznetsov, Nikolai, 163
Kwantung Army, Japanese garrison, stationed in Manchukuo, 234, 239, 241–3, 246

L'Action Française, 199, 201, 207
L'Avenir du Bassin d'Arcachon, 203
L'Echo de Bougie, 203
L'Eclair, 204–5
L'Espagne Antifasciste, 207
L'Express du Midi, 201
L'Homme Libre, 208
L'Humanité, 39 48, 144, 201
L'Oeuvre, 199
La Conquista del Estado, 76, 78
La Croix des Pyrénées-Orientales, 206
La Dépêche de Toulouse, 204, 207
La Gaceta Literaria, 75
Labour Party, 27, 205, 271
Lajolo, Davide, 141–3
Languedoc, 204
Largo Caballero, Francisco, 21, 27, 100, 119, 160, 180, 184–5, 257, 273
Laval, Pierre, 220
Le Figaro, 199
Le Libertaire, 199
Le Petit Méridional, 204
League of Nations, 116, 119, 123, 263, 294
Lebrun, Albert, 26
Ledesma, Ramiro, 75–6
Lefebvre, Georges, 13
Lega italiana dei diritti dell'uomo, 272
Legaz Lacambra, Luis, 82
Léger, Alexis, 198
Lenin, Vladimir, 18, 22, 152, 166, 181, 221
León, María Teresa, 174, 176–8, 180–4
Lerroux, Alejandro, 116, 180
Levi, Carlo, 272–3
Levi, Gino, 273
Levi, Giuseppe, 273
Levi, Mario, 274
Lewine-Szmukler, Sonja, 43
Libertad, 76–7
Ligue des droits de l'Homme, 210
Lippi, V. Diana, 147
Litvinov, Maxim, 24, 27
Lo Cascio, Paola, 142, 269
London Non-Intervention Committee, 162
Lussu, Emilio, 271, 282–3
Lyon, 207, 277

Maccabi Movement, 41
Madrid, 1–3, 7, 21, 26–8, 36, 49, 56, 60, 64, 68, 75, 84–5, 94, 98–100, 102–3, 106, 114–122, 127, 153, 155–6, 158–63, 165–7, 174, 176, 180, 184–5, 198–203, 206–9, 211, 227, 235, 237, 243–6,252–3, 256, 258–62, 264, 282–3, 293
Maeztu, Ramiro de, 78
Maisky, Ivan, 123, 162, 221
Majorca, 48, 139
Makaseev, Boris, 157
Malaga, 94, 260
Malatesta, Errico, 271, 279
Manchukuo (1932–1945), Japanese puppet state in Manchuria, 234, 237, 239, 241–2, 246
Mannheim, 75
Manuelskii, Dimitri, 155
March on Rome, 75
Margaritas, 65, 97, 104, 111

Marquis Contadero, 121
Marquis of Quintanar, 121
Martínez Barrio, Diego, 15
Martínez Unciti, María Paz, 99
Marty, André, 164, 208
Marwick, Arthur, 13
McNeill-Moss, Geoffrey, 27
Mediterranean, 10, 40, 75, 82, 123–4, 138–9, 244, 258, 260
Mein Kampf, 76, 78
Mental maps, 117
Mila, Massimo, 269–70, 273
Millán-Astray, general José, 2, 62
Ministry of Navy, 146
Ministry of Communications, 146
Ministry of Folk Culture (Minculpop), 137
Ministry of Internal Affairs, 198, 201
Ministry of War, 146
Minniti, Fortunato, 141, 143
Miravitlles, Jaume, 39, 144
Modena, 144
Mola, general Emilio, 15, 44, 57–8, 60–1, 63, 70
Molotov, Vyacheslav, 83, 161, 185
Monforte de Lemos, 86
Mongolian People's Republic, 241
Montaner, colonel Francisco, 57
Monteiro, Armindo, 123, 125–6
Monti, Augusto, 273
Moradiellos, Enrique, 222, 228
Morel, Henri, 202
Moreno Fernández, Francisco, 57
Moriya, Seiji, 243–4
Moscow, 7, 26, 37, 40, 116, 146, 153–7, 159–68, 175–7, 180–3, 187–9, 208, 222, 261
Mother's Work for National Education, 127
Moutet, Marius, 199, 202
Mouvement contre la guerre et le fascism, 210
Mujeres Libres, 96, 101, 103, 110
Mundo Obrero, 43, 103, 153
Munich, 16, 78, 82, 226
Mussolini, Benito, 7, 22, 27, 47, 69–71, 75–6, 79, 84, 127–8, 133–40, 142–3, 147, 199, 222, 225, 227, 235, 270, 272, 279

Nanetti, Nino, 277
National Socialism, 6, 75–8, 80, 82–3, 86, 217
Naval rescue and evacuation of Spanish Nationalist and Republicans, 257, 259–60, 263
Nazi/Nazism, 2, 4–6, 23, 26–7, 35–6, 41–2, 44, 49, 61, 70–1, 75–84, 86, 123–5, 127, 153, 156, 162, 176, 199, 201, 206, 218–22, 226–7, 233–4, 237–8, 247, 275, 292
Negrín, Juan, 20, 100, 124, 176
Nelken, Margarita, 15, 101
Nemes, Sándor, 42
New Economic Policy, 18, 28
Nice, 138, 277
Nippon Gaik Ky kai (Japan Association of Foreign Relations), 239
Nippon katorikku shimbun (Japan Catholic Press), 240
Nishiura, Susumu, 8, 238–9
Nitti, Francesco Fausto, 271
NKVD, People's Commissariat for Internal Affairs, 158, 181, 183, 185, 187, 190
Nomonhan (Khalhin-Gol) incident (1939), 246
Non-Intervention Agreement, 122–3, 156, 162, 201–3, 207
Non-Intervention Committee, 162, 206–8, 210, 251
NSDAP (Nazi party), 70, 75, 78–81, 83–4, 234
Numancia, 180

Operation X, 156, 162, 165, 167
Orgaz, general Luis, 57, 61, 63
Orlov, Alexander, 158
Ortega y Gasset, José, 75
Orwell, George, 28, 190–1
OVRA, 273, 286
Oyarzun, Román, 69

Pacciardi, Randolfo, 279
Palazzo Venezia, 133
Palestine, 5, 10, 34–5, 38, 40–5, 47–50
Palestine Communist Party, 34–5
Pantelleria, 139
Parma, 145
Parnakh, Valentin, 190
Partido Comunista de España (PCE), 14, 18, 153–5, 176

Pascua, Marcelino, 160–2
Paseos, 17, 27
Pasquali, Camillo, 287
People's Commissariat for Foreign Affairs (NKID), 152–4
People's Commissariat for Internal Affairs (NKVD), 158, 181, 183, 185, 187, 190
Perpignan, 202
Pétain, Philippe, 140
Pius IX, 248
Platone, Felice, 284
Poland, 43, 47, 83, 243
Ponte, general Miguel, 57, 63
Popular Army, 21, 163
Popular Front, 4, 7–8, 14–15, 17, 23–6, 28–9, 36–9, 59, 64, 79, 115, 118–19, 153–6, 183–4, 190, 198–202, 204–5, 209, 211, 220, 223, 242, 245, 253, 269, 294
Portsmouth Treaty (1905), 241
Portugal, 5–7, 57, 63, 66–7, 114–128, 222, 225, 235, 257, 260, 291
Portuguese Estado Novo ('New State'), 114–15
Portuguese Legion, 125, 127
Portuguese Military Observation Mission, 125
Portuguese National Syndicalists ("Blue Shirts"), 118
Portuguese Viriatos, 122, 127
Portuguese Youth, 127
POUM (Partido Obrero de Unificación Marxista), 14, 17, 100, 205
Pradera, Víctor, 69
Pravda, 157, 166, 178–179, 181, 188–9
Preston, Paul, 9
Prieto, Indalecio, 15, 116, 257
Primo de Rivera, general Miguel, 37, 57, 59, 62, 258
Primo de Rivera, José Antonio, 1–2, 6, 66, 68–9, 78, 97, 114, 174, 252
Primo de Rivera, Miguel, 97, 153
Primo de Rivera, Pilar, 93, 97–8, 106, 262

Queipo de Llano, general Gonzalo, 57, 60–1

Radical Party, 25, 200
Radio Barcelona, 146, 278
Rádio Clube Português, 121–2
Rakhmanov, Vadim, 189
Rato, Ramón de, 77
Ravenna, 145
Red Cross, 104, 209–10, 252–6
Redondo, Onésimo, 75–6, 98
Reggio Emilia, 144
Renault, 209–10
Republican Party, 145, 263
Requetés, 64–5, 67–8, 122
Rhodes, 139
Rijeka, 138
Rincón de Arellano, Adolfo, 84
Roatta, general Mario, 71
Robertson, Esmonde Manning, 138
Robi (firelight), 240
Rodezno, conde de, 66–8
Rodrigo, Javier, 141
Rodríguez Tarduchy, Emilio, 83
Rolland, Romain, 175
Romania, 138
Rome, 1, 9, 70–1, 75, 79, 125, 133, 135–6, 138, 225–6, 246, 273
Rosenberg, Alfred, 78, 84
Rosenberg, Marcel, 158–61
Rosselli, Carlo, 270–1, 274, 276–9
Rosselli, Nello, 279
Rossi, Ernesto, 272
Roussillon, 207
Rovighi, Alberto, 140–1, 143, 145–6
Ruiz (Archbishop of Hita), Juan, 273, 280, 283
Russian Revolution, 13–4, 241, 269
Russo-Japanese War (1904–1905), 241, 295

Saavedra Lamas, Carlos, 253, 255, 257–8
Sabbione, Paolo, 273
Sakai, Yoneo, 235–6, 245
Saliquet, general Andrés, 57
Salvemini, Gaetano, 272, 285
San Pietro in Vincoli, 145
Sánchez-Albornoz, Claudio, 121
Sangróniz, José Antonio, 62
Sanjurjo, general José, 6, 56–7, 120, 270
Sanz Bachiller, Mercedes, 98
Sardinia, 139
Savich, Ovadii, 157
Savoy, 138
Sección Femenina de la FET, 93, 97
Second International Congress of Antifascist Writers, 182–3, 189

Secretariat for National Propaganda (SPN), 116–17, 121
Sellier, Henri, 199
Serafima Ilinichna Gopner, 184–5
Serrano Suñer, Ramón, 56, 59, 69, 117, 125, 261–2
Seventh Party Congress, 156
Shirai, Jack, 236
Sicily, 139
Simpson, Wallis, 220, 225
Sino-Japanese War (1937–1945), 235–6, 242–3, 246, 249
Society for Cultural Relations with Foreign Countries (VOKS), 154, 187–8
South Manchurian Railway Company, 241
Soviet Union, 2, 5, 7, 9, 25–9, 36–7, 39, 84, 86, 119, 123, 152–5, 158, 160–1, 165, 174–8, 182–6, 188–9, 199, 202–3, 206–7, 209–11, 232
Spain, 1, 3–10, 13–19, 22–9, 34–6, 38–9, 41–2, 44–5, 47–50, 57, 59–61, 66, 68–71, 76–85, 94, 96–7, 100–1, 103–4, 106, 110, 114–29, 138–43, 145–6, 152–60, 162, 164–8, 174, 176–82, 184–5, 188, 190, 198–211, 216–28, 232–3, 235–47, 251–2, 257–62, 264, 296–70, 273, 275–9, 238–5
Spanish Civil War, 1, 3–8, 13–14, 16, 25, 28, 79–80, 86, 93, 95, 109, 114, 127–8, 138–40, 142–3, 145, 152, 155–7, 167–8, 174, 178–9, 184–5, 198, 200, 216, 218, 220–1, 224, 226, 232–3, 235, 242, 251, 269–70, 278–9, 292, 294
Spanish Communist Party (PCE), 14, 18, 39, 153–5, 166–7, 176, 185, 190
Spanish Foreign Legion, 122, 236
Spanish Popular Front, 14, 25–6, 154, 183, 269
Spanish Republic/ Republican government/ Republican Spain, 1, 3–5, 7–8, 14–29, 34–6, 45–6, 48–50, 57, 59, 63, 69–70, 79, 94, 96, 101, 108, 110, 114–15, 119–20, 123, 126, 145, 152–3, 155–68, 176–7, 180, 185, 188, 198–9, 201–11, 217, 219, 222–4, 243, 251, 253, 255, 257–9, 262–3, 269–71, 277, 285
Spanish Socialist Workers Party (PSOE), 100, 153, 176
Spartakiads. 37
Spengler, Oswald, 75, 78
Stalin, Joseph, 4, 7, 19, 22, 24, 39, 152, 155–6, 158, 160–2, 164, 167–8, 175, 177–86, 188–90, 221, 243, 247, 292
Stefani, Filippo, 140–1, 143, 145–6
Stern, Ludmila, 187
Stewart-Murray (Duchess of Atholl), Katharine, 217
Stohrer, Eberhard von, 80
Sudeten crisis, 126
Sunyol i Garriga, Josep, 37

T-26, Soviet tank, 163, 167, 238–9
Taisei yokusankai (Imperial Rule Assistance Association), 233, 247
Tâmega (Viscount), Riba, 119
Tarchiani, Alberto, 272
TASS, 157
Tattinger, Pierre, 205
teatro de urgencia, 180
Teotónio Pereira, Pedro, 119–20, 125
Third Republic, 25
Thomàs, Joan Maria, 1, 4–5, 56, 294
Thorez, Maurice, 204, 208–9
Tito (Josip Broz), 24, 164
Tocqueville, Alexis de, 13
Togliatti, Palmiro, 18, 177, 185
Tōjō, Hideki, 238, 242, 247
Torpedo boat Tucumán, 257–264
Tōseiha (Control Faction), group of officers in IJA, 232–3
Toulouse, 201, 203
Traquardi, Nello, 272
Treaty of Friendship and Non-Aggression, 126
Tribunale Speciale, 282
Tunis, 43
Tunisia, 138–9
Type I tank, German tank, 238

Ughetti, Tullio, 144
UGT (Unión General de Trabajadores), 14, 19, 100, 153
Union Anarchiste Française, 199, 205
Unión Internacional de Escritores Revolucionarios, 176
Union Republicaine, Democratique et Sociale, 203

United Kingdom, 23, 25–6, 124, 218
Urraca Pastor, María Rosa, 96–7, 108, 110
Urrutia, Federico de, 79, 83
USSR, 18–19, 22, 26–7, 127, 152–4, 156–9, 162, 166–7, 175–8, 180–3, 185–7, 189, 232–4, 237–8, 241–4, 247

Valdés, general Luis, 63
Valencia, 83, 85, 94, 97, 145, 158, 182–4, 189, 235, 256–60
Vallejo Nágera, Antonio, 64, 84
Vallejo, Eugenio, 20
Varela, José Enrique, 122
Velacoracho, Carmen, 83
Venturi, Franco, 273–4, 276
Vichy, 140, 288
Vidali, Vittorio, 277
Vienna, 41, 43, 49, 66, 82
Vigódskiy, David, 179, 189
Viñas, Ángel, 4
Vittorio Emanuele III, 134
VOKS, All-Union Society for Cultural
von Ribbentrop, Joachim, 83, 117
Voroshilov, Kliment, 152, 161, 164, 168

Wehrmacht, 2, 82–3, 85–6, 155, 234
Weiss, Nahum, 49–50
Winter Palace, 159
Winterhilfe, 81
World Labor Athletic carnival, 40
Wuhan, 243–5

Yamamoto, Shin'jirō, 240, 244
Yanguas Messía, José de, 61–2
Yehzov, Nicolai, 181, 183
Yugoslavia, 24, 42, 138
Yzurdiaga, Fermín, 69

Zay, Jean, 202
Zentrum party, 75–6
Zola, Emile, 175
Zugazagoitia, Julian, 161

Printed and bound by CPI Group (UK) Ltd, Croydon, CR0 4YY

13/09/2026

14961102-0001